THE ARCHITECTS' LIBRARY
Editor: F. M. SIMPSON, F.R.I.B.A.

THE ARCHITECTS' LIBRARY
Edited by F. M. SIMPSON, F.R.I.B.A.
Professor of Architecture in the University of London
Medium 8vo.

A History of Architectural Development.
By F. M. SIMPSON, F.R.I.B.A. Three Volumes.

Vol. I. ANCIENT, EARLY CHRISTIAN, AND BYZANTINE. With 180 Illustrations. 12s. 6d. net.

II. MEDIÆVAL. With 257 Illustrations. 21s. net.

III. RENAISSANCE IN ITALY, FRANCE, AND ENGLAND. With 268 Illustrations. 21s. net.

Building Construction.
Vol. I. By BERESFORD PITE, F.R.I.B.A., F. T. BAGGALLAY, F.R.I.B.A., H. D. SEARLES-WOOD, F.R.I.B.A., E. SPRAGUE, Assoc.M.Inst.C.E., etc. With 249 Illustrations. 18s. net.

II. By J. H. MARKHAM, A.R.I.B.A., HERBERT A. SATCHELL, F.R.I.B.A., Professor F. M. SIMPSON, F.R.I.B.A., and others. [*In preparation.*

THE ARCHITECTS' LIBRARY

A HISTORY OF ARCHITECTURAL DEVELOPMENT

IN THREE VOLUMES

VOL. III

THE RENAISSANCE IN ITALY, FRANCE, AND ENGLAND

BY

F. M. SIMPSON

ARCHITECT

PROFESSOR OF ARCHITECTURE IN THE UNIVERSITY OF LONDON; FELLOW OF THE ROYAL
INSTITUTE OF BRITISH ARCHITECTS; SOMETIME PROFESSOR OF ARCHITECTURE
IN THE UNIVERSITY OF LIVERPOOL; ROYAL ACADEMY
TRAVELLING STUDENT, 1884

WITH 268 ILLUSTRATIONS

WILDSIDE PRESS

PREFACE

This volume treats of the Renaissance in Italy, France, and England. The temptation was strong to include other countries, but if more than a most cursory account of these had been attempted, the space allotted to the three mentioned must have been considerably curtailed, or else the volume would have swollen to unconscionable proportions. After all, Italy and France were the two main arteries through which the Renaissance flowed, and nearly all the phases of development can be traced in them alone. French work has been treated in this volume with considerable fulness, partly because it has long been a special favourite of mine, and partly because hitherto no reliable books on the subject in English have been available. In Germany, Spain, and the Netherlands, as in England, the Renaissance was always struggling, never absolutely free. In all it was hampered at first by vernacular traditions, and when it finally threw those off, original development was checked, to a great extent, by the overpowering influence of Italian design.

The present volume, like the previous volumes, seeks to illustrate architectural development by reference to plan, construction, materials, and principles of design. The factors that advanced or retarded it at the different centres are also dwelt upon. In one respect, however, a slight difference in treatment was necessary. In the Middle Ages all workers were in complete unison, and the identity of each was merged in his work. In the days of the Renaissance the individual was paramount. In Italy, Brunelleschi, Bramante, and Michael Angelo; in France, Lemercier and François Mansard; in England, Inigo Jones and Christopher Wren, mark the different stages of advance. For this reason, except in the chapters dealing specially with plan and construction, development is mainly traced by a consideration, in approximately chronological order, of the buildings of these great masters and of others hardly less famous.

More than ten years have elapsed since I began this history. The delay in completion is partly owing to pressure of other work, which necessitated constant breaks, and partly to the enormous amount of ground which had to be covered. When I commenced I thought I had the necessary material to hand. England I knew, the greater part of France I was acquainted with, and I had a fair knowledge of Italy, Germany, Belgium, etc. I expected that would suffice. I was soon undeceived. Almost immediately I realized the necessity of going over again the ground I knew—which I had trod with a somewhat different aim in view—and of seeing places I had not previously visited. I cannot say that I know every building mentioned in these three volumes, but there are very few that I have not seen at some time or another, and I have renewed acquaintance with many in recent years.

I am much indebted to the following for kind permission to reproduce drawings of theirs: Mr. A. T. Bolton, Mr. W. R. Davidson, Mr. J. A. Gotch, Mr. C. J. Longman for two illustrations from his father's "The Three Cathedrals dedicated to St. Paul in London," and Mr. Arnold Mitchell; also to Mr. B. T. Batsford, the Editor of the *Building News*, and the Editor of the *R. I. B. A. Journal*. Mr. Leslie Wilkinson, my colleague at University College, has also kindly lent me some of his excellent sketches, and has also redrawn some of the sketches made by me reproduced in this volume.

I take this opportunity to express to Messrs. Longmans, Green & Co. my thanks for the courtesy and consideration they have always shown me.

UNIVERSITY COLLEGE,
   GOWER STREET, W.C.,
      September, 1911.

CONTENTS

	PAGE
PREFACE	v
LIST OF ILLUSTRATIONS	ix

CHAPTER
- I. INTRODUCTORY 1
- II. THE HISTORY OF THE RISE OF THE RENAISSANCE IN FLORENCE . 13
- III. EARLY FLORENTINE PALACES (1430–1520) 30
- IV. THE SPREAD OF THE RENAISSANCE IN NORTHERN ITALY (1450–1520) 47
- V. THE CENTENARY OF THE RENAISSANCE: SECULAR BUILDINGS (1500–1580) 68
- VI. LATER SECULAR BUILDINGS 107
- VII. THE PLANNING AND GENERAL ORDINANCE OF RENAISSANCE CHURCHES 118
- VIII. RENAISSANCE DOMES, THEIR DESIGN AND CONSTRUCTION . . . 152
- IX. THE EARLY RENAISSANCE IN FRANCE 168
- X. THE ARCHITECTURE OF THE LOUIS (c. 1625–1780) 200
- XI. THE RENAISSANCE IN ENGLAND 226
- XII. INIGO JONES, SIR CHRISTOPHER WREN, AND LONDON CHURCHES . 270
- XIII. FROM SIR CHRISTOPHER WREN TO SIR WILLIAM CHAMBERS; A CENTURY OF ENGLISH ARCHITECTS AND THEIR BUILDINGS (c. 1670–1770) 301
- XIV. THE NINETEENTH CENTURY IN ENGLAND: A POSTSCRIPT . . . 330
- INDEX 339

LIST OF ILLUSTRATIONS

CHAPTER II.

FIG.		PAGE
1.	FLORENCE CATHEDRAL: PLAN	15
2.	FLORENCE CATHEDRAL: AS REPRESENTED IN THE FRESCO IN THE SPANISH CHAPEL, IN THE CHURCH OF SANTA MARIA NOVELLA . .	15
3.	PAZZI CHAPEL, FLORENCE: PLAN AND SECTION (*L. Wilkinson*) . .	18
4.	PAZZI CHAPEL, FAÇADE AND CHURCH AND CLOISTERS OF SANTA CROCE, FLORENCE . . . . *facing*	18
5.	PAZZI CHAPEL, FLORENCE: INTERIOR . . . . „	18
6.	SANTO SPIRITO, FLORENCE: PLAN AND SECTION	20
7.	SAN LORENZO, FLORENCE: PLAN	21
8.	SAN LORENZO, FLORENCE: INTERIOR . . . . *facing*	22

CHAPTER III.

9.	PALAZZO RICCARDI, FLORENCE . . . . *facing*	32
10.	PALAZZO QUARATESI, FLORENCE, WITH PALAZZO NONFINITO BEYOND „	32
11.	PALAZZO PITTI, FLORENCE: PLAN	33
12.	PALAZZO PITTI, FLORENCE: SKETCH OF WINDOWS	34
13.	RUSTICATIONS OF FLORENTINE PALACES	35
14.	BANNER HOLDER AT CORNER OF PALACE IN THE VIA MAGGIO, FLORENCE	37
15.	SECTIONS THROUGH THE UPPER STOREYS OF THE RICCARDI AND STROZZI PALACES, FLORENCE	39
16.	PALAZZO MONTALVI, FLORENCE . . . . *facing*	40
17.	PALAZZO RUCELLAI, FLORENCE . . . . „	40
18.	PALAZZO PANDOLFINI, FLORENCE . . . . „	41
19.	PALAZZO BARTOLINI, FLORENCE: WINDOWS . . . . . . „	41
20.	PALAZZO BARTOLINI, FLORENCE: WINDOW AT SIDE	41
21.	PALAZZO STROZZI, FLORENCE: PLAN	42
22.	PALAZZO PANDOLFINI, FLORENCE: PLAN	43

CHAPTER IV.

23.	PORTA DE' BORSARI, VERONA . . . . *facing*	53
24.	SANTA MARIA PRESSO SAN SATIRO, MILAN, AND SACRISTY: SECTION .	55
25.	ABBIATE GRASSO, NEAR MILAN: ENTRANCE PORCH	56

LIST OF ILLUSTRATIONS

FIG.		PAGE
26.	Santa Maria delle Grazie, Milan: Plan of East End	57
27.	Santa Maria delle Grazie, Milan: Section through East End	58
28.	Como Cathedral: Window in South Aisle	59
29.	Prigioni, Brescia	*facing* 60
30.	Colleoni Chapel, alongside Santa Maria Maggiore, Bergamo	,, 60
31.	Palazzo Bevilacqua, Bologna: Rustication of Walls	61
32.	Palazzo Vendramin Calergi, Venice	*facing* 62
33.	Ducal Palace, Venice: End of Courtyard	,, 64
34.	Scuola di San Rocco, Venice	,, 64
35.	Renaissance Capitals (*from Sketches in the Uffizi Gallery, Florence, after Professor Donaldson*)	66

CHAPTER V.

FIG.		PAGE
36.	Palazzo Venezia, Rome: Arcading at Side of Courtyard	70
37.	Palazzo della Cancelleria, Rome: Portion of Façade	72
38.	Palazzo della Cancelleria, Rome: Details of Façade	73
39.	Il Tempietto, San Pietro in Montorio, Rome: Plans and Section	74
40.	Santa Maria della Pace, Rome: Cloisters	*facing* 74
41.	Palazzo Borghese, Rome: Courtyard	,, 74
42.	Santa Maria della Pace, Rome: Plan	75
43.	Belvedere Courtyard, the Vatican, Rome (*as designed by Bramante*)	*facing* 76
44.	Palazzo Maccarani, Rome	78
45.	Palazzo Sacchetti, Rome: Elevation	80
46.	Palazzo Sacchetti, Rome: Plan	80
47.	Palazzo Farnese, Rome: Plan	81
48.	Palazzo Farnese, Rome: Portion of Elevation and Details	82
49.	Palazzo Farnese, Rome: South Front	*facing* 83
50.	Palazzo Farnese, Rome: Courtyard	,, 83
51.	Villa Farnesina, Rome: Plan	84
52.	Palazzo Pietro Massimi, Rome: Details of Entrance Peristyle	85
53.	Palazzi Pietro e Angelo Massimi, Rome: Plans	86
54.	Palazzo Pietro Massimi: Elevation	87
55.	Palazzo Pietro Massimi: Entrance Doorway	88
56.	Palazzo Pietro Massimi: End of Courtyard	*facing* 88
57.	Palazzo Pietro Massimi: Loggia at End of Courtyard	,, 88
58.	Sagrestia Nuova, San Lorenzo, Florence (*L. Wilkinson*)	89
59.	Biblioteca Laurenziana, Florence: Plan of Entrance Vestibule and Staircase (*L. Wilkinson*)	90
60.	Biblioteca Laurenziana, Florence: Sketch of Vestibule (*L. Wilkinson*)	*facing* 90
61.	Piazza del Campidoglio, Rome: Plan	92
62.	Palazzo Caprarola: Bird's-eye Sectional View	*facing* 93

LIST OF ILLUSTRATIONS

FIG. | PAGE
- 63. PALAZZO DEI CONSERVATORI, ROME: PLAN AND ELEVATION . . . 93
- 64. VILLA DI PAPA GIULIO, NEAR ROME: PLAN 94
- 65. VILLA DI PAPA GIULIO: COURTYARD . . . . *facing* 94
- 66. PALAZZO BEVILACQUA, VERONA . . . . ,, 94
- 67. PORTA DEL PALIO, VERONA: ELEVATION . . . . . . ,, 95
- 68. PORTA DEL PALIO, VERONA: PLAN . . . . ,, 95
- 69. PALAZZO CANOSSA, VERONA . . . . ,, 97
- 70. PALAZZO CORNARO DELLA CA' GRANDE, VENICE . . . . ,, 97
- 71. LIBRERIA VECCHIA, VENICE . . . . ,, 98
- 72. BASILICA PALLADIANA, VICENZA: PLAN 100
- 73. BASILICA PALLADIANA, VICENZA: ELEVATION 101
- 74. CASA DEL DIAVOLO, VICENZA: ELEVATION 102
- 75. PALAZZO THIENE, VICENZA 103
- 76. VILLA CAPRA, VICENZA: PLAN, ELEVATION, AND SECTION . . . 104

CHAPTER VI.

- 77. SCALA DI SPAGNA, ROME: PLAN AND SECTION 108
- 78. PALAZZO GIUSTIZIA, MANTUA . . . . *facing* 110
- 79. PALAZZO PITTI, FLORENCE: WING OF COURTYARD . . . . ,, 110
- 80. PALAZZO UGUCCIONI, FLORENCE . . . . ,, 112
- 81. GRAN GUARDIA ANTICA, VERONA . . . . ,, 112
- 82. PALAZZO BARBERINI, ROME: PLAN 113
- 83. PALAZZO DELL' UNIVERSITA, GENOA: PLAN AND SECTION 116
- 84. PALAZZO DAVIA, BOLOGNA . . . . *facing* 116
- 85. PALAZZO MARTINENGO, BRESCIA . . . . ,, 116

CHAPTER VII.

- 86. SANTA MARIA DI LORETO, ROME: PLAN 119
- 87. SS. FRANCESCO E PAOLO, VITERBO, AND MADONNA DELLA STECCATA, PARMA: PLANS (*A. T. Bolton*) 120
- 88. SANTA MARIA DI LORETO, ROME (*L. Wilkinson*) . . . . *facing* 120
- 89. SANTA MARIA DEGLI ANGELI, FLORENCE: PLAN 121
- 90. MADONNA DELL' UMILTA, PISTOJA: PLAN 122
- 91. SANTA MARIA DE' MIRACOLI, ROME: PLAN 123
- 92. SANTA MARIA DI MONTE SANTO, ROME: PLAN 124
- 93. MADONNA DI SANTO BIAGIO, MONTEPULCIANO (*L. Wilkinson*) . *facing* 125
- 94. SANTA MARIA DELLA CONSOLAZIONE, TODI (*L. Wilkinson*) . . ,, 125
- 95. SAN SEBASTIANO, MANTUA: PLAN 125
- 96. SANT' AGNESE, ROME: PLAN 126
- 97. SANTA MARIA DELLA SALUTE, VENICE: PLAN 127
- 98. SAN GIORGIO MAGGIORE, VENICE: PLAN 129
- 99. SANT' IGNAZIO, ROME: PLAN 130

LIST OF ILLUSTRATIONS

FIG.		PAGE
100.	Sant' Andrea, Mantua: Sections.	131
101.	Sant' Andrea, Mantua: Plan	132
102.	Side Chapels of Il Redentore, Venice, and Sant' Annunziata, Naples	133
103.	Santa Maria della Salute, Venice: Interior	facing 134
104.	San Giorgio Maggiore, Venice	,, 134
105.	Madonna de' Miracoli, Brescia: Plan.	135
106.	San Francesco, Rimini: Interior	facing 137
107.	Sant' Andrea della Valle, Rome	,, 137
108.	Buttress, Bergamo Cathedral	137
109.	San Sebastiano, Mantua: Entrance Loggia	facing 138
110.	Sant' Andrea, Mantua	,, 138
111.	San Giorgio Maggiore, Venice	,, 139
112.	Santa Maria in Campitelli, Rome (*L. Wilkinson*)	,, 140
113.	S. Peter's, Rome: Early Plans by Bramante, Peruzzi, A. da San Gallo, and Michael Angelo	142
114.	S. Peter's, Rome	facing 144
115.	S. Peter's, Rome: Piazza	,, 146
116.	S. Peter's, Rome: Transept	,, 146
117.	S. Peter's, Rome: Plan as at Present	147
118.	S. Peter's, Rome: South Elevation	facing 148
119.	S. Peter's, Rome: Interior (*Piranesi*)	,, 149
120.	S. Peter's, Rome: Plan of Pier under Dome	150

CHAPTER VIII.

121.	Sections of Domes: Il Redentore, Venice, and Il Gesu, Rome	153
122.	Plan and Section of Dome: Santa Maria della Salute, Venice	154
123.	Plan and Section of Dome of Church at Piacenza	155
124.	Section through Dome and Transepts of Florence Cathedral, and Details of Construction	156
125.	Ribs and Arched Braces of Dome of Florence Cathedral	157
126.	Section and Elevation of Dome of the Baptistery, Florence	159
127.	Section through Dome and Transepts of St. Peter's, Rome, and Details	161
128.	Section through Dome and Transept of S. Paul's, London, and Details	163
129.	Dôme des Invalides, Paris.	facing 164
130.	Le Panthéon, Paris	,, 164
131.	Dôme des Invalides, Paris: Plan and Section	165
132.	Le Panthéon, Paris: Section and Details	166

CHAPTER IX.

133.	Hôtel de Ville, Orleans	facing 172
134.	Hôtel de Ville, Beaugency	,, 172

LIST OF ILLUSTRATIONS

FIG.		PAGE
135.	Château de Chambord: Plan and Section of Central Staircase	174
136.	Château de Chambord: Dormers and Chimneys . . . . *facing*	175
137.	Château de Chambord: Dormers and Chimneys . . . . ,,	175
138.	Château de Blois: Detail of Outside Staircase . . . ,,	176
139.	Château de Chenonceaux . . . . ,,	176
140.	La Chancellerie, Loches . . . . ,,	177
141.	Château d'Azay-le-Rideau . . . . ,,	177
142.	Château de Chambord: Plan	178
143.	Château d'Angerville-Bailleul: Plan	179
144.	Château de Blois: Cornice of South Side of Court . . *facing*	180
145.	Courtyard of House at Orleans . . . . ,,	181
146.	Château de Chambord: Corner of Courtyard, showing Corridor connecting Angle Tower with Central Block . . . *facing*	181
147.	La Place S. Croix, Angers	183
148.	La Place, Lannion	184
149.	Nôtre Dame de Bon Secours, Guingamp: Interior	187
150.	Ossuary at Trégastel, Brittany	188
151.	Château d'Anet: Plan	190
152.	Louvre, Paris: Portion of South Front . . . . . *facing*	191
153.	Louvre, Paris: Detail of Pilasters . . . . ,,	191
154.	Hôtel d'Asseza, Toulouse	193
155.	Louvre, Paris: Corner of Courtyard . . . . ,,	193
156.	Louvre, Paris: Plan showing Dates of Different Portions .	193
157.	Hôtel de Vogüé, Dijon: Window-heads	195
158.	Hôtel de Vogüé, Dijon: Plan	196
159.	Palais du Luxembourg, Paris: Plan	197
160.	Tours Cathedral: Staircase in Corner of Cloisters . . *facing*	198

CHAPTER X.

161.	Church of the Sorbonne, Paris: Plan	201
162.	Plan of the Town of Richelieu	202
163.	Richelieu: End of Courtyard of House . . . . . . *facing*	202
164.	Richelieu: Porte de Chinon . . . . ,,	202
165.	Château de Balleroy . . . . ,,	203
166.	Château de Brécy: Walled-in Garden	204
167.	Château de Blois: Dome over Staircase . . . . . *facing*	204
168.	Château de Blois: Cove under Dome . . . . ,,	204
169.	Château de Blois: Gaston d'Orleans Wing . . . . . ,,	205
170.	Château de Maisons, near Paris . . . . ,,	205
171.	Château de Maisons: Plan	205
172.	Louvre, Paris: East Façade . . . . *facing*	208
173.	L'Institut de France: Plan	209
174.	Hôtel Lambert, Paris: Plan	210

xiv   LIST OF ILLUSTRATIONS

FIG.		PAGE
175.	Hôtel Lambert, Paris: Section, etc.	210
176.	Hôtel de Beauvais, Paris: Vestibule from Courtyard	facing 211
177.	Hôtel de Beauvais, Paris: End of Courtyard	,, 211
178.	Hôtel de Beauvais, Paris: Plan	211
179.	Nôtre Dame-des-Ardilliers, Saumur	facing 212
180.	Château de Versailles: Block Plan	215
181.	Château de Versailles: Portion of Garden Front	facing 216
182.	Château de Versailles: The Orangery	,, 216
183.	Entrance Gateway, Rue S. Dominique, Paris	,, 218
184.	Entrance Gateway, Rue de Grenelle, Paris	,, 218
185.	Hôtel Amelot, Paris: Plan	219
186.	Le Panthéon, Paris: Plan	222
187.	Le Panthéon, Paris: Section	223

CHAPTER XI.

188.	The Tribunal House, Glastonbury	227
189.	Christ Church, Hampshire: Screen at End of South Aisle	facing 231
190.	Christ Church, Hampshire: Tomb of Countess of Salisbury	,, 231
191.	Layer Marney Towers (Arnold Mitchell)	233
192.	Lacock Abbey, Wilts.	234
193.	Plan of John Thorpe's House	239
194.	Plan in John Thorpe's Sketch-book	240
195.	Kirby Hall, Northamptonshire (S. W. Corner)	242
196.	Kirby Hall, Northamptonshire: Doorway in Courtyard	facing 242
197.	Kirby Hall, Northamptonshire: Bay of Courtyard	,, 242
198.	Kirby Hall, Northamptonshire: Gables, West Front	243
199.	Kirby Hall, Northamptonshire: Gables, West Front	245
200.	Bolsover Castle, Derbyshire: Fireplace	247
201.	The Deanery, Carlisle: Plans	249
202.	Great Chalfield Manor: Plan, and Plan of House with Central Porch	250
203.	Kirby Hall: Plan as at Present	252
204.	Claverton Manor: Plan	253
205.	Aston Hall: Plan	253
206.	Wollaton Hall: Plan (J. A. Gotch and B. T. Batsford)	255
207.	Cothelston Hall: Entrance Gateway, etc.	256
208.	Kirby Hall: Block Plan	257
209.	Bakewell Old Hall	258
210.	South Wraxall Manor: Fireplace, etc.	facing 259
211.	Aston Hall: Long Gallery	,, 259
212.	South Wraxall Manor	259
213.	House at Higham Ferrars	261
214.	The Talbot Inn, Oundle	261
215.	Abbey House, Malmesbury	262

LIST OF ILLUSTRATIONS

FIG.		PAGE
216.	Gables, near Broadstairs, etc.	263
217.	Newton House, near Yeovil	264
218.	Corsham Court	264
219.	Moyns Hall, Suffolk	facing 264
220.	Speke Hall: Garden Front	" 264
221.	Hardwick Hall: Plaster Work	267
222.	Aston Hall: Staircase	facing 268

CHAPTER XII.

223.	Whitehall: Plan as proposed	272
224.	Whitehall: Bird's-eye View, as proposed	facing 272
225.	Castle Ashby: Screen, South Front	273
226.	Ashburnham House, Westminster: Staircase	275
227.	Banqueting Hall, Whitehall (*W. R. Davidson*)	277
228.	Kirby Hall: Front Entrance before Court	facing 278
229.	Kirby Hall: Entrance Front	" 278
230.	Ashburnham House: Doorway	279
231.	Bolsover Castle: Riding School, etc., Plan	280
232.	Bolsover Castle: Riding School, etc., Elevations and Section	facing 280
233.	The Hungerford Freeschoole and Almeshouses, Corsham: Plan	281
234.	The Hungerford Freeschoole and Almeshouses, Corsham: Elevations	283
235.	Wren's Plan for rebuilding London	284
236.	Wren's First Plan for S. Paul's Cathedral (*W. Longman*)	287
237.	Interior of Wren's Original Design for St. Paul's (*W. Longman*)	288
238.	S. Paul's Cathedral: North Elevation	facing 289
239.	S. Paul's Cathedral: Plan	289
240.	S. Paul's Cathedral: Interior	facing 291
241.	S. Paul's Cathedral: Section	291
242.	Wren's City Churches: Plans of S. Benetfink, S. Antholin, S. Stephen, S. Martin, S. Mary-at-Hill, S. James, and S. Bride	293
243.	Wren's City Churches: Steeples of S. Bride, S. Martin, S. Mary-le-Bow	296

CHAPTER XIII.

244.	Greenwich Hospital	facing 303
245.	Greenwich Hospital: Plan	303
246.	Hampton Court: South Front	facing 304
247.	Hampton Court: Fountain Court	" 304
248.	Blenheim: Elevations (*R. I. B. A. Journal*, 1890)	facing 306
249.	The Radcliffe Library, Oxford: Plans	308
250.	Palladian Bridge at Wilton	facing 309
251.	Prior Park, Bath	" 309

as in Milan Cathedral, outside influence dictated the form; entablatures, modified it is true, but of unmistakable origin, were still placed above arcades, as in the late days of the Empire—the interior of Florence Cathedral (see Vol. II. Fig. 235) is one instance out of many; carving continued ever reminiscent of the acanthus leaf the Romans loved for their capitals; and the dome, as the crowning finish to a building of monumental character, remained in the Middle Ages almost as popular as it had been in the time of Hadrian.

Italy's position in the fifteenth century.

To understand the position Italy occupied at the commencement of the fifteenth century, it should be remembered that although the country was a disunited one, split up into several independent kingdoms and republics, and consequently not possessing possibly the same political power as France, Spain, or England, and unable to put equally large armies into the field, its cities, owing mainly to their independence, were in a far more advanced state of civilization than the cities of other countries. Their inhabitants enjoyed a degree of comfort and luxury unknown elsewhere. The pre-eminence of Italy continued until the end of the sixteenth century. Then its commerce declined, and other countries obtained supremacy. Symonds[1] states that early in the fourteenth century the streets and squares of Italian cities "were everywhere paved with flags," and he compares with them "the unpaved lanes of London and the muddy labyrinths of Paris." The dignified traditions of Roman planning had never been entirely abandoned in Italy, and the noble paved Roman roads still existed, branching in all directions. To these traditions are due the fine scale of open spaces, such as the Piazza in front of S. Peter's, the Piazza del Popolo—from which starts the old Via Flaminia—the Piazza del Campidoglio on the Capitol and its approaches, and numerous other squares in Rome as well as in other cities. Traditional also are the staircases, like the Scala di Spagna, Rome, of the eighteenth century (see Fig. 77), and the terraces and flights of steps which form so striking a feature of many an Italian garden.

Influence of literature.

In literature Italy was far ahead of all other countries years before the Renaissance dawned. The contemporaries of Dante elsewhere were but monkish chroniclers. Petrarch and Boccaccio head the long list of succeeding poets. Most Italians wrote poetry in the fifteenth and sixteenth centuries, and the few who did not could appreciate and loved to recite the poems of others. The

[1] "Renaissance in Italy: The Fine Arts," by John Addington Symonds.

revival in literature preceded what is known as the Renaissance in architecture, but it is a mistake to say it occasioned it. It helped to popularize it, especially in the second half of the fifteenth century, when the educated delighted in habitually writing and speaking in Latin, but in the two or three previous decades, when the architectural movement commenced and the first steps were taken towards acquiring a more thorough knowledge of classic art, the influence of literature on architectural advance was not great. It is true that the revived demand for classic writings undoubtedly led to more attention being paid to classic monuments; and the palaces in which the Cæsars lived, the theatres in which the plays men were recommencing to read had been acted, the covered colonnades under whose shelter poets, philosophers, and wits had recited, disputed, and sparkled, all the buildings, in fact, representative of life in the old cities under the long passed civilization, must have acquired fresh interest in consequence. Petrarch and Boccaccio may, as stated by Symonds, have "turned the whole intellectual energy of the Florentines into the channels of Latin and Greek scholarship," but architecture had for centuries nursed the germ of classic, and all the literary scholarship in the world could not have changed the current of another art, if its tide had not already turned in the same direction.[1] Seldom, if ever, does a movement take place in one art without a corresponding movement in others. Such movements are "in the air," and whence they started is generally difficult to say. Because they find expression first in one particular art, they do not necessarily have their rise in it. A poet can write a poem, a painter paint a picture, without outside support or assistance; an architect cannot build without a client. Moreover, in the fourteenth and fifteenth centuries architecture and sculpture were one; and before deciding that absolute priority is to be awarded over them to literature, it is well to remember that Niccola Pisano was born more than fifty years before Dante, to take the John of the Baptist of each branch.

The renaissance in literature was an absolutely new birth,

Renaissance in architecture a reaction.

[1] The most remarkable instance of something more than a classic germ existing in the thirteenth century, and of the power of the Italian craftsmen of the day to reproduce faithfully and feelingly Roman forms, is manifested at S. Lorenzo fuori le mura, Rome. The front of the narthex of that church consists of a peristyle of columns having capitals of the Ionic order which are as well carved as though they had been executed 1000 years before. According to Cattaneo the capitals date from 1216–27.

because the germ of literary scholarship had been entirely lost. The renaissance in architecture was but a reaction; a reaction against Gothic, and, to some extent, against the corrupt forms of Classic which before Gothic was introduced had passed muster. Herein lies the most important difference between the relation of architecture and of literature to the movement known as the Renaissance.

Vernacular traditions, Basilican and Byzantine.

A further difference worth noting is that in architecture classic traditions were not the only ones that had survived. During the two centuries, the thirteenth and fourteenth, in which alone had Gothic architecture obtained any footing in Italy, Basilican and Byzantine traditions, both founded on Classic art, had never been thrown over entirely.[1] The basilican plan and ordinance continued to be employed for churches in Central and Southern Italy long after Gothic had crossed the frontier. Thus, S. Croce, Florence (c. 1300, see Vol. II. Fig. 240), is structurally and in plan a basilican church, although its arches have a wider span than those in earlier churches, and they are pointed. Byzantine influence lasted longer in some parts than in others, and longest of all in Venetian territory, in the cities of Apulia, and in a few other towns, such as Pisa, which had close relations with the Eastern emperors. It made itself felt strongly in a variety of ways all through the twelfth century, and even later to a more limited extent.[2] Owing to Byzantine buildings chiefly the dome retained its position in Italy all through the Middle Ages. This feature originated in the East, and it was the Eastern builders that, after the fall of Rome, again popularized it in the West, as at Ravenna, in S. Vitale, at Milan, in S. Lorenzo, and in churches in Southern Italian towns too numerous to mention. A long sequence connects the Pantheon, Rome, with Brunelleschi's triumph at Florence. Through the centuries domes continued to be built in Italy. The twelfth-century dome of Pisa Cathedral,

[1] Romanesque architecture made little impression south of the Apennines; Bologna is about as far as it penetrated, and there it flourished only tentatively. It consequently exercised no influence on the Renaissance of Florence and the other cities of Central and Southern Italy.

[2] In cathedral bronze doors especially. Some, like those at Benevento, are said to have actually been designed and made at Constantinople. Others, like the famous ones at Trani and Ravello, are the work of Barisanus of Trani, and belong to the last quarter of the twelfth century. The art of bronze founding—early brought to a high pitch of excellence, as the famous doors and frame of the Pantheon, Rome, testify—was practised in Italy largely by the Byzantines, and remained a living art long after it had reached its zenith under Ghiberti.

the thirteenth-century dome of Siena Cathedral, that of the early part of the century following at Orvieto Cathedral, are amongst the most notable of existing connecting links. The huge church of S. Petronio, Bologna, was planned at the end of the fourteenth century to have a central dome, and the Florentines intended the crossing of their cathedral to be domed also, although luckily the execution thereof was deferred for more than half a century.

Not one influence, therefore, but three influences, and possibly more, helped to mould architectural design in the early days of the Renaissance, *i.e.* through the greater part of the fifteenth century. This contention cannot be insisted upon too strongly. It accounts for much that otherwise would appear phenomenal. To ignore it is to endow Brunelleschi and his immediate followers with almost superhuman powers, and to suggest that he and they evolved plans and forms out of their inner consciousness to a far greater extent than artists at any other period have been able to do. Brunelleschi reintroduced pure Classic detail; he profited greatly by his study of Roman construction; but he also continued in his work existing traditions. Not Gothic traditions, because those he neither understood, nor gave a thought to. He was a sculptor before he was an architect, and in sculpture the influence of Niccola Pisano was supreme from the middle of the thirteenth century onwards.

The feeling in Niccola Pisano's work is mainly Classic, owing to his admiration for and careful study of antique reliefs and sculpture generally. One of his most distinguished pupils, known as Andrea Pisano, who died *c.* 1349, "carried the manner of his master to Florence, . . . and in the first gate of the Baptistery he bequeathed a model of bas-relief in bronze, which largely influenced the style of masters in the fifteenth century."[1] Andrea's most famous pupil was the artist best known as Orcagna (died *c.* 1369), whose *chef-d'œuvre* is the tabernacle over the high altar in the church of Or San Michele, Florence, which was finished in 1359, only eighteen years before Brunelleschi was born. The achievements of these men and the dates when they

Influence of the Pisani.

---

[1] Symonds says that the work of Giovanni Pisano, Niccola's son, shows more Gothic feeling than his father's, but the influence of Classic composition is nevertheless visible in it, and in many respects it differs from the work of contemporary architects and sculptors of more northern countries. Giovanni's best-known achievement is the west façade of Siena Cathedral, and he, or his pupils, also "beautified" the little S. Maria della Spina at Pisa. Both examples are gingerbread Gothic, and to northern eyes at least eminently unsatisfactory.

worked are of considerable importance. A boy's natural instinct is to turn to small and delicate details of art rather than to buildings as a whole; and Brunelleschi was probably more attracted by the former than by the latter. His training also in a goldsmith's bottega would lead him in the same direction. It is no exaggeration therefore to say that from the first he was imbued with Classic feeling—certainly to a far greater extent than with Gothic. His contemporaries were similarly placed and influenced. For him and for them it was no break to turn to pure Classic art; it was a natural step. If Gothic had been alive in Italy, as it was in France and England, some wonder might be felt that the Renaissance spread so rapidly and so universally. Moreover, if the public generally had been opposed to Classic literature, or even merely indifferent to it, the enthusiasm of artists for Classic architecture might have suffered some check. But as already mentioned, the very opposite was the case. Amongst poets, writers, merchants, princes, as well as painters, sculptors, architects, admiration for the old authors was great. The arts of architecture and literature were consequently able to advance side by side in perfect harmony.

The "Grecian" cult.
The authors read at first were mainly the Latin ones. Interest in Greek literature was but slight until a somewhat later period. Petrarch had done his best to foster it, but the "Grecian" cult cannot be said to have started before 1438, when the Eastern emperor visited Florence, and a council was held at Ferrara to try and effect a union between the Greek and Roman Churches. Three years later it met at Florence, on the invitation of the astute Cosimo de' Medici, who saw political, commercial, and æsthetic advantages in establishing relations with the Eastern empire. The conference brought together a number of learned men from the East, but otherwise accomplished little. The conquest of Constantinople by the Turks in 1453 had more important results. It drove from that city numerous Greek scholars, who, with such manuscripts and works of art as they had been able to save, found a welcome and a refuge in Italy, and especially at Florence. Their scholarship it was that led the Florentines to a true and correct understanding of ancient Greek literature, but cannot be said to have had more than a small and very indirect effect on the revival of Classic architecture in Italy. That was already in full swing.

Bottega training.
A difference worth noting between the artistic craftsman of

Italy in the fourteenth and fifteenth centuries and his contemporary in more northern countries is that the latter followed but one craft; he was a mason, a carpenter, a glass stainer, a painter. The Florentine followed many. He undertook, as chance offered, the work and duties of an architect, painter, sculptor, bronze founder, or goldsmith. His versatility was largely owing to the nature of the "botteghe" in which men obtained their training. Each bottega was literally a shop in which the work was widely varied, and where the master took orders for, and he and his apprentices carried out whatever clients were willing to entrust to him.[1] An apprentice in those days learnt many trades. He did not start his career by announcing his desire to learn any one particular art or craft. If he had his prospective master would have told him, in polite, pure Tuscan, that he was mad and fit only to sweep crossings. Identically the same training was gone through by Botticelli, Orcagna, Ghiberti, Brunelleschi, Ghirlandajo, Luca della Robbia, Benvenuto Cellini, and others. Michael Angelo started as pupil to Ghirlandajo. It is a wonderful picture which these men, with their mastery of many arts, present; a picture which, under present conditions, can hardly be witnessed now. Some finally achieved success in one art, others in another, but all were trained in several. Orcagna besides obtaining distinction as a sculptor and worker in materials, studied painting, practised as an architect, and was no mean poet; Ghiberti is best known as a modeller and bronze founder, but he also painted—in fact, his sculpture is generally pictorial. He was also an architect, but in this branch he failed. Luca della Robbia was essentially a modeller, and his panels of choristers and of children dancing for the organ gallery intended for Florence Cathedral, although in marble, are plastic in treatment. He is best known by the coloured and glazed earthenware he originated and made. Cellini's salt-cellars have become world famous; to such an extent that one is liable to forget that he could model life-size figures as well as any, as his bronze Perseus in the Loggia dei Lanzi proves. Ghirlandajo, on the other hand, although he started as the others did, soon confined himself to painting, and Donatello, that exquisite sculptor, failed when he attempted architectural design, as is shown by the doorways flanking the small chancel

---

[1] Symonds describes the situation bluntly when he says, "Painting and sculpture in Italy were regarded as trades, and the artist had his bottega just as much as a cobbler or a blacksmith."

in the Sagrestia Vecchia of S. Lorenzo, Florence.¹ Brunelleschi, Michael Angelo, and the most wonderfully versatile product of the Renaissance, Leonardo da Vinci, are others, referred to later, who practised all or most of the arts.

Merits and demerits of Bottega training.

The merits and demerits of the Bottega training were about equally balanced. It taught men on traditional lines, and as all workers went through the same course, many actually side by side, absolute harmony in the different branches of art was assured. The courses probably differed slightly in the different botteghe, although much the same work could be done in all. Thus, some shops apparently had a special reputation for large-size figures; others for delicate small figures in precious metal, or for coins and medals, or for flagons and tankards, or rings, brooches, and pretty trinkets generally. In some mural painting was the forte of the master, who handled the brush better than the tools. But in all, men obtained an absolutely sound and broad practical training, and a thorough acquaintance with "materials, instruments, and technical processes of art." The training represented the survival of the Mediæval apprenticeship system, but differed from it in its comprehensiveness. On the other hand, whilst broad in this respect, it was narrow in another sense. It confined men too much to detail. Being manual, it offered few opportunities for mastering big problems of design. It was suitable for sculptors and painters, but was not calculated to produce architects. Amongst the many who started in these workshops the two who achieved greatest distinction in architecture were Brunelleschi and Michael Angelo, and the latter hardly counts as he left Ghirlandajo when he was sixteen. Brunelleschi succeeded in spite of this training, not because of it. He was more than a mere worker and designer in material. Not so versatile as Leonardo da Vinci, he was still an accomplished and well-read man. He made a special study of perspective, and evolved what Vasari calls "a perfectly correct method of applying it; a truly ingenious thing, and of great utility to the art of design." He was a mathematician, and devoted himself especially to geometry; he mastered the Scriptures so well that he could hold his own in theological discussion with dignitaries of the Church, and he early studied the works of Dante.² In other

---

[1] The building was designed by Brunelleschi, but Donatello added the doorways without his knowledge, the result being a quarrel which severed the long friendship of the two men.

[2] His father, a lawyer, originally intended him to follow his own profession.

INTRODUCTORY

words, he received, or obtained for himself, as liberal an education as the times allowed. This supplied him with the sound foundation without which he could not possibly have succeeded as he did. His bottega training helped him but little. His success was mainly due, apart from his scholarly attainments and native genius, to his careful and thorough study of the masterpieces of antique art. He studied as an architect should study, not so much small detail—in his subsequent work he often left that to others—as the construction and planning of buildings, and the big problems of design which really constitute architecture.

Painting is the art in which the Italians of the Renaissance earliest achieved distinction, and it was the painters who first threw over the traditions of the bottega training and cut themselves adrift from the workers in the other arts.[1] The divorce of painting from the sister arts of architecture and sculpture, now alas! general at least in England, may be said to commence with the foundation of a school for painters at Padua by Francesco Squarcione about the year 1430. Squarcione, who seems to have had no reputation himself as a painter, set his students to draw from the antique, and supplemented this study by thorough and scientific instruction in the science of perspective.[2] But the chief blow to the bottega system was given by Cosimo de' Medici, a few years later, by the founding, in the gardens of his palace at Florence, of his Neo-Platonic Academy, which included a training in all the arts. The introductory period of the Renaissance ends with the starting of this Academy, and with the death of Brunelleschi, which took place in 1446. The great artist's pioneer work was then bearing fruit, and the principles he had striven for were universally accepted. After his death ancient classic detail alone was followed to the exclusion of all other. What he and his successors and followers accomplished is traced in the succeeding chapters.

Divorce of painting from the sister arts.

Before treating of their work, however, a few words may not

---

[1] Symonds says that Italian painting has exercised most influence on subsequent art; but it is a question if it has exercised more than Italian Renaissance architecture. The enormous vitality of the latter and its sure foundation on ancient art, have enabled it not only to spread rapidly but also to survive. From it has sprung, ever since the fifteenth century, save during the revivalist movements, the architecture of the civilized world.

[2] The part perspective plays in early Renaissance painting is often very great. Its use, or rather abuse, in early buildings is referred to later (see pp. 54 and 64).

be out of place regarding the condition of affairs in Italy before the Renaissance dawned, and the reasons why it started in Florence, and why most of the early workers in the movement were Florentines.

Leading powers in Italy.

The town of Florence, modern by comparison with most Italian towns, succeeded Pisa as the most powerful city in Tuscany about the end of the thirteenth century. Situated on the fertile plain of the Arno, the passage of which river it commanded, it gradually developed its resources and expanded its borders. Its citizens, grown rich by commerce and conquest, soon turned their attention to making up leeway in culture; with such success that early in the fifteenth century the Republic of Florence had become not only one of the most powerful states in Italy, but also the acknowledged chief centre for everything appertaining to literature, poetry, and the fine arts. Besides Florence itself, the Republic included the towns of Pistoja, Prato, Pisa, Cortona, Leghorn, etc., the harbour of the last-named being a valuable possession which gave it a direct outlet to the sea. The other great powers in Italy of this period were the kingdom of Naples, the duchy of Milan, the republic of Venice, and the Papacy. In 1377 the Pope had returned to Rome from exile at Avignon, and gradually the old city emerged from the misery and low estate to which it had been brought by constant wars and local dissensions, and once more took its rightful place amongst the cities and powers of Italy.

An artistic age.

Whistler declared that "There never was an artistic period. There never was an Art-loving nation."[1] His statement, however, can be challenged as regards many periods in the world's history; for example, Egypt, in the time of the Ramesidæ, Athens, in the age of Pericles, and Florence in the fifteenth century. If Symonds' remark that every Italian was a perfect judge of art, "from the Pope upon S. Peter's chair to the clerks in a Florentine counting-house," has to be received with some reserve, most people will endorse his brilliant testimony to the period of the Renaissance in Italy as "an age of splendid ceremonies and magnificent parade, when the furniture of houses, the armour of soldiers, the dress of citizens, the pomp of war, and the pageantry of festival were invariably and inevitably beautiful. On the meanest articles of domestic utility, cups and platters, door-panels and chimney-pieces, coverlets for beds, and lids of linen chests, a wealth of

[1] In his "Ten O'clock."

artistic invention was lavished by innumerable craftsmen, no less skilled in technical details than distinguished by rare taste."[1] At the same time there were doubtless Florentines who cared nothing about art—as in a warlike race there are to be found some who have no stomach for fighting—but the long list of patrons of art in Florence, and the achievements in art accomplished there, show that the artistic feeling was widespread.

The government of Florence rested in the hands of the seven great "Arti," or Guilds—the wool dressers, cloth dressers, money changers, lawyers, silk merchants, apothecaries, and furriers. All the leading merchants and traders were members of one or other of these societies. The craftsmen's guilds were minor ones, and were affiliated to the greater guilds; the goldsmiths, for instance, being under the protection of the silk merchants.[2] The wealthy burghers were the patrons, as was only natural in a commercial city, and the architects, sculptors, painters, goldsmiths, etc., were their employees. The guild that exercised most influence over art in the city was the Arte della Lana, or guild of wool dressers, under whose care especially was placed the building of the dome of the cathedral, including the obtaining of the funds necessary for that purpose.

The Arti of Florence.

Although Florence was a republic, one Florentine family in particular stands out above all others as not only the most powerful in the history of the city, but also as one of the most famous in the annals of the whole of Italy. The Medici were originally merchants in Florence. Acquiring great wealth and influence they rose rapidly, and practically became absolute rulers of the town. Nor was their influence confined to Florence alone. Younger sons either became heads of other states, like Lorenzo, Duke of Urbino (1492–1519), or else went into the Church and achieved the highest honours, like Giovanni, proclaimed pope in 1513 and famous as Leo X., or like Giulio, later known as Clement VII. The daughters of the family in many cases married royalty; the most famous being Catherine, wife of Henry II., King of France. The best known of the Florentine rulers are Cosimo, died 1464, the founder of the Platonic Academy and the world-renowned Biblioteca Laurenziana, who was the patron of

The "Medici."

---

[1] "The Fine Arts," p. 3.
[2] Brunelleschi, besides being a member of the goldsmiths, was enrolled in the silk guild, but similar honour was accorded to but few of his artist contemporaries.

Brunelleschi, Michelozzo, and of artists and the arts generally; and his grandson Lorenzo (1449–92), known as Il Magnifico, who, besides achieving great reputation as a statesman, wrote poetry, and was a patron of poets. After his death the fortunes of the Medici somewhat declined, but for over two hundred years, until the race became extinct in 1737, it remained the ruling dynasty in Florence.

CHAPTER II

THE HISTORY OF THE RISE IN FLORENCE

THE work now to be considered requires in some respects different grouping from that already dealt with in the two previous volumes. In discussing the buildings of the Middle Ages it is often difficult to decide to whom should be given the credit for any design. The master mason responsible for it was merely chief amongst his fellows; otherwise he differed little from them. He had received the same education as they; had begun like them on the bottom rung; was recompensed for his work in similar fashion, although no doubt on a somewhat higher scale; and owed his position entirely to having proved his superior skill as a designer or constructor. Diligent research has brought to light the names of some of these master builders, those employed on cathedrals or large churches; but the majority have yet to be discovered, and the authors of smaller buildings and fittings are almost unknown. In mediæval architecture, therefore, the individual counts for little. His identity is merged in his work. The names Robert de Coucy, Robert de Luzarches recur to few; but Reims and Amiens Cathedrals are known to every one. By them and by other important buildings one traces architectural development.

<small>The Mediæval architect.</small>

In the Renaissance, on the other hand, the individual counts for much. Designers came to the front, and became a thing apart from the workmen who carried out their designs. Abuse has been levelled at the movement in consequence. The method in vogue before it commenced has been lauded at its expense. But one thing is certain : if the personality of several great artists could not have asserted itself; if the life in Florence and other large Italian cities had not given these artists the opportunity to proclaim their personality, and to rise above the ruck of mediocre workmen, there might have been a Renaissance in architecture—since that was desired by a cultured, artistic people,—but instead of decades, centuries would have passed before it was definitely

<small>The Renaissance architect.</small>

established. When one thinks of Italian Renaissance architecture, one's first thoughts go to Brunelleschi, Alberti, Bramante, Peruzzi, Michael Angelo, Palladio, and others almost as famous. Their lives and achievements illustrate the advances made from time to time. For this reason, in this and subsequent chapters, save in those dealing solely with developments in plan and construction, the buildings which have been selected as illustrative of each period, and to exemplify progress, are grouped mainly under the names of their authors.

Filippo Brunelleschi (1377–1446). Baptistery doors competition.

Brunelleschi's early training in a sculptor-goldsmith's workshop and his scholarly attainments have already been referred to. Little is known about what he accomplished as a sculptor and bronze founder before 1400; but his reputation even then must have been considerable, as he was enrolled a member of the Silk-workers Guild in 1398, and in 1401 was one of the half-dozen sculptors invited to compete for the second pair of bronze doors for the Baptistery of Florence.[1] In this competition, luckily for architecture, he failed; Lorenzo Ghiberti's panel being placed first and his second; although the judges hesitated considerably before coming to a decision.[2] His failure decided him to devote himself to larger problems of design, and with this purpose in view he started for Rome in 1403 with Donatello, then a lad of sixteen, as his companion.

Brunelleschi at Rome.

At Rome Brunelleschi remained four years; some authorities say without a break, others that he returned to Florence for a few months after a year and a half's sojourn. It is immaterial which is true; all agree that the period he spent studying in Rome was considerable. During that time he supported himself partly on the proceeds of a property he had sold before leaving Florence, and partly by working at his craft of sculptor-goldsmith. Vasari gives a vivid picture of the life he led there. He measured and drew the plans and construction of all kinds of buildings, "temples, round, square, or octagon, basilicas, aqueducts, baths, arches, the Colosseum, amphitheatres, and every church built of bricks, of which he examined all the modes of binding and clamping, as well as the turning of the vaults and arches." At the back of

---

[1] The first pair had been executed by Andrea Pisano in 1336.

[2] The terms of the competition were that each competitor should cast and model in bronze one panel to a given shape and size representing Abraham's sacrifice. The trial panels by Ghiberti and Brunelleschi are now preserved in the Bargello, Florence. Brunelleschi's panel is certainly the more striking, the modelling of the horse in the foreground being particularly powerful.

his mind was ever the desire to complete the cathedral in his native city. This was his great ambition; and few men have set before themselves one definite object in life, and have had to wait longer for its realization.

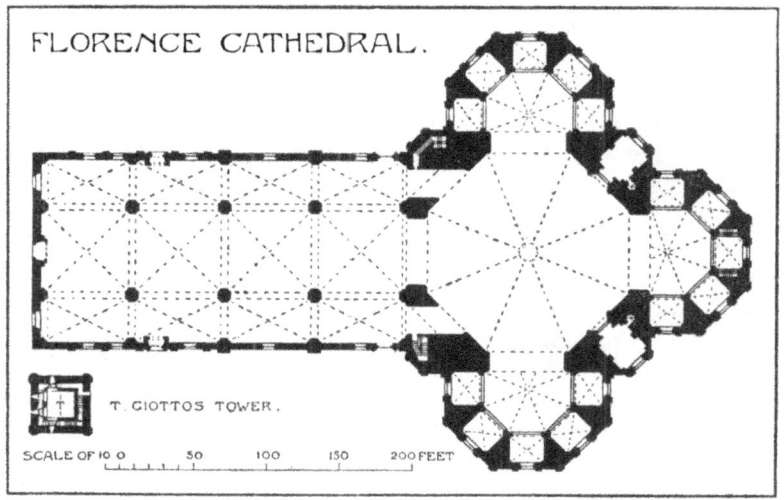

Fig. 1.

The Cathedral of Florence was begun by Arnolfo in the last few years of the thirteenth century, and was unfinished at his death in 1311. After the plague of 1348, which corresponds to our "Black Death," the walls of the nave were raised, and the building otherwise enlarged. In 1366 an assembly of architects settled the plan of the eastern arm, and probably decided also the shape of the dome which was to cover the great octagon. But that dome was never built. The three octagonal apses, or tribunes, surrounding the central octagon were covered in, and the walling of the octagon was carried as high as the cornice which ranges with the cornice above the clerestory of the nave. Then the work stopped. The intention evidently was to start the dome from that level. This is confirmed

Florence Cathedral.

Fig. 2.

by the view of the cathedral pictured in one of the well-known frescoes in the Capella degli Spagnuoli in the church of Santa Maria Novella.¹

<small>Conference *re* dome.</small>

The next conference was held in 1407, and this brought Brunelleschi post-haste back to Florence, full of projects and ideas. What these were he, wise man as he was, kept in the main to himself; the only ones he divulged being that the dome should be raised on a drum 15 braccia high, and that eight circular windows should be inserted in the drum, one on each side.² The next ten years he spent partly in Rome and partly in Florence, devoting all his spare time to perfecting his scheme. During this period the drum he insisted upon was built, and he made drawings for the completion of those portions of the east end which were still unfinished, notably the upper parts of the small apses between the tribunes. These were carried out. In May, 1417, the authorities paid him for this work, and tried to worm out of him how he proposed to construct the dome. This for some time he refused to state; refused also to show the models he had prepared. The chief difficulty to be overcome was the one the Romans had been confronted with, and had solved so satisfactorily, namely, how to construct a dome of vast dimensions without elaborate and expensive centering. Brunelleschi claimed that he could dispense with centering; could build "without any framework whatsoever." His assertion was regarded as an idle boast, and was received with ridicule. In reply he asked for another competition. This resulted in a variety of proposals being put forward by other men, mostly impossible. The only one that might have been practicable was that a central column should be erected, and the masonry of the drum during construction strutted up from that; somewhat on the lines of the central revolving post which the Byzantine builders in the East had used for constructing small stone drums.³

---

¹ The date of the frescoes is not known for certain. Vasari says they were painted by Taddeo Gaddi, who succeeded Giotto as architect of the cathedral. The picture is evidently not of Arnolfo's church, but of the Duomo, as proposed to be enlarged in the fourteenth century.

² The Florentine braccio was 23 inches, and this is of some interest as showing that old Roman measures were still current. A standard Roman measure was the square brick used in concrete walls and vaults for bonding (see Vol. I. pp. 117–121). This, according to Middleton, was 2 Roman feet square, *i.e.* 23 English inches. The braccio is still sometimes employed in Italy as a measure.

³ See Choisy, "L'Art de bâtir chez les Byzantins." The most fanciful

THE HISTORY OF THE RISE IN FLORENCE

The new competition was announced on August 19, 1418, and the designs and models were submitted before the end of the year. One was "a model in brick and mortar, without scaffolding," by Brunelleschi. Leader Scott states that [1] "in Signor Cesare Guasti's collection of archivial documents regarding the building of the Duomo, we find that from October to December, 1418, several of the masters . . . were receiving payment for building a model in masonry of Brunelleschi's plan for the cupola." According to the same writer, "this brick model, which was built on the Piazza del Duomo, remained there until 1430, when the Opera ordered its destruction." These statements dispose of the hitherto accepted belief that Brunelleschi declined entirely to disclose his scheme before the work was entrusted to him, but he doubtless kept secret many of its details.

Finally, after much discussion and waste of time, Brunelleschi, in 1420, was appointed architect to complete the dome. But the members of the building guild—the Arte dei Maestri di Pietra e Legnane—and many of the citizens were up in arms at what they termed the rashness of entrusting so important and difficult a work to one man. In consequence of their agitation, Ghiberti, his old competitor for the gates of the Baptistery, was appointed as his colleague. Brunelleschi was bitterly disappointed; but the story told about the way that, three years later, he got rid of his rival is characteristic of the man. Knowing that Ghiberti had no constructive skill, at a critical moment when the dome had started and the workmen were waiting for orders, he took to his bed, and announced that he was seriously ill. To all requests from the Syndics and workmen for instructions he replied, "Consult Ghiberti." The latter, helpless and incompetent, resigned; and Brunelleschi promptly recovered. From 1423 until his death he had sole charge of the work. When he died the dome was finished with the exception of the lantern, for which he left a model (still preserved) and complete written instructions.

Brunelleschi appointed to build the dome.

From the statements that he made in writing from time to time to the Syndics and committees, it is certain that Brunelleschi knew from the first what he intended to do, and if he had been

suggestion of all was that a mound of earth of the requisite size and shape should be formed, which could be cleared away when the dome was built; and that coins should be imbedded in the mass as an inducement to boys to help in its clearance.

[1] "The Cathedral Builders," by Leader Scott, p. 340. She quotes from Signor Cesare Guasti's "La Cupola di Santa Maria del Fiore," pp. 34, 35.

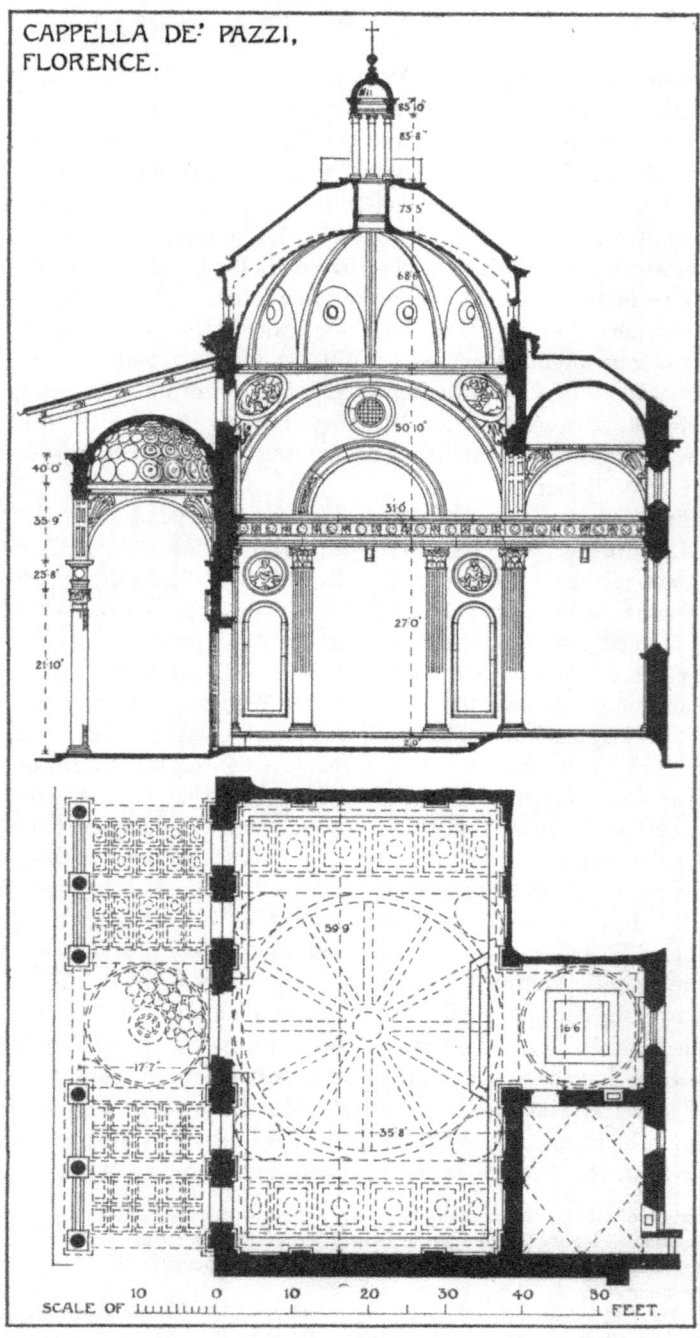

Fig. 3. (*L. Wilkinson*.)

Photo: Alinari.

FIG. 4.—CAPPELLA PAZZI, AND S. CROCE, FLORENCE.

Photo: Alinari.

FIG. 5.—CAPPELLA PAZZI, FLORENCE.   [*To face p.* 18.

trusted the dome might have been commenced many years earlier. There is no need to state here his proposals, because, except in a few details of minor importance, they were carried out as described in Chapter VIII. Whether his scheme was chiefly the result of his study of Classic methods of dome construction, or whether he followed mainly old vernacular traditions which had been abandoned, but not altogether forgotten, during two centuries of Gothic building, is also discussed there.

Much the same question arises over the dome of the Pazzi Chapel, alongside Santa Croce, Florence. The probability is that in this instance the form adopted was the result of lingering Byzantine and Romanesque traditions. The dome starts from pendentives, without a drum, but is not a true hemisphere. It is divided by ribs into twelve concave compartments.[1] As in S. Vitale, Ravenna, and numerous Romanesque churches in Italy and Germany, it does not show externally, but is covered by a flat pitched roof, the timbers of which rest on a circular wall, which is carried up to receive them. In plan the chapel consists of a narthex, nave, and small square chancel. In addition to the central dome, there are domes over the chancel and entrance bay of the narthex, whilst the rest of the church is barrel vaulted. The façade is chiefly remarkable for the happy blending of arch and lintel construction. The effect of weakness which sometimes results from such a combination is prevented by the panelled masses above the columns. These also neutralize the lateral thrusts of the barrel vaults over the ends of the narthex, and impart real and apparent stability. As an architectural composition it is one of the most beautiful ever devised.[2]

Dome of Pazzi Chapel.

Two other ecclesiastical examples by Brunelleschi, the churches of San Lorenzo and Santo Spirito, Florence, demonstrate the third

Brunelleschi's churches.

[1] Other Renaissance domes, similar in form to the dome of the Pazzi Chapel, are over the Sacristies of S. Lorenzo and S. Spirito, Florence, and S. Satiro, Milan (see Fig. 24), the church of S. Maria delle Carceri, Prato, and are sometimes found in later churches. These domes can be compared with the dome over the sixth-century church of S. Sergius and Bacchus, Constantinople, and the semi-dome over the great apse in Hadrian's Villa, Tivoli, in which example each alternate compartment is concave (see Vol. I. Fig. 96).

[2] Mr. C. H. Moore, in his "Character of Renaissance Architecture," designates the carrying of a barrel vault on an entablature above columns "bad architecture." He states that an "order has no power of resistance to the thrusts of vaulting," but inasmuch as the entablature intervenes, and the lateral thrusts are neutralized, there is little difference between this front and a wall pierced with openings which carries a barrel vault.

influence mentioned as conspicuous in early Italian Renaissance, viz. the basilican, and therefore may be considered now. These churches have little in common with later examples. His first work at S. Lorenzo was the north sacristy, or Sagrestia Vecchia. This and the chapels and transepts of the church were finished before his

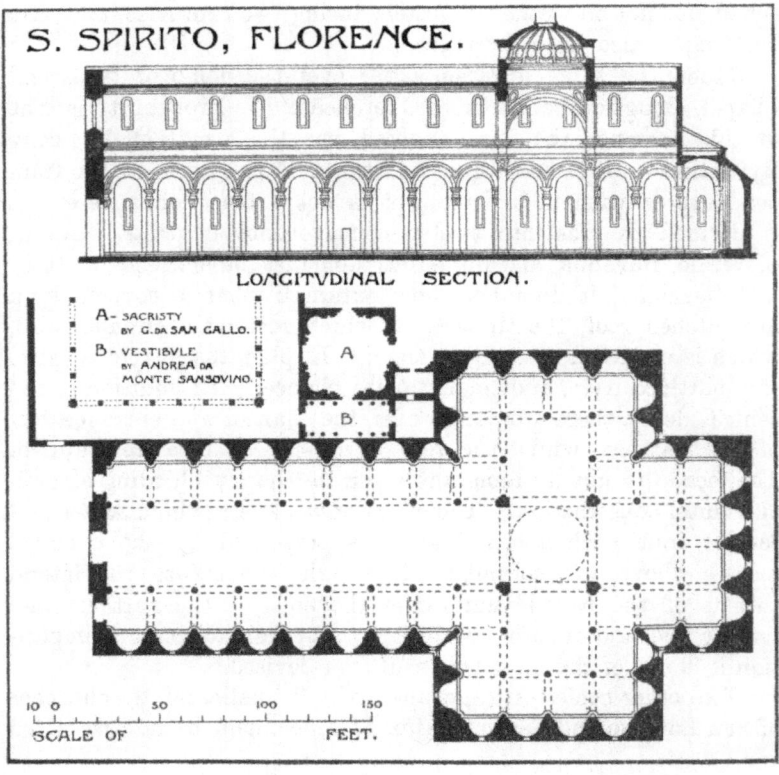

Fig. 6.

death, but the nave was not commenced until after. It is doubtful if any portion of S. Spirito was built during his lifetime. In the fifteenth century, churches, as well as palaces, often took long to build, and there was frequently considerable delay in making a start. S. Spirito is cruciform in plan, and in this respect departs somewhat from the usual basilican type, and approaches nearer to northern mediæval churches. Otherwise it differs little in size, construction, and internal ordinance from S. Lorenzo.

S. Lorenzo follows very closely the early basilican churches in Rome.[1] The chief difference is that the crossing is covered by a dome on pendentives necessitating both longitudinal and transverse arches for its support. The aisles are divided into bays by

S. Lorenzo.

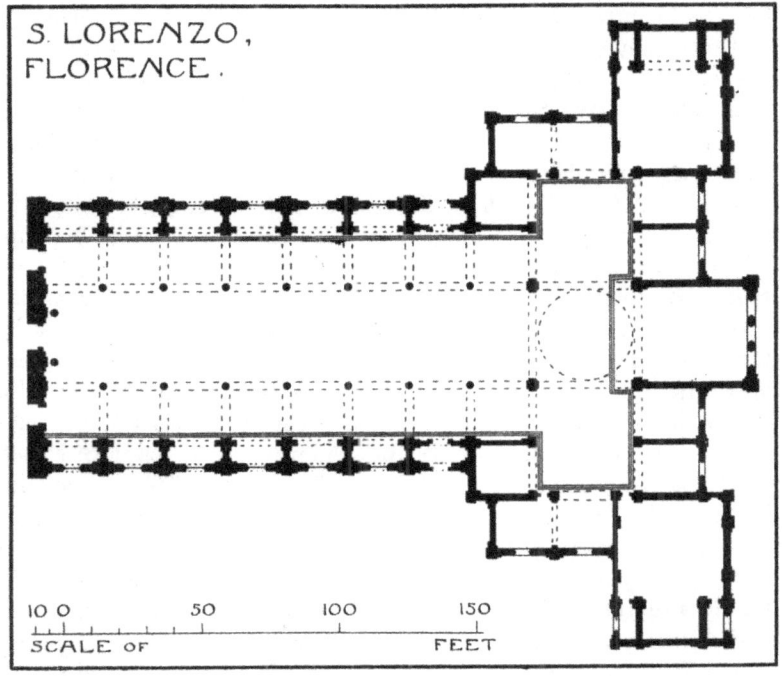

FIG. 7.

transverse arches, and each bay is domed. In basilican churches aisles have either continuous intersecting vaults, as in S. Maria Maggiore, Rome, or else flat ceilings. Apart from detail, these are the only discrepancies. Nave, chancel, and transepts are covered by flat timber ceilings heavily coffered, the arches of the arcades are semicircular, the bays numerous and close together, and above the arches is a continuous entablature over which is a clerestory similar to that in basilican churches. The splendid mosaics, however, frequently found in the latter are wanting. Pictorial painting had destroyed the older art.

[1] It is said to be built on the site of an early church, but it is doubtful if old foundations had anything to do with Brunelleschi's plan.

22   A HISTORY OF ARCHITECTURAL DEVELOPMENT

Spacing of bays.

A comparison between the plans of S. Lorenzo and S. Croce, Florence (see Vol. II. Fig. 240), shows how completely Brunelleschi departed from the spacing of Italian Gothic churches. The nave of each church has eight bays (exclusive of the bay at the crossing in S. Lorenzo), but whereas those of S. Lorenzo are barely 22 feet centre to centre, the total length being 175 feet, in S. Croce they are over 40 feet, and together measure 325 feet.[1]

Entablatures over columns.

Fault has been found with Brunelleschi for the squares of entablature above the columns in both S. Lorenzo and S. Spirito. If precedent be any excuse he could claim it to a limited extent; as in early churches and also in antique buildings similar squares are to be found. But it is difficult to recall a single example in either class in which isolated columns, crowned in this fashion, stand in a row carrying a series of arches. In S. Costanza, Rome, there are coupled columns (see Vol. I. Fig. 140) with entablatures above; and in many Roman buildings columns similarly treated stand in front of piers or walls and carry the springing of vaults, as in the basilica of Constantine (see Vol. I. Fig. 81), the baths of Diocletian, etc. In basilican churches a like treatment is not uncommon under the triumphal arch, as in S. Maria in Trastevere, Rome (see Vol. I. Fig. 118). The Byzantine builders also generally inserted a dosseret above capitals, and in both Italian and Southern French Romanesque, an extra abacus is frequently added in place of a dosseret. The later mediæval builders in Italy did much the same thing. During the thirteenth and fourteenth centuries arches in that country rarely sprang direct from a capital. Generally there was an intervening die with a capping moulding, as in the Loggia dei Lanzi, the nave of Florence Cathedral, etc. The inclusion, therefore, by Brunelleschi of an entablature was more in the nature of a survival than a revival. He probably felt, as others had before him, that a Corinthian capital, with its weak and curving abacus, is about as unsatisfactory form as could well be chosen from which to start an arch. An entablature at all events provides something square at the springing; and when the whole is so exquisitely proportioned as in S. Lorenzo criticism is disarmed. Moreover, there was an additional reason for its insertion in that church. Brunelleschi required an entablature along the aisle walls from

[1] Compare also with the plan of Florence Cathedral (Fig. 1). In old basilican churches the bays are seldom more than 12 feet centre to centre; even in S. Paolo fuori le Mura, Rome, they are only 13·4.

Photo: Alinari.

FIG. 8.—SAN LORENZO, FLORENCE.

[To face p. 22.

which to start his transverse arches and domes. He also wanted pilasters between his recesses. These and the columns of the arcades had to be the same height; so either the wall entablatures had to be omitted, or else entablatures placed above the columns. The architects who followed Brunelleschi not only accepted this superimposition, but made it a rule. Later generations, however, have not endorsed it. An entablature is still regarded as an essential over piers carrying arches, but is rare now above columns performing the same function, unless they are in pairs. In the latter case, as in the courtyards of the Borghese Palace, Rome (see Fig. 41), the Palazzo Marino, Milan, etc., an entablature, or some substitute, is absolutely necessary to unite the columns at the top and form a solid and continuous springing for the arches. In many such examples the three divisions of an entablature are merged into one—as had been done centuries before the Renaissance in the caryatid porch of the Erechtheum (see Vol. I. Fig. 61)—and the height of the super feature thus somewhat reduced. This was particularly well managed by San Gallo in the piers of the courtyard of the Farnese Palace, Rome (see Fig. 50).

A favourite device of Brunelleschi's was to dispense with any moulding or impost at the springing of an arched opening, and to continue the architrave at the sides round the head. He followed this in the side chapels and in the sacristy of S. Lorenzo, in the church of the Badia of Fiesole, on one of the hills above Florence, in S. Spirito, in the windows at the back of the narthex of the Pazzi Chapel, and elsewhere. *Traits of Brunelleschi's work.*

For the continuous entablature he had a great fondness. Along the aisles of S. Lorenzo, and in the sacristy of that church; in the narthex and round the interior of the Pazzi Chapel, he carries his cornice, frieze, and architrave without a break; notwithstanding that in all cases there are pilasters at intervals below the entablatures, and over these, above the pilasters, transverse arches. There is nothing, therefore, to carry the eye upwards and connect the two, save that in the Pazzi Chapel and in the sacristy of S. Lorenzo there are medallions in the frieze. In the church itself the frieze is plain. Brunelleschi has been blamed for this composition, but unjustly. Of two evils choose the less. A small break in the frieze and in the lowest member of the cornice might have been no drawback, but he appreciated too well the sense of breadth and repose which a continuous entablature *Continuous entablature.*

gives to depart from it without very strong reasons. The Romans seldom broke their entablatures, never at their best period; and the glorious lines of the Colosseum and Theatre of Marcellus were probably ever in Brunelleschi's mind.

Brunelleschi's achievements.
Brunelleschi owes the commanding position he occupies as the first of a long line of distinguished architects of the Renaissance to his great constructive skill, his thorough study of ancient work, his indomitable pluck, and his confidence in his own powers. When Pope Eugenius IV., noting his small stature, asked sarcastically, "Are you the man who can move the world?" he is said to have replied, "Show me where I can fix my lever, and this moment your Highness shall see what I can do."[1] His confidence enabled him to undermine the authority of the Arte dei Maestri di Pietra e Legnane, to use its members as his servants, and to establish the difference between a designer and those who carry out a design. He had the knowledge and power necessary to ensure that his work should be executed as he wished. His contemporaries ended by acknowledging his superiority. Not many of his buildings were finished during his lifetime; the exceptions being the Pazzi Chapel, the sacristy and chapels of S. Lorenzo, the piazza of the Foundling Hospital, and the fortifications which on more than one occasion he was called upon to design and superintend. The dome of Florence Cathedral lacked its lantern at his death, and S. Lorenzo to this day is without a façade. In domestic work he had no better luck. A start had been made on the Pitti Palace (see p. 32), but the Palazzo Quaratesi (see Fig. 10) apparently had not even been commenced. His many absences from Florence, for both public and private reasons, and the large amount of time he gave to personal superintendence of the building of the cathedral dome, also prevented his giving full attention to such works as progressed during his lifetime. But, except in one or two instances which are recorded, his designs were evidently executed without alterations. His command over pure Classic detail was great, and his treatment of it essentially original. He was no mere copyist. The introduction of the cherub heads in the frieze above the columns of the façade of the Pazzi Chapel (see Fig. 4) was a happy inspiration without a parallel in Roman work. In some respects his detail is superior to the models he followed; it is often, in fact, more reminiscent of Greek forms than of Roman. The feeling in the façade of the

[1] Milizia, "Lives of Celebrated Architects," p. 186.

Pazzi Chapel as a whole is Greek, notwithstanding the introduction of the arch. He may have absorbed his feeling from the study of fragments of pure Greek art in Rome, or of the temples of Magna Græcia. On the other hand, the great refinement and delicacy of his detail may be chiefly the result of his innate feeling for the beautiful.[1]

Finally, he was most fortunate in the colleagues whom he chose to collaborate with him. Donatello executed for him the cherub heads on the frieze over the columns in S. Lorenzo, and other work in the old sacristy of that church, and with the assistance of Desiderio da Settignano carried out the medallions in the frieze round the Pazzi Chapel inside, and those in the frieze above the columns of the façade (see Figs. 3 and 5). To Donatello also are attributed the shields on the Palazzo Quaratesi. In the Ospedale degli Innocenti, Andrea della Robbia added the well-known circles of babies in swaddling clothes, and it must be admitted by doing so gave distinction to what otherwise would have been a somewhat tame, albeit delicate and refined, design. Collaboration amongst architects and sculptors in the fifteenth century was common; and in entrusting detail work to others Brunelleschi only followed the general custom. He seems, however, to have carried it farther than most. He could have done the work himself, probably as well as they, but he preferred to devote his energies to the bigger problems of architectural design. It is this that chiefly distinguishes him from his fellows. He was a designer in great; and his delight was in form and mass rather than in detail.

His collaborators.

The most famous by far of Brunelleschi's immediate successors is Leon Battista Alberti. A member of a noble, almost princely, family, he was scholar, priest, architect, writer, and painter. He was born in Venice in 1404, a natural son of Lorenzo Alberti, then in exile. His delight in classical literature was as great as his admiration for Classic architecture. He wrote in Latin habitually; he preferred to speak it, and his buildings, far more than Brunelleschi's, show a deliberate attempt to revive ancient forms and methods of design. His best known literary effort is his ten books on architecture (really ten chapters), written in

L. B. Alberti (1404-72).

---

[1] The same feeling is even more apparent in Donatello's detail; for instance, in the mouldings round some of his reliefs, and notably in his famous singing gallery designed for the cathedral of Florence, and now in the cathedral museum. A cast of this is in the Victoria and Albert Museum.

1452. After his death and the discovery of printing (see p. 105), it was printed in 1485, was translated into Italian in 1550, and long remained the standard work. Amongst his other publications is a book on painting. His training was quite different from Brunelleschi's. He was no craftsman; neither had he the other's constructive skill. To a great extent he left the carrying out of his designs to others; notably to Bernardo Rossellino and Luca Fancelli, both architect-sculptors of some repute.[1] That he made the designs himself is undoubted. Both the domestic and ecclesiastical buildings attributed to him show a distinction and an originality which separate them from the work of his contemporaries. His Palazzo Rucellai (see p. 39) differs considerably from other Florentine palaces, and his churches at Rimini and Mantua became the models for later architects.

Other early Florentines.

Brunelleschi and Alberti were essentially architects. Their training was dissimilar, their acquirements were different, but each in his own way possessed the power of dealing with large problems. These two men stand out pre-eminently as leaders. But amongst their contemporaries and immediate successors were many artists of great ability, lacking only that rare distinction which belongs to but one or two men in a century. Their reputation has to some extent suffered eclipse by the splendour of the architectural achievements of their successors of the sixteenth century. That is frequently the fate that befalls pioneers. Those who with difficulty clear the path have too often to submit to the mortification of seeing others stride along it easily, passing them on the road of their own making. When judging of men's accomplishments, the conditions under which they worked should be taken into consideration. If this is done the immense contribution made to architectural development by many Florentines of the fifteenth century will at once be apparent. At no period in the world's history was versatility so general, and the average standard of accomplishment so high. The artists now to be mentioned were without exception the outcome of the bottega training, and their work illustrates its virtues and its shortcomings. In this chapter little more than their names and chief works are given; their buildings in most cases are referred to subsequently.

[1] Rossellino superintended the Palazzo Rucellai and other early works, Fancelli, S. Andrea, Mantua, and most of the later.

Michelozzo Michelozzi is one of the best known. The pupil of and collaborator with Donatello, and assistant also to Ghiberti, he designed the Palazzo Riccardi (see Fig. 9), the first of the great Florentine Renaissance palaces, and many other important works. Michelozzi (1396-1472).

The Rossellini were a family of brothers, all skilled as artists. Bernardo Rossellino (1409-64), the best known, commenced the rebuilding of S. Peter's, Rome, for Pope Nicholas V., but the only portions of his design executed were the foundations of a great western apse. About 1460 he built the Cathedral and several public buildings at Pienza for Pope Pius II. (Æneas Sylvius Piccolomini), whose birthplace it was. All are in the Piazza del Duomo, and together form a striking group. He carried out the Rucellai Palace for Alberti; designed various buildings in Rome for Pope Nicholas V., and by some is credited with the Piccolomini Palace, Siena, although this was not built until after his death (see p. 45). The Rossellini.

Benedetto da Majano began life as a carver and wood inlayer. He excelled especially in "intarsia," as the stalls in the sacristy of Florence Cathedral show, but he subsequently abandoned this work, and devoted himself to architecture and sculpture. He designed the Strozzi Palace (see p. 32) and the particularly graceful loggia to the church of S. Maria delle Grazie, on the outskirts of Arezzo. His skill as a sculptor is well shown in the richly carved marble pulpit in S. Croce, Florence. He was *par excellence* the all-round craftsman of the early Renaissance. His brother Giuliano da Majano is best known by the Porta Capuana at Naples—which must not be confounded with the larger but much inferior Alfonso's archway in the same city, sometimes also attributed to him. It is Spanish in its richness, and Spanish also in the way this richness is framed by the heavy towers which flank it. B. da Majano (1442-97).

The two names that stand out most prominently amongst Florentines in the last quarter of the fifteenth century are Giuliano da San Gallo (1445-1516) and Simone Pollaiuolo (1457-1508), better known as Il Cronaca. They collaborated over the Sacristy of the Church of S. Spirito, Florence. Giuliano and his brother Antonio San Gallo—the latter is not to be confounded with his nephew, the more famous Antonio known as the younger —were apprenticed by their father to a woodcarver, and woodcarvers they were before they attempted architectural design. Even after they had both achieved considerable success as The San Galli and Cronaca.

architects they did not abandon entirely their earlier calling.¹ Like Benedetto da Majano, they could turn their hands to almost everything. From the carving of the Figure on the Cross to the designing, superintending, and repairing of fortifications, all came natural.² Both built churches, palaces, bridges; were consulted by popes, dukes, and kings. For eighteen months Giuliano was architect of S. Peter's, Rome. Their versatility was not on so high a plane as Michael Angelo's or Leonardo's; they produced no great masterpieces; but the brothers stand together as two typical all-round men of the Renaissance.

Renaissance not "imitative."

The above are only a few of the many who, besides filling Florence and other Tuscan cities with beautiful buildings, fine carvings, and other works of art, helped to carry the new spirit south to Rome, north to Milan and Venice, and the string of towns lying between. Their work and that of the great masters of the Renaissance has been described as "imitative."³ All good art is imitative in a sense. Few, if any, men of distinction, no matter how famous, have not been influenced either by contemporaries or immediate predecessors, or by work done centuries before they were born. In the Middle Ages the influence was recent; in the days of the Renaissance chiefly remote. No doubt it is better, whenever possible, to help forward a living existing style than to resuscitate a buried one. But when—as was the case in Italy at the end of the fourteenth century—there is no existing style worthy of the name, men show their originality and artistic sense—their common sense one might add—in peering back into the past to see if they cannot discover a sound foundation on which to build anew. That is what the Renaissance men did. Their looking back was no check on their advance; in fact, their advance could not have been so great but for their retrospection. The French proverb "Il faut reculer pour mieux sauter" is excellent advice, and they followed it. They did not copy or imitate, they adapted. They regarded old buildings as a painter or sculptor regards the antique. And much in the same way as a sculptor combines study of the antique with study from the life,

---

¹ Large crucifixes in wood seem to have been their forte. Some of these still exist.

² Each in turn was superintendent over all the fortifications of the state of Florence.

³ Fergusson in his "History of Modern Architecture," p. 2, refers to the earlier styles as "True Styles," and to the Renaissance as the "Copying or Imitative Styles of architectural art."

so the architects blended their antique with the requirements of the time.

If Greek, Roman, Byzantine are "true styles" as Fergusson terms them, wherein does revival make them less true? Only when they prove unsuitable for the habits of a people, for the climate, for the materials available, the state of the labour market or other economic conditions. No unsuitability resulted in a single instance or a single building of the early Renaissance. The climate and materials were the same; the habits and labour market had changed only to the extent that made some adaptation of the styles advisable. This they received. And so well were the adaptations and necessary modifications made that Renaissance churches, palaces, public and private buildings, were not only satisfying at the time they were built, but, save in a few minor details, are still suitable for worship, use, or habitation. The vitality that the style continues to possess is more than sufficient justification, if one be needed, for the movement set on foot by Brunelleschi, Alberti, and other Florentine architects of the fifteenth century.

CHAPTER III

EARLY FLORENTINE PALACES (1430–1520)

Main divisions.
RENAISSANCE secular buildings can be grouped under one or other of two main divisions. This grouping applies not only to Florence, but to the whole of Italy and practically to all countries and to all periods. The first includes those buildings which externally have no columns or pilasters. Their fronts rise sheer from the ground, the wall surfaces unbroken save by windows and other openings. In most cases they are crowned by a massive cornice, proportionate to the total height of each, irrespective of the number of its storeys. To such buildings the term "astylar" is sometimes given—from "ἄστυλος," which signifies literally "without pillar or prop"—but it is somewhat twisting the meaning of the Greek word thus to apply it, or its derivative. The second division includes those buildings the wall surfaces of which are divided panelwise by pilasters or by columns, generally attached, supporting entablatures. In some towns one type predominates, in other towns the other; whilst in many cities throughout the world examples of both types are about equal in number.

Pilastered fronts.
The pilastered treatment of a front is capable of considerable variety. The most common is for each storey to have its own range of pilasters or columns supporting an entablature; in other words, each storey has its own "order." In other buildings columns or pilasters run through two or more storeys, but in no Florentine example was this treatment adopted until the middle of the sixteenth century. Alberti was the first to introduce it in the west front of S. Andrea, Mantua (see Fig. 110), and it became a favourite with later architects for both churches and domestic buildings. In the examples of the first quarter of the sixteenth century in which it is employed, the entablature generally crowns the building; but in the work of Michael Angelo, Palladio, and others the main cornice is often placed

EARLY FLORENTINE PALACES

below the top storey, the latter being treated differently as an attic. The "attic" was doubtless suggested by old buildings in Rome, and especially by the Triumphal Arches which almost without exception possess this feature.

In many pilastered fronts the columns or pilasters start from the level of the first floor, the ground storey being merely either plain or rusticated. Sanmicheli was especially fond of this arrangement, which has much to recommend it; as the greater simplicity of the lower part gives an air of solidity and strength to a building and also emphasizes the richness above (see Fig. 81). Rusticated basement.

In the secular buildings of Florence the Renaissance early found expression; and yet in them, even more than in churches, traditional methods of building and of architectural design are apparent. Through the Middle Ages Florence was one of the best built cities in the world. Its streets, although narrow, were lined by lofty stone houses, and had been paved as early as the thirteenth century. Amongst the pre-Renaissance palaces still standing the largest and most important is the Palazzo Vecchio, built by Arnolfo, the architect of the cathedral, about 1298. Its design is typical. The walling throughout is unevenly coursed rock-faced sandstone. Its three main storeys are divided from one another by horizontal string-courses which form the sills below the windows. The windows of the principal floor are each of two lights, under a heavy semicircular arch, the intrados and extrados of which are not concentric. At the top are boldly projecting machicolations. Other contemporary buildings are similar in character. Tradition in secular buildings.

The most characteristic Renaissance palaces in Florence follow closely, except in detail, the Palazzo Vecchio. All are without columns or pilasters on their façades, and consequently belong to the first of the two divisions under which, as has already been stated, Renaissance buildings can be grouped. The earliest and best known are the Palazzo Riccardi (formerly Medici) built about 1430 by Michelozzi for Cosimo de' Medici, and the Palazzi Pitti and Quaratesi (now De Rast), both designed by Brunelleschi a few years later, the latter for one of the Pazzi family. The first design for the Riccardi palace was also prepared by Brunelleschi, but Cosimo regarded it as too palatial, and it is stated that the architect destroyed the model he had made in a fit of temper. But the model had certainly been shown to his patron; had been seen probably by many of the artists in Astylar palaces.

Florence—although Brunelleschi was ever chary of making known his intentions—and without disputing Michelozzi's claim to be the author of the existing Riccardi, one may hazard the suggestion that his design for that building may to some extent have been influenced by the model Brunelleschi destroyed.

In the Palazzi Riccardi and Quaratesi are the same three divisions as in the Palazzo Vecchio, marked by like stringcourses, and similar spacing and treatment of the windows, the detail round the lights alone being different. Crowning the Riccardi palace is a great cornice; at the top of the Quaratesi are boldly projecting eaves. These take the place of the machicolations of the earlier building. But all three crowning features produce much the same effect, as in all strong effective shadows are cast, those of the old palace differing only from the others in being more broken. Comparing the three palaces named there can be no doubt which are the finer; no hesitation in proclaiming the great advance made by the Renaissance architects. The Palazzo Vecchio is merely straightforward building; its bulk alone the attraction. The other palaces are fine architectural achievements, perfectly proportioned and possessing refined and beautiful detail. The proportions of the Riccardi especially could hardly be improved upon. The storeys have the gradation in height so necessary for effective design, and the great cornice gives scale and majesty.[1] The Palazzo Strozzi, the foundation stone of which was laid in 1489, comes next in importance. It bears a strong resemblance to the Riccardi, and was designed by Benedetto da Majano. Benedetto dying in 1497 the top range of windows and the crowning cornice were added by Cronaca.

Palazzo Pitti. The Palazzo Pitti, as designed by Brunelleschi, was not the huge affair that now bears the name. He died soon after it was commenced, his patron Luca Pitti was banished some years later, and the building passed in the sixteenth century into the hands of a branch of the Medici by whom it was extensively enlarged. The principal front now is about 475 feet long, more than thrice what was intended originally, and the wings and courtyard at the back are additions by Bartolommeo Ammanati. Besides being

[1] The Riccardi palace was originally only about two-thirds its present size, and the main entrance was in the centre of the front. The palace was bought by the Riccardi and enlarged by them in 1714, when they incorporated the building alongside. This accounts for the existence of two courtyards. The additions have been so well managed that no one would imagine that the front was not all of one date.

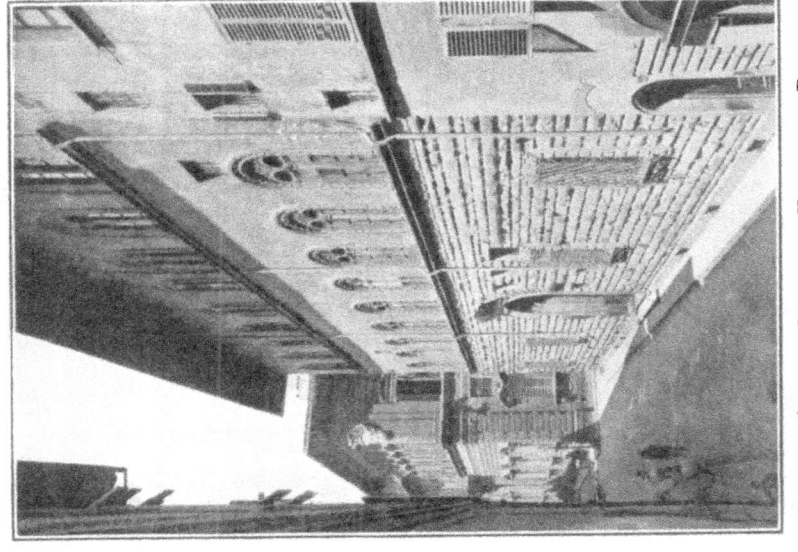

Fig. 10.—Palazzo Quaratesi, Florence. Palazzo Nonfinito beyond. [*To face p. 32.*

Fig. 9.—Palazzo Riccardi, Florence.

enlarged, the front has been spoilt by the addition of balconies at each floor level and at the top. But its grand and rugged simplicity and noble scale are apparent still; and its original beauty can be realized if one shuts one's eyes to some of its features and exercises one's imagination regarding others no longer existing.

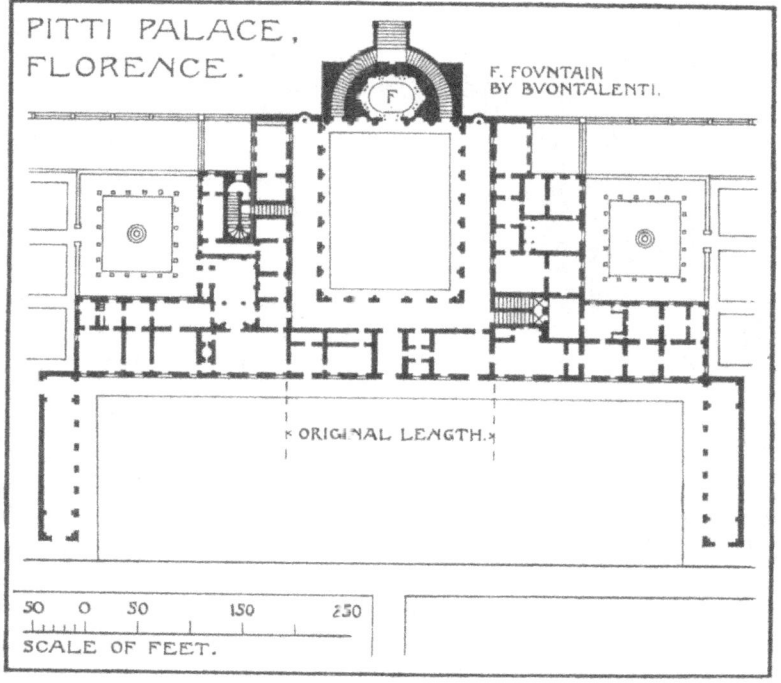

Fig. 11.

The front included originally only three openings on the ground floor, and seven bays above, instead of the existing twenty-five. But as each of the three storeys averages nearly 40 feet in height, and each bay is 24 feet centre to centre, Luca Pitti's estimate of his requirements was evidently no very modest one. The semicircular headed window recesses are each 24 feet high by 12 feet wide; the simple ratios of 1 to 1 and 1 to 2 being evidently strictly followed. The windows themselves are only about half the width of each recess, the surrounding walling being smooth stone. Scale is given to the building generally, and the recesses in particular, by pilasters on the jambs of the latter,

Façade of the Pitti.

which by their smoothness and lightness also relieve the ruggedness of the mass of walling. Above the three storeys an open loggia was originally intended, similar to the one above the Palazzo Guadagni, built by Simone Cronaca about 1490. Loggie affording protection from the sun rays and the weather were not uncommon in Florence, and a loggia would have added distinction to the Pitti, and have been a particularly suitable finish, owing to the commanding position the palace occupies on a hill above the town.[1]

FIG. 12.

The bold massive walling of the ground storeys of the Riccardi and Quaratesi palaces, and of the whole front of the Pitti palace, was an Etruscan tradition, handed down through the centuries by successive generations of Florentines. At Fiesole, at Volterra, Cortona, and other cities close at hand, are still many remains of walls, gateways, etc., of great massiveness, the work of the early settlers. In many of the old towns of Etruria are also several equally massive Mediæval buildings. The Palazzo Ricciarelli at Volterra, with its three storeys of pointed arched openings with heavy voussoirs, is a typical example. The country round Florence, especially southwards, abounds in quarries of exceedingly hard sandstone, eminently suitable for rock-faced walling and rustications. In the lowest storey of both the Riccardi and Quaratesi palaces, and also in that of the charming little Palazzo Strozzino, nearly opposite the great Palazzo Strozzi, the stone is coursed, but the courses are not equal in height or uniform in projection: in fact in all three buildings the walling is even rougher than in the Palazzo Vecchio. As a substructure

---

[1] In Signor Giacomo Brogi's "Disegni di architettura Civile e Militaire" (1904) from the Uffizi Gallery, a drawing (No. 95) by Bernardo Buontalenti is reproduced of the front of the Pitti palace as originally intended, which shows the design as stated above.

on which to build—and it must be remembered that in Florentine palaces the ground storey was used for much the same purposes as basements are now, the living-rooms commencing on the first floor

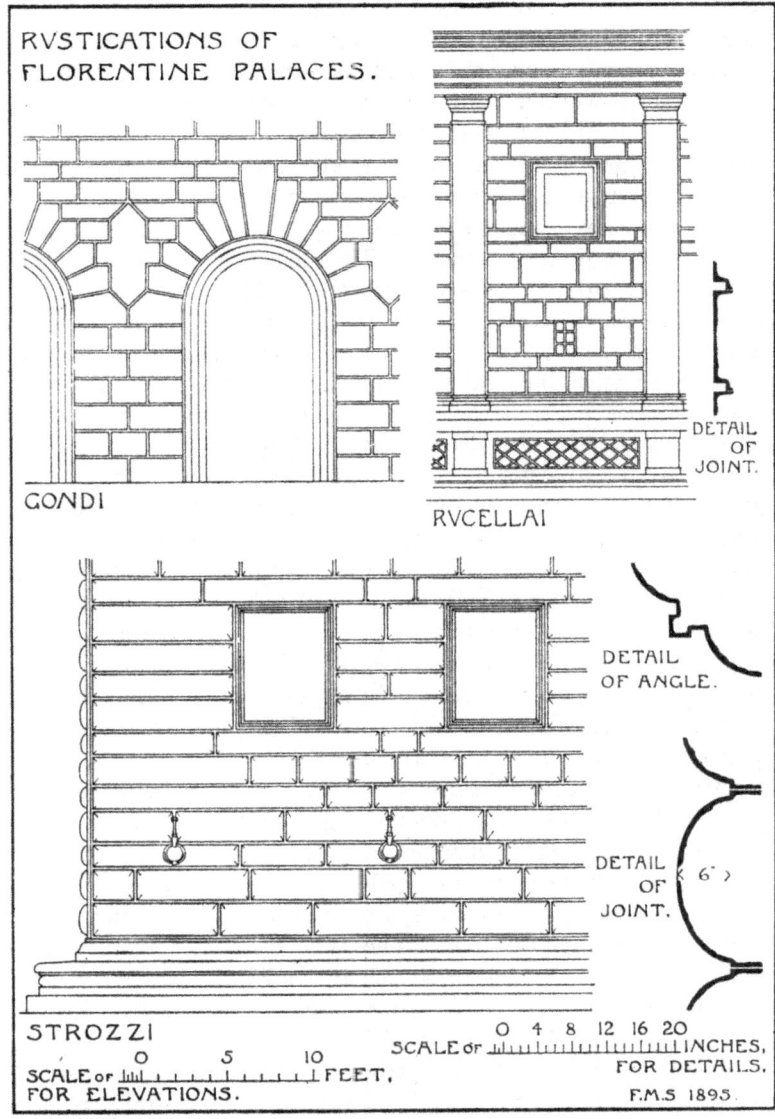

Fig. 13.

—as a podium on which to raise the house proper above the ground, nothing could be better than these walls of roughly hewn stone, pierced sparsely for light. The walling of the upper storeys of the Riccardi has received greater care. On the first floor the rustications are merely raised an inch or two above the narrow sunk margin which surrounds each stone, whilst on the floor above all the stones are smooth and flush. In the Palazzo Strozzi the rustication is worked carefully, and with some uniformity, on each storey. The projection of the rustication above the draughted margin is greatest on the ground storey, being from 5 to 6½ inches —the differences are due to the varying heights of the courses— less on the next, and least on the third. The frieze below the great cornice alone is smooth. The effect is more laboured than in the Riccardi, and less satisfactory. Monotony, however, is avoided as the different courses are by no means equal in height, and the stones vary very much in length. It was left for later men to discover, with doubtful advantage, that in rusticated walling all courses must be equal in height, and all "perpends" carefully kept. In the Palazzo Gondi, by Giuliano da San Gallo, built c. 1490-4, this insistence on regularity and uniformity is carried so far that between the heads of the windows of the first floor the stones form a pattern. In the Palazzo Antinori, one of the most charming of smaller palaces, the rustication is the same on all three storeys, and is similar to that of the middle storey of the Riccardi palace. This building has boldly projecting eaves in front, which cast a fine shadow, and illustrate well the truism that the cheapest ornament a building can have is shadow. Not a little of the charm of the Antinori is due to the irregular placing of the entrance doorway. The design is generally attributed to either Giuliano San Gallo or Baccio d'Agnolo; but its refinement and also a few of its details suggest Cronaca, whose Palazzo Guadagni it resembles in some respects.

Stucco and sgraffito.   All the above-mentioned palaces, with the exception of the Quaratesi, the two upper storeys of which are stuccoed, are stone faced throughout. Of the same type are many other palaces which are similar in design, except that only the jambs and arches of windows and doorways and the angles of the buildings are rusticated. In the latter position the stones generally form pilasters. The rest of the walling, even the ground storey, is sometimes smooth stone, as in the Palazzo Bartolini, but more frequently either stuccoed or finished in sgraffito. The upper storeys of the Palazzo Guadagni are faced with the latter, but the design is somewhat commonplace. A far better example of this work is on the Palazzo Montalvi, in the Borgo degli Albizzi (see Fig. 16).[1]

Stuccoed walls were frequently finished smooth and painted in fresco. A well-known instance of a building so treated is the Palazzo Antellesi, in the Piazza S. Croce. Painted walls, however, were not so common in Florence as in other towns in which stone was not so easily procurable. In Genoa and Verona walls were generally painted; and in the latter town especially are still many examples of quite small buildings treated in this fashion.

Painted walls.

The façades of Florentine palaces of the astylar type are always simple in design, and broad in treatment, whether of stone throughout, or stone and stucco. Apart from the great cornice—which does not always exist—there is little that can be called ornament, except bits of carving in the window heads, and the shields bearing the arms of the noble owners. Florentine shields have a form and character of their own, especially early fifteenth-century ones. Many were executed by well-known sculptors, like those by Donatello on the Quaratesi palace. They are generally placed on the angles of a building above the first floor, as on the Riccardi, Quaratesi, Strozzi, Guadagni, etc. Occasionally they are over windows, as in the Rucellai palace, or between them, as in the Antinori palace and the Palazzo Piccolomini, Siena. Between windows are often bronze torch or banner holders, and near the ground bronze rings for tying up horses are frequently fixed in the stonework, as in the Strozzi palace. These holders and rings are simple but charming examples of

Simplicity of design.

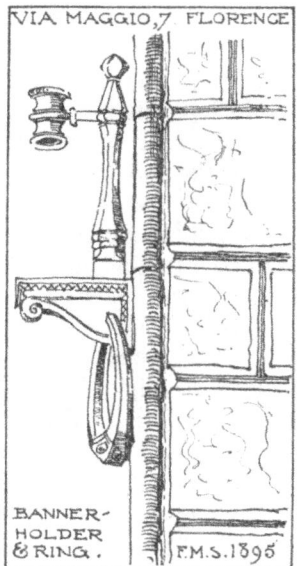

FIG. 14.

[1] In sgraffito work, plaster in different thicknesses of two or more colours—counting black and white as colours—is applied to the wall, and the design is obtained by cutting away the last coat, generally white, to show a coloured coat below. The portion of the top coat left forms sometimes the pattern, sometimes the background.

38 A HISTORY OF ARCHITECTURAL DEVELOPMENT

craftsmanship. The holders recall what the buildings must have looked like, when brave banners floated from the walls, and the ruggedness of the stone was lit up by flaming torches. Genuine works of art are also the bronze corner lanterns, some of which still remain. Those on the angles of the Strozzi palace by Niccolo Grosso (called il Caparrà) are especially good.

Sense of stability.
Whistler said of Velasquez that he made his people "stand upon their legs." There is the same feeling of fine stability about Florentine palaces. In most early examples projecting stone seats take the place of plinths. In the Riccardi palace the seat is broken into a series of seats by the arched recesses and openings; in the Strozzi and Guadagni palaces it is continuous, except where the doorways come. Whether these seats were for the retainers only, or for the populace generally, is doubtful—probably the former—but certainly no more satisfactory base for a building has ever been devised.[1]

Lighting of upper storey.
In other countries in which rooms are lower than in Italy, and larger windows are required, the huge Florentine cornice would interfere seriously with the lighting of the rooms behind; and even in Italy itself difficulties sometimes arise because of it. In the Palazzo Riccardi the rooms on the top floor are so lofty that there was more than sufficient space for the cornice above the windows, which, as is usual in hot climates, do not reach more than half the height of the rooms. The Palazzo Strozzi, however, has an extra upper storey of small importance, which only comes over the outside half of the building. This is covered by a lean-to roof, which starts from behind the great cornice, and is lighted by windows which face towards the courtyard. To light similar attics in other buildings, or else to light the upper parts of lofty rooms, later architects often inserted windows in the frieze. This expedient was introduced by Peruzzi, in the Villa Farnesina, Rome, and was followed by Sansovino in the Library, Venice, etc. (see Fig. 71); but it is doubtful if in any instance the result is altogether satisfactory.

Pilastered fronts.
The earliest and best-known palace of the second type referred to at the commencement of this chapter, in which pilasters and entablature break up the wall surface, is the Palazzo Rucellai. Each storey has its own order. The palace was designed by Alberti, and was commenced in 1451. The carrying of it out was

[1] They are now largely used by the flower-sellers; and the contrasts between the bright flowers and the grey stone behind are often most striking.

entrusted to B. Rossellino, who repeated the design, with modifications, in the Palazzo Piccolomini at Pienza.[1]

Delightfully simple and with beautiful detail, the front of the Palazzo Rucellai owes its success largely to the slightly greater width given to the two bays in which are the entrance doorways, and to the emphasis given to these bays by the shields over the first-floor windows. The pilasters are far from being aggressive, as their projection is only a trifle more than that of the rustications; and Alberti wisely followed Brunelleschi in making no

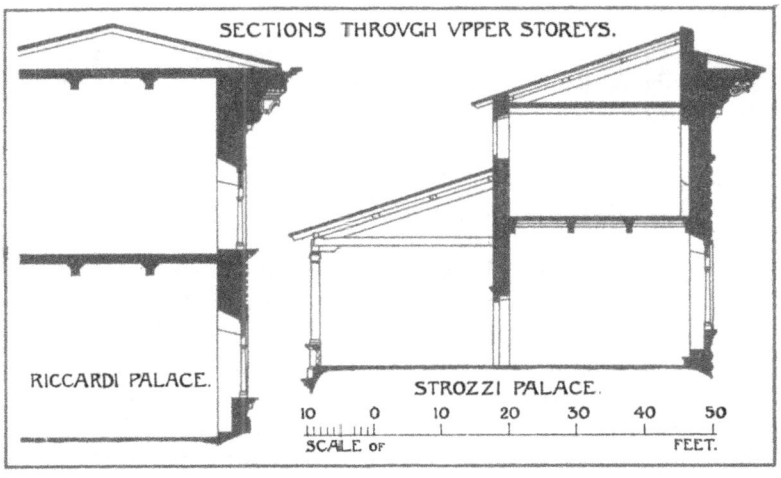

Fig. 15.

breaks in the entablatures above them. The rusticated courses themselves are pleasantly irregular (see Fig. 13). The chief difficulty in designing a façade such as this, with tiers of pilasters and entablatures ranging with each separate storey, is how to treat the topmost entablature so that it shall not overpower the pilasters immediately below, and yet shall be sufficiently important and bulky to serve as the crowning cornice. Alberti adopted the same expedient as the architect of the top storey of the Colosseum (see Vol. I. Fig. 98). He made this entablature only a trifle higher than the other entablatures, but gave it far greater projections,

[1] The design of the Rucellai is sometimes attributed to Rossellino, but the manifest inferiority of his building at Pienza, as regards its proportions, spacing of pilasters, etc., disproves this. The Piccolomini is a copy of the Rucellai without the touches which give distinction to the latter.

40 A HISTORY OF ARCHITECTURAL DEVELOPMENT

and introduced corbels into the frieze. The corbels unite the three divisions of the entablature, and give it the appearance of one great cornice. This was the first occasion since the Colosseum was built that this expedient had been adopted, but it has been followed since many thousands of times.[1]

The Palazzo Rucellai is small compared with the three greatest of Florentine palaces, the Riccardi, Pitti, and Strozzi; but its three storeys are of very respectable height, being respectively 28, 21, and 20 feet. The total height is thus 69 feet, which compares with the 83 feet of the Riccardi, the 116 feet of the Pitti, and the 105 feet of the Strozzi. The cornice of the Rucellai palace is 3·10 high, or about one-eighteenth of the total height; that of the Riccardi is nearly 10 feet, or about one-eighth; that of the Strozzi 7 feet, or one-fifteenth, counting the cornice only, or 12 feet, or about one-ninth, if the frieze is included. The Pitti palace lacks a great crowning cornice.

Fenestration.

In the Riccardi, Strozzi, Pitti, Rucellai palaces—in fact, in nearly all early Florentine Renaissance buildings, as well as in the still older Palazzo Vecchio—the arches and jambs of windows are part and parcel of the surrounding walling.[2] The windows themselves are generally of two lights, separated by a central shaft. Each light, as a rule, has a semicircular head, occasionally pierced, but more frequently merely sunk, so that the opening itself is square-headed. In the tympanum above the lights, under the enclosing rusticated arch, is, in most cases, a circle containing carving. A very solid effect is the result. The appearance of solidity was increased by the glazing, which, so far as can be gathered from existing remains, consisted frequently of a series of roundels in heavy lead cames.

Window arches.

A peculiarity of nearly all the arches over windows and other openings in early work is that the intrados and extrados are not concentric. This applies to buildings faced entirely with stone, as well as to those the walling of which is stuccoed. It is most noticeable in the latter. In all examples the intrados is semicircular, but the outline of the extrados varies. In the Riccardi, Pitti, Strozzi, etc., it is semi-elliptical; in the Palazzo Ricasoli-Zanchini, etc., it is pointed; in the Guadagni palace, and in many

---

[1] In some Romanesque buildings, notably those in Lombardy, a modified form of this type of entablature is met with, frequently with rough pilasters below; but neither entablatures nor pilasters are of correct classic proportion or detail.

[2] The Palazzo Quaratesi is an exception, but its walls are stuccoed.

Photo: Brogi.
Fig. 16.—Palazzo Montalvi, Florence.

Fig. 17.—Palazzo Rucellai, Florence.

[*To face p. 40.*

Fig. 18.—Palazzo Pandolfini, Florence.

Fig. 19.—Palazzo Bartolini, Florence.

[*To face p.* 41.

EARLY FLORENTINE PALACES

later examples, it is slightly ogeed, this being the only variety that is unsatisfactory. Otherwise the device is sound structurally, pleasing in appearance, and, moreover, traditional. It occurs in many Italian Romanesque churches in Central and Southern Italy, notably at Bari; and in mediæval domestic work in the Palazzo Vecchio, as before mentioned, in the pointed headed windows of the Palazzo Ricciarelli, etc. The windows of the Palazzo Rucellai, Florence, and the Palazzo Piccolomini, Siena, are exceptions. In these two palaces the intrados and extrados of heads are concentric.

Of a totally distinct type are those windows, mostly square headed, whose openings are cut off from the surrounding walling by pilasters or columns at the sides, and an entablature, or at least a cornice, above, with or without a pediment over. They are framed in voids. Most of the windows in Roman buildings are of this character, and the type was general in the north before it appeared in Florence. *Windows as voids.*

Vasari says that the first building in Florence with windows thus treated was the Palazzo Bartolini, built about 1520 by Baccio d'Angelo, *(ngio)* and that the architect was ridiculed severely in consequence by the wits and lampooners of the day.[1] They are mullioned and transomed, and therefore do not appear so much like voids as later windows in which these stone divisions are lacking. It seems probable that most framed-in windows in sixteenth-century Italian palaces had mullions and transoms originally which were cut out later when the desire grew for the large casements opening inwards now so characteristic of continental buildings. The windows at the side of the Bartolini palace, with the family motto "Sed non dormire" on the transoms, are particularly refined and graceful. *Palazzo Bartolini.*

Fig. 20.

The other early building in Florence with framed windows is *Palazzo Pandolfini.*

---

[1] He retaliated by carving on the frieze over the doorway of the palace, "Carpere promptius quam imitari."

the Palazzo Pandolfini. This is of sterner stuff. Designed by Raphael, or so it is said, on the occasion of his visit to Florence in 1515, to advise about the completion of the church of S. Lorenzo, it was not commenced before 1520. The work was carried out under the direction of Giovanni Francesco da San Gallo, and after his death by his brother Bastiano. Few palaces in Italy are finer in scale and proportion. The lettering on the frieze can compare with that on the attic of the arch of Titus, the finest instance of

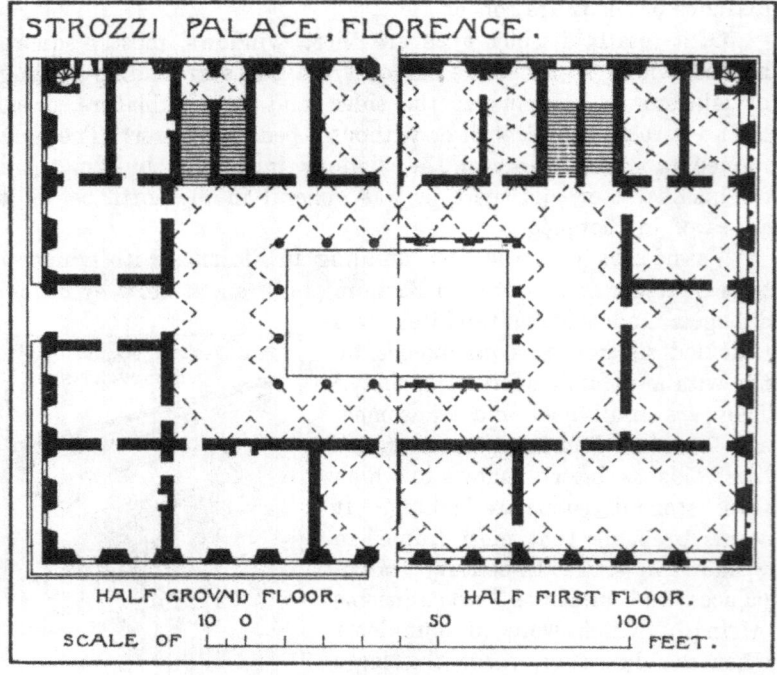

FIG. 21.

bold lettering in existence (see Vol. I. Fig. 101), and the crowning cornice is worthy of the frieze.[1]

Plans.

There is no striving after the picturesque in the plans of Florentine palaces; no itching desire for projections and breaks and little irregularities. When irregularities occur, which is rare, they were forced on the architect, and were regarded by him as

[1] Worthy in design that is, as only the lower members are stone, the modillions and upper members being wood. M.D.XX is the date cut on the building.

defects to the concealed, much in the same way as a deformity in a child is regarded by its mother. Symmetry and its correlative dignity were aimed at, and in all cases achieved. The plan of the Palazzo Riccardi, the first of the Renaissance palaces, was evidently regarded at the time as a great step in advance. Its main disposition of a central courtyard was generally followed in other buildings. The plan of the Strozzi palace may be taken as typical. The building is a rectangular block with one side and both ends

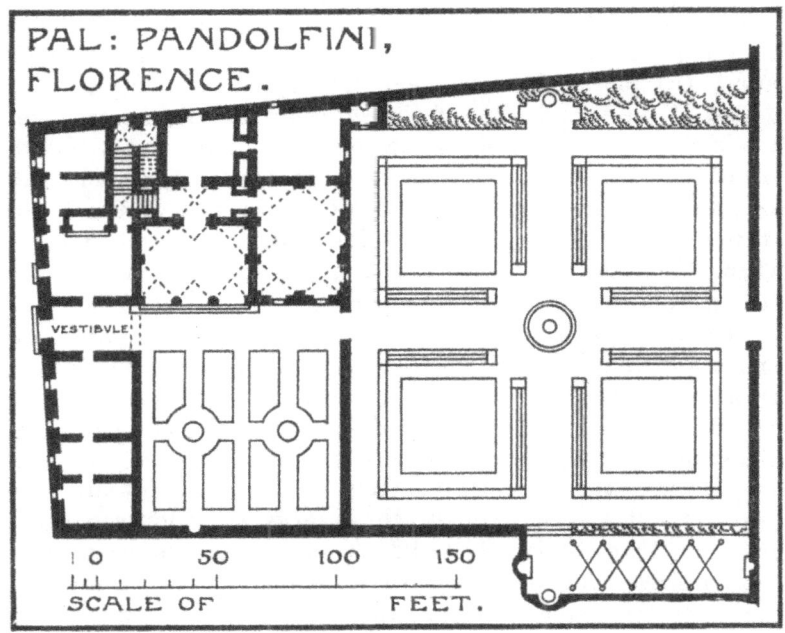

Fig. 22.

standing free. The doorways are central on each of the main fronts, and lead into a paved courtyard surrounded by an arcaded covered way vaulted in plaster.[1] The arches spring from columns, as was always the case in the earlier Florentine arcades, whether round palace courtyards or church cloisters, but in the gallery arcade on the first floor, which was added by Cronaca, piers are substituted. From the ground-floor arcades two great staircases

[1] The groin lines of the vaulting are always emphasized, when nearing the apex, by "pinching" out the plaster on either side, otherwise they would be lost entirely.

lead to the upper floors, and land opposite the wide ends of the upper galleries. Opening out of the galleries are the reception and living rooms. Nothing can be simpler, and yet nothing could be more stately. Even the smallest palaces, with few exceptions, have a courtyard. That of the Strozzino is only about 22 feet square, and yet possesses considerable dignity. The Palazzo Pandolfini differs somewhat in plan from the usual arrangement, and has no central courtyard. On the other hand, it possesses a garden. The site is an irregular one, but the irregularities are cleverly masked. The front door opens into a vaulted vestibule; on the right hand is a one-storey outbuilding, the top of which forms a terrace, and on the left, just beyond, is a loggia. The design of the balustrading of the terrace, with its recesses, is not the least happy portion of the composition. In the Palazzo Gondi Giuliano da San Gallo departed from the typical Florentine plan in placing his principal staircase along one side of the court, instead of at right angles to it. Its balustrade is consequently visible from the court, and makes a very effective picture, one that reflects great credit on the architect.

Models. An interesting sidelight on architects' methods of preparing and presenting their designs is shown by Vasari's constant references to "models." Mention has already been made of the models prepared by Brunelleschi for the dome and cupola of Florence Cathedral, and for Lorenzo de' Medici's palace. According to Vasari, the two elder San Galli, Giuliano and Antonio, were famous for this work. He says the latter was "no less competent in the art than Giuliano himself." Of one model he records that "its masterly construction excited much admiration"; of another, made for the Duke of Milan, that the duke "was filled with astonishment and admiration, as he beheld the fine arrangement and commodious disposition of the different parts, and the rich decorations everywhere applied with the utmost propriety and judgment." A third model of a palace was sent as a present to the King of France. The models evidently were very wonderful productions, and took a long time, even years, to make.[1] That the San Galli made them with their own hands seems certain. Their early training as joiners fitted them well for such work.

Architect-clerks of works. The methods of conducting their work followed by members of the building guilds, and the custom which prevailed in Florence

[1] See Vasari, vol. iii. pp. 98, 99.

in the fifteenth century of well-known architects carrying out the designs of others, often make it difficult to apportion rightly the credit for many of the early buildings of the Renaissance. Alberti especially left the superintendence of work largely to others. But the men who acted as superintendents were men of ability, and considerable distinction, and not merely clerks of works or foremen. The archives of Milan Cathedral show the high esteem in which Francesco di Giorgio, of Siena (see below), and the Florentine architect, Fancelli—who acted for Alberti in the construction of the chapel of the church of the Annunziata, Florence, and at S. Andrea, Mantua—were held. In 1490 the Council could not decide which design to adopt for the completion of the dome of the cathedral. They referred the matter to the two architects mentioned, and invited them to Milan, Giorgio from Siena, and Fancelli from Mantua—where he was in the duke's service—to decide this important point. After their decision was given and accepted, the Council further honoured Giorgio by conferring on him the title of honorary architect of the cathedral. This incident shows conclusively that although Fancelli certainly, and Giorgio probably, worked for other architects, their reputation was considerable, and not merely local.[1]

In many other towns in Tuscany the palaces bear a close resemblance to those of Florence. This is especially the case at Siena. The early examples there show the same simple, broad treatment, the same fine scale, and equally massive walling. The Palazzo Piccolomini follows closely the Riccardi and Strozzi palaces. According to De Montigny[2] it was built by Giacomo Piccolomini, brother of Pius III. and nephew of Pius II., early in the sixteenth century. Other authorities say Pius II. himself caused it to be built after 1460. The shields of both popes are carved on the front, and it seems probable that the building was commenced by the one and finished by the other. The crowning cornice and frieze are very similar to those of the Palazzo Strozzi, and, if De Montigny is correct in his statement, were evidently copied from the Florentine building. The Piccolomini may have been designed by Bernardo Rossellino, who carried out the Palazzo Rucellai for Alberti, and designed the group at Pienza, or else by Francesco di Giorgio (1439–1502). Both men were protégés of the Piccolomini family, which may account for the confusion

Siena.

[1] See Leader Scott's "Cathedral Builders," p. 370.
[2] "Architecture Toscana," by Grandjean de Montigny.

regarding the authorship of several buildings.[1] As Rossellino died in 1464, and Giorgio not until nearly forty years later, the latter may have followed the former on many. Architects in those days did not, as a rule, leave careful instructions, drawings, etc., how their work was to be finished, and in many instances original intentions were evidently not adhered to.

[1] De Montigny ascribes not only the Piccolomini at Siena to Giorgio, but the Pienza buildings as well.

CHAPTER IV

THE SPREAD OF THE RENAISSANCE IN NORTHERN ITALY (1450–1520)

IN the fifteenth century the Florentine Republic included most of the principal cities in Central Italy, whilst the greater part of Northern Italy was divided between the Duchy of Milan and the Republic of Venice. The long arm of the Papacy also reached northwards; and some cities, such as Bologna, and, at one period, Ravenna, came under its sway. Milan embraced Lombardy and a few towns on the western side; and Venice included Vicenza, Padua, Verona, Brescia, Bergamo, etc., and, in addition, towns on the east side of the Adriatic, along the coast of Dalmatia, and many settlements in the Morea and on the islands of the Græcian Archipelago. The trade of Venice with the East reached its zenith in the fifteenth century, following the crushing defeat inflicted on its chief rival, Genoa, in 1380. But its supremacy was soon to be challenged. The rise of the Ottoman Empire, followed by the capture of Constantinople by the Turks in 1453, whilst it assisted the spread of learning in Italy, was a serious blow to Venice. Early in the sixteenth century the Turks captured most of its possessions on the mainland of Greece, and later it lost also to them the Greek islands. It is to the credit of Venice that she, almost alone amongst the Western powers, tried to check the spread of Turkish influence on the sea, although with but partial success.[1] But worse than loss of colonies was to follow. The decline of Venice dates really from the discovery by Vasco da Gama of the all-sea route to India round the Cape of Good Hope, which diverted the trade with the East from the Mediterranean to the ports of Portugal. In addition to the greater northern powers were also smaller territories, more or less independent. Such

---

[1] It was a Venetian shell that unfortunately exploded the powder magazine which the Turks had placed in the Parthenon and occasioned such irreparable damage to that building.

were the states of Mantua and Ferrara, at which towns the courts were hardly inferior to the court of Milan itself.

Commenced at Milan.

The Renaissance in the north may be said to have commenced at Milan, owing largely to the Duke, Francesco Sforza, who had seized the duchy when the old ruling family, the Visconti, became extinct. He extended a warm welcome to the Florentine sculptor, Antonio Averlino, better known as Filarete, on his arrival in the city in 1451. Despot as he was, Francesco was a patron of the arts; and strangely enough more in sympathy with the new movement in architecture than with the old; notwithstanding that in his chief city, Milan, the largest cathedral in the world was nearing completion in the Gothic style. The exile at Venice of Cosimo de' Medici in 1433, accompanied as he was by Michelozzo, might be regarded as a preliminary introduction, but both duke and architect returned to Florence in the following year, and although it is stated that Michelozzo, whilst at Venice, prepared several models and designs—one being for the monastery of S. Giorgio Maggiore—none appears to have been carried out.

Filarete.

Filarete was born in Florence about 1400, and remained in that city until about 1433. For the next twelve years he was in Rome, where amongst other work he executed the fine bronze doors for S. Peter's, which now form the central entrance to the church.[1] From Rome he went to Venice, and there designed and carried out a processional silver cross for the Cathedral of Bassano. Then furnished with a letter of introduction from Piero de' Medici to Francesco Sforza, he started for Milan. In that city he remained until his death in 1465, some say 1469. The Duke evidently proved a good patron. In 1452 he recommended him as architect for the work at the cathedral. The Council dared not decline altogether, but evidently did not relish making the appointment, and two years later found an excuse for dispensing with his services. He was probably not much in sympathy with the work in progress, and his constructive skill may have been small, so possibly the Council had good reason for their action. But Filarete soon obtained compensation. In 1456 he was appointed architect for the Ospedale Maggiore at Milan. He records that on April 12, 1457, the first stone was solemnly laid with great pomp. The building, or rather its front,

---

[1] The doors were executed for old S. Peter's, which was then standing. They are well illustrated by many photographs in "Filarete, scultore e architetto del secolo XV." W. Modes, Roma, 1908.

for the courts were built later and were designed by others, was his chief architectural achievement.[1] The plan for the new town, the Citta di' Sforvinda, which Francesco Sforza proposed to build, is interesting. Its main lines consist of two intersecting squares enclosed within a circle. In the centre is the principal square, surrounded by the most important buildings, and from it radiate the main streets leading apparently to the different entrance gateways.

Near the end of his life, 1460-4, Filarete wrote "Il trattato d'architettura." The first chapter, or book, opens with a criticism on the "modern" style. The heading of Book II. is " L'architetto è come la madre, che genera l'edificio, e il Signore committente è il padre." He is said to have illustrated his work by 250 drawings, some his own designs, others of old buildings in Rome, including the Colosseum, Mole of Hadrian, etc. Many of the designs were castles in the air, but some are apparently for buildings in Sforza's city which was never built. He was evidently a man in advance of his times. Although Alberti's pilastered Palazzo Rucellai was not commenced until 1450, Filarete, in his book, shows designs for pilastered façades; and what is more curious still, includes several detail drawings for windows framed in by pilasters and entablatures in the fashion that did not become general for fifty years, and was quite unknown in Florence at the time his book was written. One good drawing of the hospital, reproduced in Signor Modes' volume, shows his Florentine training and the result of his studies in Rome, and proves that if he had had his way the building would have been in purer Classic. In the Gothic tracery and pointed heads of the windows of the principal floor, Filarete was probably carrying out the wishes of others, and not following his own instincts.

Filarete's "Trattato."

The details of Filarete's career have been stated at some length, because they illustrate how the Renaissance spread so rapidly throughout Italy. Filarete was but one of the numerous bands of what may be termed sculptor-architects of fortune who, starting from Florence, went from town to town, from court to court, ready to work for any one who would pay them. They brought with them the seed of the new movement, and it fell on soil ready to receive it. Not only at Milan were the ruling

How the Renaissance spread.

[1] The Palazzi Bolognini and Isolani, Bologna, are credited to him by some writers. Both are illustrated in "Die Renaissance in Italien," by A. Schütz, Hamburg, 1882.

princes eager for change. The families of the Gonzaga at Mantua, the Este at Ferrara, the Malatesta at Rimini and Pesaro were quite as ready; and at their courts poets, painters, architects, and men of science were welcome. A bond between Mantua and Ferrara was the famous and beautiful Isabella d'Este, sister of Alfonso, Duke of Ferrara, and wife of Giovanni Francesco, Marquis of Mantua. She was the friend and correspondent of the most distinguished men of her time. Her daughter Elizabeth married Guidabaldo, Duke of Urbino, at which city the court, owing largely to Elizabeth's presence, was, during the latter half of the fifteenth century, celebrated as the most polished, artistic, and refined in Italy. The Medici at Florence evidently regarded the spread of the Renaissance as redounding to their credit, and did all that lay in their power to forward it. The alliance between Milan and Florence, and the visit of Galeazzo, Duke of Milan, son of Francesco, to Florence in 1471, doubtless gave impetus to the movement. The residence of Bramante and of the versatile Leonardo da Vinci at Milan added stimulus. Giuliano da San Gallo also spent some time in the town, apparently in 1487, the year that Leonardo probably settled there.[1] The latter left in 1499, his famous Last Supper in the refectory of S. Maria delle Grazie having been finished in the previous year.

Change about 1480.

Until about 1480 all the architects building in the style in the north were Florentines: Alberti at Rimini and Mantua, Fancelli at Mantua, Filarete and Michelozzo at Milan. The latter, about 1465, built the Capella Portinari attached to the church of St. Eustorgio. That Michelozzo did not have his own way entirely, but had, like Filarete, to submit to northern interpretation of his ideas, is shown by the windows, which are Gothic in character.[2] But a change was coming. Characteristic entries in the archives of Milan Cathedral demonstrate that the tide was turning. One entry records the difficulties the Council experienced after 1481 in obtaining architects competent to carry on the work at the cathedral, and refers to inquiries made at Strassburg and elsewhere for skilled men. Another in 1490 mentions the sending of five sculptors to Rome for ten years to study the antique; so that they could return competent to train

---

[1] An entry in the cathedral annals of the following year records a payment in advance to Leonardo for a design for the completion of the cathedral dome (Leader Scott, p. 369).

[2] A model of this is in the Victoria and Albert Museum.

workmen on Classic lines. By the end of the fifteenth century the rising generation of Italians had lost all interest in Gothic, and nearly all trace of it had disappeared from their work.

The chief reasons why the change did not take place earlier in the north are that mediæval traditions were strong there, and the building guilds powerful and conservative. Romanesque churches such as S. Ambrogio, Milan, S. Michele, Pavia, S. Zeno, Verona; public buildings such as the Palazzo Communale at Piacenza, the Palazzo Pubblico at Cremona; the Gothic palaces of Venice; and last, but not least, the Cathedral at Milan, were monuments which could not be lightly forgotten or ignored. The building guilds were conservative because their members had served their apprenticeship in one style and were naturally loath to change. In Florence the mason's guild was comparatively weak, and Brunelleschi not only compelled its "Masters" to work under his orders, but also declined to become a member. His opposition to the guild and victory over it resulted in its absolute collapse. But the Lombard guild was far stronger, and there was no Brunelleschi to dispute its ruling. Owing largely to its influence Filarete had been turned out of the cathedral post, and later it obliged him to share not only his work on the Hospital, but his salary as well, with two other architects, men of position in the guild.

<small>Traditions and building guilds strong.</small>

The method of training apprentices at Milan differed somewhat from the Florentine method. At Milan the goldsmiths' workshops were not the training-ground. The more mediæval system prevailed, and boys served their time on buildings under the direct care of the master of the works. They were selected by the authorities for tuition under certain masters, and their fees paid.[1] The heads of the different guilds in the northern towns not only judged whether apprentices, when their time was finished, were fit to be admitted to membership, but also criticized one another, and sometimes met in solemn conclave to pass judgment on a member's work. Personal jealousy no doubt sometimes dictated an objection, but at the root of most fault-finding was the honest desire of the leaders of the building craft in each town to maintain a high standard of excellence, and to see that their patrons, the public, got good money's-worth. In Venice, as in Milan, the guild was also strong, and, unlike the

<small>Apprenticeship in Milan.</small>

---

[1] "The School of Bramante," by Baron H. von Geymüller, *R.I.B.A. Transactions*, vol. vii., New Series, p. 134.

Florentine guild, it continued strong after the advent of the Renaissance. It numbered amongst its members the family of the Lombardi, who designed the best of the early Renaissance buildings in Venice, and also Jacopo Sansovino, the Florentine, who was head of the guild between 1527 and 1534.

Influence of material. Although the Renaissance started in Florence, and many Florentines did pioneer work outside the Republic, it must not be taken for granted that northern work is therefore merely a copy of Florentine. It differs from it in many respects, and the differences are often far from being blemishes. They are mainly due, in the first place, to the preponderance of mediæval traditions in Milan and Lombardy generally, and the admixture of Gothic and Byzantine traditions in Venetian territory, and in the second, to material. In Florence stone was plentiful, and large blocks were easily procurable. No other material had been used there to any extent from time immemorial. In other towns of Central Italy, Siena, Pisa, Orvieto, etc., marble was employed in its place. In the north stone had never been the principal material. That had been brick. The valley of the Po, between the Alps and the Apennines, which embraces the towns of Milan, Pavia, Piacenza, Cremona, Mantua, Ferrara, etc., is a huge clay field. Many early buildings of Lombardy are entirely of brick; others of brick in combination with either stone or marble, as at Verona especially. The Venetians had no good building material close at hand, but they had early learnt the Byzantine expedient of a brick carcase concealed by marble veneer. This coloured all their subsequent work, both metaphorically and literally.

Influence of northern Roman remains. There is a third reason for the differences between northern and southern design, which is frequently ignored, although it is perhaps the most important of the three. This is the character of the antique Roman work in the north. Roman architecture is so frequently judged by the important remains in Rome itself and in its vicinity, that one is apt to overlook the fact that in distant provinces the buildings often differ considerably in scale and in detail from those of the capital. Even at the time when Roman detail was purest, the age of Augustus, the differences are noticeable. In the Arch at Rimini, built *c.* B.C. 27, the proportions are much lighter, the detail more delicate. The height of the entablature is to the height of the column as 1 to just over $5\frac{1}{2}$, whereas in the nearly contemporary Temple of Castor and Pollux, Rome, which is generally quoted as the perfection of Classic

Fig. 23.—Porta de' Borsari, Verona.

[*To face p. 53.*

proportions, the entablature is to the column as 1 to not quite 4.[1] The order of the Maison Carrée, Nîmes, it is true, has more the proportions of the Roman temple, but the entrance gateways at Autun, Burgundy, again have the lighter touch.

Amongst provincial examples the building that exercised most influence in the north was the Porta de' Borsari, Verona. The lowest storey is of the time of Augustus, and in some respects resembles the arch at Rimini. The upper storeys were built by Gallienus in A.D. 265, when he restored the walls of the city. Its influence was partly due to its position in the centre of a tract of country in which Roman remains were few—Verona stands half-way between Milan and Venice—and partly because it is a complete façade with windows in the upper storeys. Its scale is comparatively small; its proportions and details are not pure; its semicircular headed windows are enclosed either by a moulded architrave which forms a rectangular frame, or else by pilasters at the sides and an entablature above; and pediments are used ornamentally, attached to a wall behind. These are its characteristics; and they are also amongst the characteristics most closely associated with the Renaissance of the north. *Porta de' Borsari.*

Owing probably to the Porta de' Borsari the framed in treatment for windows was general in Northern Italy some years before it appeared in either Rome or Florence. In fact in a modified form it had been common there all through the Middle Ages. In mediæval buildings in Verona, Venice, etc., simple windows generally consist merely of a single light, or two or more lights side by side, with semicircular, pointed, or foliated heads, surrounded by a square-headed frame, sometimes moulded, more often formed of the "billet" design which appears so frequently in S. Mark's, Venice. All the Renaissance men had to do was to alter slightly the detail, and the result was a return to the windows of the Veronese gateway. *Framed in windows.*

Mention has already been made of the start of the Renaissance at Milan under Filarete. Its subsequent development was mainly under Bramante, who ranks with Brunelleschi and Alberti as one of the three greatest architects of the early Renaissance. *Milan.*

---

[1] Both these examples are of the Corinthian order. 1 to 4 is the ratio approved by Palladio, Vignola, and other writers of the sixteenth century, although some English architects of the eighteenth century, Gibbs for instance, prefer 1 to 5.

54   A HISTORY OF ARCHITECTURAL DEVELOPMENT

Bramante.

Bramante was born in 1444, probably at Fermignano, near Urbino. Like so many other Italians of his time his early bent was towards painting, which he studied first under Piero della Francesca, and afterwards at Mantua under the majestic Andrea Mantegna. What his architectural training exactly was is unknown, but he must have come under the influence of Luciano da Laurana, the architect of the ducal palace at Urbino, which was building when Bramante was a young man. He also probably knew Alberti, who lived some time at Mantua, when Bramante was working under Mantegna, but there is no evidence that he was ever the pupil of the former.[1] About 1472—possibly a year or two later—after some time spent in various cities in Lombardy, he settled at Milan. In 1499, on the downfall of his patron Lodovico, Duke of Milan, he went to Rome, and there he lived until his death in 1514.[2]

Bramante's two periods.

Bramante's architectural work divides itself naturally under two heads: firstly, his buildings in Northern Italy, and secondly, those built after he had taken up his residence in the capital. From 1500 onwards, brought directly under the influence of the antique remains in Rome, his manner gradually changed; and although at first there are still signs in his Roman buildings of northern influence, they soon disappeared, and his matured style differs considerably both in scale and detail from his earlier.

His buildings in the north.

Most of his buildings in the north show evidence of his training as a painter. The candelabra-pilasters with which he decorated the outside of S. Maria delle Grazie, Milan, are painted decoration carried out in marble. The chancel painted in perspective in the Church of S. Maria presso S. Satiro, Milan—the site not allowing room for a proper chancel—was a painter's trick, learnt from his two masters in painting, both of whom excelled in the art and theory of perspective. Alberti's influence on him is shown chiefly in the Palazzi Cancelleria and Giraud, Rome, which are referred to in the next chapter. The west front of his church at Abbiate Grasso, not far from Milan, is sometimes instanced as having been inspired by the west front of S. Andrea, Mantua, but this is doubtful. It is certainly vastly inferior in design. The two tiers of coupled columns on each side, from which the arch

[1] Alberti's S. Sebastiano, Mantua, was begun in 1460, and his S. Andrea in 1472.

[2] Messrs. Blashfield in their edition of Vasari state that he visited both Rome and Florence in 1493, and Baron von Geymüller expresses his belief that Bramante knew the capital before he went to live there.

springs, are poor substitutes for Alberti's fine pilasters, and the arch has no abutment, and would long since have collapsed if

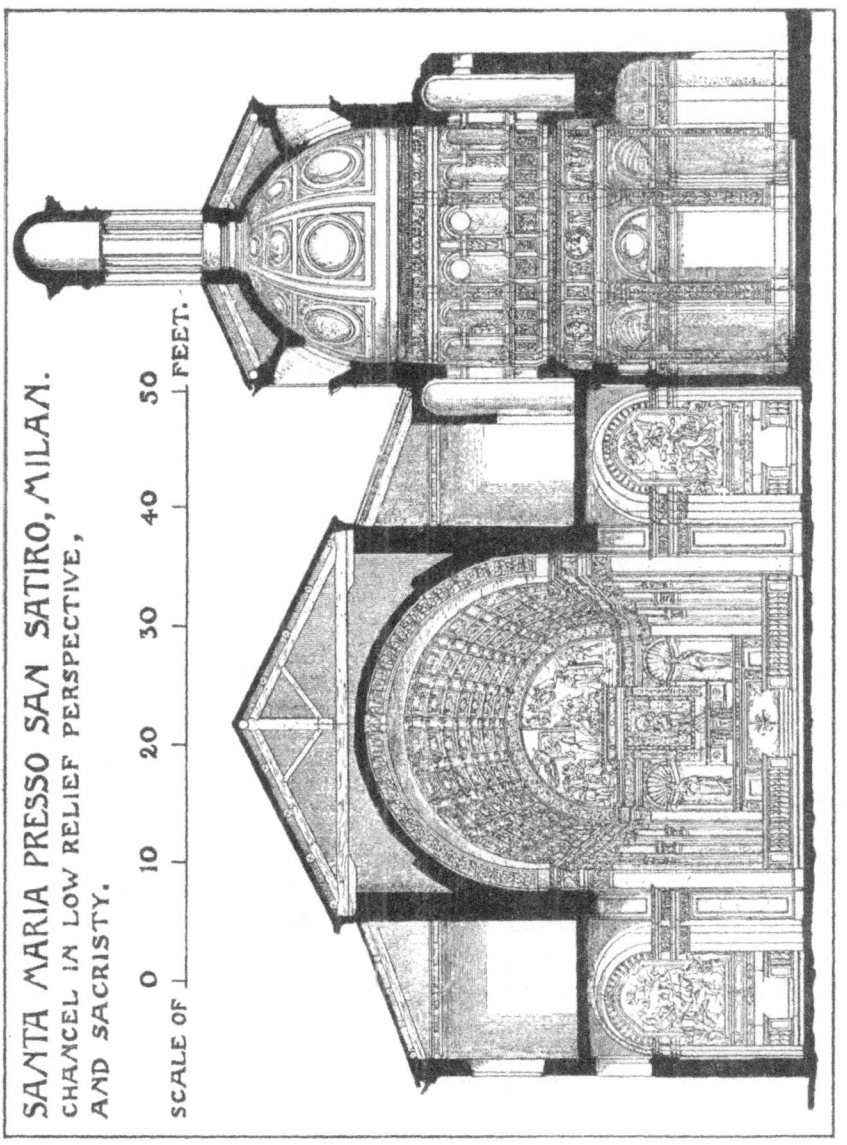

Fig. 24. (Cassina.)

SANTA MARIA PRESSO SAN SATIRO, MILAN. CHANCEL IN LOW RELIEF PERSPECTIVE, AND SACRISTY.

SCALE OF 0 10 20 30 40 50 FEET.

it had not been for an iron tie-rod. The design and construction are Romanesque, not Classic; and Bramante more likely got his idea from the twelfth-century two-storied porches of the Cathedrals of Verona and Piacenza than from Alberti's church.

His early manner.

Bramante's earlier manner is best seen in the Sacristy of the Church of S. Maria presso S. Satiro (c. 1485), and the eastern part of S. Maria delle Grazie (c. 1490).[1] The S. Satiro Sacristy is an octagonal domed building, chiefly remarkable for the rich and

Fig. 25.

elaborate detail of its interior: not the least striking portion being the frieze dividing the upper and lower storeys, with its terra-cotta busts inside wreaths, flanked by children, the work of Caradosso. At the angles are bent panelled pilasters. The effect of these is satisfactory because their panels are filled with carved ornament, which hides what would otherwise have been an objectionable line down the centre of each.[2]

[1] For a complete list of Bramante's buildings, see "Les projets primitifs pour la Basilique de S. Pierre, etc.," by H. von Geymüller.

[2] This is one way of treating pilasters on the inside angles of an octagonal building; another, pairs of pilasters flanking the angles, was followed in the

To the Gothic name of Santa Maria delle Grazie, Milan, Bramante added the well-known east end, consisting of a central square with semicircular apses to the north and south, and a long chancel eastward. The walls are thin, and, the strong corners notwithstanding, it is doubtful if they could have supported a masonry dome. Whether he intended one or not is uncertain. The sixteen-sided lantern, with its flat-pitched roof, which covers and protects the inner dome, is quite in accordance with northern

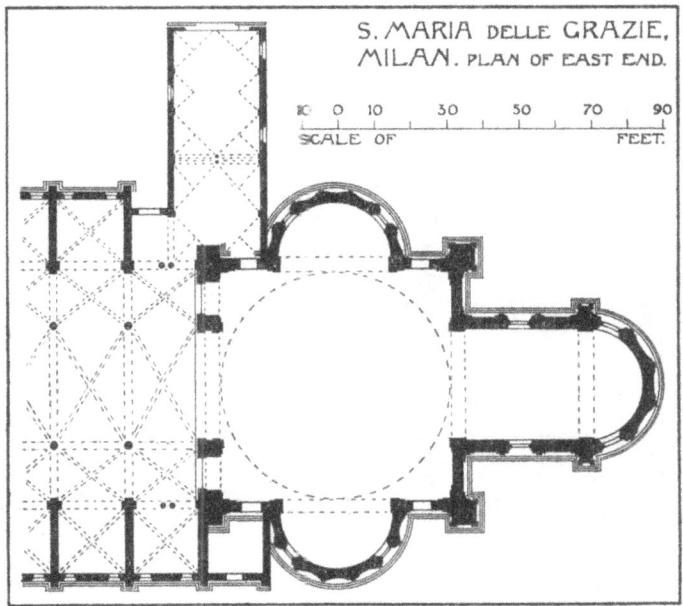

FIG. 26.

traditions; but it was added by others after he left Milan. Each side of the upper storey is pierced by a circular window; and these sixteen windows correspond with an equal number of openings in the inner dome. Fascinating as the exterior is, in its mixture of marble, terra-cotta, and brick, it is not a good influence. The simplicity of the rectangular windows and recesses in the lower portion is delightful, and shows that the architectural side of Bramante's mind was awakening; but beautiful though some of the detail is above, the storeys do not combine to form a happy

Sacristy of the Church of S. Spirito, Florence; and a third, the least satisfactory, is to place single pilasters across the angles.

composition.[1] In the interior is seen that favourite device of the architect's—two concentric archivolts, at some distance from each other, united by a series of circles, which fill the space between them. A modified version of this design, with radiating quad-

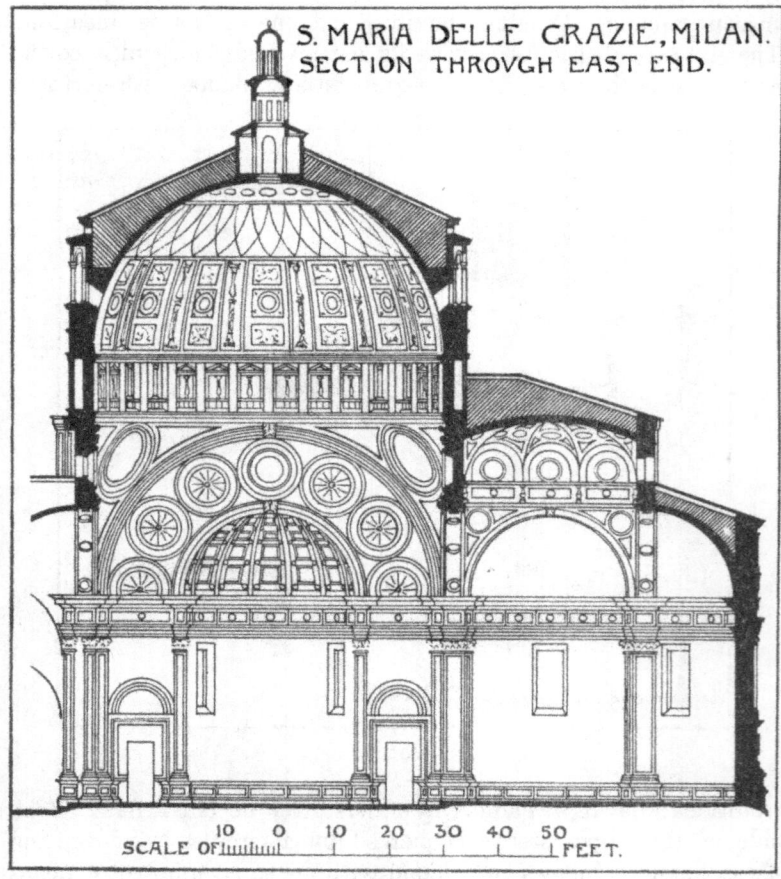

Fig. 27.

rangular panels, instead of circles, occurs over the south door of Como Cathedral, which von Geymüller says Bramante began on June 6, 1491.[2] His share otherwise in the cathedral is somewhat

---

[1] According to Baron Geymüller, only the lower portion is Bramante's.
[2] For a full account of Bramante's system in design, including the double archivolt type, see "The School of Bramante," in the *R.I.B.A. Transactions*, vol. vii. New Series.

hypothetical; but the same authority attributes to him three windows on the south side. The latter illustrate forcibly one of the most important differences between Gothic and Classic windows. The beauty of a Gothic window lies mainly in the ramifications of the tracery in its head; its frame is generally simple, sometimes it has none at all. In a Classic window, on the other hand, the frame is everything, the opening but a semicircular or square-headed void. The Como windows, with their side pilasters and entablatures and pediments, are particularly rich. The church inside is chiefly remarkable for its size, to which scale is given by the delicacy of the framed openings at the triforium level, and by the small pierced circles above which light the vaults. The eastern portion is triapsal in plan, in this respect resembling S. Maria delle Grazie, Milan, and was probably designed by Bramante's followers at Como, Tommaso Rodari and Cristoforo Solari, two well-known members of the Lombardic guild.

FIG. 28.

To them and to other "masters" is due the work at Pavia, Bergamo, Brescia, and other northern towns, executed in the last quarter of the fifteenth century, and in the first two decades of the following. That these men were good builders and excellent craftsmen is undoubted. They had served their apprenticeship and learnt their trade. But they fell between two stools. They had to abandon the style in which their forefathers had worked, and in which they themselves had been trained, and to design in a new. No wonder they failed. Their skill as craftsmen enabled them to master the detail of the new movement, to invest individual parts of a building with beauty, but not to master its underlying principles. Their work lacks rhythm, and frequently repose. Much of it is overloaded with ornament. Its beauties and its defects can be studied and admired or not, as each pleases, at Brescia, in the porch of S. Maria de' Miracoli, the Municipio, and the old Prigioni, the last one of the simplest, and therefore

Work of the "masters."

amongst the best, of northern buildings; and at Bergamo, in the façade of the Colleoni Chapel, attached to the Church of S. Maria Maggiore. This is a wonderful example of "sculptors' architecture," and as wonderful in colour as in ornament. Pink, white, black, red, and grey marbles are mingled in elaborate profusion. The northern architects were particularly fond of colour schemes in marble. In Fra Giacondo's "Loggia" at Verona the marble columns in front are alternately dark grey and pink, and marbles of both colours are also used for the architraves and soffits of the arches. But the example that surpasses all others in unarchitectural richness is the west front of the church of the Certosa, near Pavia. The body of the church was commenced in the last few years of the fourteenth century, but its front was not begun until 1473. The design of this is stated to be by Guiniforte Solari; but portions of it are also attributed to Gio. Antonio Amadeo, who designed and executed the Colleoni Chapel, Bergamo, and to Borgognone, a painter, and others.[1] Many artists evidently had a finger in the pie, and if documentary evidence did not prove this, the building itself would. The front is "paved" with sculptured frames, lovely in themselves as individual examples of the sculptor's art, but altogether lacking in cohesion.

Bologna.

Bologna deserves a separate heading, as, coming halfway between Florence and Milan, it reflects the characteristics of both cities. Many of its palaces externally follow those of the former town in scale and simplicity of design, but their material is chiefly brick. Stone is used for ground-floor storeys, but not with the rugged carelessness that gives such charm to many a Florentine building. The Bolognese, like the workers in most other northern cities, "worried" their stone. They shaped and worked it as though their delight was in the forms they could produce in it, and not in the material itself. The failing is very marked in the façade of the Palazzo Bevilacqua, otherwise the most successful of early palaces in the town. The extent to which this "jeweller's" treatment can be carried is illustrated in the Palazzo dei Diamanti, Verona, in which the stones are exact squares, except the quoins, which are oblong, and each is cut in facets. The windows of the Palazzo Bevilacqua are similar to those in northern towns, and have none of the Florentine feeling. In the courtyard is seen

[1] Leader Scott (p. 378) says that "Borgognone was only invited to the Certosa by the Prior in 1490, when the façade was well begun."

Fig. 29.—Prigioni, Brescia.

Fig. 30.—Colleoni Chapel, alongside S. M. Maggiore, Bergamo.

[*To face p.* 60.

the doubling of the bays of the arcade on the upper storey, which was a favourite device of northern architects. Bramante carried it to Rome, and introduced it, with considerable improvements, in the cloisters he designed for the Church of S. Maria della Pace (see Fig. 40).

Venice, 1470–1520.

Venice is the third great centre of the early Renaissance. The movement started there later than at either Florence or Milan—in fact, hardly a trace of it existed before 1470; and even in buildings of the following two or three decades in which it is present considerable adulteration is apparent. Venice resisted it so long because it had its own style—one as unique as it is beautiful—unique inasmuch as it was a blend of Byzantine and Gothic. This retained sufficient vitality to colour everything, until Sansovino and Palladio introduced the matured Renaissance from Rome. Even after the middle of the sixteenth century traces of the earlier style lingered in the designs of local men.

FIG. 31.

Early churches.

Of semi-Renaissance churches built prior to 1520 there is little of much value. The aisleless church of Santa Maria dei Miracoli, won in competition by Pietro Lombardi in 1481, owes its beauty mainly to its marble veneers and patteræ, and consequently more to Byzantine and Lombardic traditions than to the influence of the new movement. The dome which covers the chancel is raised on a drum above pendentives, and externally recalls the domes of S. Mark's. The rounded top of the nave roof and the semicircular gable at the west end appear strange to Western eyes, accustomed to pointed gables and pitched roofs, but the latter would have appeared equally strange to the Venetians. S. Mark's had accustomed them to the rounded form, which is general in Byzantine churches. The roof and the gable at the west end of S. Zaccaria are similar. The front of this church is an example of tiresome repetition of order above order,

62   A HISTORY OF ARCHITECTURAL DEVELOPMENT

and of the poverty in scale which is characteristic of much of the earlier work in Venice.

Palaces.

The great charm of Venice is the life on its canals; and, excepting S. Mark's, its chief architectural attraction is the numerous palaces of all dates which line them. The substitution of a waterway for dry land had little or no effect on either their planning or general design. The entrance doorways are generally of good dimensions, although possibly not so large as in Rome and Florence, where allowance had to be made for horsemen and for the unwieldy coach of the period. Many palaces have a courtyard; but few courtyards have the open arcading which gives such distinction in other cities. The most striking and characteristic feature of the fronts is the balcony overlooking the canals; sometimes only at the first-floor level, sometimes above in addition. These balconies played a large part in the life of the city. Before them by day and by night passed, in irregular procession, the noiseless gondola with its living freight, formerly the sole conveyance of the town.

Spacing of windows.

The method of spacing the windows in palace façades is worth noting. In most buildings elsewhere windows are spaced either equally or else irregularly. In Venice the spacing has regularity but not equality. The windows in the centre are grouped closely together, and are flanked, in the majority of cases, by single windows, separated from the others by a wider margin of walling. This peculiarity is not confined to Renaissance palaces, but exists also in the earlier Romanesque and Gothic ones. It may have originated from the fact that in many of the latter—the Palazzo Cà d'oro, for instance—the central openings are fronts of recesses which form balconies, the windows being behind. The effect is most satisfactory. The ends frame in the central part, and the angles are strong and solid, the latter an important necessity in all buildings.

Vendramin palace.

Of fifteenth-century Renaissance palaces, the most beautiful and also one of the earliest is the Palazzo Vendramin Calergi on the Canal Grande. It was built in 1481 by either Moro Lombardo or his brother Pietro, the latter the most famous of the family of the Lombardi. It has few of the faults of its period. The windows, grouped as above described, are each of two lights and in design are similar to Florentine windows, except that the circles above the lights and the spandrils under each enclosing arch are pierced. More light was a necessity in Venice than in

Photo: *Alinari.*

Fig. 32.—Palazzo Vendramin Calergi, Venice.   [*To face p. 62.*

Florence. Dull, gloomy days are far from uncommon there, although Venice owes much of its beauty to its humidity, which results in atmospheric effects unparalleled in Europe for brilliancy.[1] Between the windows of the two upper storeys of the Vendramin palace are columns, single between the central windows, in pairs flanking the end ones. These carry continuous entablatures. The top entablature has not the strength of the great crowning cornice of Florentine palaces, but it neither looks weak, nor does it overpower the columns below. On the ground storey are panelled pilasters. Panelling of pilasters is essentially a northern Italian practice, seldom followed in either Florence or Rome in the fifteenth and sixteenth centuries.[2] Alberti was perhaps the first to introduce it in the pilasters on the west front of S. Andrea, Mantua. From Venice, Milan, Bologna, etc., it passed to France, where it forms a leading characteristic of nearly all the buildings of the time of Francis I. The Palazzo Corner Spinelli was built about the same time as the Vendramin, and is similar in design, but smaller and somewhat simpler. It has only two central windows, and lacks columns between them. The lowest storey, consisting of a low ground floor and mezzanine, is of rusticated stone of almost Florentine severity.

Alongside S. Mark's stands the Ducal palace, the courtyard of which is a mixture of many styles. The so-called Giant's Staircase, and a portion of the side of the court against which it stands, are the work of Antonio Riccio (or Rizo), and were executed in the last few years of the fifteenth century. The design of the staircase is simple and beautiful, but its marble panels, panelled balustrade, and general feeling are more Byzantine than Renaissance. Sansovino did his best to ruin the staircase when he placed his two large figures—which give it its name—above the top step. As an example of how good work can be unsuitably placed this would be hard to beat. The end of the court beyond was designed by

_{Ducal palace.}

---

[1] Bright sun alone does not produce such brilliant effects. In a clear atmosphere its rays are too dazzling. The greyer the atmosphere the more brilliant the effects may sound paradoxical, but the statement is true. Nowhere can finer colour be seen than in London, especially on a November afternoon when the sun is setting down the Strand or beyond Westminster Abbey.

[2] Panelled pilasters are far from common in ancient Roman work. The Arch of Hadrian, Athens, and the Baths of Diana, Nîmes, are two antique examples in which the treatment occurs. In the Athenian example the pilasters at the angles are panelled like those on the Venetian palace. At Nîmes the design of the panels is unusual and exceptionally delicate and beautiful.

Guglielmo Bergamasco, a native of Alzano near Bergamo. Few of the early Renaissance architects in Venice seem to have been Venetians. The Buoni, who started the additions to the ducal palace, were from the west, probably from Como. Martino Lombardi, or Solari, to give him his original name, was from Carona in the Bergamasque Alps. He was the father of Moro and Pietro, and the first of the family nicknamed the Lombardi after their native state.[1]

Scuole di S. Marco and S. Rocco.

The two buildings which express most forcibly the faults of early Venetian art are the Scuola di S. Marco and the Scuola di S. Rocco, although the detail in itself is good in both. The former is attributed to Martino and his son Moro. Two of the windows on the first floor bear a strong resemblance to the central windows of the Porta de' Borsari (see Fig. 23), and were, if the date generally given be correct (1485), the first to have pilasters at the sides and an entablature and pediment above. The semi-circular gables over them recall S. Mark's. The most objectionable features on the building are the perspective panels on the ground-floor storey. Such effects are permissible in painting and in intarsia work, but are altogether out of place in serious architecture. All the fifteenth-century architects from Brunelleschi onwards made a careful study of perspective, but Brunelleschi and the Florentines generally used it as a helpmate; they never allowed it to become their master. The Scuola di S. Rocco was one of Pietro Lombardi's latest works. It was continued after his death in 1521 by his grandson Santo. It may be regarded as the last word of the "masters" of the building guild, who were forced by circumstances stronger than they to work in a style they were out of sympathy with and did not understand. This "tentative" Renaissance lasted in Venice about fifty years, from 1470 to 1520–30. Before it finally disappeared Bramante's S. Peter's was rising in Rome, and Sanmicheli at Verona, Peruzzi and Antonio San Gallo at Rome, and Sansovino at Venice itself had carried the Renaissance to a culmination.

Summary.

To summarize this northern work; in comparison with the earlier Florentine it is lighter, more fanciful, more elaborate. It is to the latter what Greek Ionic is to Greek Doric. The Florentines regarded ornament as a jewel which should be framed, and

[1] The Solari was a great building family. Other members of it were employed on Como Cathedral and the Certosa, Pavia.

Photo: Alinari.
FIG. 33.—DUCAL PALACE, VENICE, COURTYARD.

Photo: Alinari.
FIG. 34.—SCUOLA DI SAN ROCCO, VENICE.

[*To face p.* 64.

therefore used it sparingly. The Venetians, Milanese, and Veronese scattered it with lavish hand. The Florentines were, probably, better figure sculptors, but it is doubtful if as carvers they compared with the northern craftsmen. One reason for this is that much of the detail in the churches and palaces of Florence is executed in grey sandstone (*pietra serena*); in Venice and most of the other towns in the north the material is marble. Another is the close intercourse between Venice and the East, especially with Greece. There can be little doubt that this exercised considerable influence. To instance capitals alone. In Brunelleschi's Florentine buildings capitals are mostly copied from antique Corinthian examples in the porticoes and peristyles of Roman temples: the Pantheon, Mars Ultor, Castor and Pollux, etc. This is the characteristic Roman type. In the north this type hardly existed, and consequently does not apear in Renaissance work. Its place is taken by modified versions which have come to be regarded as creations of the architects of the fifteenth century. As a matter of fact, these varieties probably owe their origin to Greece; which, even after it became subject to Rome, maintained its artistic supremacy. The arch of Hadrian at Athens, besides showing greater refinement and delicacy, combined with much lighter proportions than contemporary buildings in Rome, has capitals above the pilasters on the lower storey which are full of the feeling generally regarded as entirely Renaissance. In the British Museum is a little antique marble capital, classed as "probably Greek," which, if its antiquity were not assured, might be included amongst Venetian examples of the fifteenth century. In the same Museum are similar and larger capitals from the upper order of the interior of the Pantheon, Rome, which differ only from these in a coarseness of execution of which no Renaissance sculptor would have been guilty. Many northern Renaissance capitals again are based on Romanesque examples, especially in the smaller towns. Of this character are some at Lugano, in Italian Switzerland, which, but for a certain refinement, might be classed as belonging to the twelfth century. After Brunelleschi and his contemporaries, Florentine sculptors turned their attention more to the type of which the capitals from the inside of the Pantheon are examples, and abandoned the heavier and more "correct" Classic. But they seldom succeeded in equalling the Venetians in the variety and delicacy of their carving.

The Renaissance of Northern Italy owes its good points

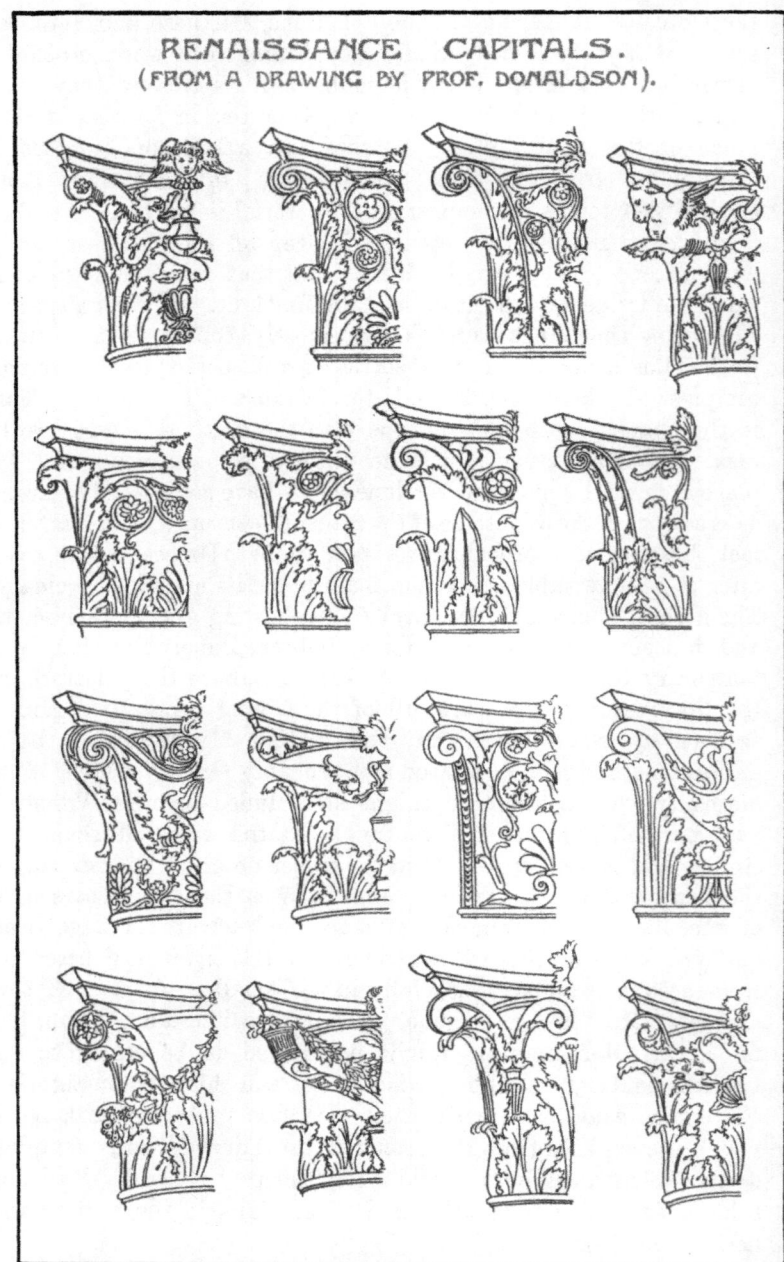

Fig. 35.

mainly to the skill of its craftsmen and the beauty of its materials; as a style it is dangerous to follow. If an attempt be made to do so with inferior craftsmen and coarser material, the result is failure. It was this Renaissance of the north, and not the Florentine or the Roman, that first found its way into France, England, and Germany

CHAPTER V

THE CENTENARY OF THE RENAISSANCE: SECULAR BUILDINGS (1500–1580)

Introduction.

FLORENCE alone can claim the honour of being the birthplace of the Renaissance, but its centenary was celebrated all over Italy. One hundred years after Brunelleschi's design had been accepted for the dome of the cathedral the movement reached its zenith; not in one city alone, but throughout the country. From 1520 to 1570 is its most glorious period; when its leading architects were in their prime, and its most famous buildings were erected. The culmination was reached in Italy before the Renaissance even started in England; and the principles upheld by Peruzzi, Sanmicheli, Palladio, Michael Angelo, etc., were already regarded as out of date in their native home before they were brought by Inigo Jones to our shores.

Uniformity in design.

Throughout the fifteenth century local characteristics are everywhere strongly marked; in the work of the centuries following they are barely perceptible. Different towns, it is true, still show distinctive traits, but these are either due to restrictions imposed by material, by site irregularities or special conditions—Genoese palaces run up the sides of hills, Venetian palaces are built at the water's edge—or else are owing to the genius of a few men who made certain cities their homes. The personal equation looms even bigger in late work than in early; and Rome, Verona, Venice, Vicenza, and some other towns can all show masterpieces, similar in their underlying principles, but full of personal originality and individual charm.

Rome chief centre.

Rome is frequently cited, with Florence, Milan, and Venice, as a centre at which great architectural advance was made, and from which ideas radiated. This is not true in the sense that a like statement is true of Florence, or even of the other towns named. Rome to some extent took the lead in the sixteenth century, partly because of the prospects of employment held out to artists, by popes, cardinals, and the Roman nobility, which brought them to the city in large numbers, and partly because at Rome alone could men study properly the remains of antiquity. The dream of every student of architecture at that time was to see for himself the great buildings of the past. These were as great an attraction as the prospect of work. Rome thus became the chief art centre of Italy, but not in the same way as Florence a century before. In Florence art developed and advanced through the genius of the Florentines themselves. In Rome developments were due entirely to outside talent.

With the possible exception of Giulio Romano (1492-1546)— and he did not come on the scene until late—no architect of the sixteenth century born in Rome reached first rank. Giacomo della Porta and Girolamo Rainaldi can hardly be placed there. All the artists who most distinguished themselves in Rome were born elsewhere. Bramante and Raphael were natives of Urbino; Peruzzi was born near Siena; Sansovino, Michael Angelo, and Antonio da San Gallo were Florentines; Giacomo Barozzi, better known as Vignola, came from Vignola, near Modena. Even the architects who achieved most success in Rome in the seventeenth century, Carlo Maderno, Bernini, Borromini, Fontana, etc., were not Romans by birth. Moreover, as the examples referred to later will show, such traits as may be regarded as most characteristic of Roman buildings—secular at least—are hardly those most prominent in other cities. In Rome the so-called "astylar" style was the one generally adopted for façades, and columns and pilasters are the exception, save in courtyards. Bologna and a few other cities agree with Rome in this respect—they were really following Florence more than Rome—but elsewhere, at Verona, Venice, and Vicenza in particular, the contrary is the case. Rome influenced the north through its antique remains far more than through its modern buildings. Neither Sansovino, a Florentine, who spent the last forty years of his life in Venice, nor Peruzzi, a Sienese, whose practice was in many places, can be regarded as Roman influences. Sanmicheli and Palladio, the two men who, in addition to Sansovino, designed most of the finest buildings outside Rome, never practised there. They both studied there when young, then each returned to his native city.

"Foreign" architects at Rome.

In this chapter and in the following only secular buildings are included; with the exception of brief reference to two of Bramante's

Secular work this chapter.

70   A HISTORY OF ARCHITECTURAL DEVELOPMENT

ecclesiastical works. The churches of the sixteenth and seventeenth centuries are considered in another chapter.

Rome: introduction.

The revival of art in Rome was chiefly due to the Church; to the popes and cardinals. It commenced in tentative fashion under Pope Nicholas V. (1447-55), was continued by Pius II. of Pienza and Siena (1458-64), and came to a head under Julius II. (1503-13) —the Giuliano della Rovere with whom Giuliano da San Gallo travelled in France—and his successor Leo X. (1513-21) of the House of Medici. The capture and sack of Rome in 1527 by Charles V. affected but temporarily the prosperity of the city; in fact, it seems to have stimulated the popes and nobility to additional energy in all directions, and especially in building.

Early renaissance in Rome.

No mention has been made in previous chapters of fifteenth-century buildings in Rome, except incidentally, and in truth there

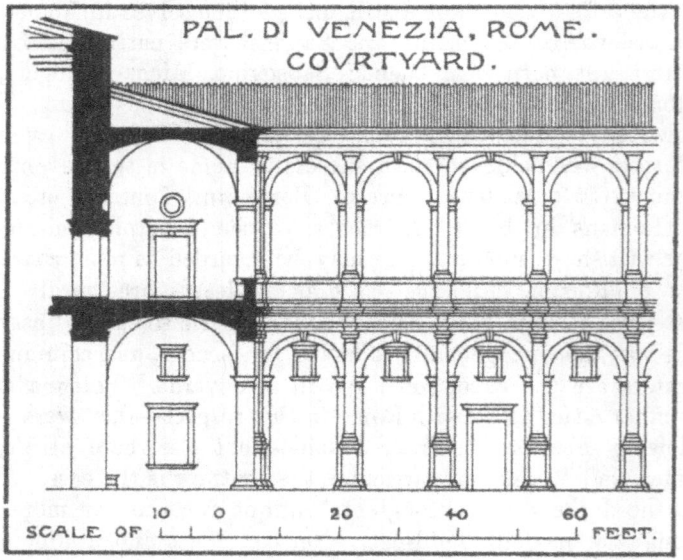

Fig. 36.

is little that calls for special mention. A few palaces, churches, restorations, and fittings can be credited to Bernardo Rossellino, Filarete, Alberti, Giuliano da San Gallo, his brother Antonio, and other Florentines. The largest and best known of early palaces is the Palazzo di Venezia, alongside the church of S. Marco. Its main front, crowned by heavy machicolations, presents little of interest. The unfinished courtyard is better. In it the Colosseum type of design reasserts itself for the first time for centuries. The arches do not spring from columns, as in the courtyards of Florence, Bologna, etc., but from piers on the face of which are attached columns.

The opening days of the sixteenth century—or the last months of the previous year—saw the arrival of Bramante in Rome. The first few years he spent there, according to Vasari, he "lived with extreme frugality," and, although he was then fifty-five, spent a large portion of his time studying and measuring ancient buildings, "not only in Rome, but in the Campagna and Naples." He certainly measured Hadrian's Villa at Tivoli—the great niche of which (see Vol. I. Fig. 96) possibly gave him the idea for the similar feature at the end of the Court of the Vatican Palace—and, when at Naples, he must have visited Paestum to see the remains of the Greek temples. *Bramante in Rome.*

The earliest building in Rome attributed to him is the Palazzo Cancelleria.[1] It was begun about 1495, before Bramante resided in Rome, but he may have prepared the design during his visit there in 1493. Although beautiful in detail it is poor in scale in comparison with his later work. This defect is accounted for if the design were made before he came strongly under the influence of the old remains in the capital. The façade is misleading, as no indication is given that behind it there are two buildings, one being a church, S. Lorenzo in Damazo, to which the smaller door gives access. To some extent it recalls Alberti's Palazzo Rucellai, Florence. But the spacing of the pilasters and the windows are different. The latter are all founded on the windows of the Porta de' Borsari, Verona (see Fig. 23), which they closely resemble, although the detail is more refined and delicate. Bramante knew Verona well, and this gateway was probably one of his chief sources of inspiration before he came to Rome. The grouping of the pilasters in pairs, with walling between, is particularly happy, the narrow spaces framed by each pair being half the width of the wider bays in which are the windows. This treatment was a favourite of his; and that fact, coupled with the design of the windows, affords presumptive proof that he was the architect of the building. The two tiers of pilasters are approximately equal in *Palazzo Cancelleria.*

---

[1] Signor Domenico Gnoli, in an article entitled "La Cancelleria ed altri Palazzi a Roma attribuiti a Bramante," gives the credit for it to Antonio Montecavallo, who superintended the work.

Fig. 37.

THE CENTENARY OF THE RENAISSANCE 73

height, but as the upper tier runs through two storeys, what might otherwise have been disagreeable proportions are avoided. The pilasters on the back and side elevations are equally spaced, and

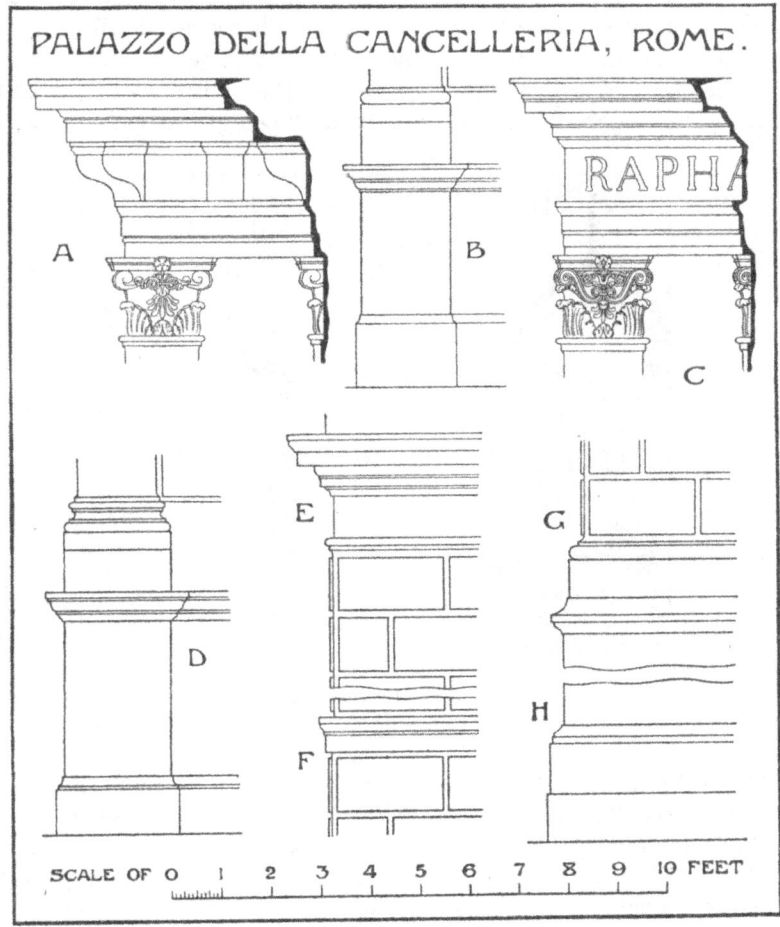

Fig. 38.

not in pairs. The walling of these portions is brick; only the front is stone throughout. Similar in design to the Cancelleria is the Palazzo Giraud (or Torlonia, *c.* 1504). The so-called Casa di Bramante, in the Via del Governo vecchio, and one or two other houses, also bear some resemblance to it, but von Geymüller says that none is by Bramante.

74 A HISTORY OF ARCHITECTURAL DEVELOPMENT

Il Tempietto, etc. Il Tempietto, in the cloisters of S. Pietro in Montorio, built about 1502, was probably Bramante's first design after his arrival in Rome. It is a little masterpiece, strongly imbued with true classic feeling and fine in scale. He intended it to be surrounded by a circular colonnade, which would have removed the feeling of isolation which the temple now has, but this unfortunately was never built. Two years later followed the cloisters of S. Maria della Pace; particularly interesting as showing that the architect

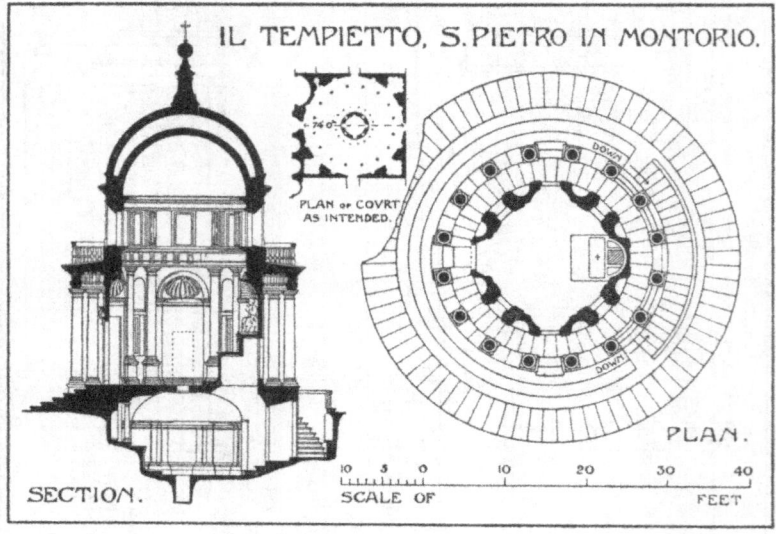

FIG. 39.

had not forgotten the northern courtyards with their intermediate columns on the upper storey, and yet had become enamoured of the Colosseum and Theatre of Marcellus type of design. The substitution of the lintel for the arch at the gallery level is a considerable improvement. The cover over the rainwater outlet in the centre of the courtyard is a characteristic little touch, evincing the care Bramante took over small detail.

Vatican. The remodelling of and additions to the Vatican was another early work of his. This included a great court nearly 400 yards long, enclosed by galleries and buildings. The ground being very uneven and the slopes acute, the court was planned on different levels; the garden of the upper part being approached from the lower by flights of steps and terraces. These unfortunately have

Photo: Alinari.
FIG. 40.—SANTA MARIA DELLA PACE, ROME, CLOISTERS.

Photo: Alinari.
FIG. 41.—PALAZZO BORGHESE, ROME, COURTYARD.

[*To face p.* 74.

now been built over, with the result that court and garden are cut off from each other and the vista from end to end destroyed.

Bramante's work at S. Peter's is considered in another chapter. That engaged most of his time until his death in 1514. His record for the fifteen years he spent in Rome is a truly remarkable one. His artistic sense is manifest in everything from the time he started practice in the north; but not until he arrived in Rome

Summary.

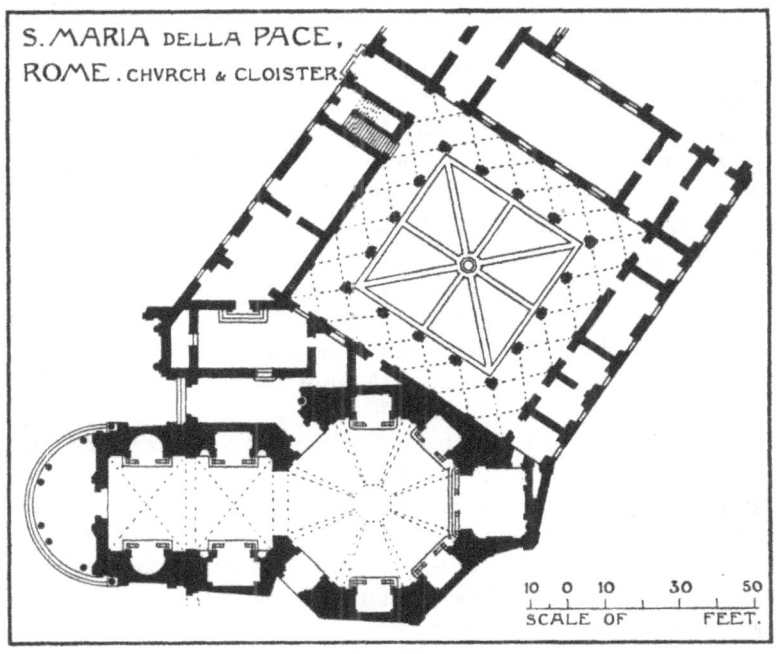

Fig. 42.

did his genius fully expand. The antique remains in the eternal city have influenced many, but on none has their influence for good been more marked. They affected him the more strongly because he was past middle age when he came under their direct sway. His appreciation of them was tempered by mature judgment. He did not rely on them alone. He had studied the art of other districts. At Milan he had been captivated by S. Lorenzo, then retaining much of its original beauty, although on two occasions or more it had been injured by fire.[1] He had also seen there the

[1] The extensive alterations which almost amounted to an entire rebuilding and changed the appearance of the church considerably, did not take place until after 1573, in which year a large portion of the building collapsed.

Cathedral rise; and there and in other cities of the north had felt some of the beauty of Romanesque and Gothic art. He was able, therefore, to pick and choose; to select the fine points in ancient work, to reject the less satisfactory, and to complement these by suggestions from other styles. His genius enabled him to blend all harmoniously; and to this happy combination is owing largely the individuality of his work.

<small>Rome, 1514–50.</small>
Bramante stands halfway between the early Renaissance and its maturity. With his death the former definitely ends, so far as Rome and the greater part of Italy are concerned. The fine buildings of the succeeding and greatest period are so numerous that it is manifestly impossible to do more than refer to a few. All that can be attempted is to draw attention to characteristics common to most, and to select one or two examples for special mention which are either essentially typical or else especially beautiful. Brief accounts of the careers of the principal architects are also added alongside the references to their buildings. So much of architectural advance was due to the individual in Renaissance days, that to appreciate fully the work of each one requires to know a little about his life and surroundings.

The Romans of the sixteenth century, like their ancestors in imperial times preferred, as a rule, grand scale to every other architectural consideration. Their next insistence was on symmetry. The latter they gained, without any sacrifice of utilitarian necessities, in a truly marvellous manner, as an examination of the plans of their palaces shows. With few exceptions their buildings are distinguished by a reticence and sobriety which does them great credit. External ornament is almost as rare in Roman palaces of the sixteenth century as in earlier Florentine. There is not, however, that strong similarity in treatment which distinguishes the fifteenth-century palaces of Florence, or even those of Venice. The principal architects, not being Roman by birth but recruited from outside, did not practice in Rome until, in most cases, their style had matured elsewhere. Close intercourse between them no doubt led to interchange of ideas, and each to some extent exercised influence over his brethren, but in the main all worked on independent lines. The result is no jumble, such as would have resulted fifty years earlier if similar independence had been exercised, because by the sixteenth century all were in accord regarding the main lines of progression necessary, and

FIG. 43.—PALAZZO DEL VATICANO, AS DESIGNED BY BRAMANTE.

[*To face p.* 76.

the only differences perceptible are those due to individual interpretation of them.

In plan Roman palaces closely resemble Florentine, and the central courtyard is a feature in nearly all. In large palaces it becomes a stately court, surrounded by paved and vaulted arcades, sufficiently high and wide to enable the coach of the period to drive round under them, and deposit its occupants under shelter at the foot of the grand staircase leading to the upper floors. On the upper floors, corridors or galleries give access to the principal rooms. The ground floor was reserved for the offices, servants, and often the stable. Over portions of it in some palaces is a mezzanine floor of low rooms, as in the Palazzo Borghese. From the stable accommodation provided one obtains a faint idea of the state kept by great Roman families. In the Palazzo Altieri there are fifty-eight stalls, in the Palazzo Doria Panfili fifty-one, in other palaces nearly as many. Their position under a house was often unavoidable, as local broils were far from uncommon in the sixteenth century, and to separate a man from his horse would have been fatal. Plans of palaces.

The greater number of palaces occupy irregular sites. Rome was a thickly populated city, with houses, especially in the central part, tightly packed along its narrow, carelessly laid out streets, and round its open spaces. Large rectangular sites were seldom procurable, even when money was forthcoming in abundance to pay for a general clearance. The skill displayed by the architects in obtaining symmetry under most difficult conditions is one of the most fascinating points about the palaces. The great Palazzo Borghese, for instance, occupies a piece of land which in outline is not unlike a leg of mutton. The narrow end, facing towards the river, contains an entrance hall and vestibule, over which is a terrace garden. In the centre of the other end is the principal entrance, from which is a wonderful vista through another vestibule and the courtyard into the large garden beyond. The court, notwithstanding the irregularity of the site, is rectangular (see Fig. 41), and the garden is symmetrically laid out. Even in small palaces a vista was obtained somehow; and when there was no space for a garden, a representation of one in perspective was often painted upon what otherwise would have been a blank wall. The Palazzo Maccarani is another wonderfully clever plan. But the most remarkable plans are those of the two palaces built side by side by the brothers Pietro and Angelo Massimi. For a Irregularity of sites of palaces.

combination of practical needs and architectural dignity and effect these are unsurpassed (see Fig. 53).

Material. Few Roman palaces are faced with stone. The angle quoins, frames, and architraves of window and other openings are of that material, and the ground storeys are occasionally of rusticated ashlar, but the walling is of brick. The bricks are long and thin, like old Roman ones, and their colour at first was probably equally delightful. But few palaces, alas! show their original colour now. In nearly all cases the brickwork is covered by coats of distemper, of singularly disagreeable hue, or else by stucco also distempered.

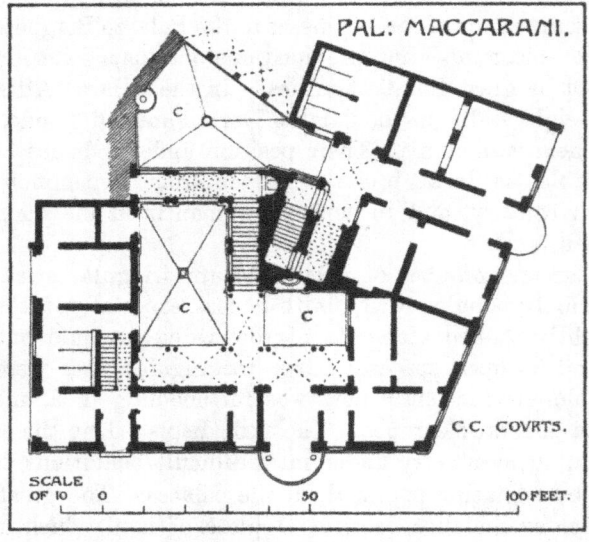

Fig. 44.

Not only is the distemper ugly in itself, but its numerous coats have completely destroyed the texture of the walling. It has filled the mortar joints to such an extent that it is difficult to see, without close examination, whether the walls are distempered or stuccoed. Red bricks apparently were generally used for facing, but yellow bricks, of a deep orange shade, were not uncommon. In the upper storeys of the courtyard of the Cancelleria the bricks are yellow, and their original colour and texture show. If the distemper could be cleaned off the walls of other palaces the improvement to each building would be great, and the gain to the whole city enormous. The fronts and courtyard walls of some palaces have stucco decoration. Of these the most elaborate is the Palazzo Spada alla Regola, the work of Giulio Mazzoni, who was more of a sculptor than an architect, as the design shows.

The façades of Roman palaces of the sixteenth and seventeeth centuries resemble earlier Florentine palaces as regards the great crowning cornice and absence of pilasters and columns, but, owing to their brick walling, and especially to their window treatment, present a totally different appearance. In Rome windows, with few exceptions, are framed in voids. The attic above the cornice, first brought prominently to the front by Michael Angelo in S. Peter's, never became popular in Rome for domestic work, although towards the end of the sixteenth century Palladio and his followers adopted it freely in other cities. It is difficult to say to whom should be given the credit of starting the type of astylar façade so prevalent in the city. Bramante certainly had no share in it; his façades are all pilastered. Not only is the date when any building was commenced a matter of some uncertainty, but in many instances authorities are by no means agreed as to who was the architect. Thus, the Palazzo Linotte is sometimes credited to Antonio da San Gallo the younger, sometimes to Peruzzi; and its date is variously given as 1515, which would make it amongst the very first of its type, and 1534; the latter by Letarouilly. The front was either never finished, or else mutilated later, but is well deserving of careful attention. The probability is that San Gallo, Peruzzi, Raphael, and others were simultaneously trying to solve the same problem and were proceeding on similar lines.

<small>Façades of Roman palaces.</small>

The Palazzo Sacchetti, which Antonio da San Gallo the younger built for himself about 1543—a noble house for an architect—may be taken as a typical example. At the top the crowning cornice; below both the first and second floor windows two string-courses, the upper in each case forming the window-sill; and between the two floors a mezzanine with windows half the size of the principal ones. The alternation of large and small windows is often most effective. But for this the façade of the great Palazzo Borghese would appear commonplace. The small windows give it scale. In provincial cities the alternation is rarer, as the buildings have seldom the height and bulk of Roman palaces. The Palazzo Farnese at Piacenza, commenced by Vignola about 1558, is an exception, and an especially interesting one, as, never having been finished, the portions built show how work

<small>Examples of astylar fronts.</small>

80 A HISTORY OF ARCHITECTURAL DEVELOPMENT

proceeded. The finest example of the type in Rome is the Palazzo Farnese, built for Cardinal Alessandro Farnese, after-

Fig. 45.

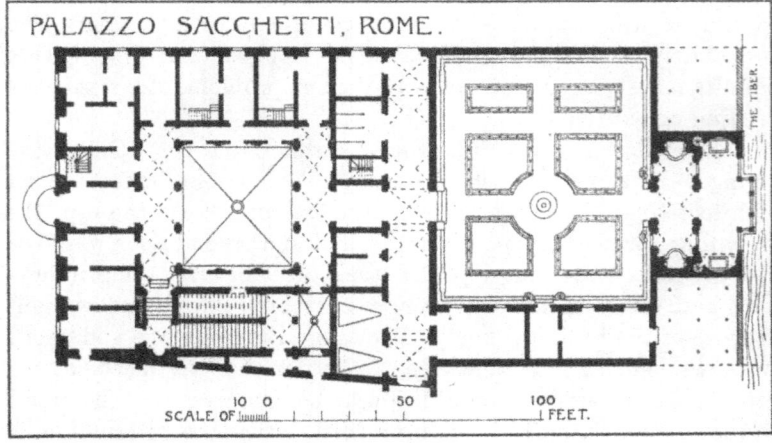

Fig. 46.

wards Pope Paul III. When it was commenced is somewhat uncertain. Messrs. Blashfield, in their edition of Vasari's Lives, state that Alessandro "bought the house which was afterwards transformed into the Farnese palace. Successive purchases of ground were followed by successive enlargements of the plan; the work began in 1517, and in 1534 Antonio da San Gallo, basing

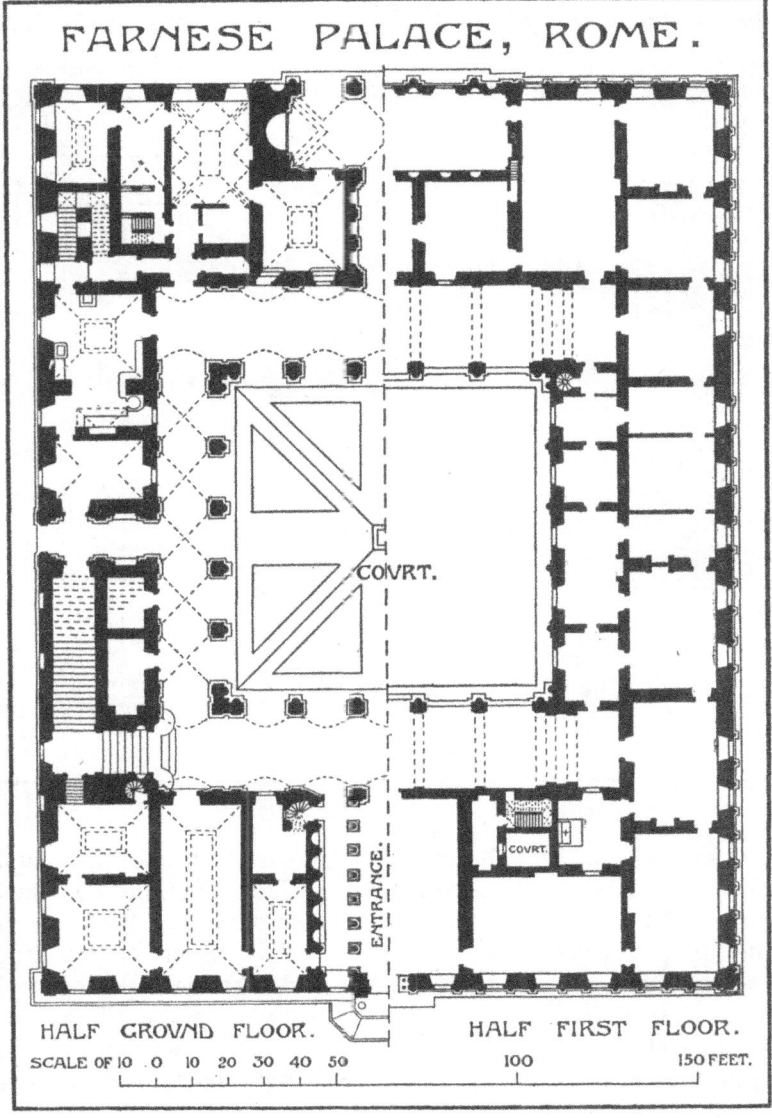

Fig. 47.

himself on the old plans made new ones." The palace is so symmetrical and rectangular, that although some of the foundations for another design may have been utilized, it is unlikely that any of the existing superstructure is earlier than the capture of Rome in 1527.[1] At the time of San Gallo's death (1546) the second storey was still unfinished. That was completed by Michael

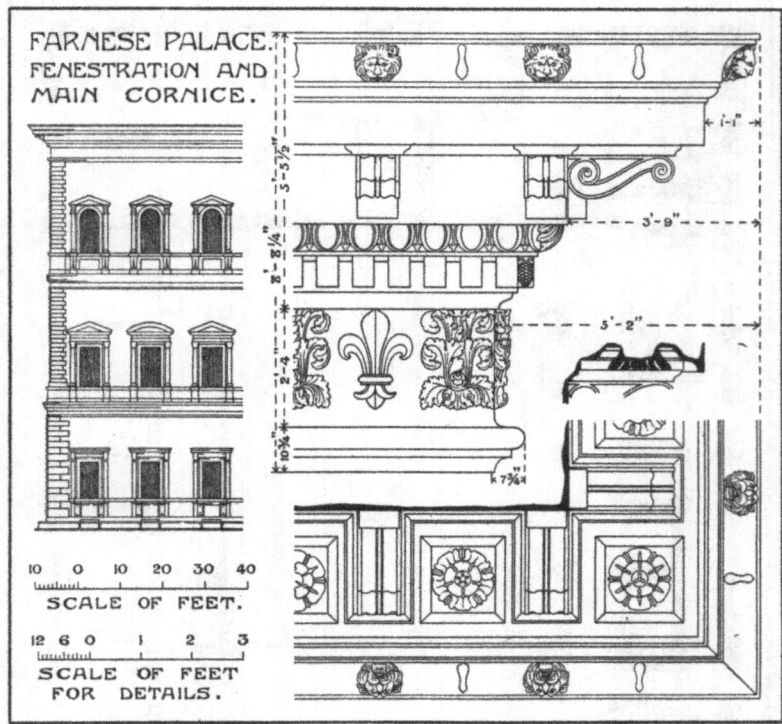

Fig. 48.

Angelo, who added the crowning cornice; and later his pupil Giacomo della Porta made some additions. In fine scale and simple dignity the main façade holds its own with the Riccardi and Strozzi palaces of Florence. The width of the walling between the windows is double the width of each opening, and the distance from the head of one window to the sill of the window above is also double the height of each window. These proportions are not apparent at the first glance; as the eye

[1] Letarouilly gives the date of commencement as 1530.

Fig. 49.—Palazzo Farnese, Rome, south front.

Photo: Alinari.

Fig. 50.—Palazzo Farnese, Rome, courtyard.

[*To face p.* 83.

rests on the spaces between the engaged columns forming the frames, and between pediment and sill, and hardly realizes the distances between the openings. To be successful this type of design demands an expanse of walling only possible in Italy and other hot countries, in which rooms require to be lofty—storerooms of great cubic capacity of air—window openings to be relatively small, and preferably not to reach too near the ceiling. In England dimensions such as those stated above cannot be expected, and such relative proportions are impossible. The only palace of this type which equals the Farnese in its proportions is the Pandolfini, Florence, but it is only two storeys in height and a smaller building in all respects (see Fig. 18). The windows in these two palaces are probably the finest in Italy of their kind. Their superiority in scale to contemporary ones in other parts of Italy—compare with Bergamasco's in the Ducal palace, Venice (Fig. 33)—is partly due to the greater skill of San Gallo and Michael Angelo, but principally to the superiority of antique examples in Rome over those of the north.[1] The south front is in some respects finer than the north. The wings which project on each side form terraces at the first-floor level, and enclose the garden which formerly sloped down to the Tiber. The centre of the front was originally open, but was filled in by della Porta in 1575. His work in itself is unsatisfactory, but his cornice over the pilasters on the second floor enables one to realize the noble scale of the main cornice round the rest of the building.

The ground and first storeys of the courtyard are arcaded, their design being strongly modelled on the Colosseum. Together they form a fine and dignified example of their type, spoilt only by the later filling in of the openings on the first floor and the insertion of windows. The upper storey, added by Michael Angelo, is not arcaded. It is chiefly notable for its pilaster on pilaster treatment, which was repeated by della Porta on the south front. This idea was evidently regarded with favour by later architects, judging by the number of otherwise plain buildings in which it is introduced. The open vestibule leading to the courtyard, with its double rows of granite columns, is exceedingly fine. Over the central carriage way is a panelled barrel vault, the sides

Courtyard.

---

[1] In the Acqueduct of Claudius outside Rome are fine examples of arched openings with side columns, and with entablature, etc., above. Their scale is bolder and their proportions more vigorous than those of the Porta de' Borsari, Verona, for instance.

84 A HISTORY OF ARCHITECTURAL DEVELOPMENT

having panelled flat ceilings. This vestibule and the two lower storeys of the court are San Gallo's work, and are alone sufficient to show that he was an architect of high order.

Peruzzi, 1481–1536.

Baldassare Peruzzi, one of the finest artists of the Renaissance, was born at Siena in 1481, and died in Rome, in poor circumstances, in 1536. Educated at first as a painter, he never abandoned entirely his early calling, although his fame is greatest as an architect. A contemporary and friend of Raphael, who was two years his junior, they collaborated together over the

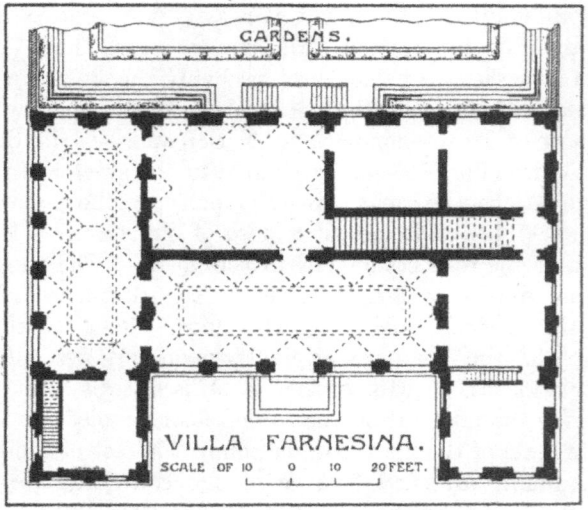

FIG. 51.

famous decorations of the Villa Farnesina or Chigi, on the outskirts of Rome, which building Peruzzi designed for Agostino Chigi, a rich Roman banker, but a native of Siena. The villa is chiefly interesting for its plan, and for the windows in the frieze of the top entablature outside, which are framed in by heavy swags. In the Palazzo Albergati, Bologna, attributed to him, are windows similarly placed.[1] Peruzzi's forte in painting was mural decoration. He excelled especially in fresco,

[1] The name and date carved on the front are "Annabale Albergati 1540," i.e. four years after Peruzzi's death. If Peruzzi designed this palace it cannot have been carried out exactly as he would have wished. The windows of the principal floor are such as a nothern architect might have designed, but hardly the architect of the Massimi palace.

chiaroscuro, and perspective. He painted few if any "pictures." Through the generosity, apparently, of his patron Chigi he was enabled to devote a large amount of time to careful study of the antique remains in Rome.[1] But his mouldings are far finer than any to be found in the old buildings in the capital. Whether he ever studied Greek buildings is unknown, but his refined and sensitive nature was akin to that of the Greeks, and led him to give to all his detail a wonderful subtlety, otherwise unknown outside Greek architecture. He had not the strength or commanding personality of a Michael Angelo —brute force it might almost be called at times —but his refinement never caused his art to degenerate into weakness.

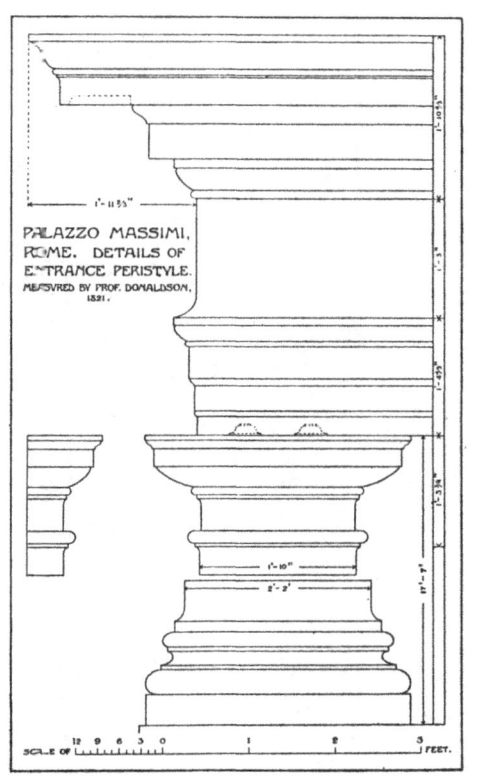

FIG. 52.

Two contemporary buildings of the Renaissance more unlike each other it would be difficult to find than San Gallo's Farnese palace and the Palazzo Pietro Massimi alle Colonne, to give it its full name, the work of Peruzzi. The former impresses by its fine scale, the latter fascinates by its perfect detail and delicate beauty. One is the work of a man of great ability, the other the *chef d'œuvre* of a consummate artist.

Palazzo Massini.

The Palazzi Massimi are two palaces standing side by side, which were built about 1532 for the brothers Pietro and Angelo. They occupy the site of an earlier house belonging to the family

[1] Many of his measurements and drawings were incorporated later by his pupil Serlio in his "Architettura," published in 1540.

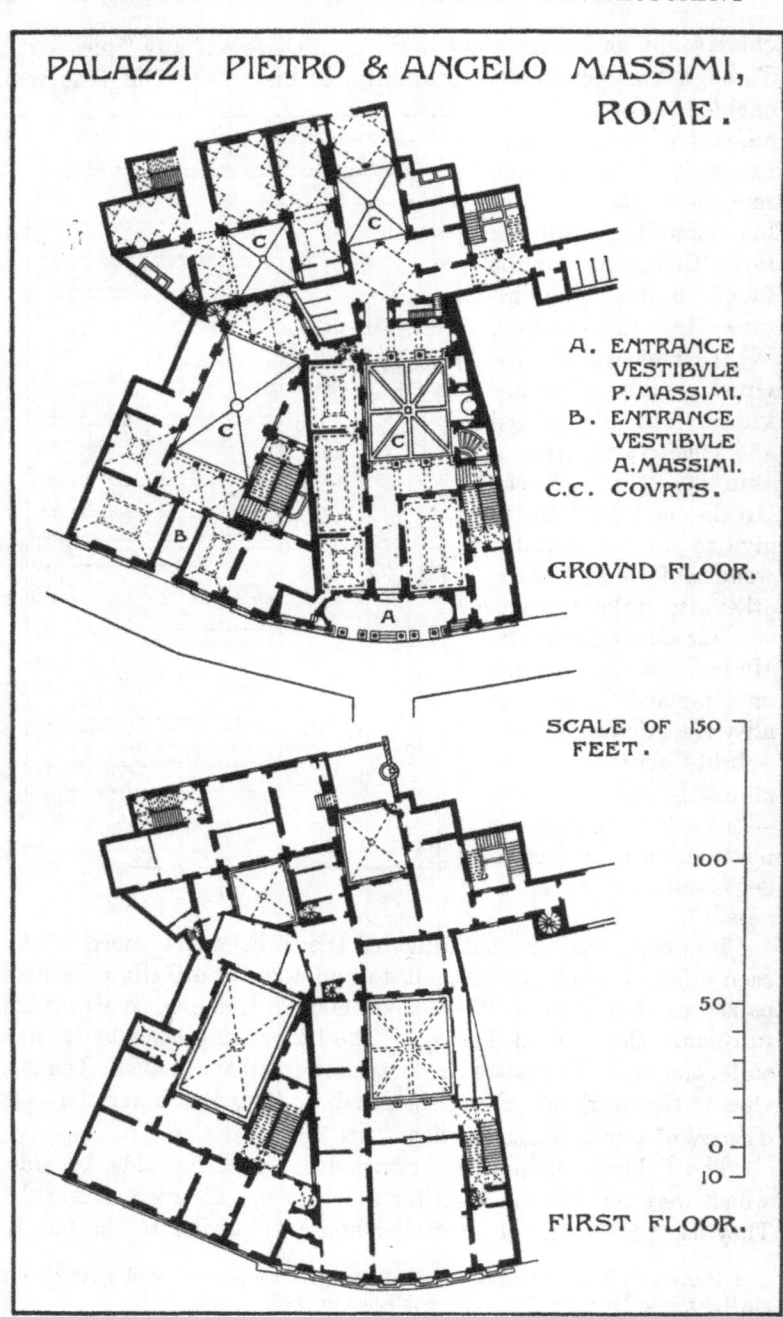

Fig. 53.

which suffered badly in the sack of Rome. The beauty of Pietro's palace has prevented full justice being done to his brother's, which is much simpler in design, whilst the planning of both is superb. The façade of Angelo's is a graceful example of the type to which the Sacchetti palace belongs, and its detail, as might have been expected from Peruzzi, is delicate and refined. The front of the alle Colonne is more elaborate and of rusticated stone throughout. Both palaces are small compared with others in Rome. Pietro's owes its charm to its proportions, to the design and disposition of

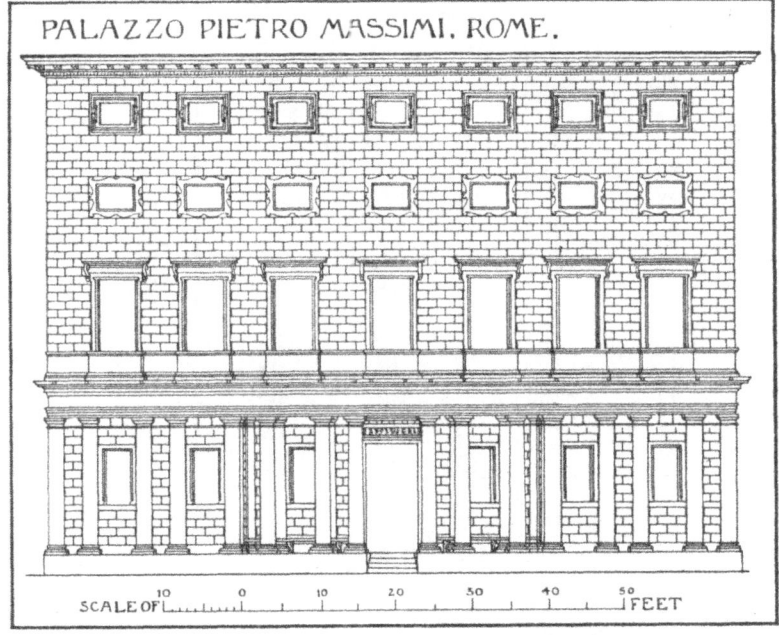

FIG. 54.

its windows, and to the colonnaded loggia which forms the entrance porch. The whole front is slightly curved, following the line of the street.[1] Peruzzi's preference for trabeate construction and his incomparable detail are well illustrated in the design of the loggia, and in the colonnades across the south end of the little central courtyard. The barrel vaults which spring from the entablatures above the columns on the ground floor of the latter

[1] Apparently the curve was an afterthought, as early plans which have been preserved show the front straight.

88 A HISTORY OF ARCHITECTURAL DEVELOPMENT

are pierced by oblong openings, to give more light to the rooms behind. It has been suggested that these are later insertions, but this is unlikely. On the contrary, it appears as though the design of the panelling of the vault was specially dictated by the necessity for providing such openings. The upper gallery at the south end with its flat panelled ceiling, white marble door-frames, and painted

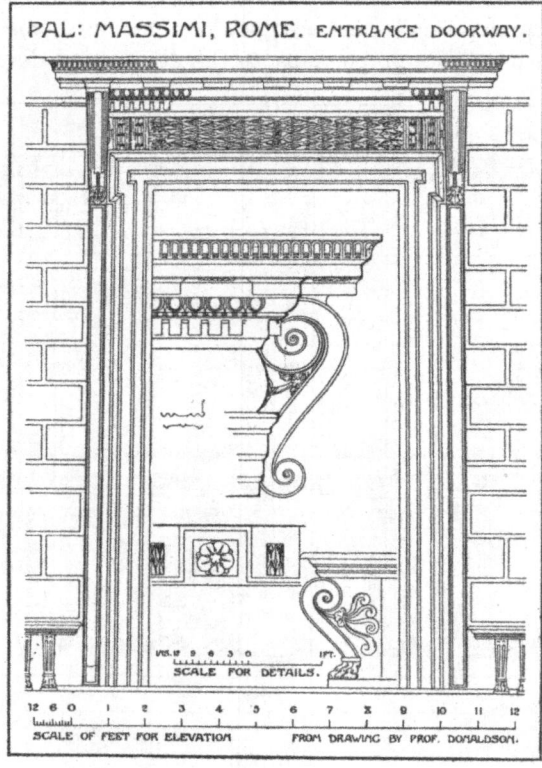

Fig. 55.

walls is one of the most interesting portions of this extraordinarily beautiful building.

The architects who, after the ones already mentioned, exercised most influence on architectural design in Rome in the first half of the sixteenth century, were Michael Angelo and Vignola.

Michael Angelo, 1474–1564.

Michael Angelo, born in Florence in 1474, was, at the age of fourteen, apprenticed to Ghirlandajo, the painter. After a short time, however, he was invited by Duke Lorenzo to take up his

Photo: Alinari.

FIG. 56.—PALAZZO PIETRO MASSIMI, ROME.

Photo: Alinari.

FIG. 57.—PALAZZO PIETRO MASSIMI, FLORENCE, LOGGIA.

[*To face p.* 88.

residence at the ducal palace and study sculpture. There he remained until the death of his patron in 1492, mastering the technique of both painting and sculpture. The greater part of his long life was devoted to these two arts, but of his success in them it is unnecessary to speak here, except so far as they touch the art of architecture.

In Florence he partly designed the second sacristy of the church of S. Lorenzo, known as the Sagrestia Nuova to distinguish *His work in Florence.*

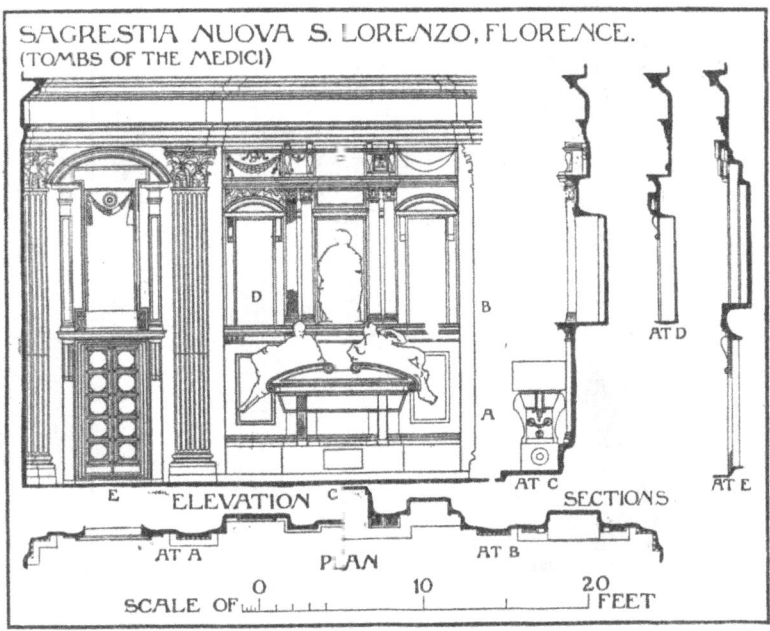

FIG. 58 (*Leslie Wilkinson*).

it from Brunelleschi's earlier sacristy. It was intended as a mausoleum for the Medici family, and was begun about 1521. Only two of the six sarcophagi he proposed to erect there were finished, but these are marvellous works, whether judged from the standpoint of architecture or of sculpture. A few years later he designed the Laurentian Library, also attached to S. Lorenzo, which was completed by Vasari. The vestibule of this is remarkable. More severe criticism has been levelled at it than at any other well-known architectural work. But throughout it bears the stamp of originality. Whether it is wise to break up a wall surface by framed niches, and by columns recessed instead of projecting, is a matter of opinion; there can be no doubt that it is permissible. A plain expanse of wall is reposeful and often desirable, but it cannot be said to be exciting, and it may be exceedingly dull. Michael Angelo's vestibule is not dull. Its columns and niches are far finer in scale and proportion than the pilasters and niches in the sacristy. The design may be a dangerous one to take as a precedent; an attempt to copy it by a less virile man might end in failure; but all who like to see a

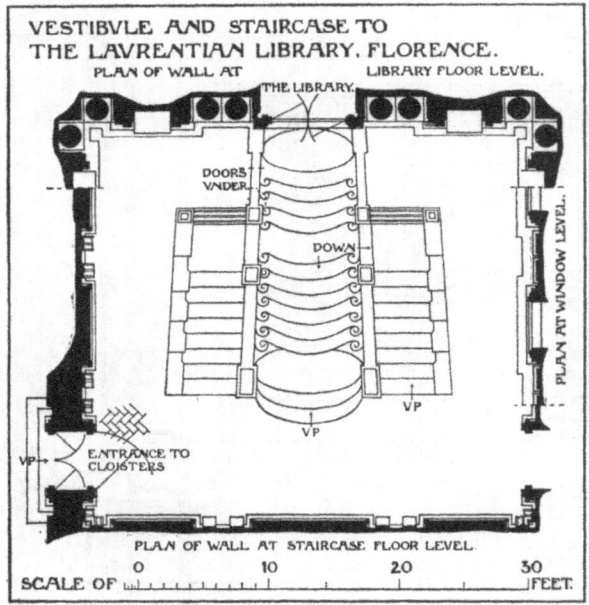

FIG. 59 (*Leslie Wilkinson*).

man's individuality paramount in his work must acknowledge that the conception throughout is great. The carrying of it out may be defective in places, but the greater part of the work was executed after Michael Angelo's death. In "sculptors' architecture" the chief defect, as a rule, is smallness of detail. The man who carved the David out of a great block of marble, and painted the ceiling of the Sistine Chapel, was not likely to fall into that error. The statement generally made about Michael Angelo is that he took up architecture late in life. This is only partially true. In the first half of the sixteenth century the

Fig. 60 (*Leslie Wilkinson*).

[*To face p.* 90.

distinctions general now did not exist. All artists of repute practised more than one art. When asked, in 1546, to continue the building of S. Peter's, Michael Angelo excused himself at first because of his age, and also because he said architecture was not the art in which he felt he most excelled. But he had already practised it, and had always been in a different position from a modern sculptor who attempts architectural composition. He had "thought" on big architectural lines; and the value of thinking without having eternally to express one's thoughts becomes evident in his next architectural venture.

This was the laying out of the top of the Capitoline hill, for which he received the commission about 1538. The result was the Piazza del Campidoglio, one of the most stately "squares" in Rome, although one of the smallest. Its irregularity adds considerably to its beauty; and the sinking of the central portion by about a foot is a great gain to the palaces on its three sides. In the middle Michael Angelo placed the fine antique equestrian statue of Marcus Aurelius, for which he designed the simple but effective pedestal. At the end of the piazza stands the Palazzo del Senatore, and on either side the Palazzo dei Conservatori and the Palazzo del Museo Capitolino. The first has a rusticated basement, above which are pilasters running through two storeys, and its merit lies in the fine outside staircase which leads to the hall on the first floor, which is part of an earlier building. This staircase and the flight of steps facing it leading up to the piazza are the only portions executed during the architect's lifetime. He designed the two buildings at the sides, but died before either was commenced. They may, however, be regarded as his work, except in respect to some of their detail, and show him at his best. The façades are identical in design. There is a breadth and dignity about each front which has seldom been equalled. Pilasters on pedestals start from the ground, run through two storeys and carry an important entablature, above which is a balustrade surmounted by figures. In no other building is this treatment more successful. The pilaster on pilaster design, already noticed in the Farnese palace, is here repeated; the result being that the windows of the upper floor stand in recessed panels. The openings to the loggia on the ground floor are spanned by lintels supported on detached columns, which flank the great pilasters and give them scale. This combination of columns and attached pilasters had never been attempted before, and is the most original portion of the

Buildings on the Capitol.

92 A HISTORY OF ARCHITECTURAL DEVELOPMENT

design. It was followed, with modifications, by later men, and might well be repeated more often in modern work.

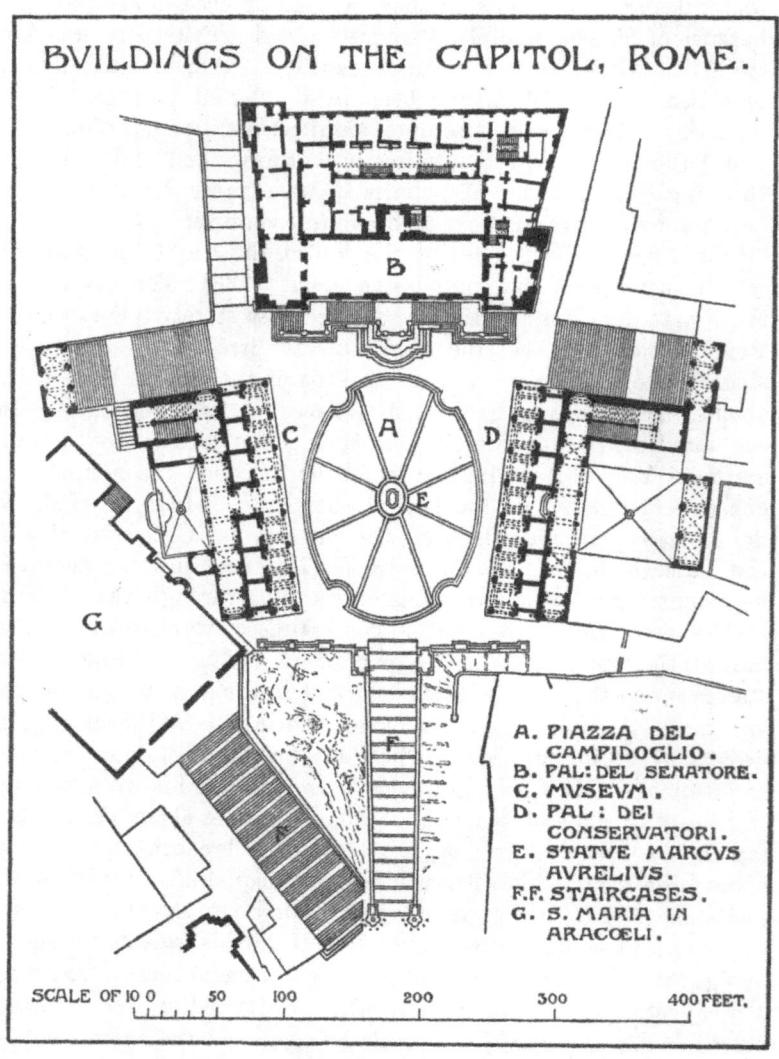

FIG. 61 (*Letarouilly*).

Vignola. Giacomo Barozzi Vignola, the author of "Regola delli cinque ordini d'architettura," designed many buildings in and about Rome and in other cities. Among his best known are the Villa di

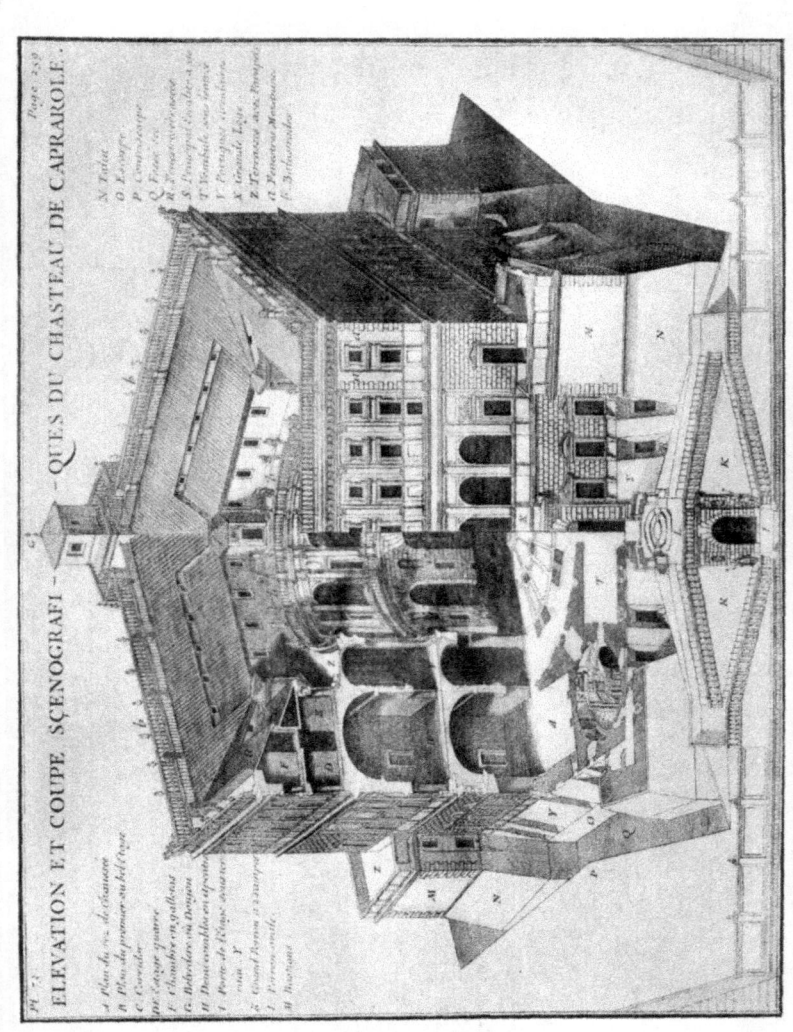

Fig. 62 (*Daviler*).

Papa Giulio, in the country beyond the Porta del Popolo, Rome; the Palazzo Caprarola, thirty miles from the city, built for Alessandro Farnese about 1547; and the Farnese palace, Piacenza, already mentioned. The Palazzo Caprarola stands on a hill overlooking the little town of the same name, and is chiefly remarkable

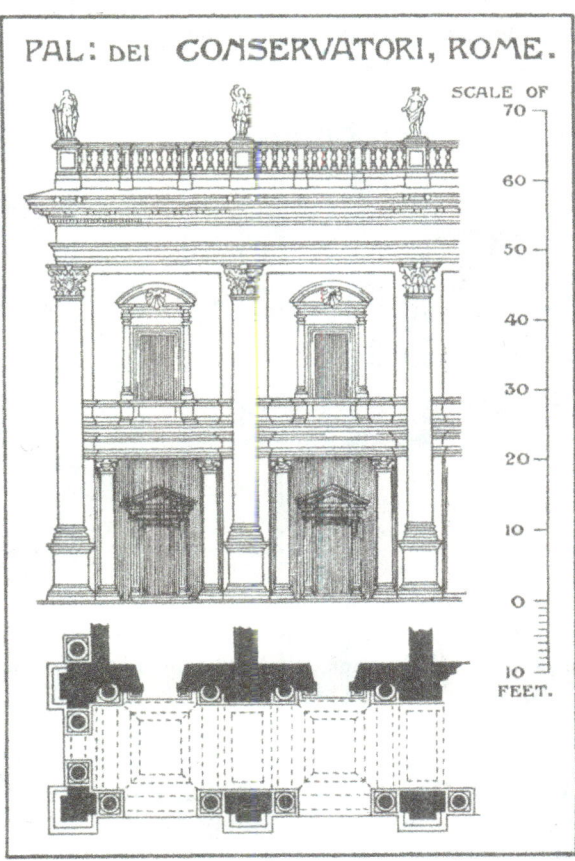

FIG. 63.

for its plan, and the laying out of its gardens, with their terraces and flights of steps. The circular court, 65 feet in the clear, which occupies the central part of this curiously shaped building, is a very fine idea, and possibly suggested to Inigo Jones the court he intended at Whitehall. The entrance front of the pope's villa is not interesting, but the design at the back, round the courtyard, is very striking; especially the ground storey with its great arched openings and peristyle of columns supporting lintels.

The lintel in buildings.
With the advent of the Renaissance the lintel to some extent regained the position it had lost in the Middle Ages. From the time of Brunelleschi it was always to the fore. Architects evidently appreciated its æsthetic superiority over the arch, and many used the two side by side in the same building. To the purist this is wrong, no matter what the result. No doubt the

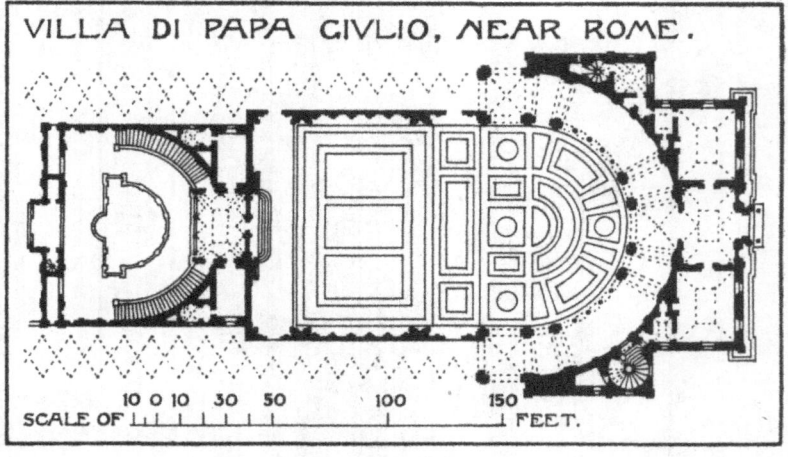

Fig. 64.

combination of lintel with arch or vault requires careful handling, but, if successful, all the more credit to the man who makes the attempt. There can be no objection to it if managed as successfully as in Brunelleschi's entrance loggia to the Pazzi Chapel, Peruzzi's loggia in the courtyard of the Massimi palace, and Vignola's Villa di Papa Giulio. A combination that is objectionable is an arch which could not possibly stand if it were not for the girder above it. That inconsistency was left for modern architects to discover. Steel and reinforced concrete, by some now regarded as bugbears, may end by being acclaimed as blessings, if their employment results in the ousting of the arch, and the general adoption once more of a trabeated system of design. That is the natural end, if these materials are used honestly. For that reason the buildings of the Renaissance architects in which the lintel is used, particularly Michael Angelo's on the Capitol hill, are especially deserving of study at the present time.

Fig. 65.—Villa di Papa Giulio, near Rome, courtyard.

Fig. 66.—Palazzo Bevilacqua, Verona.

[*To face p.* 94.

Fig. 67.—Porta del Palio, Verona.

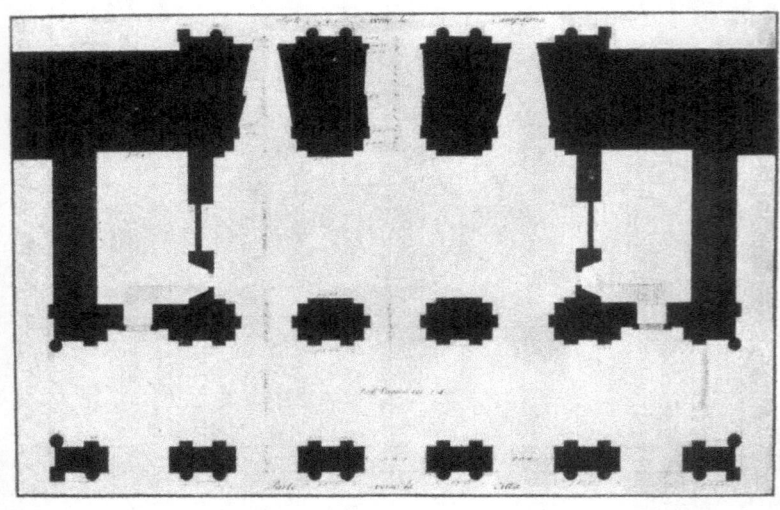

Fig. 68.—Porta del Palio, Verona.

[*To face p.* 95.

Whilst Peruzzi, San Gallo, Raphael—if he did little building his influence on architectural development was undoubtedly considerable—Vignola, and Michael Angelo were striving to advance the Renaissance in Rome, Sanmicheli, Sansovino, and, later, Palladio, with the same object in view, were equally busy and equally successful in the north. Each achieved his greatest triumphs in one city : Sanmicheli at Verona, Sansovino at Venice, and Palladio at Vicenza. *Development in the north.*

Michele Sanmicheli, born at Verona in 1484, was cradled in the profession, as both his father and uncle were architects. When only sixteen he was sent to Rome to study. Like so many of his contemporaries, much of his work was military engineering, in which he early achieved a great reputation. He was successively employed by the Papal States, Venice and Milan, to strengthen or to build anew their various fortifications. His practice in this branch coloured much of his subsequent work. Of the three entrance gateways to his native city which he designed, the Porta del Palio, Porta Nuova, and Porta S. Zeno, the first-named is an exceedingly fine design, especially on the city side. The attached columns are rusticated as well as the walling. This is amongst the earliest examples of columns so treated. Sanmicheli carried his engineering severity into the Palazzo Pompei, which is somewhat uninteresting in consequence. But he could be playful when he chose. The upper storey of the Palazzo Bevilacqua (c. 1530) is one of the richest and most varied in design in the whole range of Renaissance façades. Its bays are alternately wide and narrow, and are divided from one another by fluted columns, the flutes of each alternate pair being spiral. In each wide bay is a huge semicircular-headed window, whilst in each narrow bay there are two windows, one above the other; the lower of fair size and arched, with pilasters and a pediment, the upper ones smaller and simple rectangles. In the interior of the Capella Pellegrini, attached to the church of S. Bernardino, Sanmicheli showed to a still greater extent that he delighted in rich effects when opportunity offered and circumstances were favourable. The flutings of the columns here are also spiral. Notwithstanding his training in Rome, Sanmicheli evidently allowed his native antiquity, the Porta de' Borsari, to influence him. In the Porta some of the columns have spiral flutes, and the openings are not unlike the smaller arched windows in the Bevilacqua palace. The Palazzo Canossa is by some attributed to Sanmicheli, but it is very *Sanmicheli.*

different from his other palaces in Verona, and even if commenced by him was probably finished later by Palladio. In some respects it is the finest palace in the town. It has not the unnecessary simplicity of the Palazzo Pompei, nor the somewhat redundant richness of the Bevilacqua.

Sansovino.

Sanmicheli's immediate contemporary was Jacopo Sansovino, born in Florence in 1486. His real surname was Tatti, but he was apprenticed to the Florentine sculptor-architect, Andrea Sansovino, who took a great fancy to him, and whose name he subsequently bore. His early work was entirely sculpture, and much of it was executed in Rome, where he was taken by Giuliano da San Gallo, with whom he lived. On San Gallo leaving Rome, Bramante took him under his wing. An illness obliged him to return to Florence, but he was soon back in Rome, and, influenced doubtless by the three distinguished men with whom he had been closely in touch, he turned his attention to architecture. Of his buildings in Rome, the most important is the church of S. Giovanni de' Fiorentini, which he won in competition against Raphael, Antonio da San Gallo, and Peruzzi, a difficult trio to beat. He also designed the Palazzo Niccolini and some other buildings of less importance.

Early work in Venice.

The sack of Rome in 1527 forced him to leave the city, and he took refuge in Venice. That he had already thoroughly mastered the technicalities of building construction, and had gained repute in this respect is shown by his being commissioned, immediately on his arrival, to repair S. Mark's, then in a very bad state. He carried out the work so successfully that in 1529 the Senate appointed him Proto, or master in chief of S. Marco, a post equivalent to surveyor and architect to the Republic. In this capacity he rendered good service, opening out streets, pulling down insanitary property, and otherwise improving the city.

To his influence and example was mainly due the great advance in architecture which took place in Venice at the end of the first quarter of the sixteenth century. Before his arrival, able but indifferently trained men, such as Bergamasco, Scarpagnino, Riccio, the later Lombardi, etc., had executed the transitional work described in the last chapter. Sansovino brought with him the traditions of Florence and the glamour of Rome. He was thoroughly imbued with the Classic spirit. Moreover, he was a sculptor of first rank, a man who had held his own against even Michael Angelo.

Fig. 69.—Palazzo Canossa, Verona.

Photo: Alinari.   Fig. 70.—Palazzo Cornaro, Venice.

His first palace in Venice was the Cornaro della Ca' Grande, commenced in 1532. Whatever its faults may be, it was the first to be built in the town in pure Classic. Essentially different from earlier palaces, it served as a model for most later ones, such as the Grimani, Rezzonico, Pesaro, etc. Compared with the Palazzo Grimani, Sanmicheli's chief work outside Verona, and by some regarded as his masterpiece, it is in some respects inferior. But in comparing the two it is as well to remember that the Grimani was not commenced until 1549, seventeen years after the Cornaro. The ground floor of both palaces is exceedingly fine, the greater simplicity and repose of the earlier building being in its favour. In the upper storeys Sansovino's palace is somewhat commonplace; and although the architect has followed the traditional Venetian custom of grouping the central windows closer together than the side ones, he has not marked the difference sufficiently. Sanmicheli, in his building, repeats in both the upper storeys the alternation of large and small windows which gives such distinction to the Palazzo Bevilacqua at Verona, but has failed to retain its graceful proportions. Anderson, in his "Architecture of the Renaissance in Italy" (p. 119), says, "Peruzzi and Sanmicheli were the originating geniuses, and Sansovino the faithful follower, . . . that he had on occasions his Peruzzi manner of expression and at other times a manner which is unmistakably founded on Sanmicheli's example." Sansovino was possibly influenced by Peruzzi, whose earlier buildings he may have seen before he left Rome, but there is no evidence that he knew Sanmicheli's in Verona. Moreover, there is little likeness between the work of these two men, except such resemblances as exist in the Venetian palaces just mentioned, of which Sansovino's is the earlier by many years. Peruzzi, Sanmicheli, and Sansovino were absolute contemporaries, five years covering their births. *Palazzo Cornaro.*

The above-mentioned northern palaces are sufficient to show how greatly their designs differ from those of contemporary Roman palaces. The latter, with their framed windows and general absence of columns and pilasters, belong to a different type altogether. The further from Rome the stronger seems to have been the influence of the Colosseum and other buildings of similar design. In the capital this influence is felt only in courtyards and vestibules; in the north it rules façades as well. It appears as though the architects practising in the provinces carried away with them from Rome, as the result of their studies there, the *Influence of the Colosseum on northern façades.*

remembrance of such buildings to the exclusion of all others. The fine amphitheatre at Verona may have helped also to bend their inclination in the same direction. The selection of the semicircular head for windows in preference to the lintel, and the exclusion of the surrounding frame, practically universal in the capital, were evidently deliberate. The desire of the northern architects was to adapt the arcaded and columned treatment of old Roman buildings to modern dwellings, and to convert what had been arched openings to a corridor into windows for rooms. This was Sansovino's idea in the upper storeys of the Cornaro palace, and the intention is still more evident in the most famous of his Venetian buildings, the Libreria Vecchia, and in Palladio's *chef-d'œuvre* at Vicenza, the Basilica Palladiana.

The Library.

The Libreria Vecchia, alongside the Piazzetta of S. Mark's, was begun in 1536. Its elevations are frankly designed on the lines of the Colosseum; but they are no copy of that building, or of any other of similar character. The artist's individuality is apparent throughout. The design is far more "original" than many designs to which that term is applied, the authors of which possess neither the knowledge to enable them to follow what is good nor the good taste to reject what is bad.

Wherein it differs from the Colosseum.

In architectural compositions in which arches start from piers with engaged columns, the columns on the upper storey should be less in diameter than those below. This is the case in the Theatre of Marcellus, the best proportioned of all antique examples. If the upper pier is made the same width as the lower it is apt to look wider, in consequence of the smaller diameter of the column attached to it. If it is narrowed, the upper opening perforce becomes actually wider. Whichever method is adopted, in neither are the proportions altogether satisfactory. It was possibly some such feeling which prompted Sansovino to flank the piers of his upper storey by pairs of detached columns, one behind the other, from which the archivolts spring. The openings are consequently considerably narrowed; and yet there is no feeling that the upper supports are too heavy, as the detached columns give an appearance of lightness. This design has also the advantages that the windows can be of reasonable size, and larger spandril space left above for sculpture. The latter must have appealed strongly to the sculptor side of Sansovino's nature; but the quadrangular shape with one side curved is somewhat awkward to fill, and it is doubtful if in this respect the architect gained much. The lower

Photo: *Alinari.*

FIG. 71.—LIBRERIA VECCHIA, VENICE.

[*To face p.* 98.

storey, save for the projecting carved keystones and the sculpture in the spandrils, might be a portion of the Theatre of Marcellus—except that the front of the latter is curved—the resemblance is so close.[1] The crowning entablature is chiefly remarkable for its proportions and for the windows in its frieze. Fault has been found with the depth of the frieze, and the dimensions of the entablature generally, but it is very certain that a regulation size would have robbed the design of its distinctive character. The entablature in height is actually more than one-half the height of the columns below, and yet it in no way overpowers them. It is about one-sixth of the total height of the building, exclusive of the balustrade and figures above.

Andrea Palladio, the last of the great architects of the middle, or finest, period of the Renaissance, was born in 1518. At the age of twenty-two he went to Rome, and there he remained, with intervals of absence, until 1547. What a wonderful atmosphere of art must have existed in the Eternal city at his time, although he was too late to be fellow-student with the most famous architects of the sixteenth century. Michael Angelo had been engaged on S. Peter's for some years, and his buildings on the Capitol had certainly been designed, possibly commenced, before Palladio returned to Vicenza. The influence of the grand old man of the Renaissance over the younger man was undoubtedly strong, and, if not his pupil, Palladio was certainly his disciple. He carried back to his native town a thorough mastery of ancient work, as well as an intimate acquaintance with the best and most recent of modern buildings. *Palladio (1518–80).*

His first commission after his return was to design the two-storied arcading round the old Palazzo della Ragione, now known as the Basilica Palladiana. That soon established his reputation. The prophet was of account in his own country. It is a grand composition, with little or no trace of the pedantry which sometimes paralyzed his successors, and of which he is often accused, in most cases unjustly. On both floors he has followed Sansovino, for whose work he entertained the greatest admiration, in starting his arches from pairs of detached columns. These, however, stand *Basilica Vicenza.*

[1] Projecting carved keystones were possibly first introduced in Renaissance buildings in the Palazzo Vendramin Calergi by Lombardi. They are more common in northern palaces than at either Florence or Rome. They occur in Roman triumphal arches, as in the Arch of Titus (see Vol. I. Fig. 101), where the projection is considerable; but in ordinary antique Roman buildings, with few exceptions, keystones are flush with the other voussoirs, and are not emphasized.

well away from the piers, and not close against them, as in the Library. The intervening spaces are lintelled. The end bays of the arcading are narrower than the central ones, which are spaced to agree in width with the bays of the existing building. The detached columns in the former are consequently nearer to the piers. By narrowing the end bays Palladio not only avoided an unnecessary width for the covered pavement, but also strengthened the angles of the building. With the latter object in view, he also doubled the engaged columns at the corners, realizing how

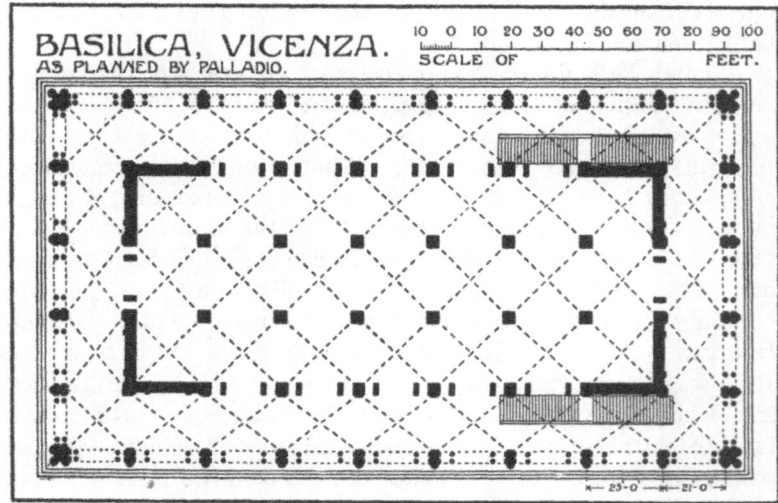

Fig. 72.

essential it was that these should not appear weak. The arcades are without sculpture, and none the worse on that account. The pierced circles above the lintels lessen the weight on them, and, in addition, give an effect of lightness to the design, truly remarkable considering their undecorated outline. In Sansovino's Library the entablatures form unbroken lines; Palladio has broken his over each column. The effect is not so bad as in the earlier Venetian buildings described in the last chapter, as the columns are engaged and not detached. But it was a retrograde step nevertheless. The great artists of the Renaissance, from Brunelleschi downwards, rarely broke their entablatures, Alberti's west front of S. Francesco, Rimini, and Michael Angelo's exterior

THE CENTENARY OF THE RENAISSANCE

of S. Peter's being exceptions, and there can be little difference of opinion as to which treatment is the more dignified.[1]

Palladio's other buildings in Vicenza are chiefly notable for their noble scale, their purity of proportion and detail, and their material, brick covered with stucco, which he was forced to use, against his wish, on the score of expense. Instead of blame for this

Other buildings in Vicenza.

FIG. 73.

he is entitled to the highest praise, for obtaining such grand effects and such purity of line with so uncongenial a material. He always used stone where it was essential, for plinths and bases; and in the Palazzo Porto Barbarano the two lowest drums of the ground-floor columns are also of stone. Palladio has been represented as

---

[1] Sansovino's Library and Palladio's Basilica should be compared with Michael Angelo's buildings on either side of the Capitol for two different combinations both interesting, of detached columns with columned or pilastered piers.

generally designing his façades with pilasters or columns carried through two storeys. As a matter of fact, although he followed Michael Angelo in his fondness for this practice, and frequently adopted it for churches, as in San Giorgio Maggiore, Venice, he seldom did so in his secular buildings. Examples of his at Vicenza of this treatment are the Palazzo Valmarano, the Municipio, or Loggia del Capitanio, and the so-called Casa del Diavolo, or Antica Posta. The last is by far the finest as regards scale, but only two bays out of the seven intended were built. These, however, are sufficient to show the design. The three-quarter engaged columns are raised on lofty pedestals which reach to the top of the ground-floor windows, some 18 feet in height. The entablature above the columns is of such vast dimensions that windows of fair size are inserted in the frieze, and yet the proportions are "correct." Between the capitals of the columns are heavy swags which start from the back volutes, and are framed by a moulding below which is a continuation of the necking of the capitals. This was a favourite device

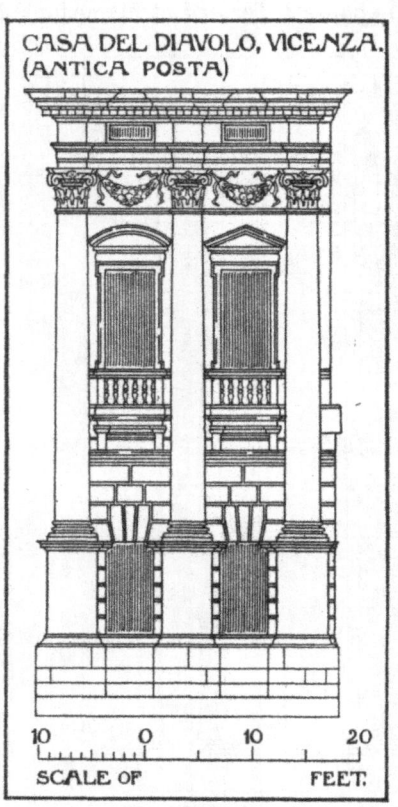

FIG. 74.

of Palladio, which he repeated in the Palazzo Thiene. But he did not originate it. Similar swags in like position occur on all the three storeys of the Vendramin palace, Venice (see Fig. 32), built by P. Lombardi nearly a century before. Apparently there is no ancient precedent for this feature, which may have been Pietro's own invention, in which case it is interesting to note that the purist Palladio was not unwilling to accept a suggestion from the work of an architect who, although a consummate artist, was little versed in Classic. In the façade of the Palazzo Valmarano flat pilasters take the place of the engaged columns of the Casa. Flanking them on the ground storey are smaller half pilasters, supporting an entablature of unusual profile, and of such slight projection that all its members, except the top moulding, stop against the large pilasters. The chief peculiarity about this façade is that these pilasters are omitted at the outer angles of the end bays. In their place on the ground floor are small pilasters, ranging with the half pilasters just mentioned, with figures above them. The effect is curious, but there was probably some special reason for it. Possibly the palace was only a portion of a scheme, perhaps the centre, and the intention was to flank it by other and lower buildings.

The Palazzo Porto Barbarano is one of the most successful of Palladio's façades with superimposed orders, the lower order Ionic, the upper Corinthian. Above the main cornice of the latter is an attic. The Palazzo Thiene shows his third treatment. The ground storey is plain and heavily rusticated, and only the upper storey is pilastered. A good effect is produced on the ground storey by the smooth walling of the tympana over the windows. As in nearly all his buildings the actual window heads are straight. Palladio, unlike Sansovino and Sanmicheli, evidently did not believe in arched window heads.

Outside Vicenza he built several villas, the most famous being the Villa del Capri, known as the Rotonda. This has been copied so frequently that familiarity has bred contempt. But it should be remembered that it was the first of its kind, and an original composition.[1]

The Rotonda.

FIG. 75.

Palladio may have had faults, but his enthusiasm for

[1] Palladio's churches in Venice are referred to in Chapter VII.

104 A HISTORY OF ARCHITECTURAL DEVELOPMENT

architecture cannot be questioned. If by his writings he somewhat reduced it to a science for others, he practised it as an art himself; and had no compunction in breaking his own rules

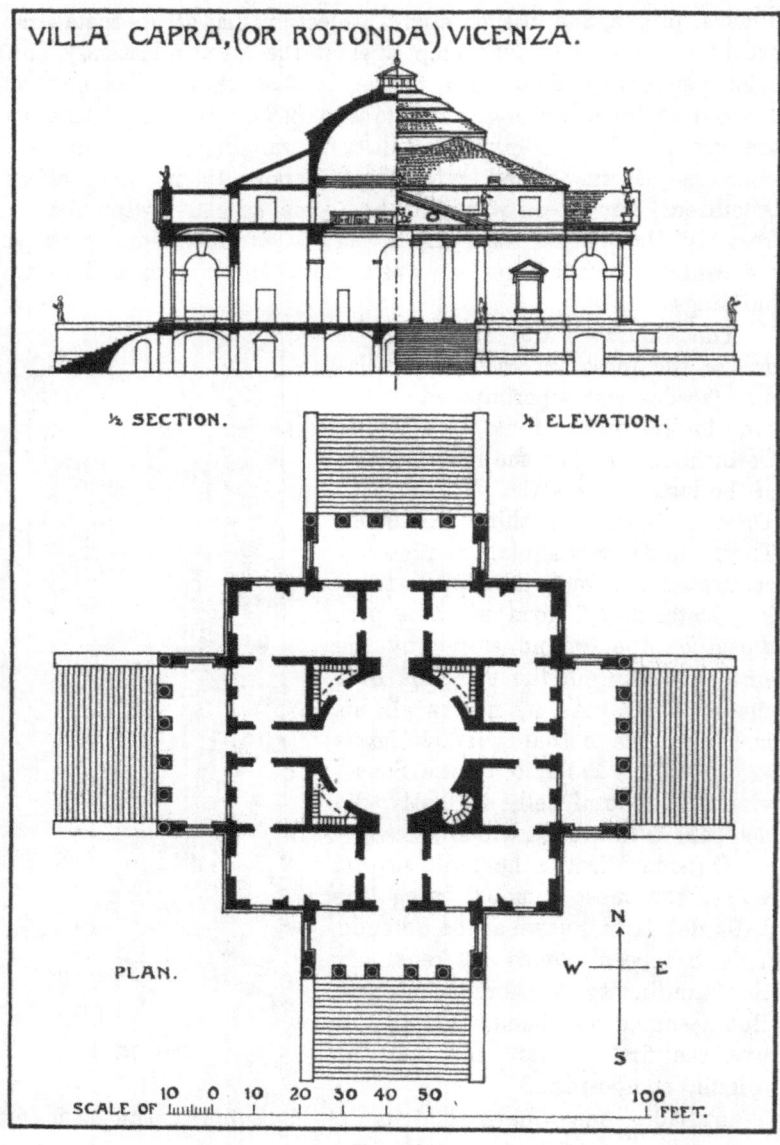

Fig. 76.

if he felt so inclined. His best-known publication is "I quattro libri dell' architettura," published in Venice in 1570. Of all books on architecture this has had, in England at least, the greatest reputation. It was by no means his only literary effort, nor was it his first. In 1554 he published "Le Antichità di Roma," the outcome of his studies there, and other publications followed. Many of the other leading architects of the sixteenth century also published books on architecture: Serlio in 1540 and 1547, Vignola in 1563, Scamozzi in 1615, etc. Printing appears such a commonplace to us now, a vital and absolute necessity that one could not possibly be without, that it is difficult to realize that when Alberti and Filarete wrote printing was barely discovered. Poor Filarete's work was never printed, and only portions of the original have been preserved.

Printing presses were started in Rome in 1467, Venice in 1469, Florence, Milan, Bologna, etc., in 1471. They were at first used in Italy solely for the Classics. Alberti's "De Re Ædificatoria" was the first architectural book to be printed, and that not until 1485, some years after his death. In the same or the next year Vitruvius' famous work, "De Architectura," the MS. of which had been known to the early Renaissance architects, was also printed for the first time. The first Italian edition did not appear until 1521, although it had been previously translated by M. F. Calvo of Ravenna, and written out for Raphael, at the latter's expense and, it is stated, in his own house, to aid him in his architectural work.[1] The publication of the old Roman's work must have been a great help; as it includes descriptions of ancient buildings, their plans and general ordinance, and much valuable information regarding their construction and decoration in addition to dissertations on the proper proportions of the "orders." But the books of the sixteenth-century architects were not altogether an unmixed blessing. They rendered gross errors in the proportions of columns and entablatures unlikely and unpardonable, but they tended to systematise design. There was a "must be," a finality about their statements which would have been positively dangerous if their authors had all agreed. Luckily each writer took a somewhat different view about what "must be." In these disagreements lay salvation. If architecture declined after their publication, the cause lay not in

Printing and its results.

---

[1] The original translated manuscript is now in the Munich Library: see editor's note to Vasari's lives, vol. iii. p. 199.

the books or their writers, but in the neglect of the later architects to study for themselves antique remains, as had been the universal custom of the band of brilliant men which preceded them. For the later men the data was ready prepared. And so they worked at second hand, and the result was sometimes second rate. At the same time it is a mistake to suppose that Architecture collapsed in Italy after the middle of the sixteenth century. Yet that is the idea conveyed in many books. The pinnacle had doubtless been reached, and pinnacles are awkward things to remain perched upon for long. A certain amount of reaction is bound to follow a great effect. But the inevitable reaction was short lived, and, as is shown in later chapters, many Italian palaces and churches of the seventeenth and eighteenth centuries compare favourably in scale, purity of design, and originality with the buildings of the previous centuries.

CHAPTER VI

LATER SECULAR BUILDINGS

BEFORE Palladio's death in 1580, there was evidence that architectural design was in danger of running to seed. That was not his fault, unless it be urged that his "puritanism" occasioned a reaction. The reaction, however, did not last very long. The worst period of the Italian Renaissance was between about 1560 and 1640. Much of the work executed then deserves to some extent the hard names which have been bestowed upon it. Decline, Decadence, Rococco, Baroque are amongst the most moderate, and they are often intensified by adjectives. But in many cases neither substantive nor adjective is deserved. Even in the most flamboyant examples there is no decline or decadence in scale. Some of the stateliest examples of planning, both of buildings and their surroundings, belong to the despised period; witness the Palazzi Borghese and Barberini, the Scala di Spagna, and the Piazza del Popolo, all in Rome, the last a noble ellipse, roughly 500 feet by 350. And the period passed, architecture once more righted itself. There is nothing that can be termed either Rococco or Baroque—whatever those terms may mean—about Bernini's Colonnade leading up to S. Peter's, Rome. The fault of many churches and houses built between 1640 and the end of the eighteenth century is that they are too sober. This may justify the term "decline," but only in the relative sense of summer to autumn.

Late efforts in any style never possess the same fascination as early efforts. The latter have a freshness, the freshness of spring, which the others lack; and surrounding them, moreover, is the glamour that attaches to pioneer struggles. One is rightly tolerant of their shortcomings in view of the difficulties their authors had to surmount. Their faults are condoned, because of what they achieved. The same tolerance cannot be extended to those who followed. The same excuses cannot be made for them. They had

Introduction.

models before them which they could copy, and, says the critic, that they failed to copy, shows that they were inferior. But that is hardly fair. To some extent later workers are entitled to more consideration than pioneers, who are ploughing virgin soil and have the whole field of design before them from which they can pick and choose. Brunelleschi, Alberti, Bramante, were thus advantaged. Their work was a help to their successors, and yet was not sufficient in amount to cripple their inventive faculties.

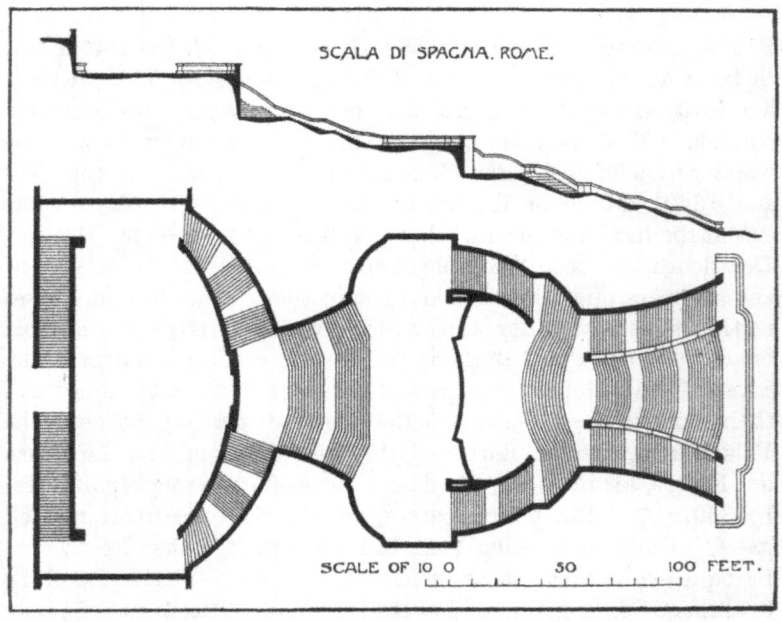

Fig. 77.

Peruzzi, San Gallo, Sanmicheli, Sansovino, Palladio, and Michael Angelo could still find many outlets for their genius. But the architects of the end of the sixteenth century and of the century following laboured under the disadvantage of appearing on the scene after the soil had been turned over many times, and had already produced noble crops. Before them were but two alternatives. Either they had to follow closely on the lines of their predecessors, laying themselves open possibly to the charge of plagiarism, or else they had at all costs, even at the sacrifice of their own good taste and instincts, to evolve something fresh and original. In despair at ever equalling what had been done before, they sometimes went to extremes; but to condemn their work wholesale, to deny them the credit for the many good qualities it possesses, and to ignore the difficulties of their position, is more than unjust, it is stupid and narrow. The early men had their faults; mainly faults of scale, of over-reduplication, and, in the north especially, of subservience of line and mass to detail. The later men have theirs, which may be broadly described as the very opposite. Their scale is always fine, their planning dignified, their massing vigorous. Their detail is sometimes excellent, but at times quite the reverse. Each building should be judged by itself; generalization, such as is often easy in mediæval work, is impossible with the buildings of the Renaissance. The personal equation is too strong.

The following are some of the principal architects who practised in Italy generally, and in Rome in particular, during the third period of the Italian Renaissance: Galeazzo Alessi (1500-72) in Genoa especially; Bartolomeo Ammanati (1511-92), Giorgio Vasari, the historian (1512-74), Bernardo Buontalenti (1536-1608), one of the most brilliant of the later school—these three chiefly in Florence; Giacomo della Porta (1541-1604), Domenico Fontana (1543-1607); Vincenzo Scamozzi (1552-1616), the last named mostly in the north; Carlo Maderno (1556-1629); Girolamo Rainaldi (1570-1655), and his son Carlo (1611-91); Giovanni Lorenzo Bernini (1598-1680); Francesco Borromini (1599-1667); Baldassare Longhena (1604-75), chiefly in Venice; and Carlo Fontana (1634-1714). To condemn these men *en masse* as decadent is a misuse of the term. The "decadent" is one who throws over tradition and scoffs at all accepted canons. These men did neither. Inequality in their work may be admitted. The best made mistakes, Bernini as often as any. There was no one commanding personality to set and maintain a high standard; no Brunelleschi, Bramante, or Michael Angelo. So whilst some late buildings compare favourably with any built before, others fail to reach a high level. *Architects of the sixteenth and seventeenth centuries.*

The first of the offenders was probably Giulio Romano (1492-1546), who chronologically belongs to the middle period. Considering when he lived he ought to have known better. His Palazzo del Tè, an extensive one-storied villa outside Mantua, has some dignity, and his Palazzo Giustizia, in the same town, although licentious, is so powerful and so fine in scale that one pardons, almost *G. Romano.*

rejoices in, the exuberance of its colossal Hermæ on the upper storeys. But little good can be said for the courtyard of the Ducal palace, Mantua, attributed to him, with its badly proportioned, twisted, and spirally fluted columns, and its heavy rustications. Twisted columns are charming on a small scale, as in some twelfth-century cloisters, but a minuet is not a suitable dance for an elephant, neither is the treatment accorded at Mantua suitable for columns of heavy Tuscan proportions.[1] After Romano's time figures somewhat similar to those on the Palazzo Giustizia are not uncommon on façades, but in few instances are they so effective. The front of a house which gives its name to the Via degli Omenoni, Milan, has eight huge figures on the ground storey, two turning into pilasters at the waist, and six at the knees. This is one of the most flamboyant of existing instances of this form of decoration.

Courtyard, Pitti palace.

Little excuse can be made for Ammanati's courtyard of the Pitti palace, Florence (c. 1568). The architect had the noble, simple front as a guide; and yet, either through fear that his work might appear lacking in boldness by comparison, or else sheer bad taste, he produced one of the most unsatisfactory of Renaissance façades. Every portion is heavily rusticated, walling, engaged columns, arches, lintels. The ground storey is better than the upper storeys, as, following in this respect Brunelleschi's window recesses in front, Ammanati made the jambs and soffits of the openings on this floor smooth.

Rustications.

In the courtyard of the Pitti rustication of stonework is carried further than in any other building; and it may not be out of place here to trace how the custom arose and developed. In early Renaissance buildings walls are generally rusticated, as already mentioned in the description of Florentine palaces. But rusticated columns and pilasters are rare.[2] One of the earliest instances occurs on the ground storey of the Palazzo Piccolomini, Pienza, where the pilasters are slightly rusticated to agree with the walling, which resembles that of the Palazzo Rucellai, Florence. The pilasters on the upper storeys, however, are smooth. Sanmicheli, in his Porta del Palio, Verona (c. 1524), carried the rustication of

[1] In Raphael's cartoon of Peter and John healing the lame man at the gate of the Temple, the columns are twisted and portions spirally fluted. Giulio possibly got the idea from Raphael, whose pupil he was; but what will pass muster in tapestry may be unsuitable for a building.

[2] Excluding the quoins of stuccoed buildings which in some cases might be termed pilasters.

Photo: Alinari.
FIG. 78.—PALAZZO GIUSTIZIA, AND BASILICA PALATINA, MANTUA.

Photo: Brogi.
FIG. 79.—PALAZZO PITTI, FLORENCE, WING OF COURTYARD.

[*To face p.* 110.

the walling round the engaged columns (see Fig. 67). He also rusticated the pilasters on the lower storey of the Palazzo Bevilacqua, Verona (c. 1530) (see Fig. 66). Sansovino rusticated the columns flanking the windows of the Zecca (or Mint), Venice (c. 1356), and those on either side of the ground-floor windows of the Palazzo Cornaro, Venice (c. 1532). The engaged stone columns of the Palazzo Elefantussi, Bologna, are rusticated entirely, the wall behind being brick. In all the above-mentioned examples, however, the projection of the rustication is slight, and the form of the column or pilaster preserved. Palladio went one step further in the columns flanking the first-floor windows of the Palazzo Thiene, Vicenza (c. 1556). He made each alternate course square, thus breaking completely the outline and cylindrical form. On the outskirts of Siena is a charming little building, the Villa Santa Colomba. Raschdorff attributes it to Peruzzi.[1] The top storey can hardly be by him, and it is possible that the whole front is by another architect, and belongs to the latter half of the sixteenth century. On the ground floor the columns and pilasters are rusticated from base to capital with square blocks; on the first floor similar rustications reach from the bases to the springing of the arches. In this building, therefore, the treatment is complete. The effect, moreover, is entirely satisfactory. To Ammanati belongs the discredit of carrying it to extremes in the Pitti palace.

Rustication of columns is to many as a red rag to a bull. When columns are engaged, and have lost their original significance as supports, much may be said in its favour. Each alternate course at least being bonded into the wall it seems legitimate to emphasize the bond. That Palladio rusticated the columns flanking the windows in the Palazzo Thiene, however, is no proof that he approved of a similar treatment for columns in more important positions, in which, if not actually structural, they have the appearance of being so. Building in brick as he did, the temptation to leave the bricks square, and not incur the expense of rounding them, must have been great; but he did not succumb to it save in the example mentioned, for which he might plead the excuse that his columns were window frames, purely ornamental in character and in no sense structural.

The early palaces in Florence are so famous that later ones do

Late palaces in Florence.

[1] "Palast-Architektur von Ober-Italien und Toscana," by J. C. Raschdorff, 1888. In that book is an excellent photograph of the Villa.

not always receive the attention they merit. The courtyard of the Uffizi by Vasari—did not somebody call him the "worst of architects"?—is simpler, more dignified, and finer in scale than the majority of earlier courtyards. Columns supporting lintels predominate, although the great opening at the end is arched. The courtyard of the Archbishop's palace by Giovanni Antonio Dosio (1533–1609) is equally fine. By the same architect is the graceful little Palazzo Larderel.[1] The Palazzo Uguccioni, stated to be by Mariotto di Zanobi Folfi (1521–1600), has one of the stateliest façades in Florence. The ground storey is possibly earlier than the upper storeys. The grouping of the columns in pairs, and the treatment of the framed windows, show considerable originality, and the proportions throughout are excellent. But the finest of all late sixteenth-century palaces in the town is the Palazzo Nonfinito, begun by Buontalenti in 1592 (see Fig. 10). The courtyard, which is as striking as the front, is stated by Raschdorff to be by Luigi Cigoli, but he may merely have superintended its erection after Buontalenti's death in 1608, as the whole building has the appearance of being one person's design. It is commonly described as "Baroque," but the combination of strength and delicacy is most remarkable; and the originality of much of the detail undoubted. As in many other Florentine palaces the ground-floor windows of the Nonfinito have large brackets below them which reach from sill to plinth, framing in panels. These lengthen the proportions of and give greater prominence to the windows. Michael Angelo is often credited with originating this treatment; as he is said to have inserted the similarly designed windows in the ground-floor arched recesses of the Palazzo Riccardi (see Fig. 9). Both San Gallo and Peruzzi, however, possibly anticipated him.

Late palaces in Rome.
Seventeenth-century palaces in Rome may not be exciting outside, but many are skilfully planned, and contain fine staircases and grand suites of rooms. The Palazzo Borghese, designed by Martino Longhi about 1590, is the largest. Its most striking feature is the arcade round the courtyard, with its simple coupled columns two storeys high (see Fig. 41). There is not a trace of decadence or the rococco in the composition, the stateliness of which is unsurpassed in Italy. The Palazzo Barberini (c. 1627) is the outcome of a triumvirate, Maderno, Borromini, and Bernini.

[1] Dosio was evidently an architect of considerable repute, and some drawings of his are reproduced in Signor Brogi's book mentioned on p. 34.

Fig. 80.—Palazzo Uguccioni, Florence.

Fig. 81.—Gran Guardia Antica, Verona.

[*To face p.* 112.

LATER SECULAR BUILDINGS

The lower storeys of the principal façade have considerable dignity, but the design is somewhat spoilt by the upper storeys, which are unusually florid for Rome. The peristylar entrance vestibule and the staircases are extraordinarily magnificent. In both the Barberini and Borghese palaces are minor spiral staircases copied from the staircase by Bramante in the Vatican. The stairs wind

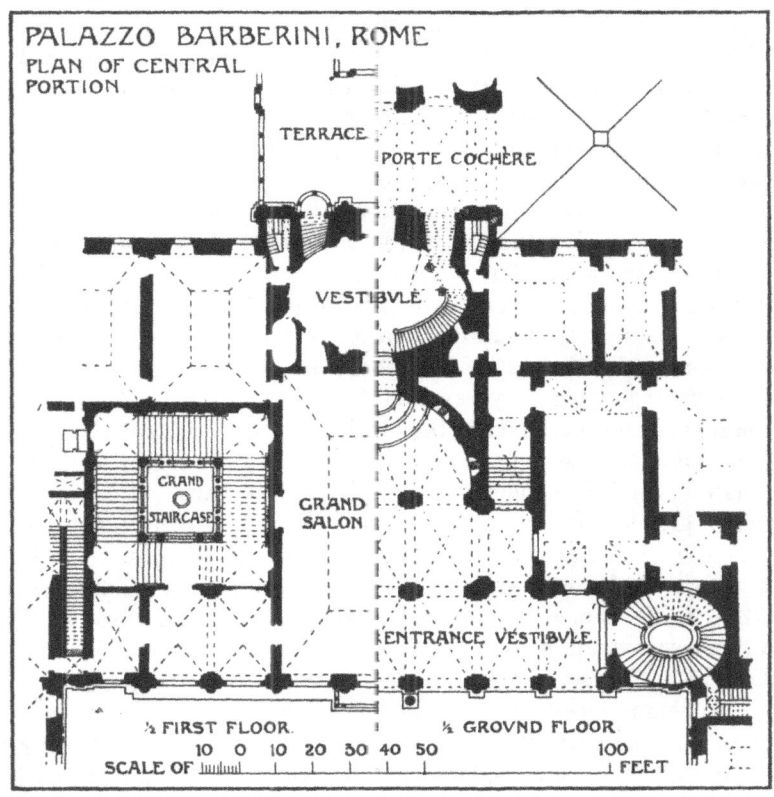

FIG. 82.

round an open oval with six pairs of columns breaking the balustrade. The south front of the Palazzo Poli, the centre of which is occupied by the Fontana di Trevi (*c.* 1735), is Michael Angeloesque in scale. It differs from the Farnese and other great Roman palaces in that between the windows are straight-sided Corinthian pilasters which start from a basement, and carry an entablature, of which, however, only the cornice is continuous.

VOL. III. I

The rococco character of the fountain mars what otherwise would be quite a fine front.

Late building in the north.
Whilst the architects in Florence and Rome were, in the main, following the traditions of Peruzzi, San Gallo, Michael Angelo, etc., in the north, as was only natural the influence of Palladio, Sansovino, and Sanmicheli was paramount. At Venice, Scamozzi, in 1584, repeated, in the Procurazie Nuove, the design of the Library, but spoilt it by an additional storey. Longhena also followed Sansovino in the Palazzi Pesaro and Rezzonico (both c. 1650), the model this time being the Palazzo Cornaro della Ca' Grande. The main façade of the Pesaro palace, with its heavy keystones and figures in unnecessarily high relief in the spandrils, is not altogether satisfactory. Its side is better, as the design of the front is repeated along it minus the sculpture. The rusticated walls and columns of the lowest storey of the Palazzo Rezzonico are really fine. This portion of the front is possibly more reminiscent of Sanmicheli—his Porta del Palio—than of Sansovino. Certainly the lintels over the central openings are better than the arches in the Palazzo Cornaro. A building in Verona undoubtedly inspired by Sanmicheli is the old Court House (Gran Guardia Antica) designed in 1609 by his nephew Domenico Curtoni. It is one of the most simple and at the same time most effective of late examples. The solid bays at the ends, framing the ground-storey arcade, give an appearance of strength and massiveness which is often lacking in buildings with arcaded fronts. The top is poor. A balustrade along the ends and on each side of the attic, which comes over the five central bays—there are fifteen altogether—would help to give a finish. Possibly Curtoni intended some such feature, but funds failed.

G. Alessi (1500-72).
Galeazzo Alessi is the best-known architect who practised mainly in the north-west corner of Italy. His principal building in Genoa is the square-planned domed Church of Santa Maria in Carignano, on a height on the outskirts. His palaces in the town are less remarkable than the villas he built outside. Of these the Villa Cambioso, and the Villa Scassi (or Imperiali) at Sampierdarena, a village at the beginning of the Italian Riviera, are the best known. The gardens of the last-named are finely designed and very extensive. Alessi's work in and about Genoa is more subdued than the secular building most associated with his name, the Palazzo Marino, Milan. Here he undoubtedly showed marked decadent tendencies. The top storey of the façade, with its

LATER SECULAR BUILDINGS

tapering pilasters and heavy brackets above, are eccentricities which have been freely copied in other countries, but which are best avoided. The broken pediments over the first-floor windows are amongst the most unsatisfactory examples of their class. In the courtyard of the palace, peculiarities in design are even more marked. Little can be said in his excuse. He was born at Perugia, and was a contemporary and friend of Michael Angelo.

The situation of Genoa is peculiar. The town is built in a vast amphitheatre, the ground rising rapidly from the harbour. Most of the principal streets run approximately parallel with the port, with the result that the houses occupy very sloping sites. This gave the Genoese architects their opportunity, of which they availed themselves nobly. They planned their buildings round courtyards at different levels with magnificent staircases leading from one courtyard to another. The slope of the ground is in some cases so steep that after passing through courtyards and up staircases, one steps out into a garden, level with the second or even third floor in front.[1] *Genoa.*

The palaces of Genoa have been stigmatized by Fergusson as displaying a "pretentious parvenu vulgarity."[2] In some of them the window heads are, it is true, treated fantastically, but the elevations of most are severely plain, the reason being that originally they were decorated with colour. Their great courtyards are amongst the most dignified and striking in the world, and are characterized also by great simplicity of design. Contemporary with Alessi at Genoa was Rocco Durago, who in 1564 commenced the Palazzo del Municipio, the plan of which is delightful. Probably finer still are the University (*c.* 1623) and the Palazzo Durazzo, both the work of Bartolomeo Bianco. The latter is almost all courtyard and staircase, and in the former the arcading surrounding the courtyard is similar in design to that of the Borghese palace, Rome, and equally effective. *Genoese palaces.*

In other northern towns there is fine late work. Two palaces, one from Bologna, the other from Brescia, are selected as fair typical examples, neither better nor worse than many others. The Palazzo Davia (or Bargellini), Bologna, is a good simple design. The colossal figures which flank the doorway and support the balcony give *Two late northern palaces.*

---

[1] Morlaix, in Brittany, resembles Genoa in its natural formation, and the local proverb there, "From the garden to the garret, as they say at Morlaix," applies equally well to the Italian town.

[2] "History of Modern Architecture," vol. i. p. 157.

116   A HISTORY OF ARCHITECTURAL DEVELOPMENT

distinction and character to the front. The legitimacy of the employment of such figures in such a position cannot be questioned. The Palazzo Martinengo, Brescia, affords more opportunity for

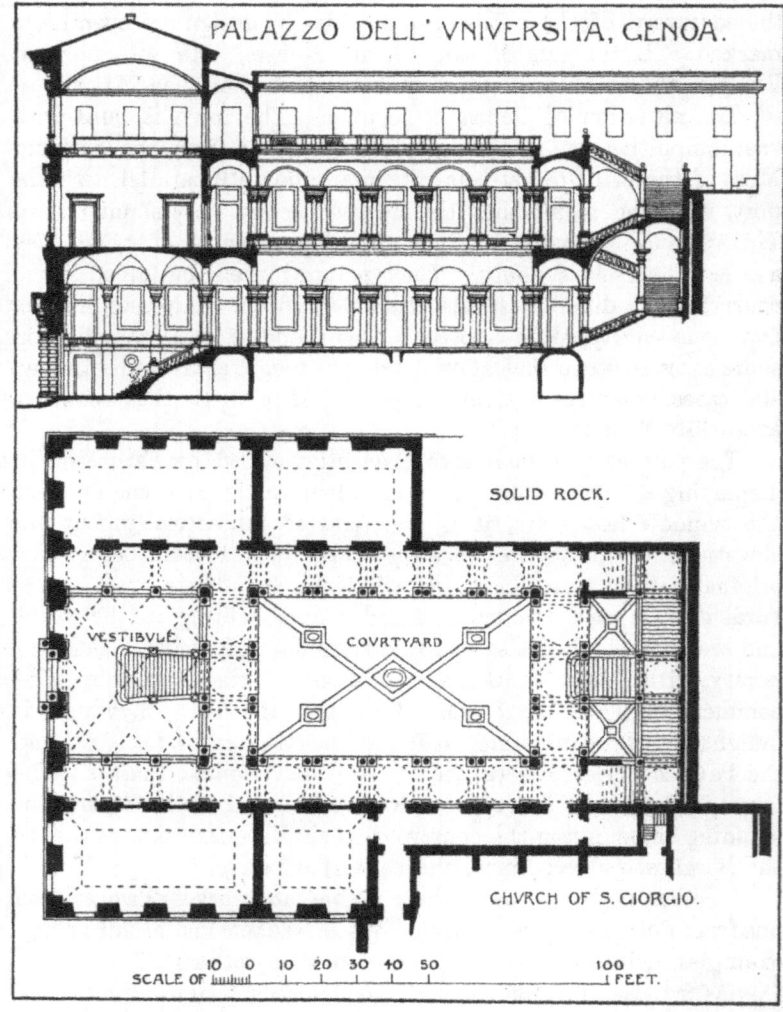

Fig. 83.

criticism, but its very faults seem to emphasize its beauties. The entrance doorways, with their recessed windows above, are fine compositions. It is easy to feel annoyed—if one is disposed to

Fig. 85.—Palazzo Martinengo, Brescia.

[*To face p.* 116.

Fig. 84.—Palazzo Davia, Bologna.

cavil—with the columns, supporting nothing but balls, which flank the ground-floor windows; with the oval windows between the balls; with the brackets on the string-course; and with the broken pediments on the first floor. But this façade is a design. The whole is carefully thought out. All the little breaks alongside the window columns, all the details throughout, have evidently received the utmost care. Whether one likes the design or not is a matter of opinion; but that it is the work of an able architect is certain.

The buildings described in this chapter belong to the declining centuries of the Renaissance, but its glory had by no means entirely departed. They show that the later men worked on traditional lines; and, in the majority of instances, avoided excess on the one hand and slavish imitation on the other. In the next chapter some of the later churches are considered; and it will be admitted by most that they also, on the whole, show a strength and restraint deserving of high praise. There are exceptions, of course. Venice in the seventeenth and eighteenth centuries had the reputation of being the most licentious of cities; and existing buildings of that period show that the licence sometimes extended to its architecture. In many towns in Southern Italy also, especially in the vicinity of Naples, there are late buildings, both secular and ecclesiastical, which do "outrage the proprieties." Such buildings, however, are rare in Rome and Florence, and by no means form the majority elsewhere.

CHAPTER VII

THE PLANNING AND GENERAL ORDINANCE OF RENAISSANCE CHURCHES

Introduction.
THE churches which have been mentioned in previous chapters mostly follow the plan and general ordinance which were vernacular in Italy throughout the Middle Ages. Except in detail, they show little evidence of a classic Renaissance. Those now to be considered belong to a different category. In them the influence of antiquity is manifest; and few of their features, proportions, and plan characteristics are not directly traceable to that source. Fifteenth-century examples are few. There was little demand at first for churches in the new manner; existing mediæval ones sufficed. The greater activity in church building in the following centuries was mainly due to the popes and cardinals, as their position strengthened and the Holy See became daily more powerful. The commencement of S. Peter's, Rome, in 1506, started a new era. The old order passed away definitely. Much of the later activity was due to the indefatigability of the Jesuits, whose churches in Rome and other cities all possess a distinctive stamp which makes them easily recognizable.

The principles of plan and general ordinance of Classic churches are so different from those generally followed in Mediæval that they merit detailed analysis.

Types of plan.
Nearly all typical examples as regards plan can be placed under one or other of two heads. The first consists of those churches compact in plan, which in the main are square, octagonal, circular, or Greek cross; the second, of those which have long naves, and, consequently, are of oblong or Latin cross form. The departure from Mediæval models is, superficially, most marked in examples of the first class; a closer examination of those of the second, however, bring out the most interesting differences. The plans of the former are founded on Pagan temples, tombs, and other Roman buildings; the Pantheon supplying the chief stimulus.

The Gothic men left the type severely alone, except in a few instances. The Byzantines welcomed it — witness S. Vitale, Ravenna, S. Lorenzo, Milan, etc.; and in the Romanesque period of Mediævalism it was freely adopted for baptisteries, and occasionally for churches. To revert to it was not, therefore, entirely a departure from tradition; but the architects of the Renaissance imbued the type with new life, and gave to it an importance which, save in the days of Imperial Rome, it had not before possessed.

The chief reason why it found favour in their eyes was that no other kind of plan is so well adapted for supporting and display- *The dome paramount.*

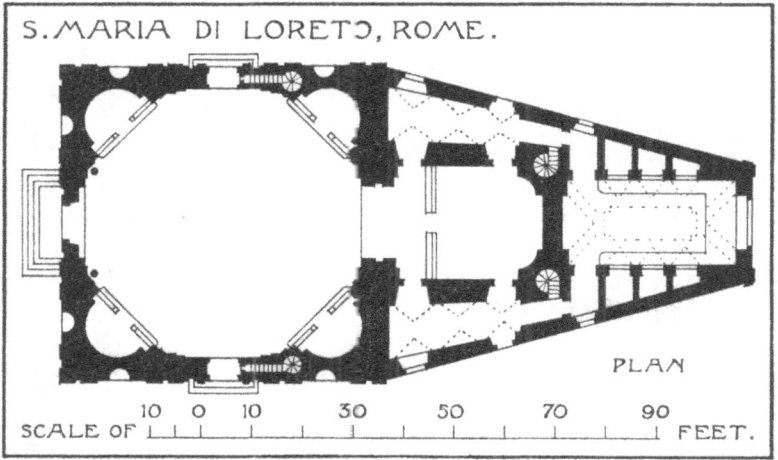

Fig. 86.

ing to advantage a central dome. Its advantages for congregational worship were a secondary consideration. The statement has been made frequently, and with truth, that the exigencies of vaulting played a large part in the development of the Mediæval church; with still greater force it may be asserted that the dome dominated the planning of Renaissance churches. Even in examples otherwise frankly basilican the square in front of the altar was seized upon as affording an opportunity for a dome, as in San Lorenzo and Santo Spirito, Florence; and in the majority of later oblong churches the whole of the eastern part was planned with that object. The desire for a dome occasioned the great eastern octagon of Florence Cathedral; and it was the building of that

120 A HISTORY OF ARCHITECTURAL DEVELOPMENT

dome which gave such enormous stimulus to the Renaissance movement.

Square plan churches.
Santa Maria di Loreto, Rome, overlooking Trajan's Forum, is one of the earliest of domed square churches on antique lines. It was designed by Antonio da San Gallo in 1507 for the guild of

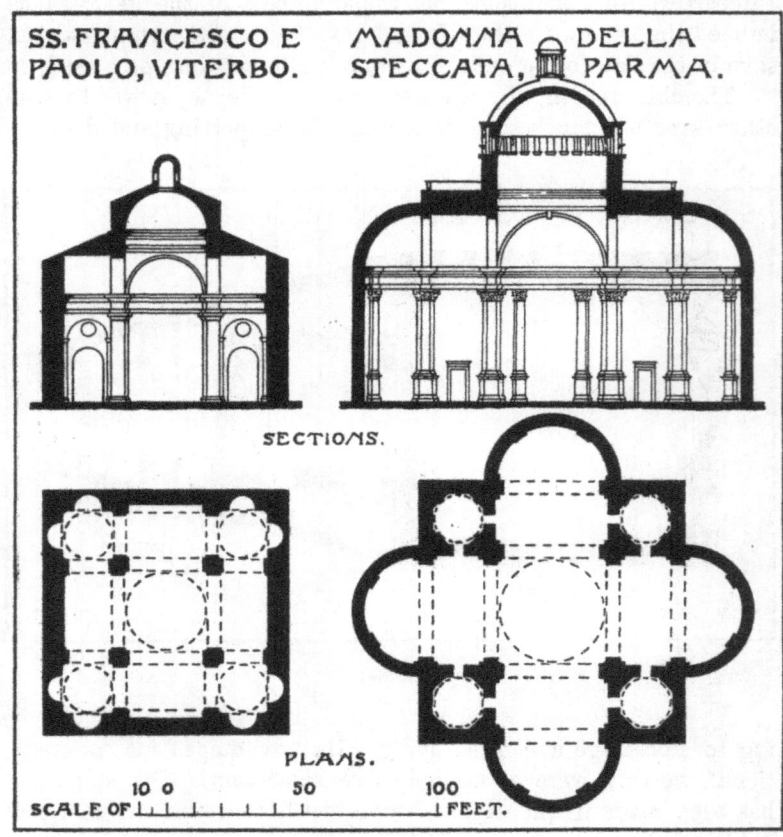

FIG. 87 (*A. T. Bolton*).

bakers. The large internal niches in the angles of the square reduce the plan to an octagon. The octagonal drum above is excellently proportioned, and the dome itself, which is of brick, is one of the most satisfactory in outline ever designed. The somewhat badly fitting, but otherwise well designed, lantern was added in 1580 by Giacomo del Duca. In S. Maria di Loreto the dome covers the whole of the main portion. In most square-planned

Fig. 83 (*Leslie Wilkinson*).

[*To face p.* 120.

RENAISSANCE CHURCHES

churches of the Renaissance the general ordinance is identical with that of S. Theodore, Constantinople (Vol. I. Fig. 161), and other typical small Byzantine churches in Greece, Turkey, Sicily, etc. Only the central square, *i.e.* one-third to one-half of the total width, is domed, the arms being generally barrel-vaulted, and the squares

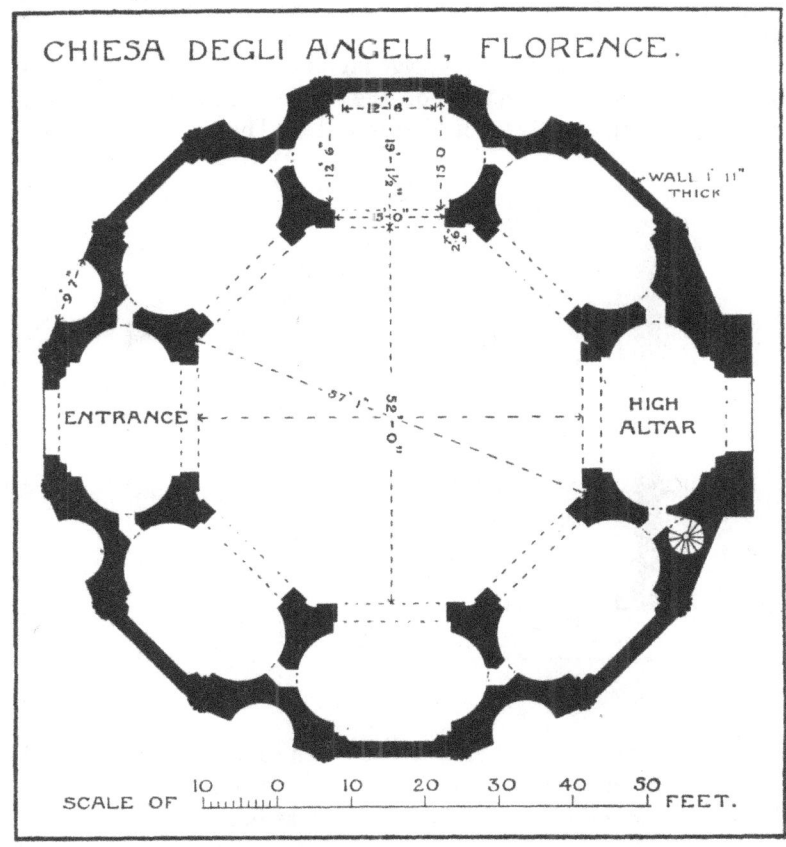

Fig. 89.

at the corners kept low, so that, externally, the churches appear cruciform. Of this character are S. Francesco e Paolo, Viterbo, designed by Vignola in the middle of the sixteenth century, the Madonna della Steccata, Parma, of about the same date, and many others. The latter church has a projecting apse on each side.[1]

[1] In plan this church resembles closely San Satiro, Milan (Vol. I. Fig. 168), and S. Germigny les Prés, France (Vol. II. Fig. 89).

122 A HISTORY OF ARCHITECTURAL DEVELOPMENT

If S. Peter's, Rome, had been left as planned by Bramante and Michael Angelo, it would have been the largest and finest of this type. As it is, the Dôme of Les Invalides, Paris, can claim that distinction. The eastern portions of Florence Cathedral (Fig. 1) and S. Maria delle Grazie, Milan (Fig. 26), may be studied in conjunction with the above, although both are additions to long naves.

Octagonal plan churches.
The most interesting of octagonal plans is that prepared by Brunelleschi for the church of the Angels, Florence. Messrs. Blashfield, in their edition of Vasari, state, "There are still remains

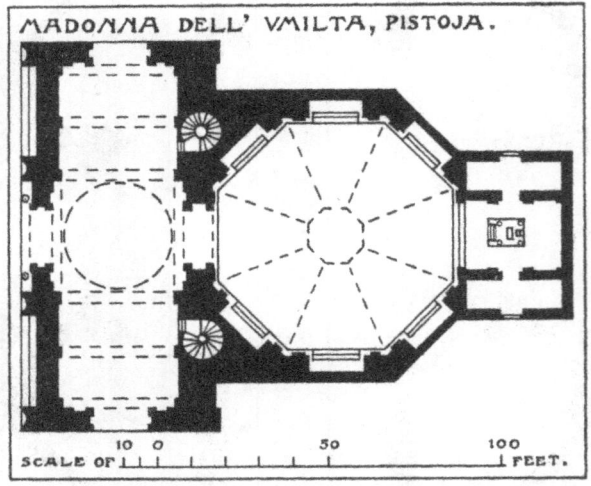

Fig. 90.

of the foundations of this church to be seen in the Via degli Alfani. ... It remained incomplete ... because the Florentines spent the money for other purposes." It is a striking example of an original application of ancient forms to modern requirements. Brunelleschi doubtless intended to construct the dome with ribs, as in the Cathedral, and the walls dividing the chapels would have afforded excellent abutment. A simpler and more ordinary plan is that of the Madonna dell' Umilta, Pistoja, built by Ventura Vittoni about 1509. The octagon is entered through a stately vestibule, the centre of which is domed and the ends barrel-vaulted. The excellence of the proportions and detail of the vestibule may be due, either directly or indirectly, to Bramante, for whom Vittoni, who is stated to have been by trade a metal-worker, executed several works in Rome in that capacity. The octagon was finished and spoilt by Vasari, who added an upper storey and the dome. The church of Santa Maria della Pace, Rome, built by Baccio Pintelli about 1487, consists of a domed octagon preceded by a nave of two bays (see Fig. 42). In the thickness of the walls of both octagon and nave are recessed chapels. The semi-circular portico at the west end was designed by Pietro da Cortona, and Bramante added the well-known cloisters.

Churches with circular plans are rare. The huge circular chancel, or chapel, which Alberti added in 1470 to the church of

Circular plan churches.

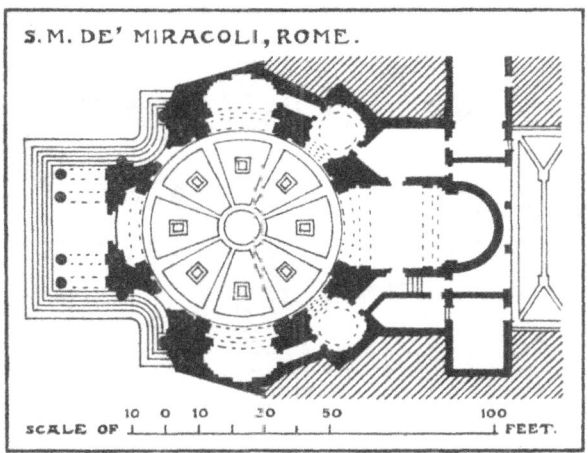

Fig. 91.

S. Annunziata, Florence, is only a portion of a church. With its thick walls enclosing niches, it is interesting as an early instance of the fascination the Pantheon exercised over Renaissance architects. A church circular internally is Santa Maria de' Miracoli, Rome, flanking one end of the Corso, where it starts from the Piazza del Popolo. Externally, it is irregular in form. Balancing it, on the other side of the street, is Santa Maria di Monte Santo, which is elliptical in plan, with numerous side chapels in recesses. Both churches were built late in the seventeenth century, and owe their designs to Rainaldi, Bernini, and Fontana. Their reputation is due more to the position they occupy than to any intrinsic merit they possess. The "Miracoli" church has an octagonal drum and dome, notwithstanding that the plan below is circular. This was so that it should harmonize better with the other church, the drum and dome of which are multangular.

Two of the largest circular churches in Italy are San Francesco di Paola, Naples, built by P. Bianchi early in the last century, and its contemporary San Carlo Borromeo, Milan, designed by Amati. Both belong to the "revival" period more than to the Renaissance. S. Francesco is frankly a copy of the Pantheon, Rome, with certain internal modifications. In the Pantheon the columns only stand "in antis" in front of the niches, and are

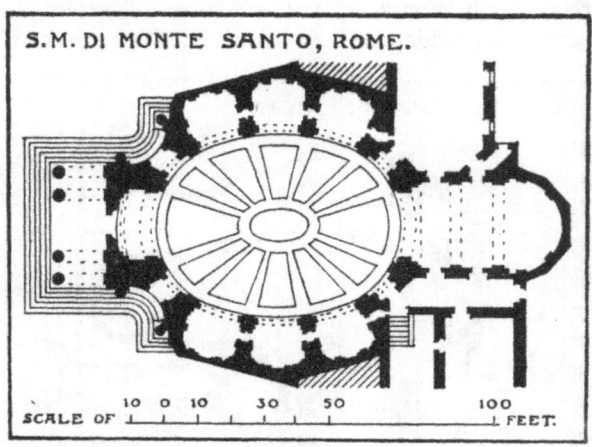

FIG. 92.

unequally spaced (see Vol. I. p. 139). In the Naples church the sweep of the columns is continuous, and the intercolumniation the same throughout. The result is monotonous, and is a lesson in how the introduction of a modification, not very great in itself, may ruin a design.

Greek cross plan churches.

The Greek cross plan was a favourite with early Renaissance architects. Brunelleschi suggested it in the Pazzi Chapel, Florence (see Fig. 3), and Alberti adopted it in its entirety for San Sebastiano, Mantua, commenced in 1460. The exterior now has a very unfinished appearance, save along one side where the entrance loggia is an attractive example of early work (see Fig. 109). Following quickly came La Madonna delle Carceri, Prato, designed by Giuliano da San Gallo and finished in 1491, and La Madonna di Santo Biagio fuori Montepulciano, commenced by his brother Antonio in 1518, and finished about twenty years later. These are approximately the same in plan

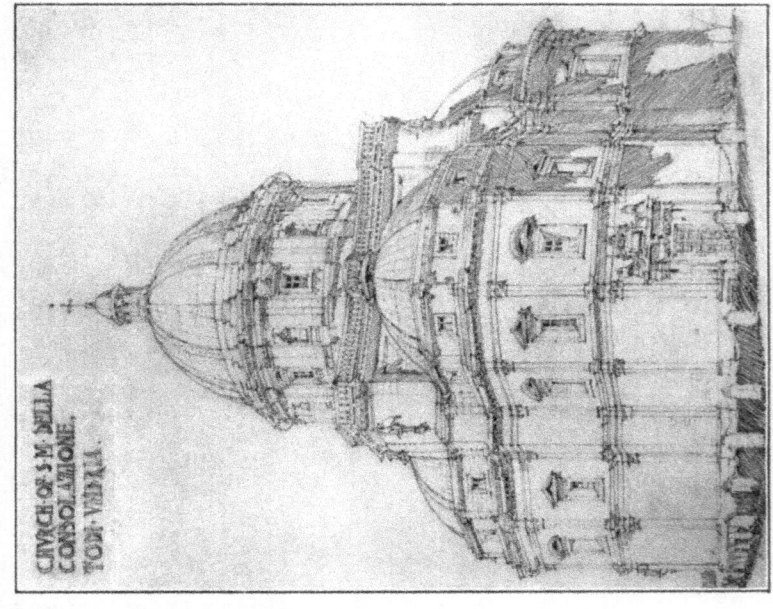

Fig. 94.—Santa Maria della Consolazione, Todi.
Leslie Wilkinson.

[*To face p.* 125.

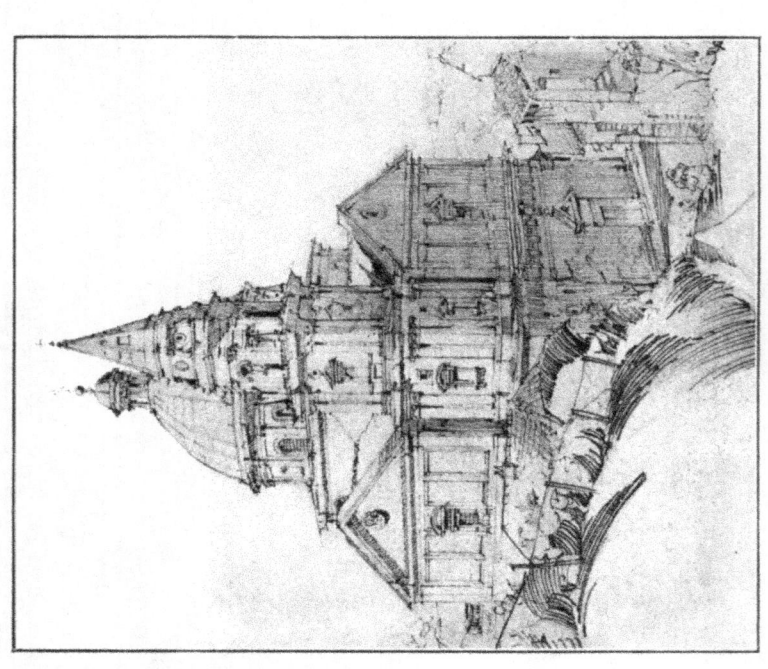

Fig. 93.—Madonna di Santo Biagio, fuori Montepulciano.
Leslie Wilkinson.

and in size; the dome of each being nearly 40 feet in diameter. In Antonio's church, however, a low sacristy projects beyond the eastern arm, and two detached towers, only one of which is finished, flank the western. At Prato the dome is similar to that of the Pazzi Chapel, and like it is concealed; at Montepulciano it is raised on a circular drum. Both internally and externally the design of the latter church is more architectural, and is evidence of the great advance made in the first quarter of the sixteenth century.

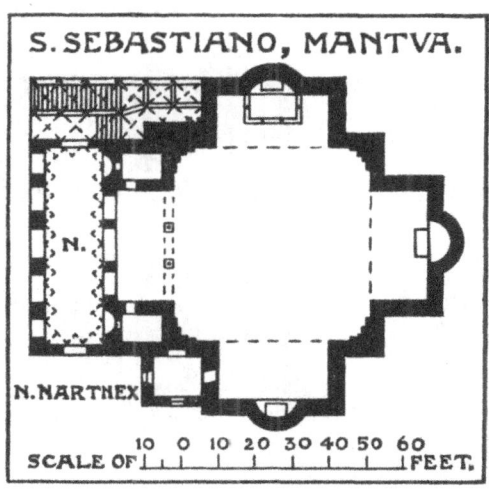

Fig. 95.

With Santo Biagio may be compared Santa Maria della Consolazione, Todi, commenced about 1508. It is now stated to be by Cola di Matteucio of Caprarola, although Von Geymüller attributes the plan and exterior to Bramante, and states that the interior was by "an inferior hand." It is a cruciform church, but apses take the place of rectangular arms. The semi-domes over these apses stop against a broad and cleverly designed square mass, the projecting angles of which contain staircases leading to the gallery surrounding the circular drum above. Few buildings are better planned and designed to show to advantage a central dome.[1] Other cruciform aisleless churches

S. M. della Consolazione, Todi.

[1] The dimensions of the church are considerable, and internally are approximately as follows: central square, 49·6 wide; height from floor to top of entablature, 51·6; to apex of semi-dome, 77·0; and to apex of central dome, 146·6, or about three times the width below.

126   A HISTORY OF ARCHITECTURAL DEVELOPMENT

are S. Giuseppe and SS. Pietro e Paolo, Siena, the small S. Crocifisso, Todi, La Madonna del Calcinaio, near Cortona, etc. The nave of the last named, however, has an extra bay, making the plan a Latin cross.

Later churches.
All the above-mentioned plans are very simple, with the exception of Brunelleschi's church of the Angels at Florence. Later churches similar in type are frequently more complicated. A few only are chosen for illustration, each possessing special traits of interest.

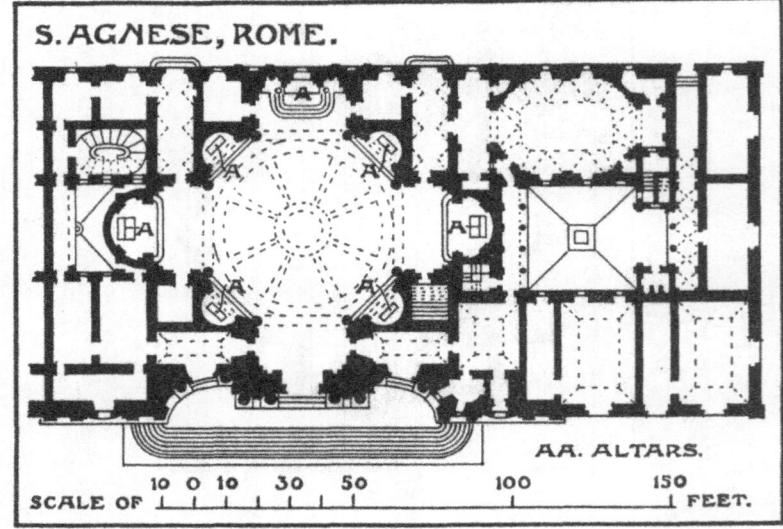

Fig. 96.

S. Agnese, Rome.
Sant' Agnese, Rome, on the west side of the Piazza Navona, was built in the seventeenth century by Girolamo Rainaldi, Borromini, and Carlo Rainaldi. The plan is a Greek cross with projecting apses to two of the arms. The angles of the central square are filled in with niches, converting it into an irregular octagon, and the arms consequently are narrower than the domed centre; in the other cruciform churches mentioned they are the full width.[1] This is the fault of the interior. The arms appear too narrow for their height; although it is curious

[1] Compare with the plans of the larger Byzantine churches, such as Daphni, S. Luke of Stiris, etc. (see Vol. I. Fig. 174), and the section of the former (Fig. 171).

RENAISSANCE CHURCHES

that in Byzantine churches, with similar plan and proportions, the narrow, lofty arms are amongst their most effective characteristics. The difference is doubtless due to the heavy entablatures of the Classic church, which form strong horizontal lines; whereas in Byzantine churches cornices are absent, and the small abacus at the springing of the arches has very slight projection. Few exteriors have been abused more roundly than the façade of this church.[1] And yet its curved wall flanked by turrets, with the

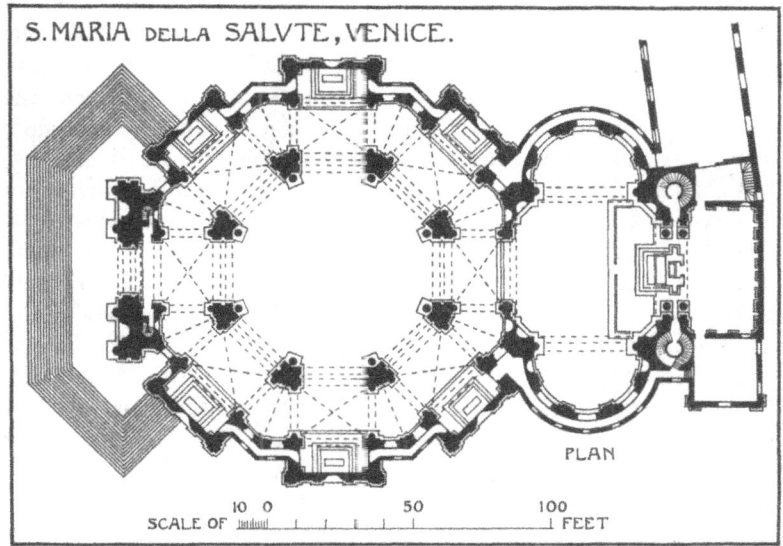

FIG. 97.

dome rising behind, possesses considerable dignity. The grouping is distinctly good. The detail may leave something to be desired, but that is a minor consideration. Detail often receives too much attention and grouping too little, because the former is on the surface and easy to perceive, whilst the latter requires looking for. Hence the reputation enjoyed by many Italian quattro-cento buildings; the façade of the Certosa, Pavia, for instance. Bad detail may spoil an otherwise good design, but no amount of good detail can compensate for poor scale and absence of idea.

Santa Maria della Salute, Venice, commenced by Baldassare S. Maria della Salute.

[1] The local joke is that the "Nile" on the fountain in the centre of the Piazza keeps his head covered because he cannot bear to look at it. A good photograph of this church is in "Baudenkmaeler Roms des XV.-XIX. Jahrhunderts," by H. Strack.

Longhena in 1631, is the best known of octagonal churches which are aisled, and probably the largest. The effect inside is one of considerable richness, not so much because of any excess of carving or ornamentation, as from the varied perspective which the plan affords. The approach to the chancel, however, is mean, merely the height of the aisles and the width of the openings of the octagon. No doubt it would have spoilt the effect of the latter if one of its bays had been made higher and wider than the others, but the vault of the eastern bay of the aisles and the arch beyond might well have been raised (see Fig. 103). When one remembers the fine effect produced by the lofty bema of the somewhat similarly planned San Vitale, Ravenna, one feels that the Renaissance architect has failed where the Byzantine succeeded. The apses which terminate the chancel are effective in themselves, but they are invisible from the octagon. As viewed from there the east end appears to consist of two rectangular rooms, with an altar under the archway dividing them. Externally the dome over the octagon, with its lantern, drums, and huge console brackets is superb. The entrance doorway is well in scale; but if the projecting chapels had been omitted, and the wall left plain as a foil and support to the mass above, the effect would probably have been far better. Over the choir is another and smaller dome, flanked by two slender campanili. The two domes are separated from each other by the width of the aisle, and the larger consequently does not appear to overpower the less.

Churches with long naves.
Notwithstanding the striking success, both externally and internally, of many of the above-mentioned examples, the exigencies of congregational worship soon obliged architects to add aisles and lengthen naves. Most typical oblong churches, however, differ only from the others in the greater length of the western arm. The eastern portions show no change, except that the chancel is sometimes extended, a similar extension, however, being far from uncommon in squarer plans. A crowning dome had still to be carried, no matter what the length of the nave. The plans of the following three churches, which in all essentials are the same as those of many other churches of the sixteenth and following centuries, are sufficient to demonstrate this: San Giorgio Maggiore, Venice, designed by Palladio in 1560; Sant' Andrea della Valle, Rome, begun in 1591 by P. Olivieri, and finished by C. Rainaldi; and Sant' Ignazio, Rome, a typical Jesuit church built between 1625 and 1675. Cut off two bays of S. Ignazio,

and the eastern apse, and the result is a square church, planned like those already considered. In S. Andrea care was taken to repeat exactly on the west side of the crossing the bay to the east. In Palladio's Il Redentore, Venice, *c.* 1576, the east end is triapsal,

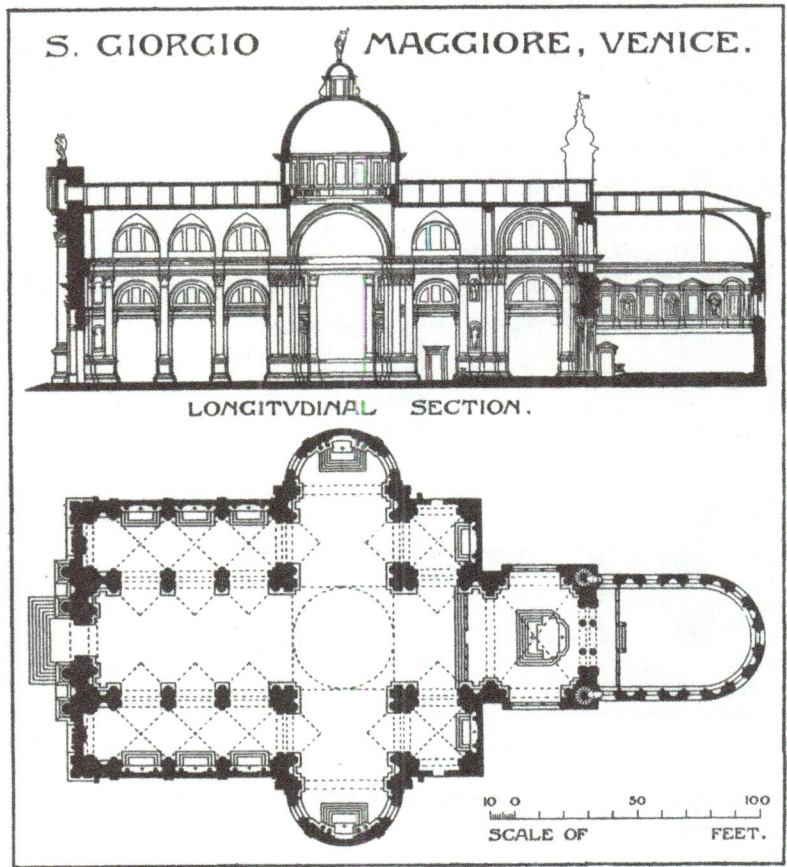

Fig. 98.

and is complete in itself; the nave, with its side chapels, appears like an afterthought.

The first oblong church to embody fully the principles of plan and ordinance characteristic of Classic churches was Sant' Andrea, Mantua, designed by Leon Battista Alberti in 1470, but not commenced until 1472, the year of his death. In Mediæval

S. Andrea, Mantua.

churches the customary internal ordinance is the triple division of the side walls of the nave into arcade, triforium, and clerestory, and the windows of the last storey reach as high as the apex of the intersecting vault. This division, somewhat differently treated, is retained in Basilican churches (see Fig. 8 and Vol. I. Fig. 109). In the majority of large Classic churches the side walls of the nave are merely one storey high, and consist of an arcade supporting an entablature which forms strong horizontal lines, and cuts off the vault above it entirely from the substructure. Above the entablature is sometimes an attic, as in S. Paul's, London, S. Roch, Paris, etc., from which the vault springs. In S. Andrea,

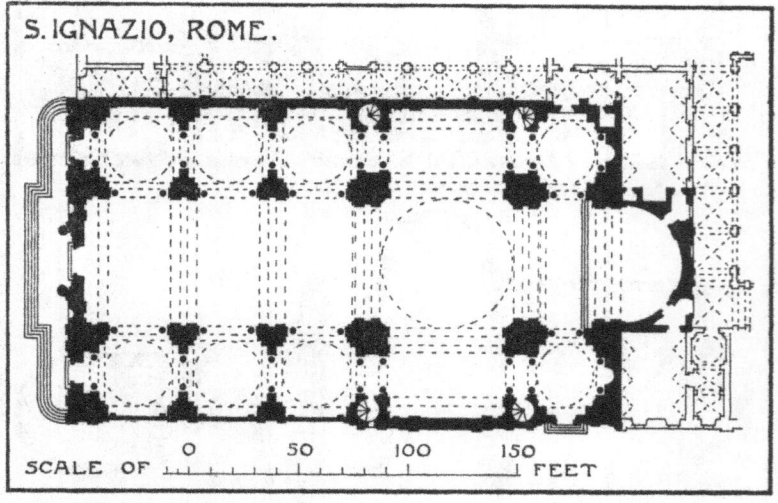

Fig. 99.

S. Peter's, Rome, etc., it springs direct from the entablature itself. In Gothic churches verticality and height were the desire. The lofty vaulting shafts and soaring vault, the mullions and jamb mouldings of the clerestory windows, the shafts of the triforium, were all designed with that object. In Classic churches the aim is for horizontality and breadth.

Vaults. In S. Andrea, Mantua, and in the transepts, choir, and portion of the nave nearest to the crossing in S. Peter's—the only portion contemplated by Bramante and Michael Angelo—the vault is a barrel vault, and consequently there are no upper side windows at all. In many other churches, above either the entablature or attic as the case may be, are windows which cut into the vault but do not reach as high as the crown. The vault is not an ordinary intersecting vault, but a Welsh-groin.[1] The windows have not the lofty proportions of Gothic; they are sometimes merely circles, more frequently lunettes; and even when lengthened, the lights are still short by comparison with Gothic ones, and the mullions dividing them broad and heavy.[2]

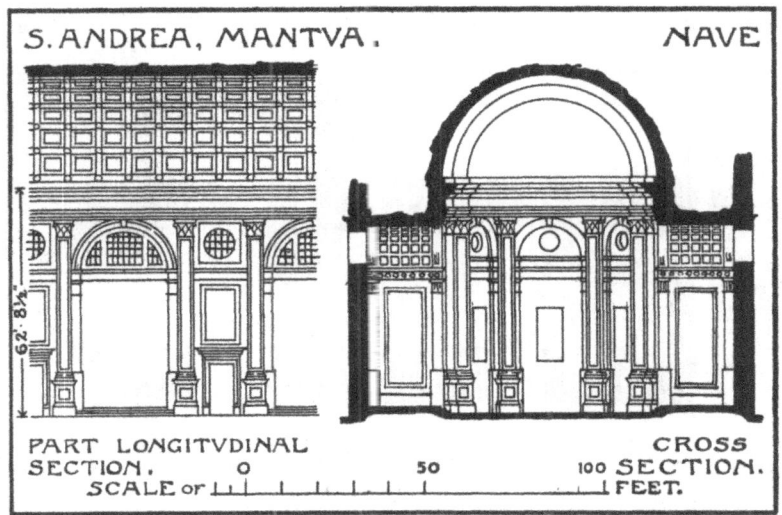

Fig. 100.

In Gothic churches the concentration of the thrusts of the ribbed intersecting vaults at certain points rendered logical the reduction of the walling to a series of piers stiffened by flying buttresses. In S. Andrea, Mantua, both entablature and vault are continuous, and any such divided substructure would have been a mistake. Alberti was fully alive to the feeling of weakness that would have resulted. He therefore planned his church with open and enclosed side chapels alternating, and by so doing was enabled to make his arched openings actually less in width than the wall between them. He thus secured an appearance of continuity below his vault, and at the same time obtained

[1] A Welsh-groin vault is formed by the intersection of two cylindrical vaults, of which the transverse is of less height than the main longitudinal vault.
[2] In France and England, as in S. Paul's, London, the windows are larger and more important than in the churches of Italy and Spain.

132 A HISTORY OF ARCHITECTURAL DEVELOPMENT

that feeling of stability and repose which was ever the object of Classic architects. The division of the nave into three great bays, the two great piers, or slices of walling, each side, the barrel-vaulted chapels, and the proportions throughout, all show that Alberti took one of the great vaulted halls of the Romans as his model, although he departed from the original in many respects. Scale is given to the nave by the pilasters at the angles of the chapels. There are two to each bay, and consequently more repetition than the division into three bays implies. The door-

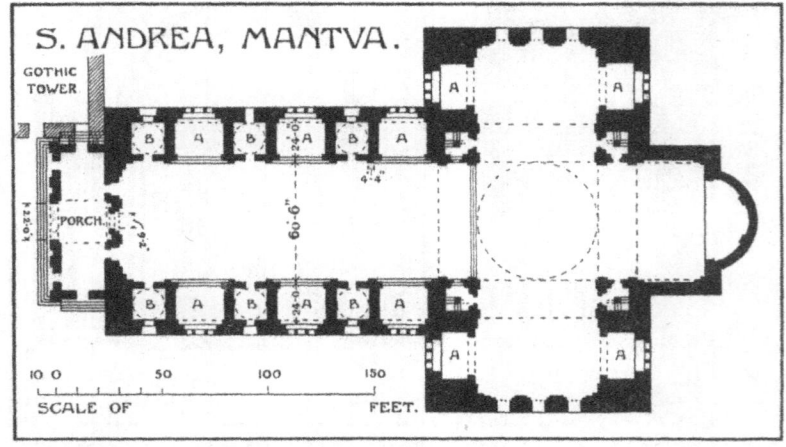

Fig. 101.

ways to the enclosed chapels with their glazed circles above—through which comes little or no light—also give scale. It is evident that Alberti had been maturing the plan for S. Andrea in his mind for some time, as in the remodelling of S. Francesco, Rimini, the foundation stone of which was laid in 1446, he tentatively introduced the alternation of open and closed chapels, and substituted slices of walling, ornamented by pilasters, for the original piers (see Fig. 106).[1]

Piers. In the majority of Classic churches the vault is a "Welsh-groin," and an appearance of continuity in the substructure was not so imperative. But there is always a vast difference between

[1] Alberti cannot be held responsible for the existing form of the angle pilasters. The sculptured panels, according to J. A. Symonds, are by Bernardo Ouiffagni and Donatello's pupil Simone, who together probably designed the pilasters to suit their panels.

Classic and Gothic churches in the number and proportions of piers. In the latter they are numerous, comparatively slender, and the spans between them small. In the former the old Roman principle of few and large supports is followed, and all spans, both longitudinal and transverse, are large, sometimes excessively so. Notwithstanding that such is the case, the proportionate width of solid to void is generally considerable. In the nave of S. Peter's, Rome, the piers are about 30 feet wide, the openings about 45 feet. In Northern Italy, and in northern countries generally, as in S. Giorgio Maggiore, Venice (Fig. 98), and S. Paul's, London (see Fig. 238), piers are narrower. But in Il Redentore, Venice, a church without aisles but with side chapels, Palladio was able to obtain the proportions which, as an enthusiastic admirer of ancient buildings, he must have preferred. He made his chapels apsidal ended, and thus secured approximately the same width of

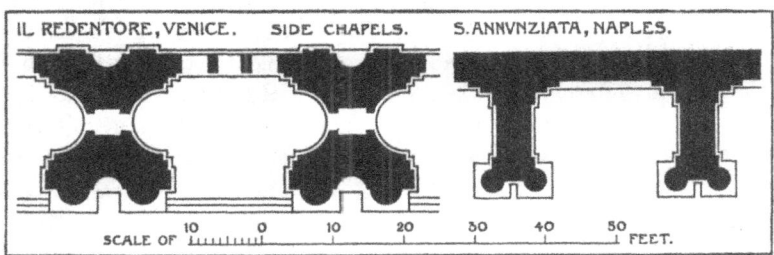

FIG. 102.

side walling as Alberti at Mantua. In other churches other methods were adopted to obtain the same result. In S. Annunziata, Naples, the width of walling flanking the openings to the chapels is far greater than the wall behind which separates them, owing to the projection of engaged columns at the angles.

In contradistinction to Gothic piers which are a succession of isolated supports, Classic piers may be described as slices of walling enriched by pilasters or engaged columns. From the pilasters on the sides, which are sometimes single, sometimes in pairs, spring the arches of the arcade. In S. Giorgio Maggiore these have their own capitals and entablatures. In the nave of S. Peter's, a cornice with a necking below forms the capital. The pilasters or columns on the face reach to the underside of the main entablature; but any appearance of verticality which they might give is more than counteracted by the stronger horizontal lines above. They may start direct from the floor, as in S. Peter's, Il Redentore, etc., or may be raised on pedestals, as in S. Andrea, S. Giorgio Maggiore, etc. Sometimes there is only one column on each face, as in S. Giorgio, or one pilaster, as in S. Roch, Paris; or there may be two columns, as in Il Redentore, etc., or two pilasters, as in S. Peter's and S. Andrea. In Palladio's two Venetian churches, the engaged columns only project half their diameter, instead of the customary three-quarters. Externally, the smaller projection might have a somewhat weak effect, but inside it is distinctly an advantage. Such columns produce a much richer effect than flat pilasters, and their projection is only a trifle greater.

Summary of internal ordinance. The plan and general ordinance described above have doubtless some faults. Owing to the great size and fewness of the divisions, Classic churches sometimes do not look their size. The Romans introduced columns between their great piers, because of their scale-giving properties. The architects of the Renaissance might with advantage have imitated them in this respect. The numerous piers in Gothic churches, and the repetition of parts generally which is one of their characteristics, undoubtedly give scale; but they tend to create a feeling of unrest. The fewer, larger piers of Classic churches are reposeful, and the large open spaces good for congregational purposes. A fine effect of size can also be produced without heavy expense. A few large piers cost less than numerous small ones. Whilst many Italian churches owe much of their beauty to expensive materials and lavish decoration, neither is absolutely necessary, as Palladio's two churches at Venice prove. Fine results are quite possible with the simplest materials and whitewash; if thought be given to the plan, and care taken with the proportions. Modern methods of building do not lend themselves to, or suggest, elaborate moulded stone work for piers, walls, and vaults. They ally us far more closely to the Roman Empire than to the Middle Ages. In adopting them, colour, ornament, precious materials need not be banished, if funds allow of their retention; but it is better to reserve them for fittings, when they will tell with greater force if the background be plain, than if it be enriched to be in what is in common parlance called "in keeping."

Exceptions. Nearly all churches commenced after the fifteenth century follow the internal ordinance described above. Most of the exceptions are in the towns along the northern frontier. The most notable of these, and certainly the most lavishly ornamented,

Photo: C. Naya.
FIG. 103.—SANTA MARIA DELLA SALUTE, VENICE.

Photo: C. Naya.
FIG. 104.—SAN GIORGIO MAGGIORE, VENICE.

[*To face p.* 134.

is the church of the Annunziata, Genoa, designed by Giacomo della Porta, the Roman architect, in 1587. The upper portion of the interior differs little from what has been stated to be customary, as above the side arches is an entablature and a Welsh-groin vault. The arches, however, spring from columns, and not from piers. Considerable pains were evidently taken to remove as far as possible the impression of a continuous superstructure and a divided substructure. The vault is divided into bays by transverse arches; below these are pilasters of slight projection reaching from the entablature to the top of the capitals of the columns; and the continuity of the entablature is broken by small breaks above the pilasters. The whole of the upper part is richly decorated

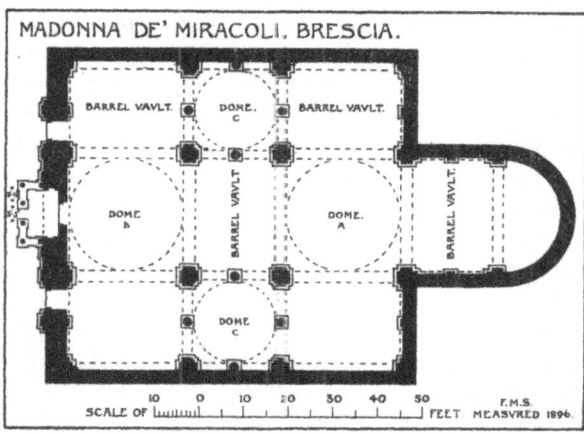

FIG. 105.

and the columns are of fluted white marble, the flutes being filled with red and other coloured marbles. In Venetian territory there are also churches whose internal ordinance is also dissimilar, but their differences are solely due to the influence of S. Mark's. Of these S. Salvatore, commenced in 1506, is the most remarkable. The nave, including the crossing, is covered by three domes, separated from one another by wide transverse arches as in S. Mark's. These are carried on slender square piers with Classic capitals and entablatures. The general effect is that the supports are much too weak, and one longs for the sturdier piers of S. Mark's, or else for the enclosed chapels of Alberti's S. Andrea. In the slightly earlier church of Santa Maria de' Miracoli, Brescia, this fault is corrected by the introduction of columns, carrying semicircular arches, between the piers. The plan of this church is as interesting as its well-known elaborate west porch, and if carried out on a larger scale should produce most striking results. The two domes of the nave are separated by a barrel vault over the intervening bay; dome A being carried higher than dome B. The domes CC over the middle bays of the aisles are smaller and lower.

Lighting. The lover of Gothic may with justice claim that the windows of Classic churches show none of the thoughtful care and elaborate skill lavished on the windows of great Mediæval cathedrals. He will also miss, as a rule, the wonderful effects of the slanting rays falling from the lofty clerestory on the south side. But if Classic windows are dull in design it matters little because, in Italy at least, they are little seen. There are frequently none in either the east or the west wall. The entablature cuts off any upper ones, and lower ones are generally hidden. Standing at the west end of S. Andrea, Mantua, no windows at all are visible, except some very unimportant ones at the east end. In this church, and in Classic churches generally, the windows in the drum and dome over the crossing provide the main lighting. The effect of the flood of light coming from one does not exactly see where is very striking, and ample compensation for any shortcomings elsewhere. The most important part of the church, including the high altar, is illuminated. In S. Peter's, Rome, practically the whole of the lighting of the western portion of the church may be said to come from the dome and drum, as the windows in the apses of the choir and transepts are comparatively small.[1]

In S. Andrea, Mantua, the "open" side chapels have each a lunette close under the vault, and in aisled churches, each bay, as in San Giorgio Maggiore, Venice, has often a similar window. Frequently, however, there are no side windows at all. Each bay of aisle or each side chapel is domed, and has its own small lantern. The aisles of the nave of S. Peter's are lighted in this way.

Exteriors. The greater number of Italian churches in towns are so hemmed in by buildings that frequently nothing is visible except the west or entrance front. The end of the choir sometimes rises above cloisters, but is seldom treated architecturally; either because funds failed or else because the authorities regarded as an

---

[1] In San Ambrogio, Milan, and in other Romanesque churches, the effect is the same; see Vol. II. pp. 169, 170.

Fig. 106.—San Francesco, Rimini.

Photo: Alinari.
Fig. 107.—Sant' Andrea della Valle, Rome.

[*To face p.* 137.

RENAISSANCE CHURCHES

unnecessary extravagance the embellishment of what they alone would see. There is no "back wall" in a Mediæval church; no corner neglected simply because it would seldom be seen. A Classic church is often all "back wall," except the actual front. Even when a church comes at the corner of two streets, and one side at least is visible to the public, an elaborate stone façade is accorded to the entrance end, whilst the sides remain in brick in very nearly carcase state. In that condition they are not necessarily ineffective. Their fine scale and simple lines often result in considerable dignity. But there is little that calls for description. In aisled churches the skeleton construction is much the same as in Mediæval days, except that buttresses are internal and not external. In this respect architects were simply following Roman precedent, as expressed in the Basilica of Constantine, Baths of Diocletian, Caracalla, etc., and also the general custom in Italy through all the centuries of the Middle Ages. Italians were ever averse to exposing and making a feature of structural necessities, and the architects of the Renaissance in particular carefully avoided any display of active strength, realizing that visible evidence of forces at work tend somewhat to produce a feeling of weakness. Their strength is always in reserve, and externally quite as much as internally they aimed at repose. For this reason flying buttresses, when they exist, are generally either hidden by lofty and continuous side walls, as in S. Paul's, London, or else are concealed under aisle roofs. When they show they seldom merit the epithet "flying." The buttresses of the Cathedral of Bergamo are of a not uncommon type; and the console shape is also frequently met with, as in the church of the Val de Grâce, Paris.

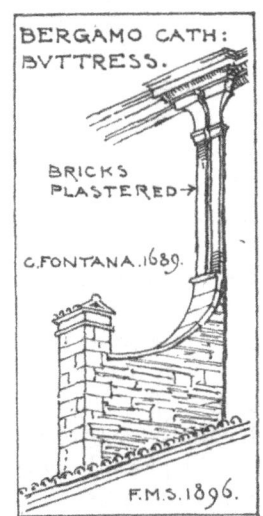

FIG. 108.

West façades.

In designing western façades for churches with either aisles or side chapels, the architects of the Renaissance were confronted by the same difficulty which had troubled their brethren centuries before. This was how to treat satisfactorily in elevation, or how to mask, the ugly sectional outline presented by a building with a lofty central nave, and side aisles of approximately half the height. They sometimes adopted the masking narthex of Early Christian churches, but rarely the twin towers of Mediæval. Their difficulties, moreover, were accentuated by their desire to use the "orders," and by the restrictions these imposed.

S. Francesco, Rimini.

The first to tackle the problem was Alberti. He solved it simply in the church of San Francesco, Rimini, by carrying one order the height of the aisles across the whole front, and over it, in the centre only, another order the width of the nave. His design was never finished, but it is clear that he intended the upper order to be crowned by a pediment, and the lower order to have two half pediments at the sides to stop the aisle roofs. This front would not have received so much attention if it had not been the first of Renaissance attempts; and if the fact had not been overlooked that Romanesque builders in southern countries frequently did much the same thing, although naturally with inferior proportions and details. The side of S. Francesco is superior in all respects to the front. Here Alberti retained the existing aisle wall of the Gothic church, but built in front of it a series of arched recesses to contain the sarcophagi of poets, philosophers, and artists, friends of Sigismondo Malatesta, Duke of Rimini, who ordered the rebuilding.

Alberti's next venture was at S. Andrea, Mantua. The situation here was complicated—perhaps it was really facilitated —by the tower of an earlier church which overlapped the front at the corner. A satisfactory façade seemed an impossibility, but the difficulty supplied the opportunity, as not infrequently happens in architecture, and Alberti filled the space available by a vast porch. This is not the full height of the church, but is of noble dimensions. In the centre is an arched opening 22 feet wide, and more than double that dimension in height, flanked by doorways which give it scale. Four pilasters, raised on pedestals, reach from the ground to the underside of the entablature, above which is a pediment, flat pitched as in Greek temples. The scheme is far grander than the one at Rimini, and historically it is of especial interest, as for the first time pilasters are carried through more than one storey. This front antedates by more than half a century similar pilaster treatment by Michael Angelo and Palladio.

S. Giorgio Maggiore.

The third notable front is that of San Giorgio Maggiore, Venice, designed by Palladio in 1560. At the end of the nave

Photo: Author.
Fig. 109.—San Sebastiano, Mantua.

Fig. 110.—Sant' Andrea, Mantua.
[*To face p.* 138.

Fig. 111.

[*To face p.* 139.

the architect placed one huge order, consisting of four great engaged columns raised on pedestals and crowned by a pediment. The ends of the aisles are much the same as at Rimini. The entablature of the smaller order at the sides is carried across the central part over the entrance doorway, the great engaged columns cutting through it. This façade must be seen to be appreciated. Photographs and drawings give no idea of its stateliness; dimensions little idea of its size. At first sight it seems such an obvious, simple thing to do, that one wonders it had not been done before, or that it has ever been departed from since. But it takes a strong man to do a simple thing; weaker men take trouble to show their cleverness. For the Redentore Church, Venice, Palladio designed a somewhat similar, but undoubtedly inferior front. The columns are not raised on pedestals, do not reach the full height of the church, and the pediment above them stops against an attic, the cornice of which ranges with the eaves of the roof. The design is more suitable for a projecting porch than for a front itself.

Notwithstanding the success of S. Giorgio, its design was seldom followed.[1] Later architects reverted to the treatment started by Alberti at Rimini, and made the centre of their façades two orders high. Of this character are the churches of the Gesù, Sant' Andrea della Valle (see Fig. 107), and Santa Maria in Campitelli, all in Rome, and many others too numerous to mention. Il Gesù was commenced by Vignola about 1568, and finished by Giacomo della Porta. The Jesuits, who in the sixteenth and seventeenth centuries obtained a commanding ascendency in ecclesiastical matters, employed this type of façade everywhere; not in Italy alone, but throughout Europe. At Paris is the church of S. Paul and S. Louis; at Avignon, in Southern France, there is a fine example, at Antwerp another, and there are many elsewhere. The aisle roofs of the Jesuit church in Rome stop against large scroll brackets. Similar brackets were first introduced in the front of Santa Maria Novella, Florence, by Alberti, or so it is stated on somewhat doubtful authority. They occur in many later churches in Italy and other countries, amongst them being the well-known church of the Val de Grâce, Paris. The façades of the other two churches were designed by Carlo Rainaldi in the middle of the seventeenth century, and resemble the Gesù, except that they have no side brackets. Their crowning pediments are

Later façades.

[1] The difficulty and expense of obtaining stones large enough may be the reason.

also somewhat barbarously broken in the manner affected by later architects, but the effect is undeniably fine.

<small>Masked fronts.</small>

In S. Peter's, Rome, and in some other large churches, mostly late in date, the sectional outline is ignored in the west front, and is masked by a narthex, porch, or portico. At S. Peter's, a narthex stretches the whole width of the church, and above it is a gallery of equal length. This is represented externally by a single order, with an attic above. Michael Angelo's original design was a projecting peristyle of fourteen huge detached columns, ten behind and four in the centre in front. In S. Paul's, London, a double tier of six pairs of detached columns stretch from aisle wall to aisle wall, flanked by towers, the wall of the nave being recessed behind the central columns to form a porch. The principal façade of San Giovanni in Laterano, Rome, is an open porch with gallery above, with columns and pilasters on its face which run through the two storeys. It was added by Alessandro Galilei in 1734, and is frankly a screen. As an example of late work it is worth recording; and although a trifle hard and suggestive of the teesquare, is fine in scale and on the whole simple in design.

<small>Portico fronts.</small>

The two churches facing the Piazza del Popolo, Rome, S. Maria di Monte Santo and S. Maria dei Miracoli, have porticoes in front; but neither church is of oblong plan, and the portico of each is merely the height of the side walls.

In the above examples, and in others that might be mentioned, the adoption of something in the nature of a "screen," saved the architects the trouble of reconciling the fronts with what came behind. They were perfectly justified in the course they took; and were by no means the first to take it. In many Mediæval churches a large portion of the *entrance* front of each is but a screen, with nothing behind it; as at Bourges, Rouen, Salisbury, Wells, etc. At Wells the result is so beautiful that nobody can cavil; at Salisbury the masking has been done but indifferently well. If the Classic men are to be blamed for their practice, the Goths cannot be allowed to go scot free. But when the result is beautiful architecture, it is better and fairer to blame neither.

S. PETER'S, ROME.

The largest and most important church in Christendom deserves something more than incidental reference. Most of the best known of Italian architects of the sixteenth and seventeenth

FIG. 112 (*Leslie Wilkinson*).

[*To face p.* 140.

centuries had a share in its building. The scheme for rebuilding and refortifying the portion of Rome which belonged to the popes, inaugurated by Pope Nicolas V. in 1452, entailed the destruction of the old basilican church of S. Peter, which had long been in a very dilapidated condition, and the building of a new church partly on its site. The pope died before his plan could be carried out, and the work was in abeyance for over fifty years. Early in the sixteenth century the project was revived by Julius II., who commissioned Bramante, at that time the best-known architect in Rome, to prepare an entirely new design for the church. The foundation stone was laid by the pope on 18 April, 1506, under the great south-west pier of the dome, known as S. Veronica's pier.[1]

Bramante's original plan (Fig. 113, A), which was proceeded with, was a square with a projecting apse on each side. Towers were intended at the four corners, and domes over the four chapels on the diagonals round the central dome. The arms were designed to be barrel vaulted as they are now. The four great piers at the crossing were began first, and before Bramante's death in 1514 they were finished, and some of the arches they support turned.[2] All effort apparently was concentrated on this portion, and no attempt made to begin the outside walls. In no other way can the discrepancies in the many tentative plans prepared by Bramante and his immediate successors be accounted for. In all, the central space remains the same, but the external walls vary considerably in outline. No foundations for these can have been built, otherwise the numerous changes could never have been suggested. Bramante either found it exceedingly difficult to make up his mind regarding the exact shape his building should take externally, or else failed to satisfy his clients. In another design (Fig. 113, B) attributed to Bramante, although the authorship is uncertain, aisles are carried round the external apses. These are retained, with modifications, in Peruzzi's plan (Fig. 113, C). Peruzzi, before

Bramante's design.

---

[1] The present S. Peter's follows the orientation of old S. Peter's and the majority of early churches in Rome; the entrance is at the east end, and the altar and choir are at the west.

[2] Vasari, p. 52, says, "In the arches of the edifice he (*i.e.* Bramante) also showed the manner in which they may be turned with movable scaffolds." The barrel vaults of the Amphitheatre at Arles, the side vaults of the Baths of Diana at Nîmes, and all the arches of the Pont du Gard, near Nîmes, are built in slices with straight joints, *i.e.* with no bond between them. The slices in the last-named are about 5 feet long. The vaults of S. Peter's were possibly built in this way, which would explain Vasari's remark.

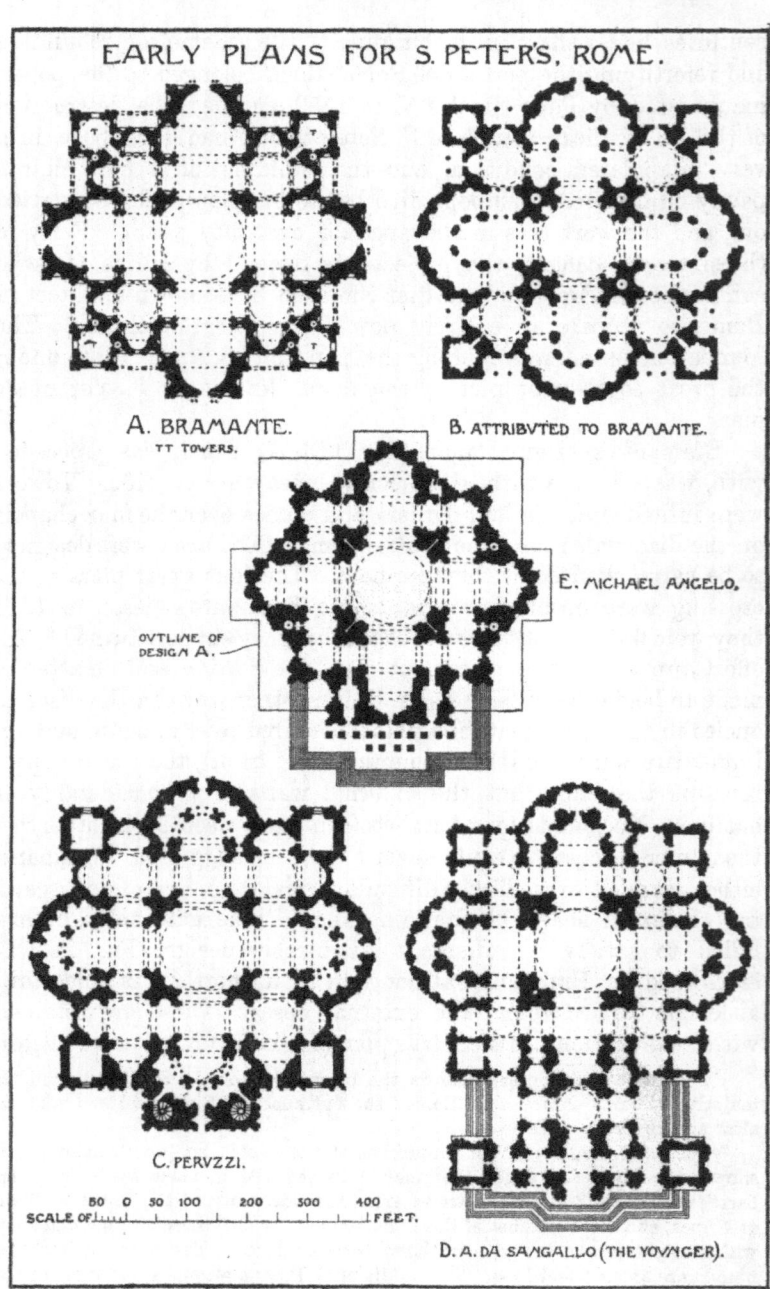

Fig. 113.

he was appointed architect to S. Peter's, acted for some years as assistant to Bramante, the latter being in bad health for a long time before his death. In all three plans columns are shown between the great piers. Bramante had probably learnt their scale-giving properties from San Lorenzo, Milan, and his study of ancient buildings in Rome would confirm him in his opinion of their utility.[1]

To Bramante belongs the credit for the plan of the central portion of the church, and the general internal ordinance, exclusive of the three end bays of the nave. He made several designs for the interior which are reproduced in von Geymüller's " Projets primitifs pour S. Pierre." One section shows two orders with a gallery above the aisles, and a quadripartite vault, another a single Doric order, with a gallery carried on columns between the piers as in Roman buildings. A third shows the design much as executed, a single Corinthian order carrying an entablature from which springs a barrel vault.

During the lifetime of Bramante, Peruzzi, apparently under his direction, made a plan with a long nave of three bays, similar in proportion and size to the Basilica of Constantine. After Bramante's death, the idea of a Latin cross was revived by his successors, Giuliano da San Gallo, Fra Giacondo, and Raphael, and plans are in existence showing long naves, which are ascribed to the two last. San Gallo retired after eighteen months, Giacondo died in 1515, and Raphael in 1520. Peruzzi succeeded, and the Greek cross again obtained the ascendancy. Design C, in Fig. 113, was probably made by him at this time. The capture of Rome in 1527 interfered considerably with the work, and delayed progress. Peruzzi, however, is said to have completed the south transept, and at his death in 1536, the barrel vaults surrounding the dome were apparently finished, and the great pendentives started. Antonio da San Gallo, the younger, was next appointed. Whatever were his faults, he was fully alive to the manifest superiority of a compact plan when a dome is the principal external feature in a design. Whilst, however, retaining the Greek cross, he suggested in front of it a huge pronaos, consisting of a long vestibule in front, flanked by detached towers, and an open porch behind, which was to be domed (see Fig. 113, D). Above the

Bramante's successors.

---

[1] Remembering the length of Bramante's sojourn in Milan, it is interesting to compare the early plans of S. Peter's, especially B and C, with the plan of San Lorenzo (see Vol. I. Fig. 154). They have many points of resemblance.

central entrance to the vestibule was to be a balcony, from which the popes could bless the people in the Piazza on State occasions. The idea was great, but unpractical. The pronaos would have been a noble entry to the largest church in Christendom, but the expense would have been enormous, and it would not have increased at all the accommodation of the church.

San Gallo's model.

San Gallo prepared a wood model of his scheme to a large scale, which is now in the model room in one of the great piers at the crossing, where also is preserved Michael Angelo's model for the dome. It is beautifully finished inside and out, and the Corinthian pilasters of the interior are shown much as at present. This is of importance, as it proves beyond a doubt that the internal ordinance was settled before Michael Angelo appeared on the scene. From the model it is clear that the pronaos would have been separated from the church to an extent difficult to realize from the plan. It would have interfered somewhat with the view of the dome from the Piazza, although not so fatally as the existing nave, but would have affected but little the view of it from the sides. As regards San Gallo's design for the church itself, the external walls are shown two main storeys in height, the lower Doric, the upper Ionic, separated by a pilastered mezzanine. The last is the chief blot. Under the dome were to be two drums, the upper set back behind the lower, each consisting of a number of arched openings with columned piers between, Colosseum fashion. The fault of the elevations throughout is over reduplication; and the criticism of San Gallo's successor, Michael Angelo, is fully justified, that the outside " was broken into too many parts, and with an infinity of columns."

M. Angelo at S. Peter's.

In 1546, Michael Angelo, at the age of seventy-one, was entrusted with the completion, with instructions to use the utmost despatch. He evidently felt that if the church were ever to be finished, its plan must be curtailed, and some of the adjuncts suggested by Bramante, and retained by Peruzzi, San Gallo, etc., omitted. He therefore cut out the squares at the external angles and the chapels alongside them, omitted the aisles round the apses, and made the latter merely the width of the arches supporting the dome. His omissions are clear from the outline surrounding his plan (Fig. 113, E). The gain in compactness was great, but much of the poetry of Bramante's plan was lost. The columns between the piers went definitely. San Gallo apparently did not propose to keep them; but their omission was a mistake. They might

Photo: *Alinari.*

FIG. 114.—S. PETER'S, ROME.

[*To face p.* 144.

easily have been retained between the great piers and the outside masses of walling, where they would have added interest and scale. Apart from the changes mentioned, the desire of Michael Angelo was evidently to complete Bramante's design as far as possible as the earlier architect would have wished. He told Vasari frequently, or so that writer declares, "that he was but executing the design and arrangements of Bramante, seeing that the master who first founded a great edifice is he who ought to be regarded as its author." Bramante had settled the internal ordinance, and that Michael Angelo left. The external ordinance is apparently entirely the latter's; but its single Corinthian order is a reproduction, to a slightly larger scale, of the order inside.[1] Fergusson, in his dislike for and desire to condemn the outside "gigantic order of Corinthian pilasters," conveys an altogether wrong impression when he states that "the great acanthus leaves of the Corinthian order, nearly seven feet in height, challenge attention everywhere." Most of the leaves are less than half that height. His dimensions may, by a stretch, be applied to the upper leaves of the capital if they are measured from the necking; but considering that these are, to a great extent, covered by the lower leaves, the statement is misleading. Their seven feet certainly does not challenge attention.

To Michael Angelo belongs solely the credit for the design of the drum and dome.[2] Bramante intended a hemispherical dome, stepped externally like that of the Pantheon, Rome, carried on a cylindrical drum surrounded by a continuous peristyle. The plain cylindrical drum immediately above the roofs—which from most points of view is invisible—was probably built before Michael Angelo took the work in hand. From this rises the drum proper, which was his design, also cylindrical, except that its curve is broken by sixteen projecting buttresses, which agree with the ribs of the dome above. On the face of each buttress is a pair of engaged columns. In the model for the dome, already referred to, curved consoles reach from the entablature above the buttresses to the springing of the dome below the ribs. These were omitted in execution. They would not have added material stability, but would have carried the eye upwards, tied drum and dome together, and intensified the pyramidal effect.

Drum and dome.

---

[1] The order outside, exclusive of the attic above and the basement below, is about 108 feet high; that of the interior is about 10 feet less.
[2] See p. 160 for the construction of the dome.

146   A HISTORY OF ARCHITECTURAL DEVELOPMENT

At Michael Angelo's death in 1564, the drum was finished, but the dome barely started. The portico in front of the principal entrance, consisting of detached columns 100 feet high, had just been commenced. Vignola succeeded, but did little except add the cupolas over two of the four squares at the angles. They are exceedingly graceful and well proportioned, and elsewhere would look well, but they are overpowered by the great dome alongside. The remaining pair were never built. The great dome was erected by Giacomo della Porta and Domenico Fontana, who departed somewhat from the model left by Michael Angelo (see p. 160). The work was begun in July, 1588, and finished in the incredibly short time of twenty-two months.

Later additions. If only the history of the building of this great church stopped here, many hundreds of pages of criticism would never have been written. Unfortunately, in an evil hour, Pope Pius V., early in the seventeenth century, decided to pull down Michael Angelo's partially finished front, and to build a long nave of three extra bays. The work was begun in 1606 by Carlo Maderno, who also designed the entrance narthex—against the interior of which nothing can be said—and built the front, utilizing Michael Angelo's columns, but making them engaged, instead of detached. In 1626 the church was consecrated, one hundred and twenty years after the laying of the foundation stone.

The Piazza. In 1666 Bernini was commissioned to lay out the Piazza and plan an approach. He could not undo entirely the harm Maderno had wrought, but in his encircling colonnade he designed the grandest example of a Doric peristyle since the Parthenon was erected at Athens. The central aisle is barrel-vaulted, whilst the sides have flat stone ceilings. The columns on the inside are 14 feet centre to centre, those on the outside have 16 feet 6 inches centres, but the difference is not markedly noticeable. This colonnade alone is a refutation of any statement that after the middle of the sixteenth century Italian architecture was necessarily debased and fantastic. Nothing could well have been simpler, and it is difficult to conceive of anything grander. What restraint the architect must have exercised! And yet in one history book Bernini is included amongst those who "practised this debased form of art . . . the Rococo or Baroco . . . which was followed in the seventeenth century." If elsewhere he indulged in extravagancies, they are washed out by this one work.

Faults in S. Peter's. That S. Peter's has faults nobody denies, but those faults are

Photo: Alinari.

FIG. 115.—PIAZZA OF S. PETER'S, ROME.

Photo: Alinari.

FIG. 116.—S. PETER'S, ROME, TRANSEPTS.

[*To face p.* 146.

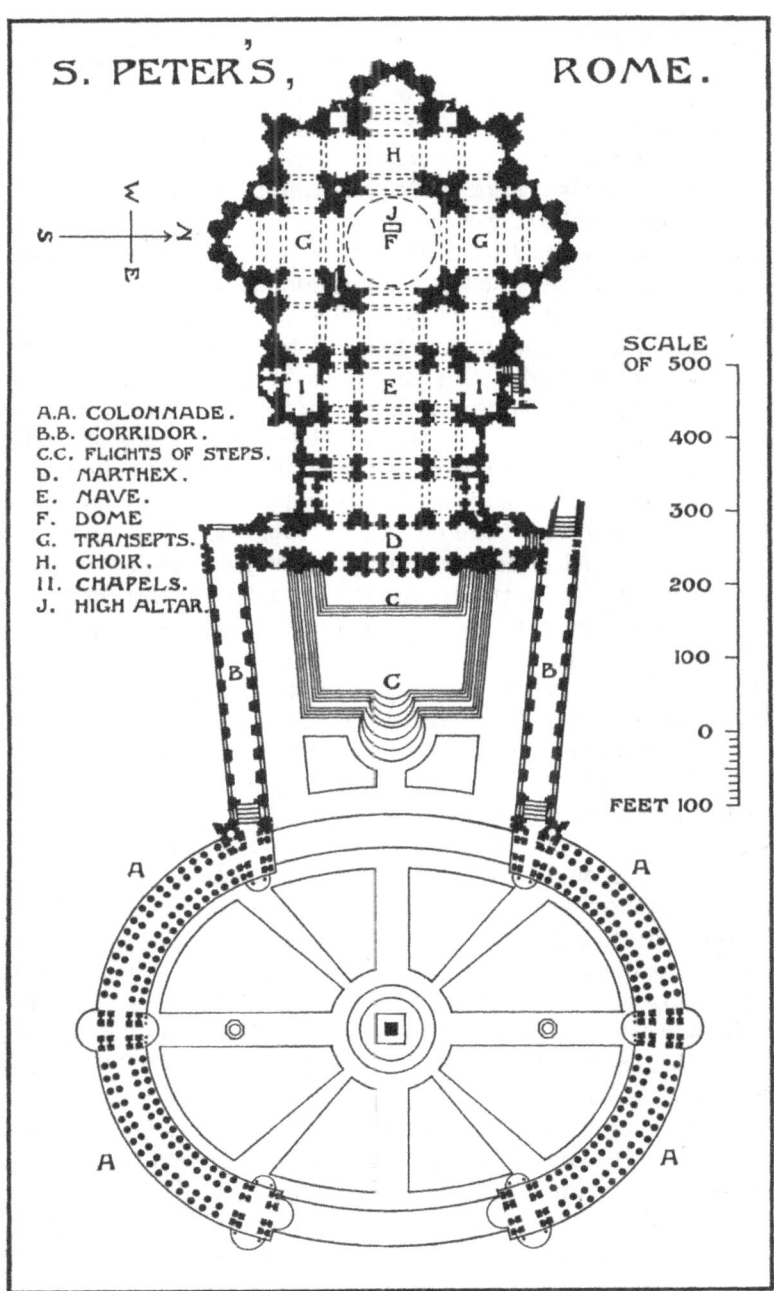

Fig. 117.

neither Bramante's nor Michael Angelo's. They are mostly in the three bays of the nave and in the entrance front. The exterior should be seen and judged from the west. Here one can realize what the effect all round would have been if Michael Angelo's adaptation of Bramante's Greek cross plan had been retained eastwards. Michael Angelo's intention was evidently to treat the external walls as a great plinth to the dome. Their parts are all designed with this object in view. The numerous straight-sided pilasters, close together and mostly in pairs, were purposely given but slight projection so that they should not appear too conspicuous, and yet should tell as vertical lines and carry the eye upwards. The projection of the main entablature is also slight—the fascias of the architrave and cornice sloping inwards considerably—and the entablature itself and the attic above much broken. An entablature with considerable projection and strongly marked horizontality would have tended to isolate the dome, and was therefore to be avoided. The numerous windows and niches between the pilasters give scale, and many are interesting in design, and recall the architect's secular buildings in Rome, on the Capitol, the Palazzo Farnese, etc. Those who believe that columns, pilasters and entablatures are unsuitable and immoral decorations for a wall surface, and find fault with the Colosseum in consequence, will condemn Michael Angelo's design. But if one admits the legitimacy of the treatment, one must also admit its success. In fact, there is no reason why one should not do the latter, whilst declining to allow the former. If there is anything in the contention that the outside of a church, or any other building, ought to express its internal divisions, few examples can be instanced which equal S. Peter's in this respect, excluding, be it understood, the added nave. The outside order agrees with the inside, the entablature marks the start of the vault, and the attic its height. One must admit that the side walls of the nave aisles and chapels are carried up higher than was strictly necessary, the walls flanking the chapels marked I on plan (Fig. 117) rising 50 feet or so above their roofs. But the whole design externally would have been ruined if they had been of less height than the walls of the transepts.[1] Little can be said in favour of the entrance front. Its chief fault is its great width. Some of the most famous of Gothic façades owe their reputation largely to the fact that they are wider than the church behind; Wells, Bourges, Rouen, are

[1] See remarks on S. Paul's, London, p. 290, about masking side walls.

Fig. 118.—S. Peter's, Rome, south elevation.

[*To face p.* 148.

Fig. 119.—S. Peter's, Rome (*Piranesi*).

[*To face p.* 149.

instances. But in all cases portions rise higher than others and form towers. In St. Peter's not only is the front much wider than the church with its chapels beyond—the width of which is already great—but the whole is of the same height. Towers were intended at the ends, and one was built and then pulled down. The contrast between the long, straight line of the parapet and the dome set back far behind is exceedingly unsatisfactory, except from a distance, when the projection of the nave is lost. When nearing S. Peter's it is best to feast one's eyes on the colonnade, and then shut them until the fine entrance vestibule is reached.

It is unfortunate that the worst portions of the church itself are those one sees immediately on entering. If one could skip the nave with its tawdry coloured marbles, and "lolling" figures, which appear to be trying to fall out of their spandrils, and go straight under the dome, or even under one of the barrel vaults surrounding the dome, one would hear less criticism and more praise. First impressions are so hard to eradicate. The great fault in S. Peter's is its sculpture; not its architecture. The sculpture throughout is unarchitectural. Figures are not framed in; they seldom fill the niches or spaces in or against which they stand or are placed. Their pointing arms and projecting legs are disturbing influences, and destroy the feeling of repose which the great architects of the Renaissance always strove for. The most offensive are the spandril figures above the side arches near the entrance, especially the figure on the left-hand side, from whose foot a globe is suspended. If these figures could be hacked off, and the white marble carvings sprigged on to the side pilasters of the piers gently removed, the gain would be enormous. Neither Bramante nor Michael Angelo would have tolerated either. The sculptured monuments and accessories also do their best to destroy scale instead of imparting it. Their authors were not content to let their work be judged by its own intrinsic qualities. They were afraid that it might not tell if they did not magnify; forgetting that all they were asked to do was to furnish the church, and that they were not called upon to compete with it in scale. *Interior.*

That S. Peter's is huge everybody knows; that it does not look its size most writers maintain. If it be judged empty, the latter contention is true; but an architect is entitled to claim that that condition is not a fair one. A church is for a congregation; and people give scale. A solitary visitor, if such were possible in S. Peter's, would be, and doubtless would feel, lost. The proper *People give scale.*

150 A HISTORY OF ARCHITECTURAL DEVELOPMENT

time to judge the church is when service is proceeding. Then it is possible to get some faint inkling of its size.[1]

Dimensions.   The following are the internal dimensions of the church. Authorities, however, differ, and more than approximate correctness must not be assumed.

Length of nave . . . 316 feet
Width of octagon . . 139 „
Length of chancel . . 158 „
———
Total length 613 feet
Width across transepts . . . . 455 „
„ of bay of nave nearest dome . . . . 79 „
„ of other bays of nave . . . . . . 87 „
Centre to centre of bays of nave (average) . 79 „
Height of nave, 151 feet to 152·6.

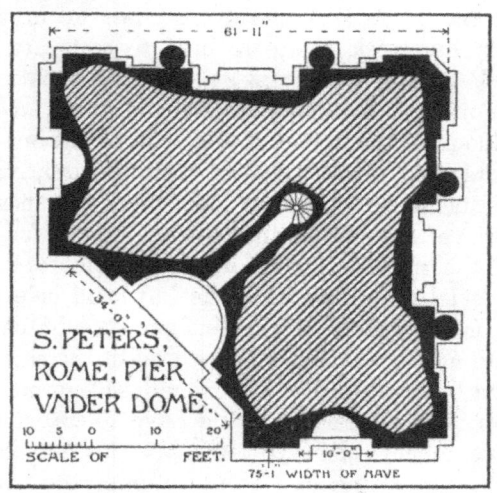

FIG. 120.

Great piers.   To realize the meaning of these dimensions is difficult. Perhaps nothing brings home more forcibly the actual size of the church than the dimensions of the great piers supporting the dome. Each pier measures over 60 feet along two sides, the width of an ordinary London street; and in area equals a fair-sized country church. In Bramante's original plan (see Fig. 113 A) they are shown less, but

[1] I realized its size one Sunday, when a congregation of 1000 to 2000, after service at the high altar under the dome, melted into the apse at the west end, leaving the rest of the church apparently empty.

before he had proceeded far he realized the necessity of an increase. Later plans show them as built, except for the niches on the outside faces which, according to von Geymüller, were filled in later by Antonio da San Gallo.[1] With such dimensions a practical necessity, it is difficult to see how the pilasters on the piers could have been smaller. In fact, under the dome they actually look too small. This is chiefly owing to the huge quadrangular pendentives above, each filled by a great circle, which crush everything below. These are the result of the filling in of the inside angles of the piers, which changed the plan from a square into an irregular octagon. No doubt the added bulk was an advantage and the carrying of the drum and dome was facilitated. But æsthetically it was an error. Nothing excels in beauty the curved lines of triangular-shaped pendentives on a large scale. Those of S. Sophia, Constantinople, are amongst the most effective features in the church. But the pendentives of S. Peter's are ugly; and if Bramante was responsible for their shape, which appears certain, this was his one mistake.

[1] See his "Projets primitifs," etc., Plate 45.

CHAPTER VIII

RENAISSANCE DOMES, THEIR DESIGN AND CONSTRUCTION

THE simplest form of dome, consisting merely of pendentives and saucer-shaped top, is used generally over aisles and side chapels in Renaissance churches in place of the intersecting vault common in Mediæval. In more important positions, the crossing of a church for instance, domes hemispherical or otherwise are carried on pendentives, as in earlier work. Most are raised on a tholos, or cylindrical drum, to give them greater height and prominence. In large Renaissance churches the drum is almost as important a feature as the dome itself, and receives special architectural treatment. When the space below is octagonal the dome is usually octagonal also, but not always; and occasionally an octagonal drum and dome are placed above a circular space, as in S. Maria de' Miracoli, Rome, although this is rare.

Windows. Windows are generally in the drum; and the surface of the dome above is unbroken, save at the apex where an open eye is covered by a lantern, as in Il Redentore, Venice. In a few instances, in addition to the windows in the drum, there are small ones in the dome, as in the Jesuit church, Rome. When there is no drum and light is a necessity, windows perforce are in the dome, as in the Pazzi Chapel, Florence (see Fig. 3). When a modicum of light is all that is required, the lantern at the crown supplies sufficient.

Materials of domes. Simple Renaissance domes are of timber, brick, or stone. The two first are covered with lead, and occasionally stone domes are also so covered. In Spain, Sicily, and Southern Italy tiles are sometimes substituted. Most effective are the many small domes of Palermo Cathedral, Sicily, with their different coloured glazed tiles.

Shapes of domes. A large proportion of domes are hemispherical. The majority of these, however, are stilted a little both externally and internally,

DESIGN AND CONSTRUCTION OF DOMES 153

to counteract the foreshortening which is inevitable when a dome of this form is looked at from below. The extrados is rarely exactly concentric with the intrados, no matter what the material employed may be. In this respect the Renaissance builders were

FIG. 121.

following precedent; as from the Pantheon, Rome, downwards the advantage of a greater thickness at the haunches than at the crown was recognized. Many domes, and amongst them some of the largest in existence, are pointed. Of these it is sufficient to mention the domes of Florence Cathedral, S. Peter's, Rome, S.

Paul's, London, Madonna del Calcinaio, Cortona, steep pitched and octagonal like Florence, S. Biagio, Montepulciano, La Superga, near Turin, the Panthéon, Paris, the last named excessively pointed, and many others.

Double domes. The majority of smaller domes consist of only a single thickness of stone, brick, or timber framing. Many larger ones, however, are of two or more thicknesses, and the dome visible from outside is not the dome seen from inside. Of this character is the larger of the two domes of S. Maria della Salute, Venice, where

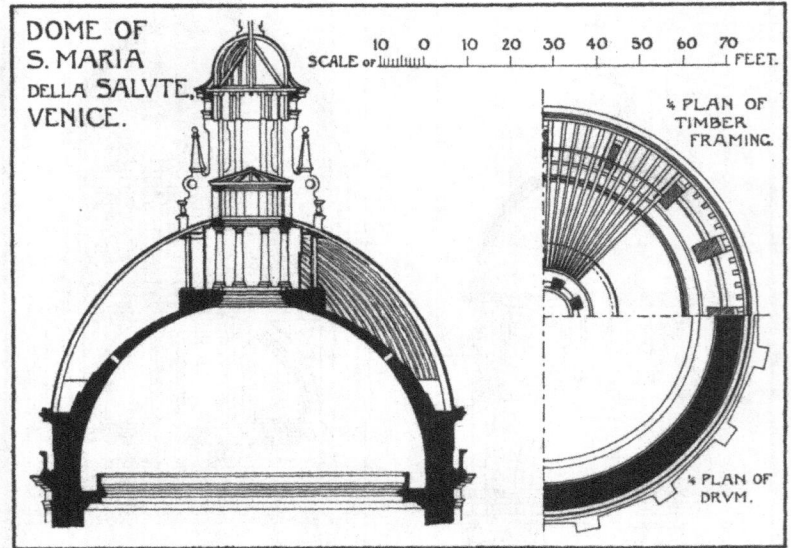

Fig. 122.

an inner shell of brick is hidden externally by timber framing. The outer covering was adopted in this and other instances partly as a protection and partly to add a few extra feet in height and give the dome additional emphasis. In the Salute church the timber framing is independent of the inner dome. In one of the churches at Piacenza, and in numerous other examples, it is carried on it. In La Superga, Turin, there are two domes, an outer and an inner, both of which start from the same springing line—the top of the attic above the drum—but are practically independent of each other. Both are pointed, the outer more acutely than the inner, and as its span is also greater, it consequently rises much higher. In the Val de Grâce, Paris, the lower dome is a complete hemisphere, and above it is an upper dome of timber the springing line of which is level with the crown of the dome below.

In some of the largest domes the construction is far more complicated. Five of the most important examples are selected here for comparison, irrespective of country. These are the domes of Florence Cathedral, S. Peter's, Rome, Les Invalides, Paris, S. Paul's, London, and the Panthéon (S. Geneviève), Paris. When domes of a single thickness are raised on drums there is sometimes a fear that the height necessary for external effect will result in

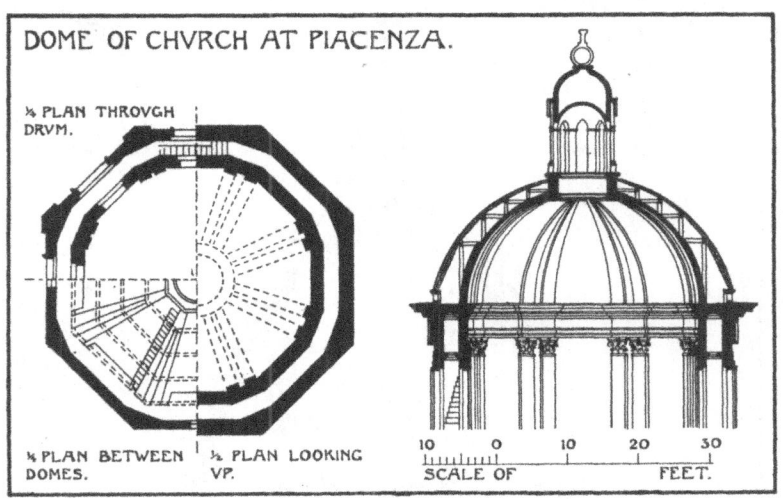

FIG. 123.

bad proportions internally. The constructions of the last three examples mentioned were adopted to circumvent this difficulty.

The pointed form was chosen for the dome of Florence Cathedral, partly because it exercises less thrust than a semicircular, and is better adapted for carrying a stone lantern, and partly because it foreshortens less rapidly, and also actually rises much higher than a hemispherical dome. Brunelleschi's ambition was that his dome should dominate the city from all points. Hence his insistence on the drum; although he was well aware that this added to his difficulties, and separated the lateral thrusts of the dome from their natural abutments. The drum, like the space below and the dome above, is octagonal in plan. It is about 16 feet thick and nearly 40 feet high; some 12 feet or so higher

Florence Cathedral dome.

156   A HISTORY OF ARCHITECTURAL DEVELOPMENT

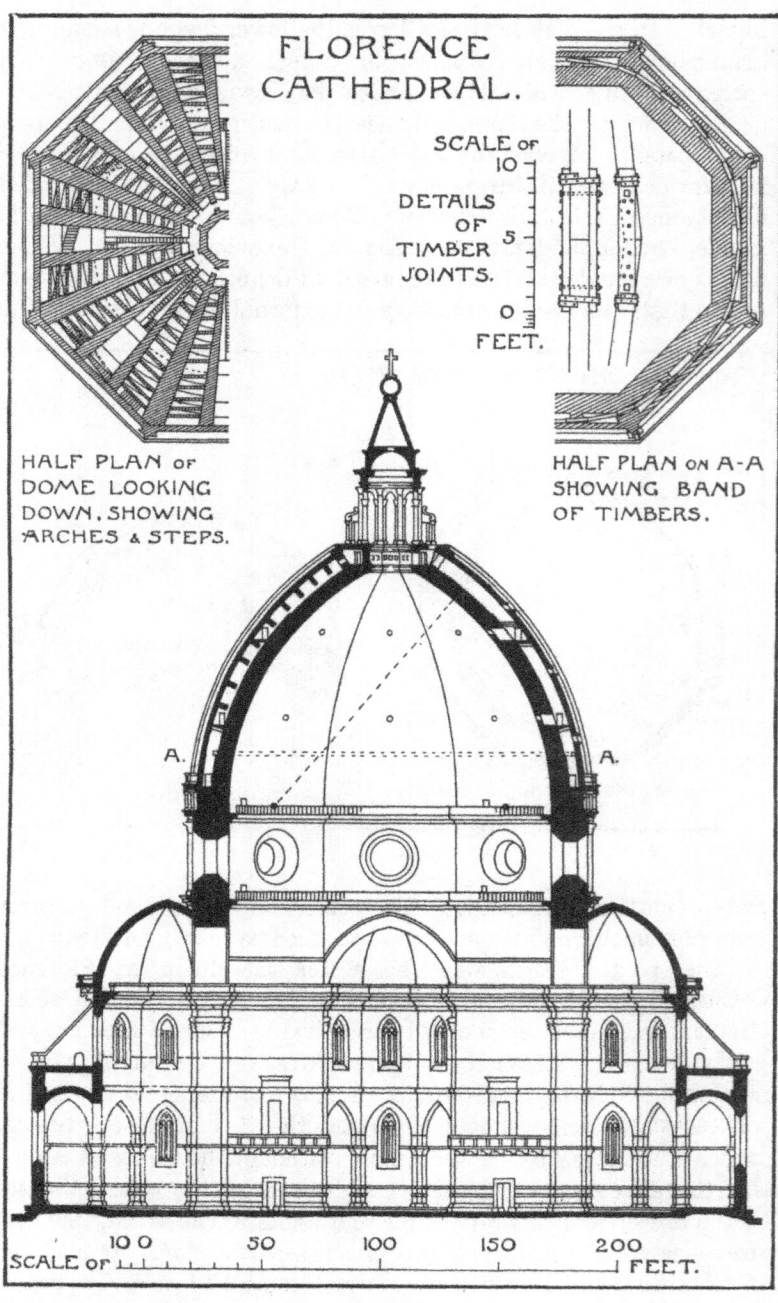

Fig. 124.

DESIGN AND CONSTRUCTION OF DOMES 157

than the 15 braccia he stipulated for when he laid his scheme before the committee. The dome is solid for the first 10 feet. This portion is built of carefully selected stones dowelled and clamped together. Above, it rises in two shells practically concentric. For about half the height these are also of stone, brick being used for the remainder. The inner shell is about 7 feet thick, the outer about 2 feet 7 inches at the base, tapering to 2 feet at the crown. The space between is from 4 to 5 feet wide. These shells, however, are not the main construction. From the eight corners rise eight great ribs, in between which are two inter-

Fig. 125.

mediate ribs on each side. All these ribs, both principal and intermediate, are the full thickness of the two shells plus the space between, in fact the angle ribs are deeper still as they project and show externally. The intermediate ribs are each about 6 feet wide at the springing, and narrow to about 2 feet at the top, where they, together with the angle ribs, butt against the octagonal ring of heavy masonry which carries the lantern. Nine flat segmental arches are thrown across from one great angle rib to another on each side. These clip and bond with the intermediate ribs, and also bond with the outer shell; thus stiffening and tieing all parts together.

Galleries.   Running round the dome, piercing the ribs, are two galleries, at, approximately, one-third and two-thirds of its height. These are constructed of large stones, which help to tie the inner and outer shells. Below the lower gallery is a bonding course of heavy timbers in 24 lengths, with timber fish-plates at all junctions bound by iron bands. These timbers are embedded in the masonry. Near the base of the dome, immediately above where the ribs separate, are chains of iron, also embedded; and there is possibly another chain above the timber band, but if it exists it is entirely concealed. These chains and bands were necessary, owing to the absence of abutment occasioned by the high drum.

Absence of centering.   Brunelleschi stated that he would dispense with centering—at least, for the lower half of the dome; and he is generally credited with having accomplished this feat, although how he succeeded is not exactly certain. He would experience no difficulty in building the solid 10 feet at the base without it, and possibly little up to the first gallery, or even to a point between the two galleries, which is about halfway. Above that he did not commit himself in his original statement. It is sometimes taken for granted that he dispensed with centering altogether. But this is doubtful. The probability is that he followed to some extent old Roman methods. The Romans used very light centers for their vaults and domes; merely sufficient to carry skeleton ribs, which, when they had set, were relied upon as permanent centers (see Vol. I. pp. 119–121). Possibly Brunelleschi acted in the same manner, building his ribs, after he had reached a certain point, in single rings, and as each ring set proceeding with the next. There is no doubt that a considerable amount of timber was employed during the building of the dome, as all accounts tell of strong platforms going across from side to side at different levels. These must have been solidly constructed, as they supported restaurants for the workmen, to save the loss of time which descending for meals and ascending again would have entailed. From these platforms a good deal of strutting-up could be done; and from them probably started light centers for the upper portions of the ribs. This suggestion does not conflict with Brunelleschi's statement, as such centering would be very different from that which the master-masons of the time said was necessary.

Stairs, etc.   The small details that make for convenience are as carefully studied in the dome as the bigger problems of construction. Access to all parts is easy, and all parts are well lighted. Flights of steps lead up to the second gallery, whence steps formed on the extrados of the inner shell lead direct to the lantern. Many small circular openings in the outer shell light the passages and staircases, and some extra light also comes from openings in the inner.

Whilst giving Brunelleschi full credit for his originality and ingenuity, it is of some interest to investigate to what extent he was indebted to earlier domes for the germ of his design. The idea may have been suggested to him either by Roman vaults and domes, with their skeleton ribs and connecting-bond courses, or else by the dome over the Baptistery in his native city, with the construction of which he must have been well acquainted. In the

Prototypes.

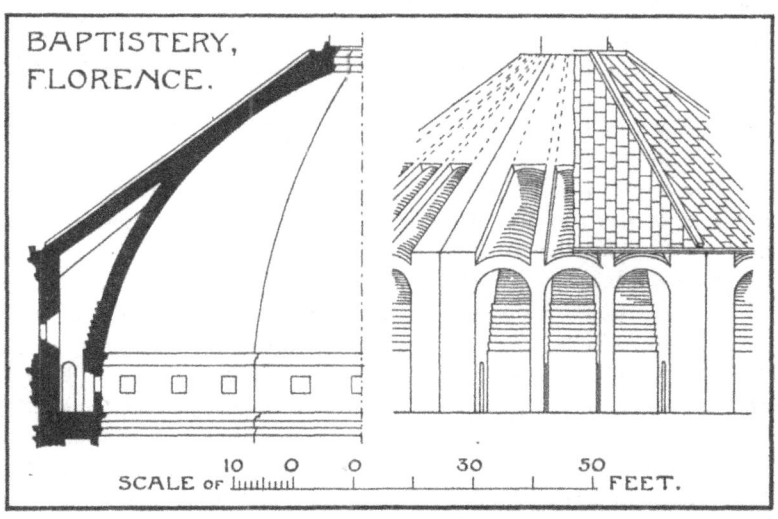

FIG. 126.

Baths of Gallienus, Rome, a decagonal building covered by a hemispherical dome, a strong rib of brickwork rises from each internal angle, the ten ribs meeting and uniting with a ring at the top round a central eye. There are also twenty intermediate ribs—which, however, stop far short of the ring—and, in addition, horizontal bonding courses.[1] Other domes in Rome are similarly designed. The Baptistery of Florence is an octagonal building of the early twelfth century, about 85 feet in diameter. It is covered

[1] Considerably more of this dome is shown in Piranesi's drawing of it, published in 1756, than exists now; and in Brunelleschi's time it was probably in a still better state of preservation.

by a pointed dome in brick, with strong angle ribs and two intermediate ribs on each side. Above the ribs start three barrel vaults, which die on to the extrados of the dome, concealing it externally, and forming a flat-pitched covering. This design could not have been adopted in its entirety for the Cathedral, as the desire of everybody was that the Cathedral dome should show as a landmark. It evidently did not satisfy Brunelleschi entirely, otherwise he would not have spent so many years in Rome studying the solution of the great problem. Still, between the two there is sufficient resemblance to claim that Brunelleschi, whilst utilizing his acquired knowledge of antique examples, was also continuing and developing methods of dome construction, which for centuries had been vernacular in Italy. The dome of the Baptistery of Florence is not the only Mediæval one built in this fashion. In the dome over the Baptistery of Cremona, built some fifty years later, the same construction was followed.

Dome of S. Peter's, Rome.
The dome of Florence Cathedral has been treated at length, because, besides being the first of the great domes of the Renaissance, it is also the most complex. The dome of S. Peter's, Rome, is somewhat similar in construction, but is circular in plan, and has no cross braces. Its diameter is about the same as that of the Florentine dome, being 139 feet internally.[1] Above the main entablature which crowns the drum is an upper drum, or attic. This attic and the haunches of the dome, as high as about 40 feet above the entablature, are solid. From that point start two shells, which are not quite concentric, the outer shell, which is much the thinner, being the steeper. Sixteen great ribs of stonework, the full thickness from intrados to extrados, bond with the shells and carry the stone lantern. The curving shells between the ribs are of brick, laid herring-bone fashion. Michael Angelo intended originally a third and inner shell, a true hemisphere, which appears in his model. This was omitted in execution. It is doubtful if it would have improved the internal proportions; but would probably have been a gain structurally, as it would have counteracted to some extent the lateral thrusts of the upper shells, and also increased somewhat the thickness of the brickwork immediately above the outer and inner entablatures. This is the weakest portion; and it is here that some of the worst cracks were discovered in 1742, when the commission was appointed to report on

[1] The diameter of S. Peter's dome is also stated to be 137·6. The Florence dome is about 138.

DESIGN AND CONSTRUCTION OF DOMES

the stability of the dome.[1] The thrusts of the great ribs are, in appearance, counteracted by the buttresses which project from the drum, but these are too low down to be really efficient. The consoles which Michael Angelo intended to place above them (see p. 145) would have remedied this defect a little, but not much. Further resistance to thrusts is afforded by the iron chains which surround the dome, imbedded in the lower half of the inner shell, one being near the springing, and the uppermost about halfway

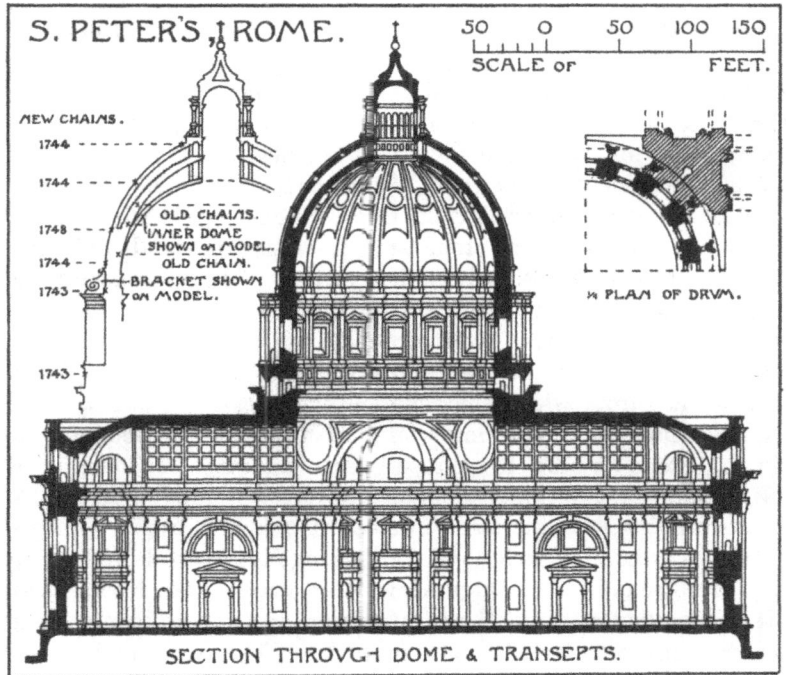

FIG. 127.

between it and the eye. Between 1743 and 1744 five more chains were added as follows: at the top and bottom of the drum, below the lantern, just above the attic, and at about half the height of the dome. In 1748 a sixth was placed between the two last.

Although the domes of Florence Cathedral and S. Peter's, Rome, have each two shells, the space between them in both examples is inconsiderable, and the shells are also united by the ribs. In the three remaining examples to be considered each

Dome of S. Paul's, London.

[1] The defects in the dome are partly due to great haste in building (see p. 146).

has three separate and distinct shells or domes, one above the other. S. Paul's, London, is the most ingenious. The dome covers an irregular octagon, formed by eight oblong piers of brick faced with stone, each averaging about 30 feet long by about 10 feet wide (see plan, Fig. 238).[1] Above these piers and the barrel vaults which spring from them rises a plain cylindrical drum, as in S. Peter's, which carries the principal drum and its surrounding peristyle. The sides of this drum are not vertical, but incline inwards, diminishing the diameter internally from 110 feet at the level of the "whispering" gallery to 102 feet at the springing of the inner dome. This "batter" is quite imperceptible outside from below, and is barely noticeable inside. The inner dome is of brick, 18 inches thick, and is pointed in outline, except that its apex is cut off by an eye 20 feet in diameter. In its haunches, which are thicker and of stone, are embedded iron chains. From the haunches rises a brick cone, also 18 inches thick, with a stone apex and five bands of stone at approximately equal distances. In each band is embedded another chain. This cone carries the stone lantern which crowns the outer dome. Its sides are pierced with numerous oval openings for light, and at the top there is an eye smaller than the eye in the dome below. From the haunch from which the cone springs rises a vertical wall, or upper drum—far more important than the corresponding attic in S. Peter's—which is pierced with windows. Connecting it with the cone and inner dome are thirty-two stone buttresses—corresponding with the same number of columns in the peristyle below—pierced by circles and by openings to allow of free circulation all round. The outer dome is of wood covered with lead. Its timbers start from these buttresses, the upper beams being carried on corbels built into the cone. The considerable space between the outer dome and the cone, occupied by these framed trusses, is lighted by the windows in the upper drum, and also by eight openings at the apex of the dome, immediately below the gallery round the lantern. These openings are barely perceptible from below, but are really of considerable size. Wren doubtless devised them in place of the customary "lucarnes," in order to retain the surface of his dome unbroken. A certain amount of light also enters this space through the eye of the inner dome and the openings in the cone.

[1] The total of the area of these eight piers does not equal the area covered by one pier of S. Peter's, Rome.

DESIGN AND CONSTRUCTION OF DOMES

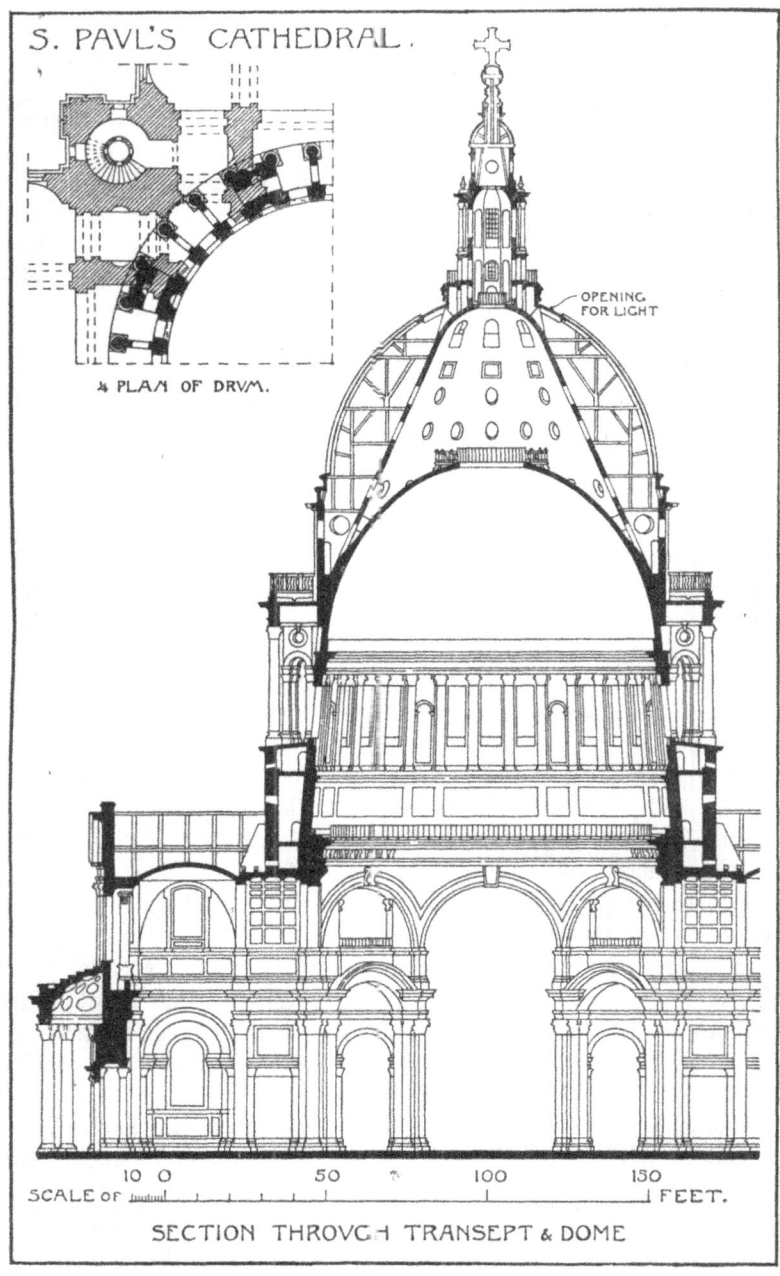

Fig. 128.

The peristyle which surrounds the principal drum on the outside is a very beautiful feature. It is also a great structural asset. Only half the columns are detached, and these only partially so, as behind them are pilasters from which arches are carried across to corresponding pilasters on the wall of the drum. In every fourth intercolumniation the columns are engaged, the space between them being filled in solid with a niche in the centre of each. Too high praise cannot be given to this arrangement. The gain in apparent strength is enormous, and in actual strength not inconsiderable. From behind the solid masses arches are thrown across to the top of the drum, providing abutment where it was most necessary, just below the haunch of the inner dome from which starts the cone. Altogether, the disposition of thrust and counterpoise is perhaps the most scientific that any building Classic or Mediæval can boast. It is a triumph to Wren the mathematician as great as the beauty which resulted from it is a triumph to Wren the architect.[1] (See also Fig. 239.)

Dome of Les Invalides, Paris. The dome of the famous church which forms part of the Hôtel des Invalides, Paris, is also triple. From an ordinary cylindrical drum starts a truncated dome, about 82 feet in diameter, which, however, is not much more than a haunch, as the upper portion is cut away to form a vast circular opening, or eye. Through this is seen an intermediate dome, elliptical in outline, which is covered with paintings. These are exceedingly well lighted by windows in an upper drum which, quite invisible from below, throw a flood of light upwards. The effect is striking. The third dome, the one that shows from outside, and its lantern are of timber framing covered with lead.

The fine appearance of the church outside is largely due to its plan, which is square, and to the two lofty drums on which the dome is raised. The arms are comparatively low and the pyramidal grouping is excellent. Not a little of the reputation the dome enjoys is due to the lavish gilding of the leadwork. This is a lesson on a large scale of how important it is that gold should be massed, if it is used at all.

Dome du Panthéon, Paris. The central dome of the Panthéon, Paris, is the smallest of the five domes mentioned, being only 68 feet in diameter. This is the

---

[1] The central dome over S. Isaac's, S. Petersburg, is an exact repetition of the triple design of S. Paul's, carried out in iron, mostly cast. The church was built by the French architect, De Montferrand, about a hundred years ago. The dome of University College, London, is another copy on a smaller scale.

Fig. 129.—Dôme des Invalides, Paris.

Fig. 130.—Le Panthéon, Paris. [*To face p. 164.*

DESIGN AND CONSTRUCTION OF DOMES 165

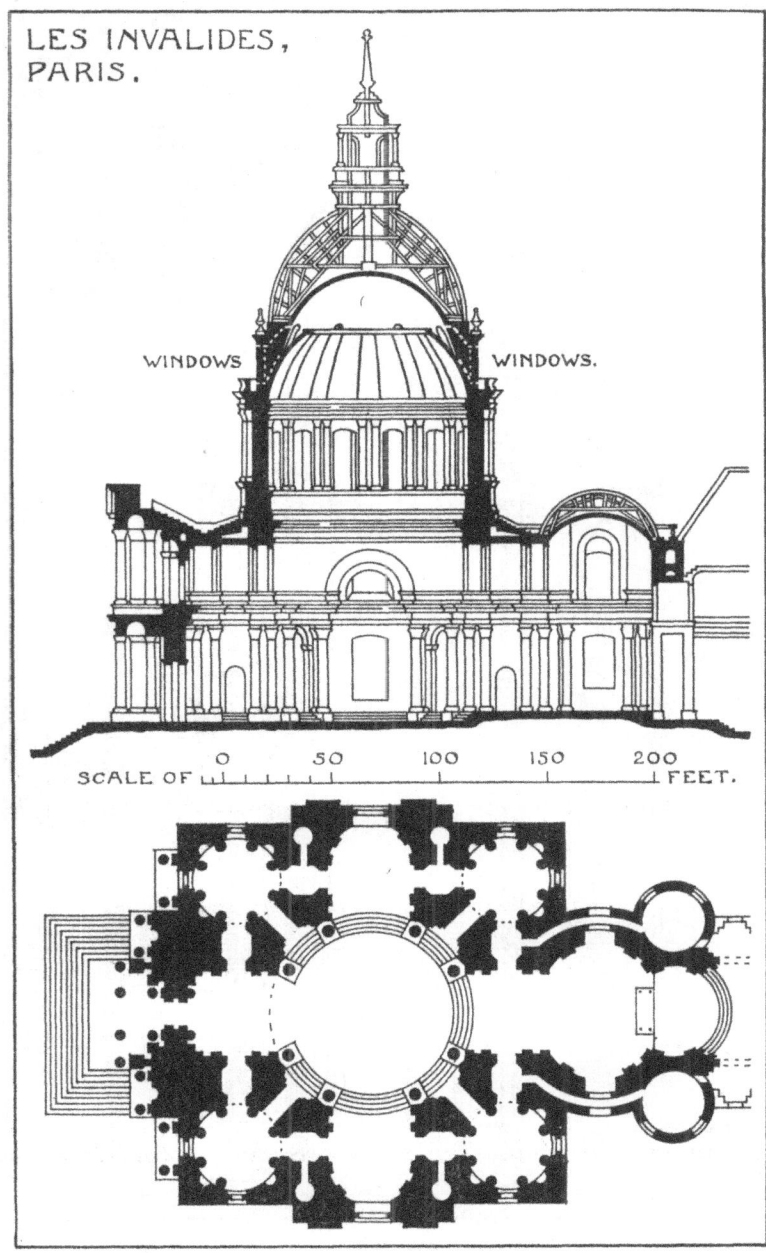

Fig. 131.

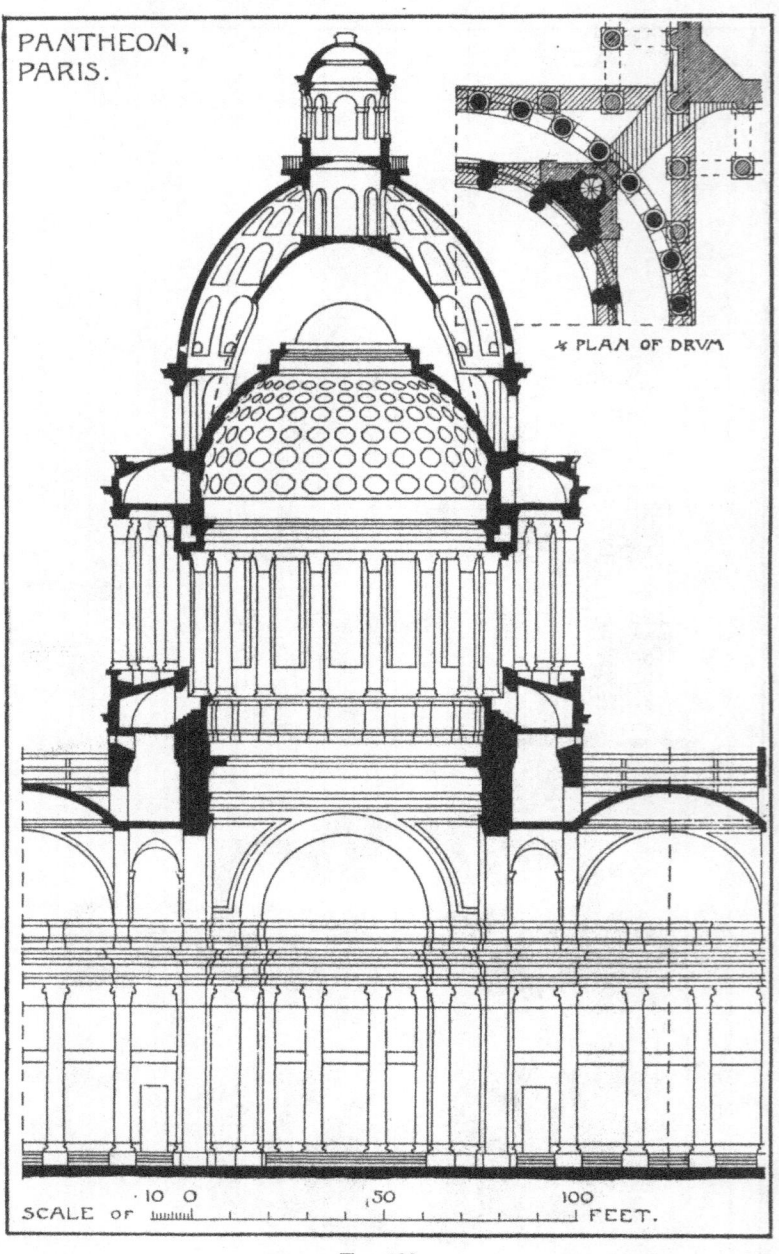

Fig. 132.

only church with the triple division in which all three domes are of stone. The lowest has an eye about 31 feet in diameter, and through this, as in Les Invalides, appears a painted dome. This intermediate dome is elliptical, but its sides are cut away to form four large semicircular-headed openings. Through these the light from the windows in the upper drum enters the church below the painted dome. The lower drum is surrounded by a continuous peristyle which neither imparts nor has the appearance of imparting the abutment that is so ably obtained by the peristyle of S. Paul's, London. The upper drum carries the dome proper. The stone lantern is principally carried on the intermediate dome, which in this respect answers to the cone of S. Paul's, London, but it receives some additional support from and is buttressed by the top dome. The construction of the church throughout is most daring, almost foolhardy (see p. 222), and the top dome is literally only a shell. At its springing it is 19 inches thick, but even this thickness is not continued throughout. Four tiers of arched recess are formed one above the other on the inside, with the result that the greater part of the dome is less than a foot thick. The dome and lantern may be safe, but they rock considerably in a high wind.[1] The dome appears a much better shape when seen from a distance than from near, when it foreshortens too rapidly. The great width of the portico also kills it when the two are seen in conjunction. A tetrastyle portico might have been an improvement. The four arms of the church are covered by saucer domes on pendentives, which are extremely graceful examples of their kind. They do not show externally, as they are under the timber roof. (See also section, Fig. 187).

[1] As I experienced one September when in the lantern.

CHAPTER IX

THE EARLY RENAISSANCE IN FRANCE

Introduction. THAT the Renaissance started later in France than in Italy is no matter for wonder. The French had centuries before perfected a style of architecture to which they were deeply attached, and the masons and other craftsmen were steeped in its traditions. For nearly a hundred years previous to the middle of the fifteenth century, however, work had been almost at a standstill. Owing to constant wars, internal feuds, and the weakness of the kings, the greater part of the northern half of the country, from the Loire to the Somme, was a desert. The peasant population had been exterminated, or had fled for shelter to the towns. The end of "the Hundred Years' War" and the accession of Louis XI., in 1461, marked a change. Gradually brigandage disappeared, and the country settled down. The land was tilled once more. Moreover, the kingdom became united under one ruler to an extent unknown previously. The great counts and dukes of the far southern and northern provinces were reduced in power and brought into line. The old feudalism of the Middle Ages was subdued and crushed; and the nobility never succeeded again in obtaining a tithe of their former strength. Under Louis XI. France embraced the greater part of what is now included under that title, Brittany being still independent, and forming the most important exception. With peace, coupled with a great revival in commerce and agriculture, came prosperity; and with prosperity a great increase in building activity. When that followed, it was natural for the craftsmen to try and pick up the threads that had been dropped in the interval. As in the land of the "Sleeping Beauty," when the sleepers awoke, the turnspit recommenced turning the spit, the women their weaving, the men their usual vocations; so in France in the middle of the sixteenth century work continued as though no break had ever occurred. Doubtless the craftsmen had heard of the art revolution in Florence; but they had had enough of revolution. Their minds harked back to the achievements and methods of their forefathers, and an Indian summer in Gothic art during the last forty years of the century was the result.

To René I., poet, artist, and art-lover, Duke of Anjou, Count of Provence, and titular King of Naples, belongs the credit of introducing the Renaissance into France, although his dominions did not come under the French Crown until after his death in 1480. The second son of the King of Naples, he knew that town well, and was also acquainted with other cities in Italy. Interesting evidence of his personal knowledge of the Renaissance movement in that country is afforded by the magnificent coloured relief by Luca della Robbia, emblazoned with the arms of Anjou and other heraldic devices which was made in honour of his visit to Florence in 1442.[1] René was a collector of medals, and in 1460 he invited Francesco Laurana, a Florentine sculptor and medallist, to his Court. Francesco lived there for seven years, but does not appear to have carried out any architectural work. In 1475, however, he returned to France, after an absence in Sicily, and between then and 1483 executed the small chapel of S. Lazare in the old cathedral of Marseilles, the tomb of the Comte du Maine in Le Mans Cathedral, and a sculptured retable for one of the altars in the church of S. Didier at Avignon. The first-named may be regarded as the earliest example of Renaissance architecture in France. It consists of a central column and two side pilasters, the panels of which are carved with Renaissance detail, supporting two arches, whilst above is an entablature, crowned by two segmental pediments. All the detail is very delicate, and more characteristically Venetian than Florentine. Laurana was evidently, like Filarete, a travelling sculptor, and one not averse to working out of his own country.[2]

Influence of King René.

King René's early welcome to the Renaissance is interesting; but it can hardly be said to have had any lasting results. It was but an episode. During the reigns of Louis XI. and Charles VIII. (1461–98), Gothic traditions still ruled. The additions made by the latter king to the castle at Amboise, soon after his marriage with Anne de Bretagne—by which alliance Brittany passed

Under Louis XI. and Charles VIII. work Gothic.

---

[1] This huge plaque is in the Victoria and Albert Museum, and is as valuable for its artistic qualities as for its historic associations.

[2] In the old cathedral of Marseilles is also a characteristic white relief by Luca della Robbia, who died in 1482.

definitely to the French Crown—show no trace of the new spirit. The little chapel of S. Hubert, within the castle precincts, is a pure and beautiful example of late Gothic, possessing withal a richness that no Renaissance building can rival. Even in the following reign, that of Louis XII., all churches and most secular buildings were Gothic throughout; for instance, the fountain called after the king at Blois; the front of the château in the same town, etc., although in the latter a few bits of Renaissance ornament have crept in as though by accident.

Expedition into Italy. The incident that hastened the spread of the Renaissance in France—it can hardly be said to have caused it, because its introduction was inevitable—was the expedition of Charles VIII. into Italy in 1494, to enforce his claim to the crown of Naples. This curious march, almost without parallel in history, was by permission, in some cases by invitation, of the different Italian powers. But both permission and invitation were bitterly regretted when it was discovered that the king regarded the greater part of the country as his by right of conquest, and that his followers behaved as though they had won great victories. No sooner had Charles entered Naples in triumph than a league was formed behind his back by the States he and his army had bitterly offended, and in the following year he was forced to cut his way back through Italy to France. Although the expedition, politically, was a failure, from the point of view of the development of French architecture it was a success. Pisa, Florence, Rome, and other cities had been entered, and their buildings, so different from any in France, must have been a revelation to the whole army, from the king downwards. At Florence especially, at that time the wealthiest and most powerful of Italian cities, the majesty of its palace façades, the richness of the internal decorations, and the skill lavished on all articles of every-day use, cannot but have opened the eyes of all to the force and beauty of the new movement. On the other hand, the power of the French king—such an army as his had never taken the field before—and the evident wealth of the French nobility, must have convinced many Italian craftsmen that there was another market for their wares, another country where they might practise their art with possibly greater profit than in their own. That several found their way into France in the wake of the army seems certain. M. Léon Palustre[1] states that the gardens and pictures appealed more to the French

---

[1] "L'architecture de la Renaissance."

than the buildings, and that the king only brought back with him gardeners, painters, and the like. He quotes letters from Cardinal Briçonnet, Bishop of S. Malo, to the queen, and from Charles himself, in which Naples is described as "ung paradis terrestre." Mention, however, is made by Commines, the historian, of "plusieurs ouvriers excellens en plusieurs ouvraiges, comme tailleurs et peinctres" brought from Naples, and it is impossible not to feel, as argued later, that much of the early Renaissance carving in France is the work of Italians.

Charles's excursion into Italy was only the first of several. His successors, Louis XII. and Francis I., on more than one occasion followed suit. Louis marched in triumph through the northern towns to the very outskirts of Venice, and Francis continued the fighting until the treaty of 1515, when he and Pope Leo X. met at Bologna with great state on both sides. These facts are sufficient to show that in the last few years of the fifteenth century, and in the first two decades of the sixteenth, the French had many opportunities of studying the buildings in all parts of Italy, and that Italians received encouragement to settle in France. The greatest Italian artist who was induced to take service under a French king was Leonardo da Vinci. Between 1506 and 1513 he was mainly in Milan, at that time in possession of the French, and three years later he came to live in France itself. But his health was failing, and his few remaining years he spent in curious scientific speculation, and troubled little about art. He died at Amboise in 1519.[1] *Later Italian expeditions.*

The real start of the Renaissance was made on the banks of the Loire. Towards the end of the fifteenth century, and during the first twenty years of the century following, this district was the favourite of the French kings. The Court was more often at Amboise, Blois, or Loches, than at Paris. Charles VIII. was born and died in the château of Amboise; Louis XII. was born and bred in the château of Blois. Orleans counted itself second to no town in France; and Tours and Loches were both places of importance. Amongst early efforts in which the Renaissance is introduced tentatively may be mentioned Louis XII.'s wing of the château of Blois, already mentioned, the Hôtel d'Alluye in the same town, the tomb of the children of Charles VIII. in Tours Cathedral, and the original Hôtel de Ville at Orleans. Louis's front at Blois is *Start on the Loire.*

---

[1] Flying machines interested him especially, and he got near to solving the problem.

Gothic, but in the panels of each alternate pier of the arcade on the courtyard side is Renaissance carving, and the capitals have the acanthus leaf the ancients loved. In the courtyard of the Hôtel d'Alluye, in the frieze separating the upper gallery from the lower arcading, are terra-cotta medallions of the Cæsars surrounded by wreaths. There can be little doubt that these are Italian, and were probably executed in Italy and thence shipped to France. The tomb of the children of Charles VIII., according to M. Palustre, was executed about 1506, under the direction of the French sculptor, Michel Colombe, by his nephew and an Italian, Girolamo di Fiesole. The same remark applies to the contemporary tomb of Francis, Duke of Brittany, in Nantes Cathedral. The design of the Hôtel de Ville at Orleans is stated to be by the architect Charles Viart. The whole is Gothic, with the exception of some capitals, and the curious arched corbel cornice which is one of the characteristics of much of the early work of the district. If the façade of the charming little Hôtel de Ville at Beaugency is also rightly ascribed to Viart, that architect must have made great progress in his study of the Renaissance during the twenty years or so that separate the two buildings. In the Beaugency building there is hardly a trace of Gothic feeling left.[1]

Italian carvers.

To what extent Italian workmen were employed on the above and on somewhat later work is uncertain. In the case of the two tombs mentioned, Frenchmen may have carved the figures, and Italians—at Nantes a compatriot of Girolamo's was also engaged—the architectural accessories. The French carvers of the period, like their brethren of England and Germany, were very expert; as is shown in the little chapel of S. Hubert, Amboise, in the doorways and porches of many late churches and cathedrals, Beauvais, Abbeville, S. Maclou, Rouen, etc., and in the fittings in these and other churches. But however expert technically a craftsman may be, he can no more carve ornament successfully in a style he has not had opportunities of studying, than an author can write in a language with which he has but a nodding acquaintance. The suggestion that Italians were the carvers of Renaissance ornament executed in France prior to about 1510 does not detract from the credit due to Michel Colombe and other French sculptors of the period. Figures, for which no knowledge of the style was necessary, are far more important than their

[1] The parapet and turrets are modern.

Photo: *Author.*   Fig. 133.—Hôtel de Ville, Orleans.

Photo: *Author.*   Fig. 134.—Hôtel de Ville, Beaugency.   [*To face p.* 172.

surroundings, which could be executed by any fairly competent carver who knew the trick. But can the Frenchmen have known it so early ? How could they have learnt it ? Not merely from descriptions; and there is no evidence that French sculptors at this period studied in Italy. There are few old Classic monuments near the Loire; the remains of Roman art in France are mostly further south. Books could not have helped them. Alberti's book and the printed Vitruvius had only been published about twenty years, and even if available, the illustrations were not such as would have enabled men, otherwise unlearned in the style, to produce that delicacy of line which is one of the characteristics of the Loire work. As soon, however, as they had a few models to guide them their progress would be rapid; and their rare technical skill would enable them to vary the design, and suggest the fresh combinations which frequently occur in French work. If it be true, as stated by M. Palustre, that the Fontaine de Beaune at Tours was designed and executed by Martin and Bastien François, nephews of Michel Colombe, in 1510-11, it is evidence how quickly French sculptors had absorbed from Girolamo di Fiesole and other Italians the essence of the style. But at the same time one hesitates to believe that so purely an Italian design can at so early a date have come from any but a native of Italy.

With the accession of Francis I. the Renaissance advanced by leaps and bounds. The movement was confined at first mainly to secular buildings, and, to some extent, to tombs and other church accessories. The clergy, as a body, remained conservative, and, as will be shown later, continued the old traditions. Francis was a great builder. Probably no other king ever had so many palaces in course of erection at one time. On or near the Loire he built the famous north wing of the château of Blois, and the greater part of the huge château of Chambord, besides additions to other royal seats in the neighbourhood. Farther north he remodelled Fontainebleau and S. Germain-en-Laye, and commenced the following châteaux: Villers-Cotterets, Madrid, la Muette, Challuau, Folembray, and the Louvre. These are mostly rather later than Blois and Chambord. Not only was Francis keen on building himself, but he inspired keenness in, or more likely demanded it from, his courtiers. They, following his example, mostly chose the Loire valley for their country houses, and as a rule made excellent choice of sites. They also built hôtels in the towns lining the river, to house them when the Court was in

Francis I., 1515-47.

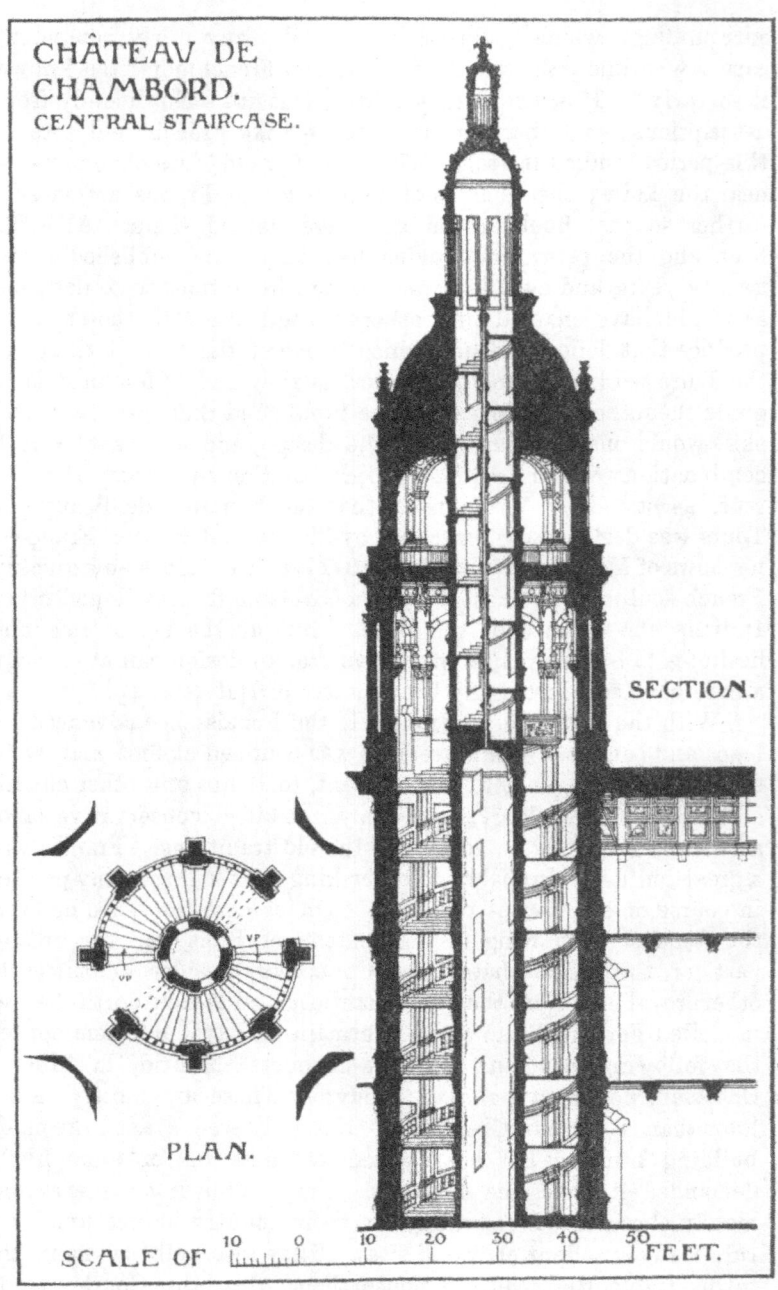

Fig. 135.

Photo: Author.
Fig. 136.—Château de Chambord, dormers and chimneys.

Photo: Author.
Fig. 137.—Château de Chambord, dormers, chimneys, etc.

[To face p. 175.

residence. Thus, Baron d'Alluye, one of Francis I.'s ministers, besides building the hôtel at Blois, already mentioned, built in the neighbourhood the château de Bury, now in ruins. The municipalities were not backward in following the example set, and the Hôtel de Villes of Beaugency, Loches, etc., belong to this period. The architectural fascination of the Loire lies not, therefore, merely in the royal castles, but also in the numerous châteaux dotting the country-side, and in the houses in the towns, although many of the last, especially at Orleans, have during the last thirty years disappeared.

Chambord and the north wing of Blois are the finest of the royal palaces in the Loire district, and Chenonceaux and Azay-le-rideau the most delightful of the smaller houses. Chambord was commenced 1519, and with the exception of a small block by Henri II., and the low buildings containing suites of rooms on three sides of the court, altered or added by Louis XIV., the whole is François premier in character. The main portion consists of a square block, with huge circular towers at the four angles, which contains on each floor a Greek cross-shaped Salle des Gardes, or reception-chamber, besides rooms in the corners and in the towers. In the centre rises the famous spiral staircase, serving all floors, with double flights winding round a circular well. The flights are so arranged that people can pass from one floor to another at the same time without either meeting or even seeing one another, except for chance peeps they may obtain through the openings in the wall surrounding the well. The well is domed above the level of the balcony flat, and over it is a newel staircase which leads to the lantern. The novelty of its arrangements caused the fame of this staircase to spread outside France. Palladio, in his " Quattro Libri," says : " This invention being new and beautiful, I have placed here the design of it." He gives a plan and section, but evidently only from hearsay, as the design is wonderfully different from the original. Only the idea remains translated into stately Italian classic. *Châteaux of the Loire.*

Probably no building in the world presents so varied and broken a sky-line as the central block of Chambord. Running all round, above the second storey, is the peculiar cornice described later, and a balustrade. Behind the latter is a flat, from which start the upper walls of the towers and other portions, all of which are set back several feet from the face of the wall below. The towers are crowned by conical roofs, each with a lantern at the summit, and very steep-pitched roofs cover the other buildings. Rising out of or breaking into all the roofs, are numerous lofty dormers and chimneys, elaborate in design, and enriched by carving and other ornamentation. In the centre of the flat is the cupola over the main staircase, with its flying buttresses and lantern carried high above everything else. The display is bewildering, and is evidence of the originality and abandon of the men who designed and carried out this important building.

At Blois, the chief feature is also the staircase, this time external. External staircases were by no means uncommon in Gothic days, and there are also several later examples, but none so rich and effective as the staircase at Blois. Facing due south, on to the courtyard, the play of light and shade is wonderful; and this, coupled with the beauty and richness of its detail, renders it one of the marvels of the early French Renaissance. Both this staircase and the one at Chambord have newels, and all the steps are winders. That is characteristic of most of the staircases of the period. Not for a hundred years or more did the French adopt generally the straight flights of the Italians. The winding newel staircase was a Gothic tradition; and although occasionally, as in the château of Azay-le-rideau, an exception is made, that only proves the rule. The other portions of the front on either side of the staircase present the usual characteristics described later. To the extreme right, the pilasters, window-mullions, etc., plain elsewhere, are richly carved; and Fig. 144 shows how in places the carving stops abruptly, as though the king had lost his interest in the work, or the carvers had gone off elsewhere. The north front of this wing, with its numerous arched balconies and loggia at top—the latter a feature borrowed from Florentine palaces—owes its reputation more to the way in which its storeys are raised high above the valley on an imposing substructure of stone, in places natural rock, than to any intrinsic merit it possesses as a design.

Chenonceaux. The main portion of the château of Chenonceaux was commenced in 1515 by Thomas Bohier, actually on the river (which flows under and round it) near the north bank. The property falling in later to the Crown, Henri II. gave it to Diane de Poitiers, who built a bridge across to the opposite or south side. On the death of the king, Catherine de' Medici, his widow, obliged Diane to exchange it for Chaumont, and in 1560 built two long galleries, one above the other, on top of the above-mentioned

Photo: Author.
Fig. 138.—Château de Blois, detail of outside staircase.

Fig. 139.—Château de Chenonceaux.

[*To face p.* 176.

Photo: Author.
Fig. 140.—Loches, La Chancellerie, and earlier building in front.

Photo: Author.
Fig. 141.—Château d'Azay-le-Rideau.

[*To face p.* 177.

bridge, her architect being Philibert de l'Orme.[1] The original building was square, with turrets at the four corners and a chapel projecting at the north-east. The extra room and bay at the south-east were probably added by Diane. The marked difference in architectural feeling between the galleries and main block is evidence of how rapidly design changed in France after the middle of the sixteenth century; although in this instance much is due to de l'Orme's superiority over his contemporaries. Interesting evidence that this advance was widespread is, however, afforded by two buildings which stand side by side at Loches. One is of the delicate François premier pattern; the other, La Chancellerie, which is dated 1551, is far more robust. There is apparently no evidence that it was designed by any architect of repute. Its most curious features are the pilasters in pairs recessed behind the projecting frames of the windows. In a vague way these remind one of Michael Angelo's treatment of the side walls of the vestibule of the Laurentian Library, Florence (see Figs. 59, 60).

The château of Azay-le-rideau was begun in 1516 by Gilles Berthelot, whose initial and that of his wife Philippe are entwined in the carving. As at Chenonceaux, the site chosen was alongside a river, the Indre, whose course has been diverted so as to surround the house entirely by flowing water. By the buildings of a country one can tell the characteristics of the people. Probably no single building in France could be instanced which illustrates so well the taste, habits, hopes, and fears of a courtier of Francis I.'s time as this gracious château. The rooms, large enough for stateliness and yet not too grand for comfort; the well-proportioned windows, not too numerous, and yet sufficient in size and number to admit plenty of air and sunshine; the terrace surrounding the house and separating it from the river-moat, and the staircase leading to it; all show that the troubled times were passing, that men were able to indulge in peaceful country pursuits, and could afford some time for ease and quiet. Chambord is a royal palace; Chenonceaux, apart from its river galleries, is small; Azay-le-rideau may be taken as the typical French country home of the early sixteenth century, which can be compared and contrasted with contemporary Italian villas, German schlösser, and with Elizabethan country houses of fifty or sixty years later. It differs from all. In stateliness it may not equal the Villa; in

Azay-le-rideau.

---

[1] The sketch (Fig. 139) was taken from where the formal garden is now. In 1879 this was all ploughed field.

178   *A HISTORY OF ARCHITECTURAL DEVELOPMENT*

homely comfort it may fall short of the English Hall. Notwithstanding its moat and machicolations, any one in danger would prefer the Schlöss. But for picturesqueness allied to a certain symmetry, for charm of position, although the country is flat, for beauty of detail and proportion and general sense of refinement, it would be difficult to find its superior in any country.

Plans.   The plans of early Renaissance châteaux and houses along the Loire are largely based on Mediæval plans. Although feudalism

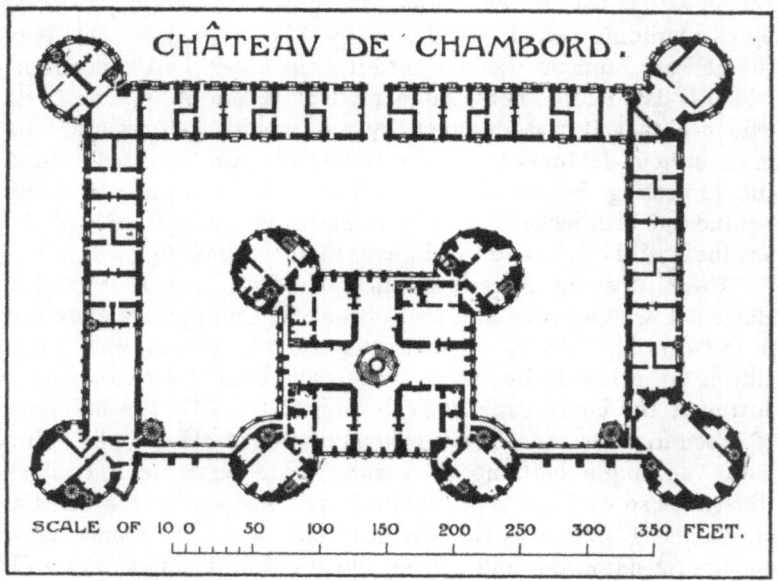

Fig. 142.

was dead, and the nobles could not defy authority as they had hitherto done, and consequently no longer regarded strength as the first essential, the times were still occasionally boisterous, drawbridges still an advantage and means for defence desirable. These causes affected planning to some extent. The builders also would not altogether abandon ancient models. In mediæval castles a not infrequent form was a triangle with a circular tower at each of the three points. One might be the keep, or that might be additional and separate. The entrance might be at one angle, or in the centre of one side; in either position it was flanked by a pair of towers. The towers were connected by buildings, or merely by walls, enclosing a court. Somewhat of this character is the plan of the château of Chaumont, built before the Renaissance began in France, although evidence of it appears in some of its decoration and ornament. The plans of later châteaux are generally square. Of this form was the château of Bury, near Blois. A square courtyard was surrounded by buildings, with a circular tower at each outer corner, and a pair of similar towers flanked the entrance, which was in the centre of one of the sides. Beyond was a formal garden, also with towers at the angles. At Chambord, the keep, or main block, already described, forms the centre of the north

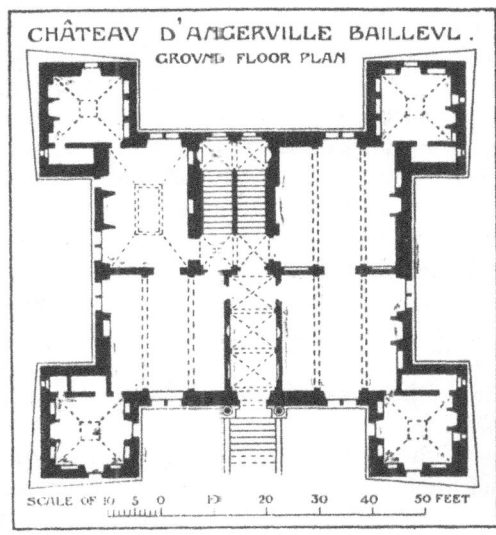

FIG. 143.

front; and the remaining portions of the front, although lofty, are little more than galleries connecting the keep with the towers at the ends. Azay-le-rideau and Chenonceaux have no enclosed courtyard. The former is an ⌐-shaped building, the latter approximately square. Tradition obliged circular towers at the corners, but at Chenonceaux, and in the western portion of Azay-le-rideau, these are small, little more than turrets, and no longer start from the ground, but from corbels a few feet above it. The château of Valençay, several miles south of Blois, boasts two enormous circular towers crowned by domes. In the château de Madrid and other royal châteaux built mainly in the second half of the sixteenth century, the angle towers are square in plan; and the same form occurs in the contemporary château d'Angerville-Bailleul in Normandy, and elsewhere. Thus was originated the "Pavillon," which plays so important a part in the domestic architecture of the seventeenth century.

Characteristics of work on the Loire.

The originality displayed in the buildings already referred to in this chapter, and in others contemporary with them, is very great. In no sense are they merely a reflex of Italian art. The old traditions of the country are still strongly apparent; although translated, as it were, into another language. Not until later in the century did these disappear, and then only gradually. Evidence of this tradition is afforded by the high-pitched roofs—often gabled in towns, in the country always hipped—in the tall chimneys, lofty dormers, similar, except in detail, to the equally striking Gothic ones at Blois, Amboise, Josselin in Brittany, and elsewhere; in the machicolations that crown sometimes only the tower, at other times extend along each face; and in the broken skyline and general picturesqueness of mass. The canopies over niches flanking doorways and windows, as in the château of Azay-le-rideau, and in numerous churches, are Gothic in essence and form, but Renaissance in detail. Many similar canopies, finials, etc., exist in Como Cathedral, the cloisters of the Certosa, near Pavia, etc. It does not follow that one nation copied the other; the transition was so natural that each may have acted independently.

Cornices.

Under a high-pitched roof the great crowning cornice of Florentine and Roman palaces would be out of place, and frequently, as at Azay-le-rideau, there is only a small moulded eaves course. The central block of Chambord, Francis I.'s wing at Blois, and the town halls of Orleans and Beaugency (see Figs. 133, 134, and 144), have, however, cornices of somewhat unusual design. In their proportions these recall the cornices of Florence; in their detail they resemble similar unorthodox ones of the early Renaissance in Northern Italy. It is possible, however, that they were derived from the corbelled over-sailing courses of earlier French buildings, such as those on the château of Amboise. Their most curious member consists of a series of small arches enclosing shells.

General ordinance.

Much the same general ordinance is found in all the façades of the first half of the sixteenth century in the Loire district. A horizontal cornice, or string-course, runs under each range of windows, forming their sill, and another string-course, or architrave, runs above the heads of the windows below. The space

Photo: Author.

FIG. 144.—CHÂTEAU DE BLOIS, CORNICE OF SOUTH SIDE OF COURT.

[*To face p.* 180.

Photo: Author.
FIG. 146.—CHÂTEAU DE CHAMBORD, CORNER OF COURT.

[*To face p.* 181.

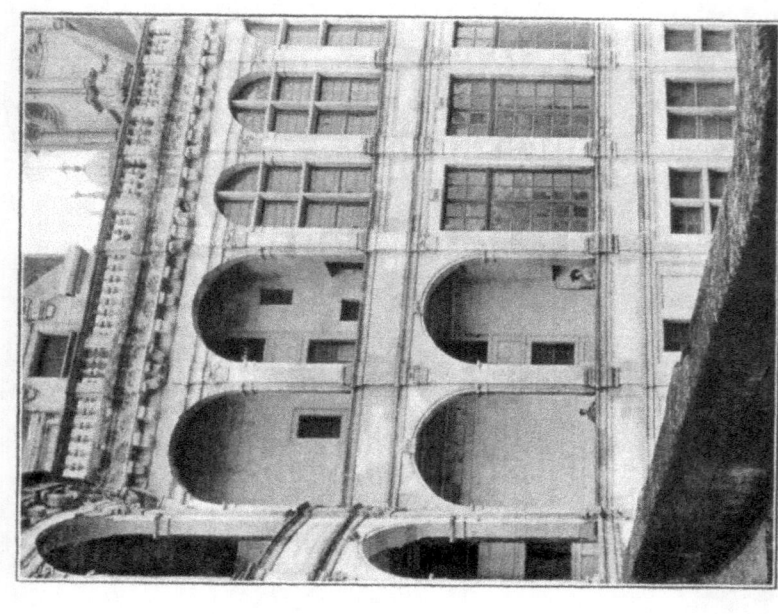

FIG. 145.—COURTYARD OF HOUSE, ORLEANS (CALLED AGNES SOREL'S).

between is treated as a deep frieze, and in not a few examples is carved. Under the entablatures so formed are pilasters; sometimes standing singly, central between windows, but more frequently placed close against the window jambs, so that each window is framed by a pair of pilasters, which form part and parcel of its design. The pilasters in some instances are plain, as at Azay-le-rideau; in others they are panelled, as in the so-called house of Agnes Sorel at Orleans, which is the more characteristic treatment.[1] Short lengths of pilasters connect the pilasters of the different storeys, breaking the frieze portion into a series of long panels, and helping to form vertical lines. The proportions of the windows themselves, with their mullions and transoms, remained for long the same as in the time of Louis XI. In many the detail also shows no change; in others, the mullions and transoms are square and unmoulded, but with the centre frequently sunk to form panels, as in Francis I.'s wing at Blois (Fig. 144). In the town hall of Beaugency and in some cases at Blois, the panels are filled with delicate carving.

In the latter half of the fifteenth century, the weak and unconstructional three-centred form of arch had become general in France, corresponding to the equally weak, contemporary four-centred arch in England. The former is used in the arcading facing the courtyard in Louis XII.'s wing at Blois, in both storeys of the courtyard front of the Hôtel d'Alluye, Blois, in the Agnes Sorel house at Orleans, and elsewhere. During Francis I.'s reign, it was supplanted by the more classical and stronger semicircular form. Few windows, however, have arched heads; they are generally lintelled. The semicircular heads of the windows and gallery openings in the upper storey of the château de Chambord, which cut in such an objectionable way through the architrave and into the frieze of the entablature above, are manifestly unfortunate alterations. They form one of the greatest defects of the building, but the original architect is not to blame. The windows at first were evidently like those below, and the openings alongside them apparently had curved sides and lintelled heads; not a very satisfactory treatment, but better than the present design.

Arches.

[1] Agnes Sorel died in 1450, seventy years or so before the existing house was built. Its front has recently been taken down and rebuilt about ten feet further back, in order to widen the road. The alteration has been extremely well done, and the courtyard, the most interesting portion, remains as before.

Badges.   One of the most delightful features in the Loire work, found also to a limited extent on buildings outside the district, is the series of royal badges and initials, surmounted by crowns, which are carved on the walls. For this French architects deserve the sole credit. No parallel is to be found in Italy; and, moreover, these badges occur in Gothic buildings in which there is little or no trace of the Renaissance. The porcupine of Louis XII., the ermine of his wife Anne of Brittany, and the salamander of Francis I., are the badges met with most frequently; and less often the swan pierced by an arrow, the badge of Francis' wife Claude, and the double pair of wings of Marie of Cleves. One of the earliest porcupines is over the small doorway of the façade of the château of Blois, in a panel framed by Gothic carving. On the same front is the crowned L. The ermine badge is sometimes represented by the animal itself, sometimes merely by its tails. In the Queen's oratory in the château of Loches, the walls are peppered all over with carved tails, and very effective they are. The salamander, happy in the midst of flames, and generally with a crown upon or above its head, is carved on all buildings erected by Francis, and on many built by his courtiers. Its existence does not prove that the building was the king's, only that it was built in his reign. On non-royal châteaux and houses it generally appears uncrowned; as at Azay-le-rideau, where the salamander and ermine appear side by side over the double entrance doorway, and the Hôtel du Bourgtheroulde, Rouen, where are the salamander and porcupine. The outside staircase at Blois is particularly rich in salamanders and crowned F.'s, and the C. for Claude also finds a place, whilst on the ceiling her emblem is carved. Henri II. signed his buildings in similar fashion, and so did his wife Catherine de' Medici, and his mistress, Diane de Poitiers. Other kings and queens followed suit, but in later work there is not that delightful abandon that distinguishes the time of Francis.

Material.   In one important respect the workers along the Loire were exceptionally favoured. The district produces an abundance of stone, perfect as regards texture, colour, and degree of softness, and without parallel for the execution of delicate detail. Similar to Caen and Bath, it is, in some respects, superior to both. It is this which gives the charm to the ordinary, simple, vernacular work of later days on both sides the river from Orleans to Saumur. The heads of the windows of the smallest cottages are often formed of voussoirs two or three feet in height. Every little house is delightful in proportion, refined in detail, designed with ease, apparently hardly designed at all, as though everything came natural in that valley known as the "Garden of France." At Angers the touch has always been bolder than further up the river; possibly because the stone is harder. The "corbel" cornice is an especial characteristic of this town, and there are many examples of it, all differing slightly. The earliest building in which it occurs is probably the Hôtel de Pincé, designed by Jean de Lespine about 1530. For roof covering the district is also favoured; it supplies the most delightful slates of any country. Very small and nearly black, they produce an excellent effect on the high-pitched roofs, and especially on the conical spires surmounting towers and turrets. The use of the material was not confined solely to roofing. At the château of Chambord the panels of the chimneys and of the pilasters flanking dormer windows, etc., are filled with slate, and look

FIG. 147.

like panels of black marble. Lozenges and circles of slate are also nailed on friezes, etc.; and although these have frequently broken away, showing that this employment of the material had its drawbacks, the result is still rich and striking (see Fig. 136). In Brittany and Normandy, where the slates are similar in size but not so black, they are largely used for protecting walls and timbers of "post and pan" buildings. There is no reason why a like treatment should not be followed in England, especially in the west, where the slates resemble those of Brittany, and in the counties served by Westmorland, where the green slate can be obtained small and of good colour and texture.

For the floors of rooms the French have ever used tiles to a

184 A HISTORY OF ARCHITECTURAL DEVELOPMENT

Internal treatment.

great extent. The suites of rooms in Francis I.'s wing at Blois are all tiled, and many of the designs are most successful, although all are restorations. Most are blue and white, with yellow in parts; and in some the H of the second Henry is introduced. In the château of Chenonceaux is some good tiling, apparently original. Rooms are occasionally vaulted, as in the oratory of the

Fig. 148.

château of Azay-le-rideau; but generally the ceilings are of framed timber. The latter have not the richness of detail which characterizes contemporary Gothic wood ceilings in England. The walls were evidently hung with tapestry, and wood panelling is rarely met with now, and can never have been general. The elaborately carved and painted panelling which covers the walls of Catherine de' Medici's sitting-room at Blois is an exception. Altogether, the

THE EARLY RENAISSANCE IN FRANCE

interior of a French château can never have boasted the cosiness of the slightly later English houses; but in a warmer climate than ours tiled floors and bare walls possessed some advantages.[1]

The men who designed these buildings are generally referred to in existing documents as master-masons, or masters of masonry. They were mostly engaged on one job at a time, to which they devoted themselves, their pay being a "livre," sometimes a little more, per day, equal to about fifteen shillings at the present time. At Chambord, Jacques Coqueau, who succeeded Pierre Nepveu (called Trinqueau) in 1538, received four hundred livres a year as "king's master mason." In an entry, however, in 1491, one, Simon Boussart, is called "maistre visiteur du mestier de maconnerie;"[2] and in 1534 J. Beaudouin was paid rather more than two livres for a plan of the Hotel-de-ville, Loches, he being described as belonging to another town. It appears, therefore, as though sometimes the men who superintended the work were not always the designers; and this receives confirmation from later entries. The term "architect" first appears about 1540, although for some time after that men continued to be called "master mason." In 1541 Serlio, the Italian, is described by Francis as "notre cher et bien aimé Bastiannet Serlio peintre et architecteur," and in 1549 Philibert de l'Orme is referred to, in connection with a payment made to François Marchand and Pierre Bontemps for work on Francis I.'s tomb at S. Denis, which de l'Orme designed, as "aumosnier du roy et son architecte." De l'Orme is elsewhere described as inspector and superintendent of the royal buildings of Fontainebleau, S. Germain-en-Laye, etc. Serlio was paid annually 400 livres for work at Fontainebleau, 225 livres as architect to Marguerite d'Angouleme, and, in addition to the above, one livre a day for a visit to any work except at Fontainebleau. Pierre Lescot, in 1546, received 1200 livres as architect of the Louvre. Later, architects' pay mounted rapidly. Salomon de Brosse, who designed the Luxembourg, Paris, got 2400 livres annually, and J. Lemercier 3000, the latter as "first king's architect." By that time, however, the purchasing power of the livre had greatly decreased, and the coin itself was of less value.

Although the Renaissance started later in most districts than

Architects.

Examples elsewhere.

---

[1] The wonderfully rich tiled floor in the principal room in the château de Chaumont is not the original floor, nor is it French. It was brought from Palermo.

[2] See "Dictionnaire des Architectes Francais," par Adolphe Lance.

on the Loire, there are very few towns in France, from Toulouse in the south to Arras in the north, from Nantes in the west to Nancy and Dijon in the east, which do not possess some examples of it earlier than 1550. Many of these towns, however, have fine earlier houses, built when Gothic was still the only style recognized throughout the country. At Bourges, the famous house of Jacques Cœur had only been finished in 1451; at Rouen, the Hôtel du Bourgtheroulde was not commenced until 1486, the Palais de Justice not until a few years later. These buildings and others similar undoubtedly delayed for some time the progress of the new movement. Notwithstanding this at Bourges, the Hôtels Lallemand and Cujas were built before 1520; and at Rouen, Roland Leroux designed, about the same time, the tomb of Cardinal Georges d'Amboise, Archbishop of Rouen, and his nephew, which is in the cathedral. To the cardinal, who was Louis XII.'s minister, is largely due the early spread of the Renaissance in France generally, and in Normandy in particular. Little remains *in situ* of his famous château at Gaillon, commenced at the end of the fifteenth century and finished in 1510, which, for richness of ornamentation, had no parallel in the country. Like so much of the work of the period, it was Gothic in the main; but here and there portions were executed in the new style—for example, the arcade now standing in the courtyard of the Ecole des Beaux Arts, Paris. The house known as the Ancien Bureau des Finances, facing Rouen Cathedral, which was built about 1510, is probably now the earliest building of the Renaissance in Normandy. Another good example at Rouen is the wing added to the Hôtel du Bourgtheroulde about twenty years later, on the front of which are some finely sculptured panels representing the meeting of Henry VIII. and Francis I. on the Field of the Cloth of Gold. The first appearance of the Renaissance at Caen was possibly in the east end of S. Pierre, designed by Hector Sohier, the best known of Norman architects of the first half of the sixteenth century. In the same town are the Hôtel de Valois, or d'Ecoville, with a striking courtyard, and four or five other fine Renaissance houses. Caen and the country round are, like the Loire, favoured in their stone, to which circumstance much of the delicacy of the detail there and general excellence of the work are due.

Brittany. The influence and taste of Anne de Bretagne account for an early start in Brittany. A little corbelled-out oriel near the

THE EARLY RENAISSANCE IN FRANCE

castle of Vitré is one of the most elaborate examples in France. The "candelabra" system of ornamentation, found in S. Maria delle Grazie, Milan, and elsewhere in Northern Italy, is frequently met with. At Vitré it occurs on two or three buildings, but the most curious instance is on the columns inside Notre Dame de bon Secours, Guingamp. The triforia of this church are almost unique, and the carving in the spandrils over the openings of cupids with outstretched arms and legs is well above the average. Many of the buildings in Brittany are in granite, which does not lend itself to delicate detail. Of this material are the calvaries and ossuaries, which are almost peculiar to the district. They are rugged and bold, but full of character. At Guimiliau and S. Thégonnec, within a few miles of each other, and at Plougastel-Daoulas, are the finest calvaries; and S. Thégonnec also has an unusually imposing ossuary. Ossuaries were sometimes built against churches, as at Trégastel. Twenty years ago they were often full to the brim with skulls and bones dug up from the graves; but apparently the custom, like the old costume of the country, is being abandoned.

FIG. 149.

The South of France, being Italy's near neighbour, and possessing many fine old classic remains, might have been expected to take a leading part in the movement. Such, however, it did not do. Laurana had sown the seed, but it had not taken root. In Toulouse, a town chiefly famous for the fine scale of its Gothic churches, there are some fairly early examples of interest, but none of importance. The best secular buildings belong to the

Toulouse.

second half of the sixteenth century, and some are later still. As a rule, they are distinguished by the extravagant richness of the window jambs and mullions. The Hôtel d'Asseza (see Fig. 154), in which this trait is absent, is the finest in the town, and is also one of the most striking of its time in the whole of France. Over the doorway to the staircase is carved the date 1555. In design the building is considerably in advance of all contemporary work in the provinces, and is superior even to the royal palaces in or near Paris, the Louvre alone excepted. Whoever designed it must have been a scholar of no mean order, as it shows a knowledge of Classic detail and proportion rare in France in the middle of the sixteenth century. The upper storey suggests an acquaintance with Palladio's basilica at Vicenza, which was only commenced in 1549. The combination of circles above lintelled openings, flanking a central arch, was, however, a favourite with Bramante, and had been used by him in the choir of Santa Maria del Popolo, Rome, early in the century.

FIG. 150.—OSSUARY, TRÉGASTEL.

Île-de-France.

The most important examples in the Île de France are the royal châteaux begun by Francis I. and continued by his successors. The château de Madrid, the most elaborate of all, no longer exists. Its façades were enriched by coloured majolica plaques by Girolamo della Robbia, who possibly also gave the original design for the building. De l'Orme and Primaticcio in turn are said to have superintended the work, and the former is stated to have protested—and very properly—against the della Robbia decoration. Of existing châteaux, Villers-Cotterets, S. Germain-en-Laye, and Fontainebleau are the earliest. Portions of the first date from about 1520, and have all the characteristics of the Loire work; but the main buildings surrounding the forecourt were added after Francis' death. The château of S. Germain-en-Laye, with its red brick and stucco in the upper storeys, and its flat roof, is not a very successful design. The remodelling of the château of Fontainebleau was commenced in 1528. According to M. Palustre, the first architect was Gilles le Breton. He built the greater part of the so-called oval court—portions were destroyed later—the wing adjoining, and commenced the great court of the Cheval Blanc. At about the same time, Pierre Chambiges, the architect of S. Germain, began the wings of the same court. Both men were master-masons of the old school, with but limited knowledge of Classic architecture. In 1540, Serlio, "notre cher et bien aimé," was invited by Francis I. to Fontainebleau, probably because of the fame he gained by his "Architettura," which had just been published. Il Rosso, the painter, who for some time had had charge of the internal decorations of the château, and also possibly designed the Grotto des Pins, was poisoned in the following year, and was succeeded by Primaticcio. What share these Italians had in the designing of the outside is uncertain. M. Palustre will allow them none, and he is probably right, and unintentionally kind to their reputations. The early fronts are no particular credit to anybody. The attraction at Fontainebleau is not so much external as internal. The decorations of the principal rooms, designed and carried out mainly by the Italians mentioned, are best worth seeing. On the death of François I., Serlio left, and was no longer employed there, although he returned in 1553, dying in the following year. Under Henri II. some work was done by Philibert de l'Orme, and extensive additions, including the Cour des Offices, were made by Henri IV. early in the seventeenth century. Succeeding kings added still more, with the result that the château is interesting as a building in which the architecture of the different periods can be studied; but externally, the effect, as a whole, is not particularly happy.

The second period of the French Renaissance may be said to commence with the building of the Louvre and Tuileries in 1546 and 1564 respectively, and to cover about the succeeding seventy years. The principal architects were Pierre Lescot (1515–78), Philibert de l'Orme (1515–70), Jean Bullant (c. 1512), and Jacques Androuet du Cerceau (1515–c. 1584). Jean Goujon and Germain Pilon were the most distinguished sculptors. *Second period.*

The best known buildings by Lescot are the original portions of the Louvre, and the hotel he built for the Président de Ligneris, now, much altered and added to, known at the Musée Carnavalet. He was a man of position, with powerful friends at Court; a member of the Parliament of Paris, and a favourite of the king. How he obtained the knowledge of architecture which *Pierre Lescot and Philibert de l'Orme.*

enabled him, at the age of thirty, to design the above-mentioned buildings is not known. Professor Blomfield suggests that the real architect of both was Jean Goujon, who undoubtedly carved

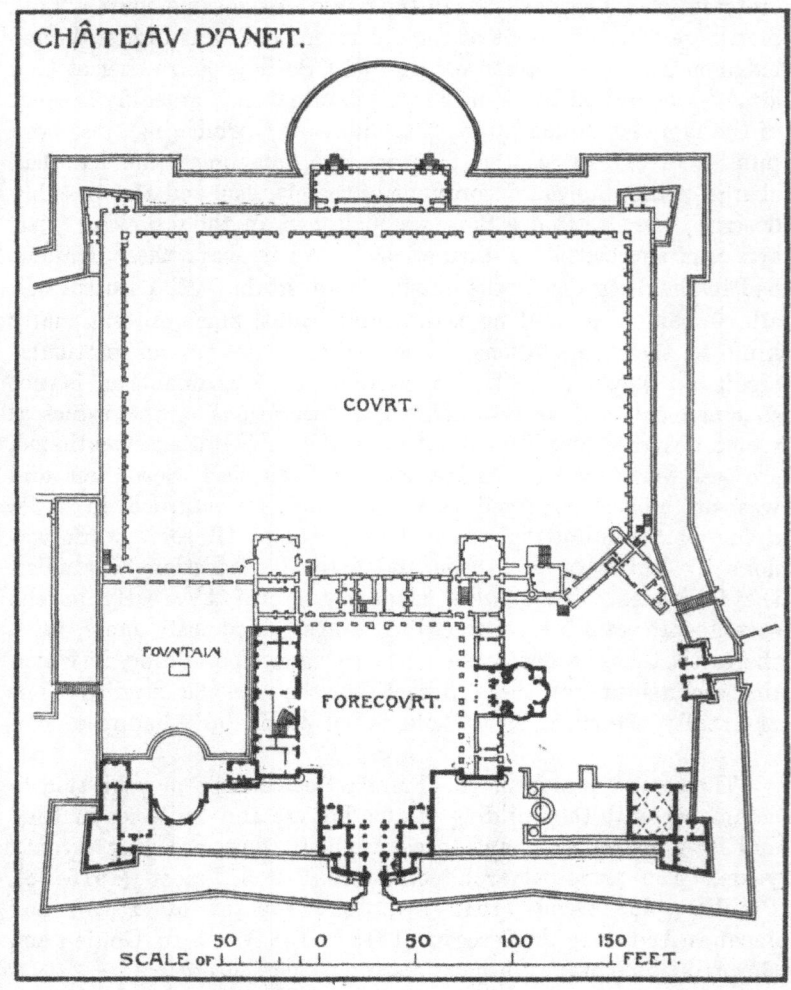

Fig. 151.

the figures which decorate the fronts.[1] Lescot certainly was appointed architect of the Louvre in 1546, and drew his pay of twelve hundred livres a year; but that in itself proved but little,

[1] See article in the *R. I. B. A. Journal*, vol. xviii. 3rd Series, p. 109.

Photo: Author.
FIG. 152.—THE LOUVRE, PARIS, PORTION OF SOUTH FRONT.

Photo: Author.
FIG. 153.—DETAIL OF PILASTERS, SOUTH FRONT OF THE LOUVRE.

[To face p. 191.

as the age was a corrupt one, and many men enjoyed sinecures whilst others did the work. At the same time, one hesitates to accept the suggestion without definite proof, especially as Goujon's position was so assured that it is unlikely he would have allowed another to obtain the sole credit for work he himself had done. There is no doubt about De l'Orme's skill as an architect. When nineteen or twenty he went to Italy, returning in 1536. In 1548 he was appointed architect to the king, and he was also architect for Catherine de' Medici and Diane de Poitiers. For the last he designed the château d'Anet, in Normandy, where he was assisted by Goujon, Germain Pilon, hardly inferior as an artist to Goujon himself, and other well-known sculptors of the day. Portions only remain *in situ* (shown black on plan, Fig. 151), but in the court of the Ecole des Beaux Arts, Paris, is part of one of the principal façades, and in the Louvre is Goujon's masterpiece, Diana and the Stag, which formed the top of the fountain in the centre of one of the courts. In 1561 the architect published his " Nouvelles Inventions pour bien bastir et à petits fraiz," and six years later " Le Premier Tome de l'Architecture." These publications show that De l'Orme, besides having a thorough knowledge of classic proportion and detail, was a master of construction. He originated the "keel" shaped roof (the form is still employed in modern work), and in his books gives elaborate instructions how it is to be framed. To him is also due the "banded" column (see Figs. 152, 153), which he claimed as his invention, first used by him flanking the doorway of the chapel in the park of Villers-Cotterets. His argument, as stated in his " Premier Tome," was that, as ancient nations had invented "orders" of columns, and had bestowed on them their names, why should not the French do the same? His design is really a modification of the rusticated column, which had been introduced in Italy some years before. The ground-floor storey of the Tuileries, now destroyed,[1] had many columns and pilasters of this character, and it continued a favourite treatment in France until the middle of the seventeenth century. The richest examples of it are on the ground-floor gallery facing the Seine, which was commenced by Catherine de' Medici to connect the Louvre and Tuileries (see p. 193). Not only are both columns and pilasters banded and carved, but the bands are continued as rustications between pilasters, and from pilasters to window openings.

[1] Two bays have been rebuilt in the Tulieries gardens.

192 A HISTORY OF ARCHITECTURAL DEVELOPMENT

Bullant and Du Cerceau.

Bullant was employed on a good many buildings, including the château d'Ecouen, on which, according to M. Palustre, he succeeded a master-mason called Billard, or Baillard, and the earlier portion of the château of Chantilly. He also published one or two books on architecture. Jacques Androuet du Cerceau is better known as an engraver and writer than architect. As a draughtsman he was a consummate artist.[1] Many of his drawings are finer than any contemporary Italian ones. He studied in Rome for two or three years, and so was well acquainted with old work; but in his buildings he failed to reproduce its spirit, although his planning, especially in the château of Charleval, is good. His first book he published in 1539, and until 1584 he was busy with new publications or new editions. His "Livre d'Architecture" was published in 1559; "Les plus Excellents Bastiments de France" in 1579. The latter is his most famous work, especially valuable as a record of many buildings which have entirely disappeared and of others which have been much altered. Du Cerceau's books and De l'Orme's helped greatly towards a proper knowledge and appreciation of classic architecture in France. Printing was of greater assistance to architects in that country than in Italy. For in the latter, old examples were numerous, and could be studied first hand; and the Renaissance was established there before printing was introduced. The excellence of the draughtsmanship of the early French publications is great. Those of the sixteenth century show signs of the superiority in this respect which is so marked in the illustrated books of the century following—a superiority the French have retained to the present day.

The Louvre.

In 1539 Francis I. decided to pull down the old castle of the Louvre, which dated from the time of Philippe Auguste; but the new building was not begun until 1546, the year before the king died. The earliest portion therefore belongs to the reign of his successor Henri II. This is the southern half of the west side of the court. After some delay, the western half of the south side was also built. The design is the work of a man of genius. It suffers from the fact that under Louis XIII. and his minister, Richelieu, the court was greatly increased in size, and consequently the different parts of the original fronts now appear a trifle small, and the delicacy of the detail is lost. But that the beauty of the

[1] See "French Châteaux and Gardens in the Sixteenth Century," edited by Mr. W. H. Ward, for reproductions of many of Du Cerceau's original drawings.

Photo: Neurdein.
FIG. 154.—HÔTEL D'ASSEZA, TOULOUSE.

Photo: Author.
FIG. 155.—THE LOUVRE, PARIS, CORNER OF COURTYARD.

[*To face p.* 193.

design was realized by succeeding architects is proved by the manner in which it was repeated in the additions. The only difference is that on the north, south, and east sides a full top storey replaces the lower attic of Lescot.[1] The superiority of the original composition is most marked. This is largely because, apart from the better proportions which the attic affords, the projecting bays are crowned by segmental pediments—on the other sides they merely finish with a balustrade like the neighbouring walling—and the roof shows, with its elaborate lead ridge, rising above an original and beautiful cresting.

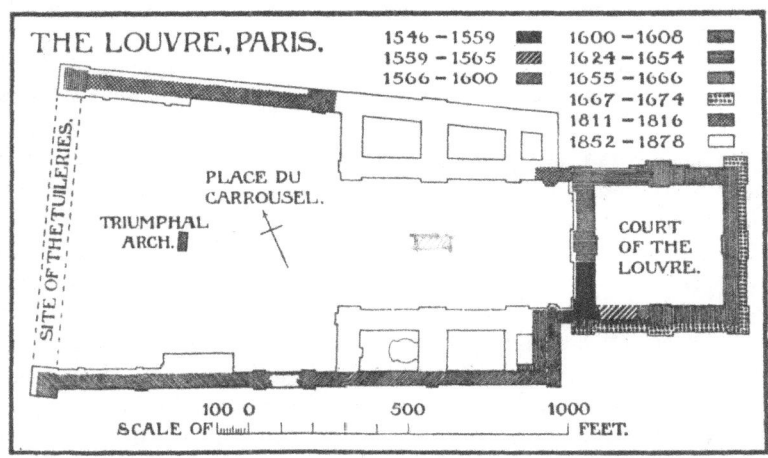

FIG. 156.

In 1564, Catherine de' Medici, Henri's wife, began the Tuileries, and shortly afterwards the one-storied gallery facing the Seine, already mentioned (see Figs. 152 and 153), and the wing at right-angles to it at the east end, from the river to the Louvre. Little more than the ground storey of the central part of the main façade of the Tuileries was designed by De l'Orme. The ends and upper storeys were added later. The building, as it stood before it was burnt in the days of the Commune, was certainly vastly inferior in design to Pierre Lescot's portion of the Louvre, but it is not fair to judge De l'Orme by what was not his work entirely; although it is doubtful if his design, carried out complete, could have compared successfully with that of the king's palace.[2]

Tuileries.

[1] See pp. 206-9 for further history of Louvre.
[2] The plan of the Tuileries, as designed by De l'Orme, is given in Blondel's "Architecture Française."

VOL. III.   O

Between 1594 and 1609 the river front between the Louvre and Tuileries was finished. To the right of the present fine central triple archway, which is modern, a mezzanine and upper floor were added over the Queen's gallery. To the left, a corresponding wing was built which, there being no gallery, differs from the other in some particulars. The mezzanine, as an independent division, is omitted, and the pilasters, which start from the ground level on the right, are raised on a basement. The alternation of curved and pointed pediments is retained, but the niches containing figures between the pedimented bays are replaced by windows. The result in consequence is less satisfactory.

Characteristics of second period.

The work of the second period shows a better perception of the principles and proportions of classic architecture, but it lacks the freshness and piquancy of the earlier work, and the strength, fine composition, and scale which distinguish that which followed. Each storey of a building, as a rule, has its own range of pilasters, above which is a well-proportioned entablature; but these pilasters are independent of the windows, and no longer frame them, as in the earlier examples. Moulded architraves round windows, however, are general, and mullions began to be omitted. Pilasters sometimes run through more than one storey, but this treatment was far from common until a hundred years later. The tall dormer assumed more modest dimensions, and ceased to be such an important feature. In the portions of the château of Chambord added by Henri II., a curved pediment of slight rise, with cresting above, replaces the lofty gable of varied outline, and the same tendency is noticeable elsewhere. The originality generally displayed is still considerable, and this is the more remarkable because no signs of the lingering Gothic traditions which coloured earlier work are apparent. The aim of the architects of the second half of the sixteenth century was to follow the ancients, and the Renaissance architects of Italy. That they succeeded in doing so without copying, on the one hand, and without descending to banalities on the other, is greatly to their credit.

Henri IV. (1589–1610).

Hard things have been written about the architecture of the end of the second period, of the time of Henri IV. Coming between the fascination of the François premier period, and the splendour and magnificence of the time of Louis Quatorze, it is sometimes misjudged. It has been accused of being grotesque and over-florid. Those who like prettiness find it dull; others

THE EARLY RENAISSANCE IN FRANCE 195

who clamour for purity proclaim it debased. As a rule, it is none of these things. Its qualities may be negative rather than positive, but its proportions and scale are good, the designs generally show ideas worth consideration, and the carving is always of a high order. Eccentricities are met with in some examples, as in the Hôtel de Ville of La Rochelle, where the

FIG. 157.

upper storey is carried on an arcade, more than half the arches of which are supported by columns on one side only, the other side springing merely from a pendant which dangles in the air. Overfloridness is also present occasionally. One of the most marked instances of this is in the façade of the château of Harfleur, which, however, is really later, as it dates from 1650. The columns and pilasters which run through two storeys are banded *à la mode*

De l'Orme, in a particularly objectionable way. On the other hand, many examples of the period can be instanced which, although rich in carving, have sufficient plain wall surface to frame satisfactorily the ornamentation, and are refined and well proportioned. There are several at Dijon, the best being the Hôtel de Vogüé, commenced in 1607. The doorway in the outside wall which gives access to the courtyard, and the windows in front at the ends of the wings, are elaborate jewels in a plain setting which shows them to advantage. The plan has many good points, and is interesting as an example of a good-sized town house of the period. The Hôtel de Sully, Paris, is another example, somewhat later in date. The front, with its two curved pediments, is fine and bold, and the courtyard well proportioned. It was designed by Jean du Cerceau, grandson of Jacques Androuet.

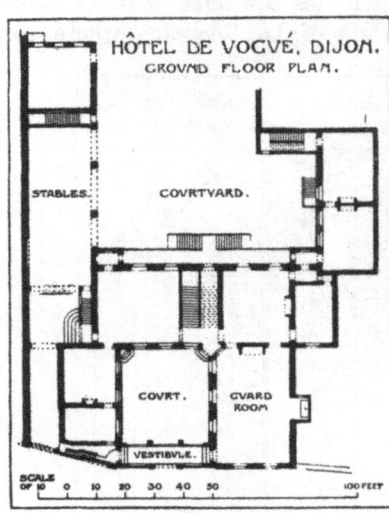

Fig. 158.

Luxembourg.

A connecting link between this middle period and the third and great period of French classic is the Palais du Luxembourg, commenced in 1615 for Marie de' Medici, widow of Henri IV. Her instructions to her architect, Salomon de Brosse—another grandson of Du Cerceau—were to copy the Pitti palace in Florence.[1] It was natural, perhaps, for both Queen Dowager and architect to prefer Ammanati's courtyard, as the more recent, to Brunelleschi's far finer façade, and the fronts of the Luxembourg in consequence are rusticated all over. The rustications in the French palace, however, are not so objectionable as in the Florentine, as De Brosse succeeded in introducing a certain amount of refinement. Most buildings of the period are planned round a courtyard, and the Luxembourg is no exception; but the pavilion grouping of the main block is somewhat unusual, and distinctly

[1] Two of Du Cerceau's sons were architects, one, Baptiste Androuet, following Lescot, in 1578, as architect of the Louvre.

effective. The gardens were very extensive, and still evince their former grandeur, although considerably reduced.

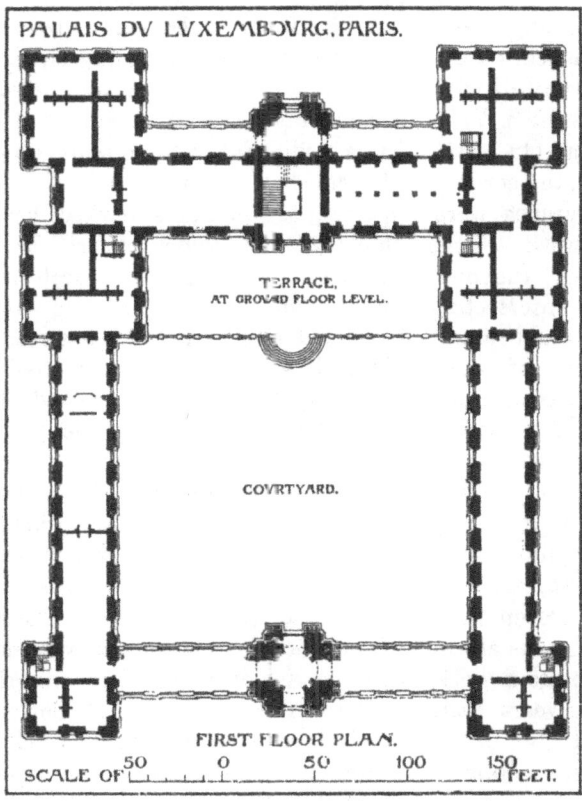

Fig. 159.

Churches of the Sixteenth Century

The Renaissance had little effect on church design in France during the sixteenth century. In churches which were unfinished the work proceeded as though the architecture of Greece and Rome had never existed, and Alberti, Bramante, and Michel Angelo had not been born. No change of importance is noticeable until after the first quarter of the seventeenth century. When additions were necessary, the new style appears half shamefacedly in detail; as in some panelling in one of the south chapels of S. Vincent,

Rouen; in the cupolas crowning the western towers of Tours Cathedral; in the extension eastward of the church of S. Pierre, Caen; in pinnacles of buttresses, and in numerous doorways, porches, etc., throughout the country. In many cathedrals and large churches are Renaissance doors of exceeding richness which harmonize well with the elaborate Gothic stonework which frames them; as at S. Vulfran, Abbeville, the south transept of Beauvais Cathedral, etc. At Tours a delightful little outside staircase was built in the corner of the cloisters of the cathedral. But when new churches were required, the builders harked back to the earlier work. Either they did not know of, or else did not believe in, the new ordinance. To them a church must still have an intersecting ribbed vault; and such being so, the plan remained as before, and the buttress and flying buttress followed as a matter of course. Triforia were sometimes omitted, columns often replaced clustered piers, and capitals disappeared; but these modifications had been introduced in the previous century, and were not due to the Renaissance.

S. Eustache, Paris.

The largest church of the century is S. Eustache, Paris. Although not commenced until 1532, and not finished until nearly a hundred years later, its plan—which is a copy of Nôtre Dame—proportions, construction, and high-pitched roof, are Gothic. Even its detail can hardly be said to be Classic. The window heads are filled with tracery, uncusped as was the custom in this bastard work, but otherwise differing little from those of a hundred years earlier. Externally, the faces of buttresses are enriched by pilasters, pilasters also are introduced between windows, openings are semicircular headed, and entablatures replace string courses; whilst internally the vaulting shafts are built up in a series of panelled pilasters, one above another, and in place of bosses where the diagonal ribs of the vault cross, are pendants; the last an idea borrowed from English fifteenth-century vaults. The interior of S. Etienne-du-Mont, Paris, which was commenced a few years later, appears rather more classic, but this effect is partly owing to the balustrated gallery between the columns, which was added in 1580, when the fine western doorway was built. If two such important churches could be built at this time in the capital in the manner described, more advanced ideas could hardly be expected from clergy and builders in the provinces. The burst of building activity in the last quarter of the fifteenth century was too recent, and its results

Fig. 160.—Staircase in corner of Cloisters, Tours Cathedral.

[*To face p.* 198.

too far-reaching for it to subside quickly. Many important cathedrals and churches were still in the making, Beauvais especially. In them change was impossible. Besides, there was little demand for new churches. The clergy were apathetic, the kings indifferent, the nobility busy with their own town and country houses, and the people satisfied. The church of S. Michel, Dijon, is more Classic than either of the Paris churches mentioned, but even that is but a mixture. The interior is chiefly remarkable for having no clerestory, although the space above the nave arcades is considerable. Its absence may be due to a suggestion obtained from S. Peter's, Rome, or S. Andrea, Mantua. In the west front a determined attempt has been made to produce a façade of the Renaissance, but one feels that the style is only skin-deep. The repetition in the design is wearisome. Portions of the front were designed by Hugues Sambin, said to have been a pupil of Michel Angelo, but there is not a trace of that master's bigness in the whole composition.

CHAPTER X

THE ARCHITECTURE OF THE LOUIS (c. 1625-1780)

No country at any period can show so sudden and marked an advance in architectural design as occurred in France at the end of the first quarter of the seventeenth century. The advance is all the more noteworthy because architecture in Italy at that period was at its lowest ebb. The French had shown, a hundred years before, that they could borrow a style from another country and endow it with a freshness all their own; but that was the easier task, in that they had their old style on which to graft the new. In the century that followed the new had in turn grown old; and to lop its unnecessary features and purify its exuberance was more difficult.

J. Lemercier (1585-1654). The credit for the achievement is mainly due to two men, Jacques Lemercier and François Mansard, or Mansart. Lemercier was the elder by some thirteen years, being born about 1585. How and where he obtained his training is somewhat uncertain, but he early became the *protégé* of Cardinal Richelieu, and his fortune was made. Richelieu was appointed a member of the king's council in 1624, and in the same year Lemercier was commissioned to carry out extensive additions to the Louvre. In 1629 he began the Palais Royal, or Cardinal, Paris, of which only the Galerie des Proues remains of the original; and about the same time the college and church of the Sorbonne, also for Richelieu. Nothing illustrates better Lemercier's superiority over his contemporaries than the design of this church. S. Eustache was being finished in the capital, and in the provinces the style followed was still transitional. Lemercier's church is Classic, and Classic of a purity unobtainable in Italy at that time, and otherwise unknown in France. The dome rises in the centre of the church, but the plan is not a Greek cross, as two of the arms are each of two bays, whilst the other pair are only of one bay each. The arches of all the bays spring from pilastered piers, and the ordinance is of the type which had previously become general in Italy, and was subsequently followed in France. The dome, like that of the church of the Val de Grâce, Paris, in which Lemercier later had a share, is double, an inner dome being covered by an outer, which rises high above it. The entrance façade and the dome are most happily proportioned, and together form a perfect architectural composition. S. Roch, begun by Lemercier in 1653, the year before he died, is not so successful either internally or externally, although a much larger church.

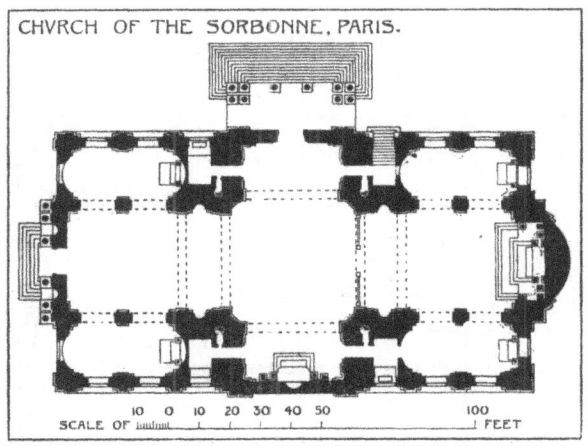

Fig. 161.

It is not often that an architect gets an opportunity of laying out a new town and designing all its houses; but that was Lemercier's good fortune. His client was his old patron, the Cardinal, who, having taken as title the name of the village in which he was born, decided to rebuild it entirely, so that it should be worthy of him, and at the same time provide lodging accommodation for important members of his retinue. For the whole town was but an adjunct to a new château, for which Lemercier was also the architect. Of this mansion little now remains beyond a domed pavilion, but the beautiful drawings of it by Jean Marot[1] show a wonderful succession of courtyards, flanked by buildings, approached from an immense circular forecourt. Allowing for the artist's exaggeration, it is evident that the whole was planned on a royal scale. The town is almost unaltered. The northern and

Town of Richelieu.

[1] "Le Magnifique chasteau de Richelieu."

southern gateways, De Chinon and Du Château, still afford access to it, and lead direct to the two squares and the Grande Rue which connects them. Two subordinate gateways have disappeared, but the moat and the enclosing wall remain. The fronts of the houses in the Grande Rue are all alike. Each has a wide archway in the centre, with two windows on each side and five windows above. The blocks of stone over the entrances were intended to be carved with the arms of the Cardinal's followers, but this has only been done in one or two cases.[1] The main cor-

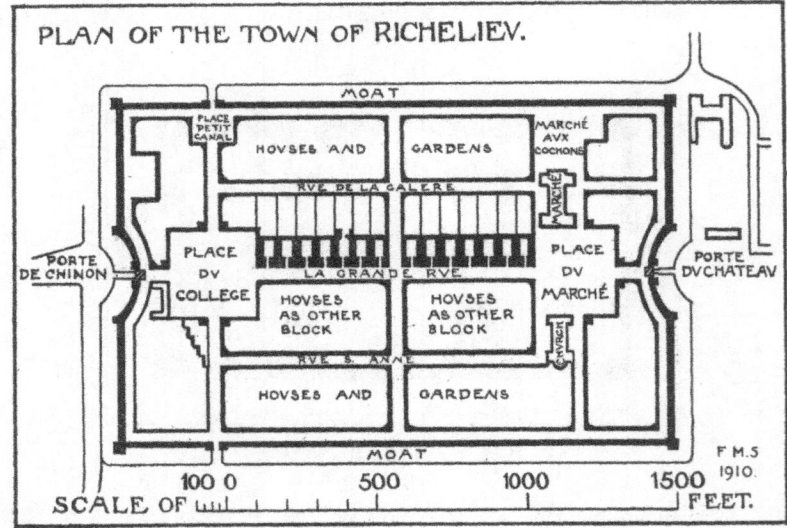

Fig. 162.

nice of the houses is continuous from end to end of the street; but the high-pitched roofs are separated, each house having its own roof, hipped on all sides—a wise precaution against spread of fire. Each house has its courtyard and garden beyond, but only one has the effective design illustrated in Fig. 163. The houses in the subordinate streets and surrounding the squares are less lofty and imposing—the windows of the upper floor breaking through the cornice—but at each corner of both squares is a larger house, similar in size and design to the houses in the main street. The effect produced by this grouping is excellent. Both squares are

---

[1] The town was unfinished at the Cardinal's death.

Photo: Author.
FIG. 163.—RICHELIEU; END OF COURTYARD OF HOUSE.

Photo: Author.
FIG. 164.—RICHELIEU, PORTE DE CHINON.

[*To face p.* 202.

FIG. 165.—CHÂTEAU DE BALLEROY.

[*To face p.* 203.

lined by trees, the successors probably of those planted by order of the Cardinal.

Before the time of Lemercier pilasters on external walls had begun to go out of fashion, and what may be called the "quoin" era succeeded. There are thousands of domestic buildings in France of the period of Louis XIII. and XIV. which would be dreary if it were not for their quoins. These come at the angles of walls, the sides of windows, and are also continued vertically from one window to another, and above the topmost windows to the main cornice. These connecting quoins are the direct descendant of the short pilasters in the Loire district, which connect the window-framing pilasters of one storey with similar pilasters above or below. All the houses at Richelieu are of this design— simple, dignified, unexciting, but very reposeful. They are well proportioned, good in scale, have well-designed cornices at the eaves, and many of the dormers, although lacking the importance of earlier ones, are not ineffective. In the entrance gates of the town occurs the broad simply channelled pilaster, which is another characteristic of seventeenth-century building, and was an especial favourite with eighteenth-century French architects.

Quoin era.

François Mansard was the son of Pierre Mansard, the king's carpenter, and so was early initiated into the mysteries of building craft. When only twenty-eight he designed the château of Balleroy, between Bayeux and Saint Lô, one of the stateliest of French country houses. It is approached by a very wide, straight village street, which leads to a bridge across a small river, on the opposite bank of which stands the château. Its appearance is very imposing. The main block consists of a lofty centre of three storeys, with dormers above, which projects a few feet in front of the rest of the façade, which is a storey lower. The central part is crowned by a steep-pitched, hipped roof, surmounted by a belvidere; and the roofs of the wings are also hipped on all sides. The whole is raised on an extensive terrace, on the front part of which stand also two one-storied outbuildings, to the right and left, which frame in the main building and give it scale. The design throughout is very simple, but shows how effective the "quoin" treatment can be when carried out boldly.

François Mansard (1598– 1666).

Another work of Mansard's in Normandy, the small château of Brécy, now a farmhouse, a few miles from Caen, shows the giant at play. The entrance courtyard is enclosed in front by a pilastered wall, with a well-proportioned central gateway; but the chief interest lies in the rectangular garden at the back. This is of no great size, but its divisions and terraces at different levels give it considerable dignity.

Châteaux Maisons sur-Seine and Blois.

Mansard's two finest secular buildings are the additions he made to the château of Blois, for Gaston d'Orléans, in 1635, and the château of Maisons, near Paris, commenced a few years later. His intention at Blois was to pull down the whole of the François premier wing on the north side of the courtyard—he did demolish a small portion—and to rebuild it to match his new west wing.

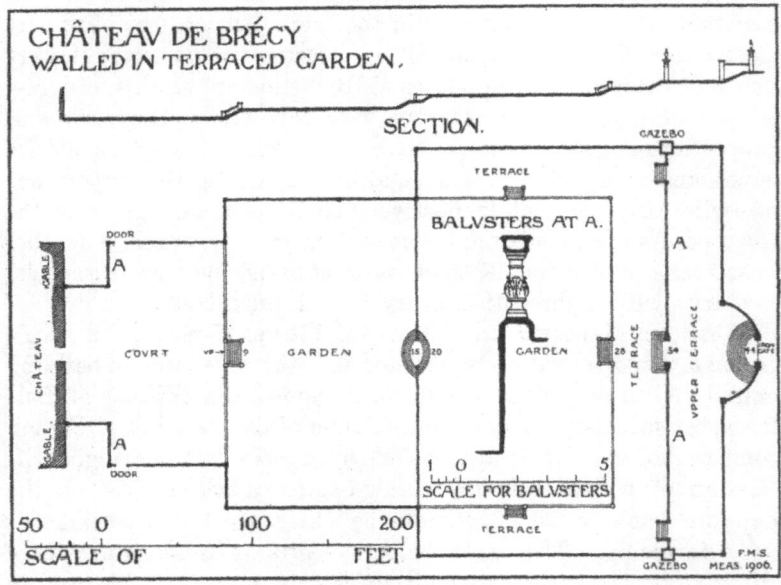

Fig. 166.

Fortunately the work never proceeded so far; as, fine though the effect would doubtless have been, the destruction of the earlier work, with its wonderful external staircase, would have been a great calamity. The courtyard side of Mansard's wing was never finished. On some of the columns the flutings are only half made, on others they are not even commenced; and the triglyphs and metopes are only partially worked on the frieze. Inside, the splendid carving in and round the panels of the ceiling of the staircase-hall is incomplete, and in places only outlined. But enough is carved to show the great beauty of the design. The façade facing the court is three storeys in height, each storey

Photo: Author.

Fig. 167.—Château de Blois, dome over staircase.

Photo: Author.

Fig. 168.—Château de Blois, panelled cove under dome.

[*To face p.* 204.

Photo: Author.
Fig. 169.—Château de Blois, Gaston d'Orleans' wing, portion of terrace front.

Photo: Author.
Fig. 170.—Château de Maisons, near Paris.

[*To face p.* 205.

having its own order. The effect is somewhat dull, and would be worse if it were not for the peristyle, curved in plan, which comes in front of the corners to the right and left. The terrace façade is far better. The ground is at a higher level than on the courtyard side, and is reached by the first flight of seven steps of the

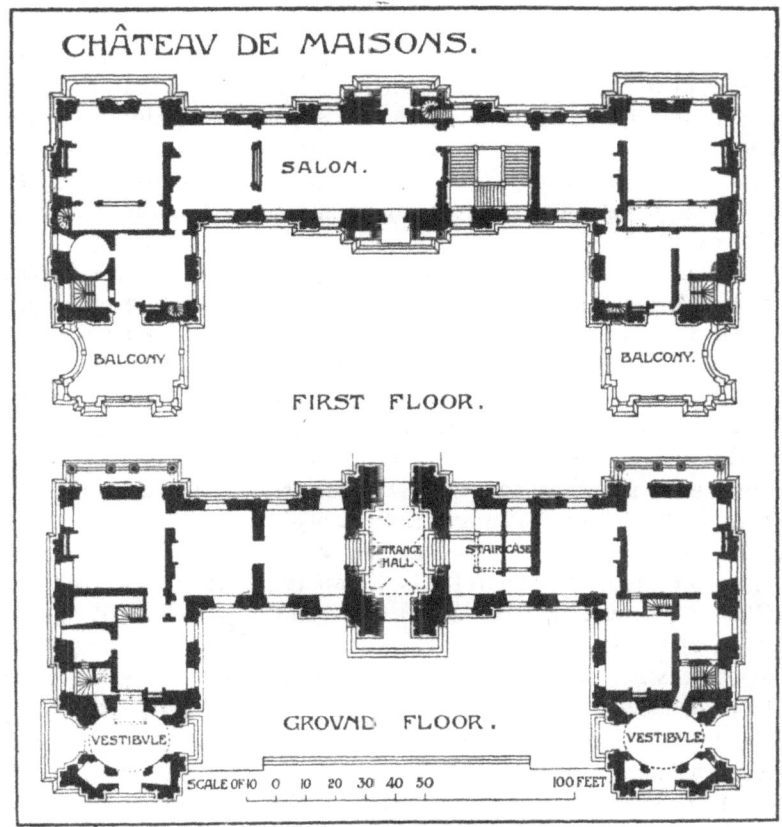

Fig. 171.

main staircase. The ground storey consequently is treated as a basement, and only the two upper storeys are pilastered. In no building, probably, is the superiority of a low, simple ground storey over a high ornamented one better demonstrated.[1] The

[1] In "Le Grand Marot" extensive gardens are represented on the south or terrace side, which, if they ever existed, are now cut through by the road, far below the level of the terrace, which runs round the castle. In the same book

château of Maisons, like that of Balleroy, faces a bridge over a river, but here the river is the Seine. In this building Mansard, as at Blois, adopted the pilaster treatment for walls. The effect, however, is much better than usual, as most of the pilasters are in pairs. The front facing the river is not so happy as the garden front; in great measure because of the side wings of the latter with their one-storeyed projections, which are terraced. These are the best features in the building, and altogether admirable.[1] The planning inside is stately; the rooms are well proportioned, and many of them retain their old fireplaces, ceilings, doorways, etc. The most effective feature of the interior is the series of groups of children in high relief, cleverly introduced as a frieze between pilasters under the ceiling of the principal staircase.

Val-de-Grâce. The most important church designed by Mansard is the Val-de-Grâce, Paris. The church and its surrounding buildings, however, had not proceeded far before the work was suspended; and when it was continued, Lemercier and, later, other architects carried it to completion. The façade of the church has not the simple dignity and fine proportions of Lemercier's church of the Sorbonne; and the heavy consoles at the sides which act as flying buttresses, are overdone. For the latter, however, Lemuet and Leduc, who followed Lemercier, are probably responsible.

Succeeding architects. Lemercier and François Mansard were succeeded by a brilliant group of men, of whom Louis Levau (or Leveau) (1612-1670), Claude Perrault (c. 1613-1688), Jean Marot (c. 1620-1679), and Antoine Le Pautre (1621-1682) are the best known. These men, together with the two first named, started the style known as Louis Quatorze (1643-1715), which, under the hands of Jules Hardouin Mansard, Robert de Cotte, and others, became somewhat stereotyped.

Completion of the Louvre. To this group belongs the completion of the Louvre; excepting the portions added in the last century. In 1624, by command of Louis XIII. and his minister Richelieu, Lemercier began the extensive additions which enlarged the courtyard to four times the size originally contemplated. He more than doubled the length of the west side, adding the central pavilion, and built

are shown belvederes on top of the central and angle pavilions, which cannot have improved the design.

[1] The château is now isolated, and where its gardens were formerly are villa residences, but a great portion of the well-laid-out park beyond remains.

nearly half of the north side. To the west he had the good taste to repeat exactly Lescot's design with the attic upper floor. To the north, he—or Levau who succeeded him, which does not appear quite certain—substituted a whole storey with a complete order. The change is no improvement. A sequence of three orders is rarely successful. The Italians showed their wisdom by seldom attempting it. The remaining sides of the court were finished by Levau, who was Mazarin's *protégé*, between 1654 and 1664. He was a safe man who could be trusted to repeat Lescot's general design and detail without modifications, the unfortunate upper storey excepted. Where he was obliged to depart from the original, as in the central bays on each side where the entrances come, he failed. The pediments over these are deplorably weak, but he was hampered by the three orders, which prevented his making the top entablature of sufficient size. By the time Levau had finished the inside of the court, the question of the outer façades, especially the long front to the east, had become acute. Levau prepared a design, but Colbert, who had succeeded Mazarin as minister to Louis XIV., would have none of it. Bernini was summoned from Rome. His proposals were most drastic; and consisted of nothing less than sweeping away all existing buildings of the Louvre and Tuileries, and starting a new gigantic palace to cover their sites, and also the ground between them.[1] Luckily his plans were not accepted. They have many fine points, but no matter how splendid the result might have been, Lescot's wing would have disappeared.[2]

As the result of much intrigue, a design submitted by Claude Perrault was finally accepted, and work in accordance with it was commenced in 1665. Perrault was famous as a physician, anatomist, and mathematician, and his interest in and enthusiasm for architecture were undoubted. He was a man of great ability; and if he really made the design for the east front of the Louvre himself, he deserves a very high place amongst architects. Doubts as to this, however, were current from the first. Jacques François Blondel, writing some seventy years after the work was done, refers to them, but characterizes as disgraceful the attempt

East façade.

---

[1] His design is reproduced in "L'Architecture Française," by Jacques François Blondel (in Vol. iv. of the republication), together with Perrault's design for a similar rebuilding.

[2] Sir Christopher Wren records, when in Paris, "Bernini's design for the Louvre I would have given my skin for, but the old reserved Italian gave me but a few minutes' view." Evidently Wren thought highly of it.

to rob Perrault of the credit. One suggestion made is that the design was really due to Perrault's brother Charles, also an amateur. This seems improbable; if one may judge from a design by Charles for a triumphal arch, illustrated in Blondel's book, which is an impossible production, bad in scale, covered with ornament, and without a trace of the reticence and dignity so conspicuous in the Louvre façade. Another suggestion is that the design was really Levau's; but that he could not claim the authorship owing to Colbert's opposition to him.[1] He apparently superintended the work, as *premier architecte du roi*, but he may have done that without having designed it. The front, with its simple, effective ground storey, noble peristyle of columns in pairs above, standing several feet in front of the wall behind, and framed by the more solid bays at each end, is far superior to anything of Levau's on the courtyard side. The divisions and decorations of the pilastered back wall are masterly. The pediment in the centre over the entrance is far finer in scale than the pediments in the court. Either Perrault was served by a very able ghost—and who that ghost can have been the list of contemporary architects fails to suggest—or else he had a marvellous genius for architecture. His plan for uniting the Louvre and Tuileries is a fine one, and there is no reason why that at least should not have been entirely his own.[2] In the seventeenth and eighteenth centuries architecture was studied and understood by other than architects. A physician, with some knowledge of it and with ideas, might make such a plan. But an elevation, with its difficulties of perspective, light and shade, foreshortened proportions, and last, but not least, fine scale, is another matter. To design one so full of dignity and originality as the east front of the Louvre, and so far in advance of contemporary work, requires greater knowledge, and knowledge of a different and more intimate kind. If Perrault possessed that his versatility must have been phenomenal.

The north and south outer façades were also carried out by Perrault, but are dull by comparison with the east façade. After these were finished, little more was done for over a century. Not until the time of the First Empire was any serious attempt made to unite the Louvre and Tuileries to the north. Between the two buildings were houses, streets, squares, a whole district of the city, and this had to be swept away. Under Napoleon I.

[1] See "Dictionnaire des Architectes Français," by A. S. Lance.
[2] See footnote on preceding page.

FIG. 172.—East façade of The Louvre, Paris.

[*To face p.* 208.

considerable progress was made, and the work was completed under Napoleon III. But what had taken more than three centuries to achieve only lasted a few years. The Tuileries was burnt in the Commune; and its ruins were cleared away in the eighties of the last century.

Levau should not be judged by his work at the Louvre. His versatility and power of design are better shown in the château of Vaux-le-Vicomte, near Fontainebleau, the plan of which is very fine; the Collège des Quatre Nations, founded by Mazarin in 1661, now the Institut de France; and the Hôtel Lambert, in the Rue de l'île S. Louis, Paris. The curved front of the Collège

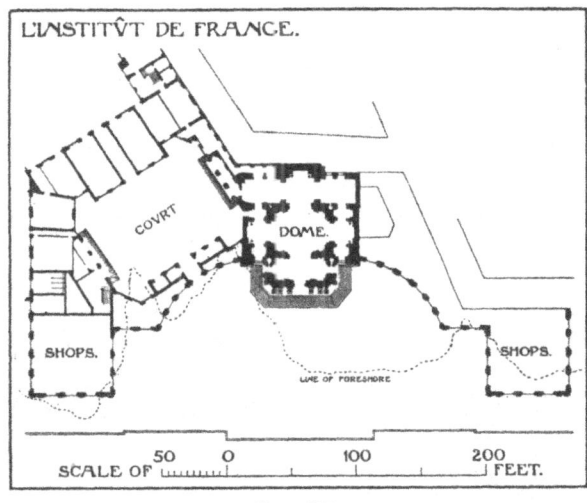

FIG. 173.

is an excellent idea, possibly suggested by the line of the old foreshore of the river. In elevation the curved portions are not so successful as the rectangular wings at the ends. The pilasters of the latter, running the full height of the building, have considerable dignity, and the detail is excellent. The courtyard has some good points, and from it the dome over the central block appears more striking than from the river. The most interesting architectural feature of the Hôtel Lambert is the outside staircase at the end of the court facing the entrance. Between the columns in front of this, however, a glass front has recently been erected which has ruined the design, although it may have been necessary for comfort.

210 *A HISTORY OF ARCHITECTURAL DEVELOPMENT*

Antoine Le Pautre.

Le Pautre's best work is the Hôtel de Beauvais, in the Rue François-Miron, Paris. In plan, it is as striking an instance as

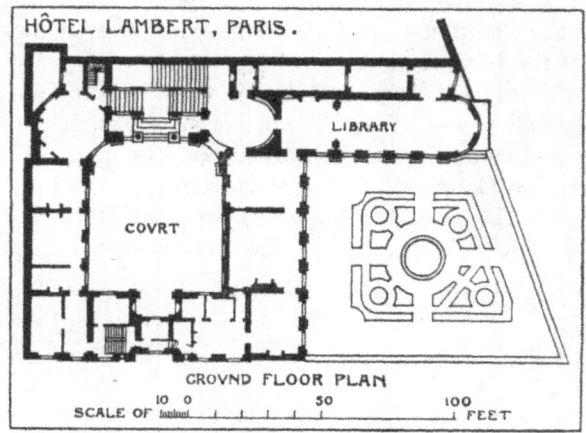

Fig. 174.

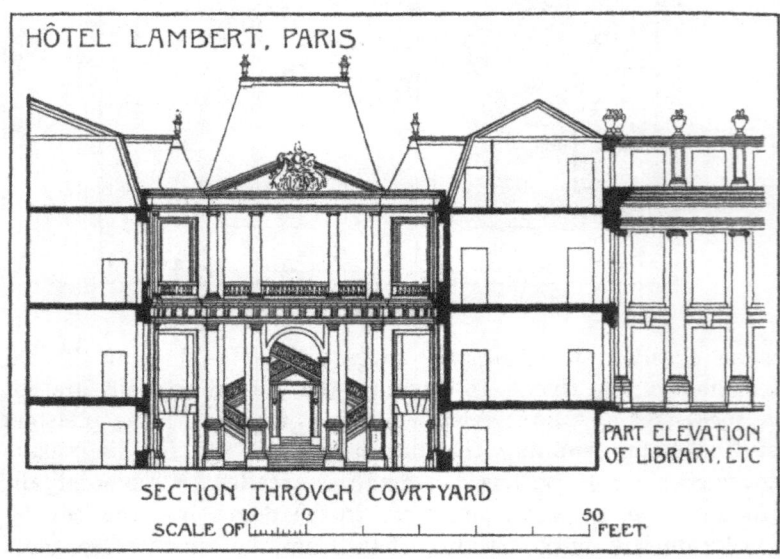

Fig. 175.

the Palazzo Massimi, Rome, of how symmetry can be obtained on an exceedingly irregular site. The elevation facing the street is now very simple, but may possibly have been different originally.

Photo: Author.
Fig. 176.—Hôtel de Beauvais, Paris, vestibule from courtyard.

Photo: Author.
Fig. 177.—Hôtel de Beauvais, Paris, end of courtyard.

[To face p. 211.

THE ARCHITECTURE OF THE LOUIS

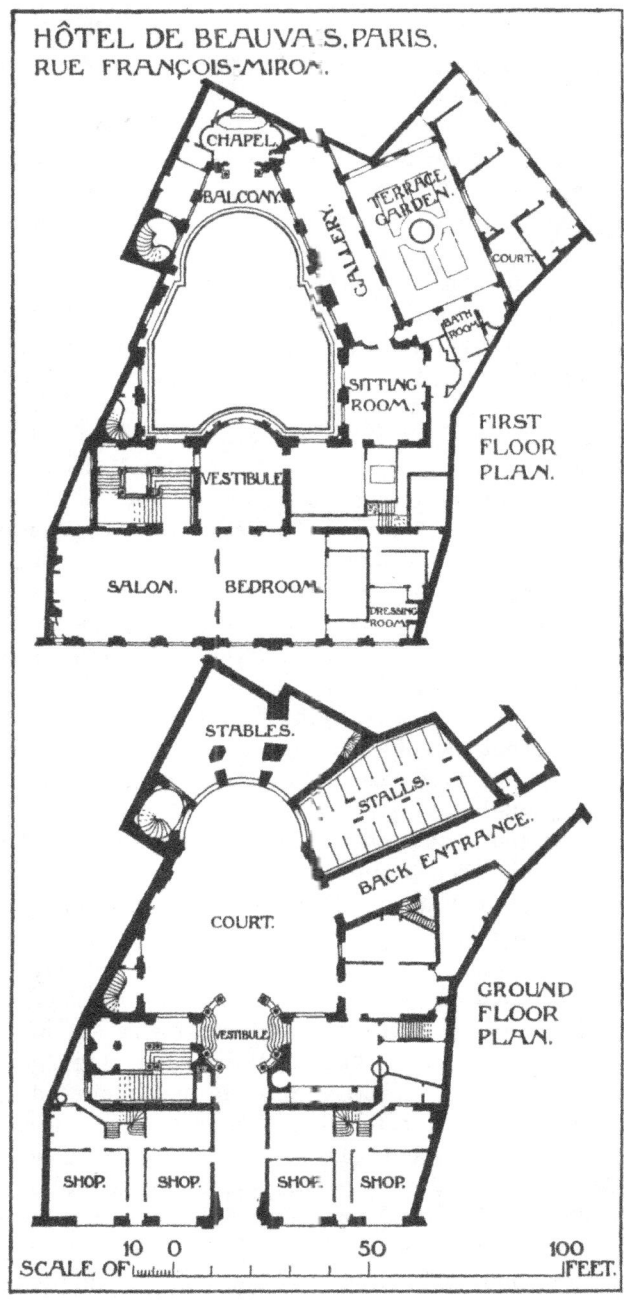

Fig. 178.

The chief interest lies in the courtyard, which is excellent both as regards plan and design. A barrel-vaulted carriage-way, under the front portion of the house, leads to an open circular vestibule with detached columns on the courtyard side. The opposite end of the court is much narrower than the entrance end, and the ground storey is curved in plan, whilst on the first floor an exceedingly well designed doorway, or window, flanked by columns, is recessed to allow of a balcony in front. An effective entablature runs round the court above the ground storey. This is continued over the columns of the circular vestibule; but in order to prevent its appearing too heavy at this point the detail is varied; in the frieze, triglyphs take the place of the bold corbel-brackets elsewhere, whilst the carving of the metopes has less projection. Altogether the design is full of interest. In 1652 Le Pautre published "Les œuvres d'architecture d'Antoine Le Pautre." This book, as might have been expected of the author of the Hôtel de Beauvais, is well worthy of study. Its great attraction, however, lies in the beauty of the draughtsmanship of the illustrations, which were designed and drawn by his brother Jean, an engraver of high repute. Some of the decorative designs in the book are incomparable. Jean Marot, like Du Cerceau, is better known by his publications than his buildings. "Le Magnifique Chasteau de Richelieu" has already been mentioned. He issued a book on contemporary French architecture (no date) which has been republished in different forms. One edition is known as "Le Grand Marot"; another, very inferior, as "Le Petit Marot." The above-mentioned books, and others published previously or subsequently, made the French absolutely independent of Italian writers, and contributed not a little towards their emancipation from Italian architecture.

Many other buildings of the seventeenth century might be mentioned. In Paris there are several due to Lemercier, F. Mansard, and others. In the provinces few towns are without examples. At Soissons, the small Pavillon des Arquebusiers (c. 1623) is an early and effective example of "quoin" design. At Noyon, near the west front of the cathedral, and at Orleans, are many stately town houses of the old nobility. Caen, Abbeville, and other towns in the north are full of similar examples. At Saumur the church of Nôtre Dame des Ardilliers deserves special mention because its nave is circular, and churches of that plan are rare in the provinces. It is nearly seventy feet in diameter

Photo: Author.

FIG. 179.—Nôtre Dame des Ardilliers, Saumur.

[*To face p.* 212.

internally, and is therefore of good size, and the dome that covers it is well proportioned. The churches and houses of this period receive scant description in guide books, are frequently entirely unmentioned, but they are well worth seeking, and better merit attention than earlier examples, possibly more "picturesque," which find a place in most sketch-books.

Jules Hardouin Mansard (1643–1708) dominates the end of the seventeenth century and the commencement of the eighteenth. He was the son of Jules Hardouin, first king's painter, his mother being a niece of François Mansard, whose surname he took. Amongst the architects of his time he does not appear to have been popular, but his unpopularity may have been due to the commanding position he occupied in the architectural world. Daviler, the author of "Cours d'Architecture," first published in 1696, and a man of considerable ability, worked for him as assistant for some time, and does not give him a good name. He records that he "wasted five years in that capacity." His principal assistant was Cailleteau Lassurance, architect of the Palais Bourbon, now part of the Chamber of Deputies, who designed many of the largest of the old private hotels in the Faubourg S. Germain. Saint-Simon, famous for his Memoirs, writing at the time of Mansard's death, insinuates that neither Mansard nor his successor, Robert de Cotte, knew anything about building, and that Lassurance was their "ghost," *qu'ils tenaient tant qu'ils pouvoient sous clef.* But Saint-Simon had a malicious pen, and his injustice towards those he disliked is proverbial. Mansard could not possibly have carried out all the work attributed to him without substantial aid, but it does not follow that his best works were not his own.

J. H. Mansard.

The list of town and country houses he designed is stupendous. He was not content with merely single buildings; he erected whole "quartiers." At Paris, the Place Vendôme (originally Place Louis le Grand) and Place des Victoires are his, in addition to other large works. To the Hôtel des Invalides, commenced by Liberal Bruant, he added the famous Dôme, his greatest artistic achievement (see Figs. 129 and 131). At Versailles he built the château, almost a town in itself.

The Place Vendôme differs from other squares in that a house is built across each of the four corners. These four houses, together with the central houses on two sides of the square, are emphasized by pediments. The other houses are balustraded on top. Otherwise all are alike, as well as the houses in the streets to the north and south. The effect is still very dignified, although minor alterations, especially in the arched openings of the ground storey, have somewhat spoilt the design. Such arched openings were a tradition in France, dating from mediæval times, and they have continued down to the present day. The actual openings were often square headed, the semicircle above being filled by panelling, or by a window lighting the mezzanine, or entre-sol, which so frequently divides the ground storey from the important first floor. In the Place Vendôme pilasters of the Corinthian order start at the first-floor level and run through two storeys to a well-proportioned entablature crowning the wall. This was the favourite treatment in Mansard's day. After his death it was abandoned in favour of the simple, straight-sided, channelled pilaster, introduced before by Lemercier and François Mansard, which is referred to later.

Versailles.
High praise cannot be given to Mansard's great building at Versailles. It is great only in size. This was his finest opportunity, and he cannot be said to have made the most of it. He was possibly hampered to some extent by an existing building by Levau which he had to incorporate, and also by instructions from the king. Whether judged from the entrance court or from the gardens, the main composition is unsatisfactory. From the court, the centre is too much recessed; from the gardens the wings look as though they do not belong to the central block. The entrance courtyard itself is planned on fine lines. Now dismal, bare, and deserted, it presented a different appearance when thronged with carriages, cavaliers, pages, and courtiers. The chief main faults of the building are, firstly, that there is no central commanding feature; and secondly, that there are no enclosed courtyards of anything approaching fine dimensions. The chapel only rises sufficiently high to produce an unsatisfactory break in the sky-line; otherwise, the building is of one height. The courts of the central block are merely light-giving areas. The chapel, judged by itself, and separated from its surroundings, is a success. It is really dignified; especially the interior, with its range of columns at the gallery level which support the main entablature from which springs the vault.

Garden front.
The garden front might have been improved if wings had been built at the ends, standing forward as far as the central block. Such wings would have enabled the length of the front to be

judged from the garden, which now is impossible, and would also have enclosed two stately courtyards, open to the garden, each about 450 feet by 300. The whole of the front is of three storeys, the top storey being an attic crowned by a balustrade. The monotony of the balustraded outline is most depressing, extending as it does for more than a third of a mile. The sculptured groups and finials above the balustrade—which are restorations—are

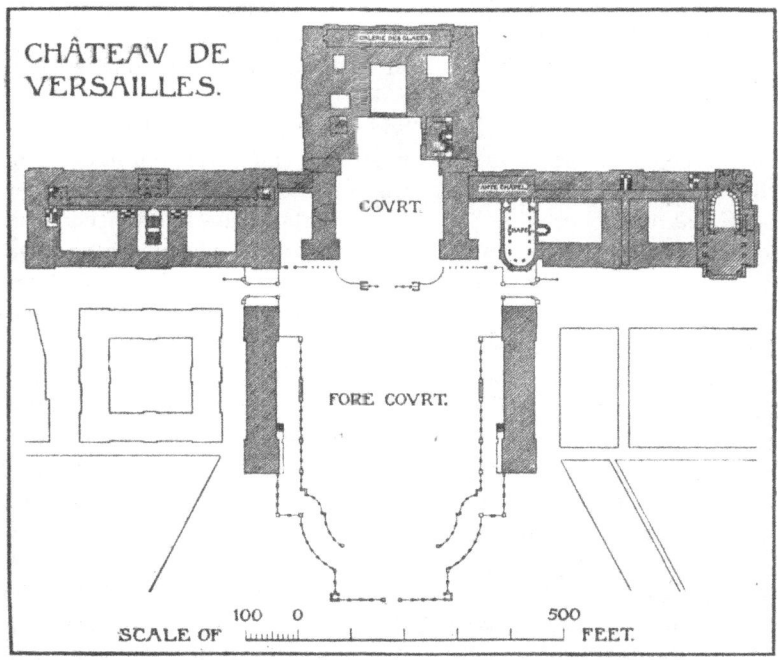

FIG. 180.

effective if a small portion of the front is taken by itself, but in the mass they are lost. The same remark applies to the projecting bays. These are only carried as high as the entablature which ranges with the first floor, and above that level consist merely of detached columns. They do not therefore tell, save in strong sunshine. In portions of the entrance front pilasters are carried through two storeys, and possibly the effect would have been better if this treatment had been adopted facing the garden. Altogether the parts are too numerous and too small, and the bays too narrow. The building, as a whole, lacks dignity, the one quality a large building should possess.

216 A HISTORY OF ARCHITECTURAL DEVELOPMENT

<small>The interior.</small>
Many rooms in the palace are individually well proportioned and of good size, but somehow they fail to impress, possibly because they are so numerous that one's sense of scale becomes confused. The Salle des Glaces is the largest and by far the most successful. That really does look large, in great measure owing to the mirrors facing the windows. Each mirror consists of many separate pieces set in narrow, gilded, metal frames, which help to give scale. The same design with single sheets of plate glass in each division would be unbearable. The private apartments of Marie Antoinette, with the later decoration of her time, form a charming suite.

<small>Orangery.</small>
At the south end of the wide terrace which stretches the whole length of the garden front, forming an extensive plateau, is the Orangery. This is a vast sunk garden, with a simple arcaded façade as a background, and great flights of steps on either side leading down to the lower level. Here one obtains, what one never obtains anywhere in the main building, an absolute sensation of size. The effect is magnificently stately, and the finest architectural picture at Versailles.

<small>Gardens, etc.</small>
The gardens at Versailles are something distinct from the palace. As a rule, garden and house help each other; are bound together, and part and parcel of one design. At Versailles it is difficult to see the gardens from the house, and practically impossible to see the house from the gardens. The royal apartments, however, being on the first floor, the former drawback did not so much matter, as from the Salle des Glaces, at all events, a fair view is obtainable. Le Nôtre, the designer of the gardens, followed his usual plan of principal parallel alleys and minor diagonal ones, with circles at most intersections. The Trianons occupy a corner. The Grand Trianon, begun by Mansard in 1688, after the château was finished, is a very clever example of an Italian villa, and consists of a single storey and a basement. It is practically two distinct buildings, joined by a loggia open on both sides. One side is arched, the other lintelled, a somewhat unusual and not altogether satisfactory combination. The outside walls are of yellow stone, the columns, pilasters, and frieze of the main entablature being pink marble. The design of the Petit Trianon is entirely different. The building is three-storied in front and two-storied at the back. It was not commenced until 1766, and is one of the best-proportioned examples of late work; delightful in detail inside and out, and a credit to its architect, Jacques Ange Gabriel.

Photo: Author.
FIG. 181.—VERSAILLES, PORTION OF GARDEN FRONT.

Photo: Author.
FIG. 182.—VERSAILLES, THE ORANGERY.

[*To face p.* 216.

With the death of Mansard, in 1708, the last of the great architects of Louis XIV.'s time passed away. His principal successors were his brother-in-law, Robert de Cotte (1656–1735), who continued his practice and completed most of his unfinished buildings, Germain Boffrand (1667–1754), Cailleteau Lassurance (d. 1724), and his son Jean (d. 1755).

Mansard's successors.

The work of the time of Louis XV. has got a bad name, but it does not deserve it. The term "Louis Quinze" is often applied to anything that is twisted and distorted in form and overflorid in decoration. Bad imitations, especially of the furniture of the period, are largely responsible for this reputation. The real thing is very different. The buildings—externally, at least—err in being too plain, if that be an error. Their façades are so simple that they are easily passed by. But a little attention bestowed upon them is well repaid. Then their beauties reveal themselves coyly one by one. In the first half of the seventeenth century the "quoin" treatment found most favour for window jambs and external angles; in the second half Mansard popularized the Corinthian pilaster. In the eighteenth century the simple, channelled pilaster is often the only sign that the outsides of buildings received any architectural thought at all. These pilasters come generally at the external angles, and also frequently flank, in addition, entrance doorways. They have no capitals, frequently no bases, and reach from the plinth to the main cornice at the eaves. They relieve in many cases what otherwise would be too great simplicity, and in all instances strengthen the corners, both literally and figuratively. Window openings, as a rule, are quite plain, sometimes without architrave at all, at other times surrounded by a plain band resting on a well-designed, moulded cill. The openings generally start from quite close to the floor, affording an opportunity for an iron grille or balcony-front to each. In many buildings these grilles are delightful in design and workmanship, and the only relief to an otherwise absolutely plain front. In the time of Lemercier and F. Mansard keystones of windows and doorways were carved as grotesque faces or masks. Some of the most effective are over the openings in the court of the Hôtel Carnavalet. In the eighteenth century they are also often carved as faces, but the object of the sculptors was to make these as "gracieuse" as possible, and women's faces predominate. Often the carving extends beyond the keystone proper, and wanders in leaves and flowers over the neighbouring voussoirs. Theoretically

Characteristics of Louis XV. work.

this may be wrong, but the work is executed with such grace and lightness of touch that a man must indeed be wedded to ruggedness who does not admit and appreciate its beauty. Sometimes the faces are omitted, and frolicsome carving alone is substituted. Brackets supporting balconies are also frequently carved. The exuberance displayed in these is less pardonable, because whatever carries, or seems to carry, weight should appear strong rather than ornamental. More licence is permissible in brackets which are purely architectural features, like those under the straight portions of the cornice of the gateway in Fig. 183. These brackets and keystones illustrate well the maxim that it is better to have little carving and have that little good, than much and indifferent. And the simplicity of the surroundings emphasizes the richness of these spots of ornamentation.

Interiors. The interiors are the very opposite of the exteriors. They are proof that the architects could revel in ornament when they chose, and to some extent prove that they deliberately used it sparingly outside. But although the interiors are so rich—so florid, if the term is preferred—they are not gaudy. The fact that all parts of a room are equally rich prevents the richness from being too apparent. It may sound paradoxical to claim that the plainer a room is the richer it often appears, but the statement is nevertheless correct. One elaborate feature may so dominate its surroundings that all else is forgotten. The plainer its setting, the more its influence is felt. If the eighteenth-century architects had held their hand at any one point, the effect of many of these old rooms would be deplorable. But they did not. Ceilings, cornices, and panelled walls; fireplaces, mirrors, and marble-topped tables; over-doors, the doors themselves, their handles, plates, and escutcheons—all are treated alike. Even the floors are elaborate parquet. And the furniture in the rooms and the hangings to the windows were in keeping. Herein lay salvation. A Louis Quinze table with curly legs or a chair of curious outline may appear grotesque in a modern drawing-room, but that is because it lacks an appropriate setting. The boudoir from the Hôtel Saint Albin, Rue Vieille du Temple, Paris, now at South Kensington, shows how richly decorated rooms sometimes were. This is Louis XVI. work, and owes its effect mainly to its paintings. In most of the old rooms in Paris, Versailles, the Trianon, etc., the woodwork is, or was, white, or that pale grey which is only one remove, although in the panels, especially the upper portions,

Photo: Author.
FIG. 183.—ENTRANCE GATEWAY, RUE S. DOMINIQUE, 16, PARIS.

Photo: Author.
FIG. 184.—ENTRANCE GATEWAY, RUE DE GRENELLE, 188, PARIS.

[*To face p.* 218.

THE ARCHITECTURE OF THE LOUIS

near the ceiling, were frequently paintings of figure subjects or landscapes.

The French architects of the eighteenth century thoroughly Plans. realized that a good plan is as much a work of art as a good elevation. The plans of the old houses of the period are most stately, and are even more worthy of study than the plans of

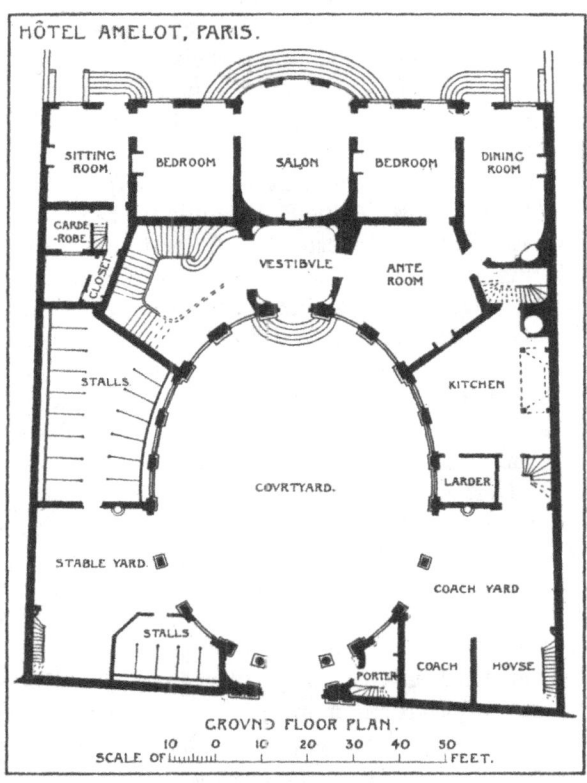

Fig. 185.

Italian palaces. They are nearer our own time and our own conditions. Their stateliness may be coupled with a certain amount of inconvenience, but, provided the latter is not too great, the sacrifice is worth making. A strong similarity runs through all. A lofty entrance gateway, generally arched and crowned by a curved cornice, leads to a courtyard. On either side of the gateway are the rooms for the porter, over which are

220   A HISTORY OF ARCHITECTURAL DEVELOPMENT

bedrooms for him or for other servants. This portion of the house is quite low, and towards the street is represented not infrequently by a blank wall, save for the entrance. Such windows as were necessary here faced the court. To the left and right are the stables and coach-houses, frequently with their own courts. The French nobility did not equal the great Roman families in the number of their equipages, but the smallest hôtels have stalls for half a dozen horses, and the larger ones could accommodate five or six times that number. Sometimes the stables are on one side, and the kitchen is on the other, far away from the dining-room. This arrangement has its advantages. Smell from cooking is kept out of the house. Satisfactory service might be difficult now, but the large number of servants kept in those days made it easy. The Hôtel d'Amelot, now 1, Rue S. Dominique, Paris, designed by Germain Boffrand, has been chosen for illustration. The plan has considerable dignity, and the service is more convenient than in most examples. Otherwise it differs little from them, save in the shape of its courtyard, which is oval instead of the more customary rectangle.

Paris hotels.

Most of the principal provincial cities in France possess examples of the eighteenth-century house, and Paris is still particularly rich in this respect. The majority are in the Faubourg S. Germain, in the streets de Varenne, de Grenelle, Saint Dominique, de Lille, etc. In the Rue du Faubourg S. Honoré are others, one being the British Embassy, which still have their gardens reaching to the Champs Elysées. Many of these old houses, especially those in the S. Germain quarter, are now Government offices. Some remain private houses, and not infrequently an old house is hidden from view and retains only a portion of its courtyard, a more modern building having been built on the remaining portion and above the porte-cochère, porter's lodge, etc. In some instances a house with its garden extended from one street to another; and on the site is now a road lined on both sides by blocks of flats. Or the site only reached half way; hence the quiet cul-de-sacs similarly lined, which are not uncommon.[1]

[1] In a map of Paris, dated "an 8" (1800), in my possession, the large private houses of the Faubourg S. Germain and their gardens are plainly shown, as well as Le Nôtre's laying out of the ground in front of the Hôtel des Invalides, and the Ecole Militaire, now built over. The map also shows the buildings, rows of houses, streets, and squares that until Napoleon's time came between the Louvre and Tuileries, extending to the Rue S. Honoré.

To turn over the pages of seventeenth and eighteenth-century books on architecture is in itself a liberal education. Marot, Le Pautre, Blondel, Mariette, etc., take one back to the days of the fine gentleman and full-bottomed wigs, to the stateliness of the time of the later Louis. Blondel and Mariette are particularly valuable for Paris and its vicinity.[1] In the book published by the latter are shown some delightfully planned gardens in the country in which symmetry is obtained on the most irregular sites. *Eighteenth-century publications.*

In the middle of the century Emmanuel Héré de Corny laid out in marvellous fashion a large portion of the town of Nancy for Stanilas, father-in-law of Louis XV. The Place Stanilas is one of the stateliest squares in France. It is open at the four corners, except that across them are very remarkable iron gates and grilles; an unusual feature, but one that lends great distinction to the surroundings. In the centre of one end is a short street leading to a triumphal arch, which forms the entrance to the oblong Place de la Carrière. At the end of the latter stands the Palais du Gouvernement, by Héré, which is connected with the houses on either side of the Place by two fine semicircles of open arcading. Altogether the planning is well worthy of study, and all the buildings of this part of the town are simple, dignified examples of the period. *Nancy.*

Under Louis XV. the Place de la Concorde, Paris, was planned by Jacques Ange Gabriel (1710–82), who also designed the two fine buildings at one end flanking the entrance to the Rue Royale. The design of these is undoubtedly founded on Perrault's east façade of the Louvre, with some modifications. The substitution of single columns for columns in pairs on the upper storey is certainly no improvement, and the arcaded ground storey, with its numerous openings, is not so reposeful as the corresponding storey of the earlier building. Behind the arcade is a covered way, which in itself is an advantage. The detail is delicate, yet forcible, and such as might have been expected from the architect of the Petit Trianon. *Place de la Concorde.*

[1] Mariette was a publisher who reproduced the works of Marot and other engravers. About 1750, he sold his plates, etc., to another publisher, Charles Antoine Jombert, who commissioned Jacques François Blondel to get out a great work in eight volumes, "Architecture Françoise" (1752-4-6), which bears Blondel's name. Only four volumes were published. Blondel is also known as the author of "De la Distribution des Maisons de Plaisance, et de la Decoration des Edifices en general," 1737 and 1738, and other works.

222 A HISTORY OF ARCHITECTURAL DEVELOPMENT

Panthéon.   The most remarkable achievement of the end of the century is the Panthéon, Paris, the work of J. G. Soufflot (1709-80). In plan it is a Greek cross, and in many respects closely resembles Justinian's church of the Holy Apostles at Constantinople, destroyed in 1464, so far as can be judged from Procopius' description of it.[1] Each arm is domed, and over the crossing rises a higher dome, the only one that shows externally. This last has already been described (see p. 164). The fault of the building is over-clever construction, which very nearly resulted in the collapse of the central portion. The four piers at this point

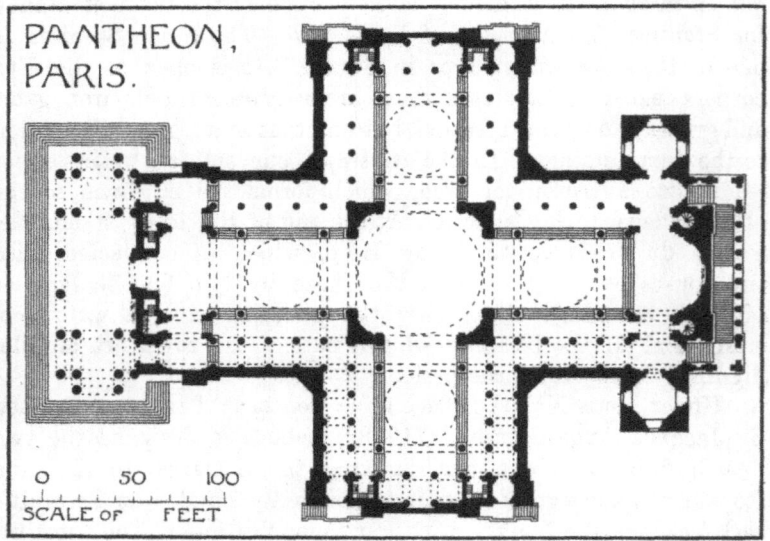

Fig. 186.

had to be strengthened early in the nineteenth century. The manner in which the wide transverse arches separating the central dome from the side domes appear to be carried mainly on small pilasters is exceedingly startling. The perspective effects are striking, owing to the ranges of columns which divide the side ambulatories from the main portions of the building, and to the peeps obtainable from one arm into another behind the piers which support the dome.[2] The main lighting is from huge

[1] See Hubsch, "Monuments de l'architecture chrétienne," Plate XXXII.
[2] The mural decorations by Puvis de Chavannes are perfect as regards decorative quality and suitability.

lunettes, placed above the side columns, which rise above the roofs over the ambulatories. These do not show at all externally, as the outside wall stands in front of them, several feet away. This wall is unpierced, and absolutely plain, save for its entablature, and the extra frieze of swags below which might with advantage have been omitted. The entrance is by a stately portico, with sculptured pediment (see Fig. 130).

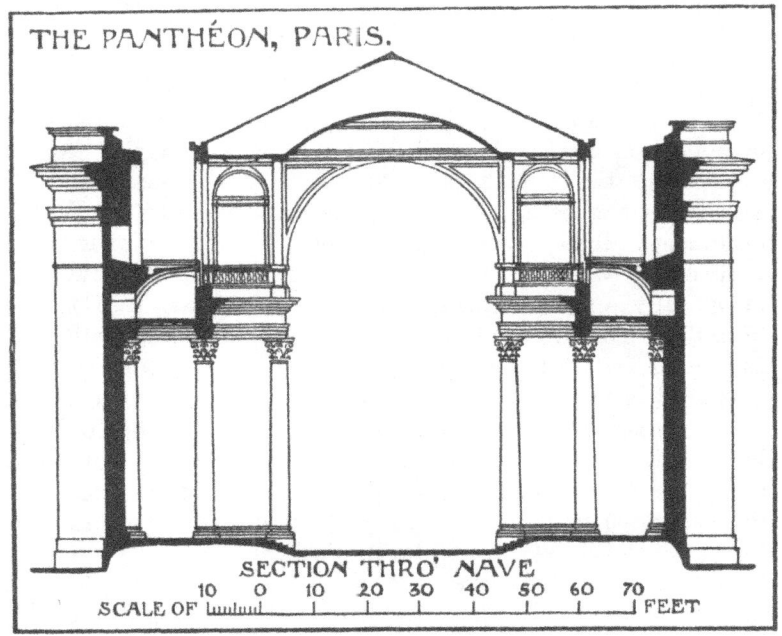

Fig. 187.

The beginning of the nineteenth century was marked in France, as in England, by a Greek revival. This extended to all the arts; to architecture less, perhaps, than to others. In the paintings of David; in the furniture known as "Empire"; in the dress of the period, it is strongly apparent. Its approach is heralded in the portico, and especially in the unpierced walls of the Panthéon. In the church of the Madeleine, designed by Pierre Vignon in 1806, it burst forth. Externally, this is a noble building, excelling the Maison Carrée, Nîmes, with which it is frequently compared, in size—its external dimensions are nearly thrice those of the older building—and in general design in that

Greek revival.

it is peripteral. In detail it almost holds its own with the other, and that is high praise. Internally, it is equally striking, and displays greater originality. Greek temples had wood ceilings; Roman temples were frequently vaulted by a barrel or an intersecting vault; the three bays of the Madeleine are domed. There are no aisles, but at the sides are shallow chapels and recesses between the internal buttresses which take the thrusts of the domes. The fronts of the recesses are cleverly treated with columns, etc., which give scale to the interior.[1]

Originality of French work.
In these two chapters on the Renaissance in France, emphasis has been laid more than once on its individuality and originality. Even in the Madeleine this is apparent, although Napoleon's command was for a reproduction of an ancient temple. At no period were the French mere followers of the Italians. The Italian Renaissance has its own merits and demerits; the French Renaissance likewise its own. No one with any knowledge of architecture will confuse the buildings of the two countries. Occasionally a design might belong to either, but that is the exception. The front of the church of S. Sulpice, Paris, for instance, is Italian in feeling, but then Servandony, who designed it, was so anxious for his work to be regarded as foreign that he Italianized his name to Servandoni. The façades of such churches as the Sorbonne, S. Roch, etc., do not differ very much from other façades in Italy, but still there is a difference. The François premier buildings are well known to most English students, but the later examples in France have hardly received the attention they deserve. In some respects they are more valuable to us than Italian buildings. They are more recent; their materials more resemble ours; the requirements of their day differed little from our requirements now. And they present such variety. They form a school in themselves. To advise careful study of them is not to recommend neglect of either Italian buildings or our own. Opportunities for studying all are now easy, and time ought to be found for all. Attention should also be given to modern work in France. Notwithstanding the political upheavals the country has experienced, her architectural traditions have remained unbroken for centuries. They have been assailed and opposed by Viollet-le-Duc and a few others, but have emerged triumphant. The Ecole des Beaux Arts has preserved them,

[1] As was the case in Roman basilicas, but the design is altogether different and more complex in the Madeleine.

nurtured them, and passed them on from one generation of students to another. To this cause is largely due the excellence of the work of the present day. It may occasionally be dull, but it is never bad;[1] and its best excels the best of any country in Europe.

[1] Except the "art nouveau" attempts, of which some deplorable recent examples may be seen in Paris and in the provinces.

CHAPTER XI

THE RENAISSANCE IN ENGLAND

Pre-Renaissance secular buildings.
NOT many secular buildings exist in England earlier than the fifteenth century, and those belonging to that century are none too numerous. In towns civic improvements have necessitated the sweeping away of the greater number; and even in the country their unsuitability for the requirements of the day and other causes have occasioned their removal. Of early examples the keeps of Rochester in Kent, and Castle Hedingham in Essex, and the so-called Jew's house at Lincoln, and another close by, are Norman. To the thirteenth and fourteenth centuries belong some Edwardian castles, Maxstoke, and notably Conway, Carnarvon, and others in Wales; and as examples of smaller houses may be mentioned the Bishop's Palace, Wells, in stone; Little Wenham Hall, Essex, in brick; the old priest's house at Alfriston, Sussex, in wood and plaster; Hever Castle and Penshurst Place, Kent, etc. Oxford and Cambridge also possess a few early examples, but most of the older college buildings at these two centres belong to the fifteenth century. Of monastic and collegiate buildings elsewhere of that date there are also a fair number. The most remarkable are possibly the Vicar's Close, Wells, and the Abbot's Kitchen and Tithe-barn at Glastonbury. The last is perfect, and the first-named is delightful in all respects, and the houses in it are still habitable. More purely secular town buildings of the fifteenth century are the George Inn and the Tribunal House, Glastonbury; the New Inn, Gloucester; the Guildhall, Lavenham, Suffolk, and some others. Through the battlements of the George Inn the stone figure still gazes on the street below, as it has done for four hundred years or more. Unaltered examples, however, are few, although in many towns portions of houses of this date remain, in many cases concealed by more modern fronts. Town houses of the Middle Ages can be better studied abroad than in England, as removals there have not been so wholesale. Brittany

is still full of many with half-timbered fronts, and in some of the towns in the south of France whole streets remain of stone houses dating from the fourteenth and fifteenth centuries, and little changed in appearance since that time. At Figeac, to the north of Albi, they are especially numerous. The ground-storey of each house consists of one or more unglazed, pointed, arched openings, which start from the ground and are shuttered at night, as they have been for centuries. Above is a comparatively unimportant

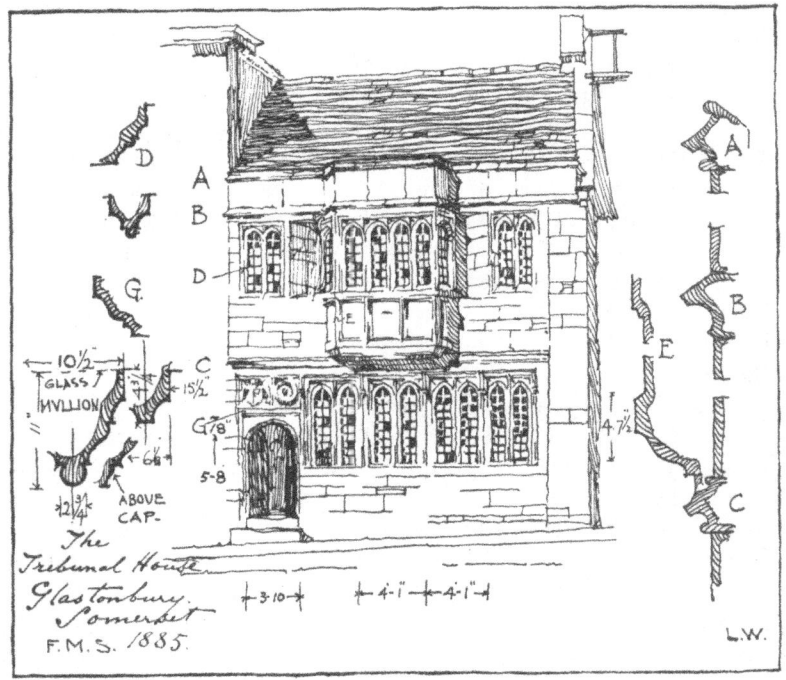

FIG. 188.

floor, lighted by plain windows; and higher still the principal floor, lofty in height, the windows in many instances having rich traceried heads. Many towns in Germany, Nürnberg, Rothenburg, Innsbruck, etc., are also rich in mediæval examples.

In fifteenth-century country houses England more than holds its own. Norfolk and Suffolk are particularly rich in this respect, and Hurstmonceaux Castle, Sussex, and Haddon Hall, Derbyshire, are well known. Of smaller houses Ockwells, Berks, Great Chalfield and South Wraxall, Wilts, and many others might be mentioned. These should not be ignored in any attempt to trace the rise of the Renaissance in England, as in plan, general design, and also in detail as well, they exercised considerable influence through the sixteenth century, and the greater portion of the century following.

The Renaissance work before sixteenth century.

During the whole of the fifteenth century, when the Renaissance was advancing by leaps and bounds in Italy, England remained faithful to her old traditions. Not a breath of the new movement wafted across the Channel. Workmen in this country followed their different callings, hardly aware of its existence; certainly without allowing it to affect their art. The style that had satisfied their forefathers sufficed for them. And no wonder. For Gothic, especially towards the end of the century, was still full of vigour. With the close of the Wars of the Roses it seemed to take a fresh lease of life, and one likely to last long. Its spirit animated all classes of buildings; from the cathedral to the wayside chapel, from the castle to the cottage. Even after the Renaissance began knocking at the door, in many places it knocked in vain. And in others, where the door was opened, it was still kept on the chain, and the Renaissance was allowed to enter but through a chink.

The start.

The Renaissance may be said to start in England with the accession of Henry VIII. in 1509. This monarch, young, generous, and impetuous, delighting in new fashions and new faces—as some had good cause to rue—was a great contrast to his austere, avaricious, and somewhat narrow father. An accomplished scholar, his interest in the revival of learning was great; and he was soon to take a leading part in the advancement of the new movement in art. That was in the air. It had long been the custom for influential Englishmen to send their sons to Italy, to study the humanities; and they, on their return, brought back glowing accounts of the condition of architecture, painting, and sculpture in that country. The laying of the foundation stone of the new S. Peter's, Rome, three years before the king came to the throne, the pomp and magnificence of that ceremony, and the new departure in architecture by Bramante, must have been well known to many in this country. Not only did Englishmen go to Italy, but, early in the sixteenth century, attracted by the splendour of the English Court, and the lavish generosity of the king, Italians began to come to England.

The first Italian of any note to arrive was Pietro Torrigiano, a fellow-student with Michael Angelo—whose nose he broke—in the Pietro Torrigiano. Medician Academy in Florence. The exact date of his arrival is uncertain, but it was probably 1510. The late king had left full instructions regarding his tomb, but these were upset by his successor, who entrusted the designing and carrying out of the work to Torrigiano in 1512. About the same time, Torrigiano designed another tomb at Westminster for Margaret, Countess of Richmond, mother of Henry VII., who also died in 1509. In the king's tomb two recumbent bronze figures, representing Henry and his queen, rest side by side on a black-marble pedestal, the sides of which are carved with wreaths, enclosing figures, flanked by bronze pilasters. In position and attitude the figures follow English traditions, but the wreaths and pilasters, enriched with Renaissance ornament, are important departures. These take the place of the panels, or niches with traceried heads, which had hitherto been customary. At the head and feet of the effigies are seated angels, balanced on the cornice of the pedestal. Their semi-detachment from their surroundings is also evidence of the new feeling, as in Gothic work, in most instances, figures are framed, and part and parcel of the architecture. But Torrigiano was a sculptor first and foremost, and the angels gave him an opportunity of showing his skill in that branch of art, which neither the effigies nor the ornamentation of the pedestal afforded. For Henry VII.'s chapel he also made "a garnishment, an awlter," and various "ymages," of which only portions now exist. Another fine work of his is the tomb of John Young, Master of the Rolls and Dean of York, who died April 25, 1516. A painted terra-cotta figure reclines in more realistic attitude than had been thought proper before, on a stone sarcophagus, delicate in detail, and with the charming lettering in which Italian artists excelled.[1] In 1518 Torrigiano visited Italy, and tried to persuade Benvenuto Cellini to return with him to this country. But Cellini, with a characteristic outburst, declined to have anything to do with "those beasts the English." Torrigiano returned here, and spent some time working on the altar; but he soon left again.[2] Other Italians of repute early employed in England were Giovanni da Majano and Rovezzano.

[1] This tomb, formerly in the Rolls Chapel, is now in the Museum of the Records Office, which occupies the site of the chapel. The two volumes of Domesday Book, it may be mentioned, are in this museum.

[2] Vasari says that he went to Spain, where, being badly treated, his violent temper asserted itself, and he was thrown into prison by the Inquisition, and died there in 1522. Other authorities say he lived until 1528.

The former made the fine terra-cotta medallion busts of the emperors set in the brickwork of Cardinal Wolsey's portion of Hampton Court, and the latter designed the elaborate tomb for Wolsey, which passed through so many and strange vicissitudes, and now exists only in scattered fragments. The panels over the entrance gateway to Lincoln's Inn, Chancery Lane, dated 1518, which are carved with the royal and other arms, are Italian in feeling. They have been attributed to Hans Holbein, but he did not arrive in England until 1526, eight years later. His sympathies were entirely with the Renaissance, but were enlisted more on the side of painting than of architecture. He painted the ceiling of the Chapel Royal, S. James's, in 1540, and is credited with a gateway to Whitehall, which stood until 1759, and other work. Like most of the artists of his time, he was interested in all the arts, and may have designed buildings in this country, especially during the first few years after his arrival, and before his reputation as a painter was fully established.

Examples, 1520-30.

Between 1520 and 1530 the Renaissance cropped up simultaneously, like flowers in the spring, in various parts of England, but especially in the southern and eastern counties nearest to the ports for the Continent. The meeting between Henry VIII. and Francis I., in 1520, at the Field of the Cloth of Gold, helped it forward considerably. Nearly all the Renaissance work of this decade, and of the succeeding twenty years or so, is by foreigners.[1] In the southern counties these men were Italians, with perhaps a few French. The Renaissance, however, was so recent in France, and in many parts still so imperfectly understood, that the possibility of there being any might be dismissed if it were not that in some English examples—Lacock Abbey, for instance—the feeling is far more French than Italian (see Fig. 192). In the eastern counties some of the workmen, perhaps, were Flemings. The proximity of Flanders, and the strong business relations between that country and Norfolk, Suffolk, etc., render this not unlikely. Moreover, the work on the east coast is somewhat different in character from that of Hampshire, Wilts, and Dorset; is coarser, less refined, and more akin to that of the Low Countries. Whatever

[1] Exceptions are the pendants and spandrils of the roof of the Great Hall at Hampton Court, which are Renaissance in character, and are stated by Mr. Ernest Law, in his "History of Hampton Court," to have been carved by Englishmen, the pendants by Richard Rydge of London, and the spandrils by Michael Joyner. These men probably worked under the direction of one of the Italians in Wolsey's employ.

Fig. 189.—Christ Church, Hampshire. Screen at end of South Aisle, dated 1529.

Fig. 190.—Christ Church, Hampshire. Chantry tomb of Margaret, Countess of Salisbury.

[*To face p.* 231.

was the nationality of these men, they were not architects, and hardly merit the title of sculptors. They were carvers, who apparently travelled from place to place, arriving with their bag of tools, and departing when any work entrusted to them was finished. They had nothing whatsoever to do with the planning, construction, and general design of buildings. That was by Englishmen, and followed in all respects what had been in general vogue for half a century or more. All the foreigners did was to enrich with Renaissance detail some of the principal mouldings and the flat surfaces separating mouldings. Their contribution was never the meat itself, but merely the salt to the meat, which added an extra savour. This is well shown at Christ Church, Hampshire. In the church there are three chantry chapels—two in the south aisle, and one, the largest, which encloses the tomb of Margaret, Countess of Salisbury, in the north. The general design of all three is fifteenth-century Gothic. The chapel at the side of the south aisle is dated 1525, that at the east end 1529. In the former there is not a trace of the Renaissance; in the latter the frieze at the top is carved with the delicate ornament of that style. In the Salisbury chapel, c. 1530, various horizontal rails, and the vertical, panelled buttresses, are carved in similar fashion. The carving on these monuments may have been executed after the Englishmen had finished their work, as the portions enriched are those which, in Gothic, are frequently left quite plain; and the intention of the original workers may have been to leave them so. In the stone screens flanking the choir at Winchester Cathedral the design is much the same as at Christ Church, and is "Perpendicular," but with a Renaissance cresting. On top of the screens are oak chests, designed and carved in the new manner. Four out of the six are original, one on the north side being dated 1525. In the church of S. Cross, close to Winchester, are portions of an elaborate oak screen, which in design and workmanship is entirely foreign and apparently Italian. The heads of the openings are filled with carved and pierced Renaissance ornament. Cowdray Park, Sussex (c. 1530)—in the corner of the county that is close to Southampton—is very good Perpendicular Gothic, but the Renaissance crops up in interesting fashion in the carving of the ribs of the fan vaulting of the porch. Perhaps the most partial indication of its presence in any building of this date in England is at Hengrave Hall, Suffolk (c. 1525-36). The house is regulation Tudor throughout, and only in the corbelling of the oriel window over the entrance doorway is there any evidence that the foreigner assisted with his tools.

Terra-cotta.

At Layer Marney Towers, Essex, and at Sutton Court, Surrey, is some interesting early Renaissance work, which differs from that already referred to in being executed in terra-cotta. At Sutton Court the mullions of the windows, the facings of the octagonal buttresses, and of the parapets, etc., are in this material. The terra-cotta was probably ordered and made abroad—very likely in Flanders—and thence shipped to England. It may have been fixed by foreigners, but not necessarily. At Layer Marney the Renaissance is limited to the mullions, transoms, and heads—all of which are very elaborate—of the windows of the entrance gateway, and the battlements, etc., of the octagonal towers which flank it. The window mullions and transoms are square and unmoulded, but are panelled, as in French work, and filled with ornament. The mullions finish with small Corinthian capitals. The rest of the building is thoroughly English. In the church near the Hall are two tombs: one to Henry, Lord Marney, the other to his brother John, who succeeded him in the title. Henry died in 1523, John in 1525; yet Henry's tomb is in terra-cotta and Renaissance throughout, whilst John's is Gothic, and similar to Sir William de Marney's tomb of c. 1414 in the same church. John's tomb was evidently left to the local workmen, who ignored —and probably rejoiced in ignoring—the new style, and harked back to that of their fathers.

1530-60.

Between 1530 and 1560 are other similar and interesting examples, but still no buildings to which the term "Renaissance" can be justly applied. The screen at King's College, Cambridge (1526-34), shows the Italian carvers at their best. No richer example exists in England, and not many are finer in Italy. In 1541 Lacock Abbey, Wilts, was acquired by Sir William Sherington, who remodelled the monastic buildings and made some additions, the most notable being an octagonal tower, crowned by a balustrade. The windows of the tower have little corbels in the heads of the lights, and some larger windows in the quadrangle have also corbelled heads. The green and yellow encaustic tiles on the ground floor of portions of Lacock may easily have been made in England, where their manufacture was well understood, although they differ from earlier English ones in the character of their design. Of the wonderful palace of Nonesuch, near Cheam, Surrey, begun by Henry VIII. about 1539, nothing now remains.

THE RENAISSANCE IN ENGLAND

It is stated to have been Gothic in design, with Renaissance ornament, and that Italians, French, Dutch, and Englishmen were

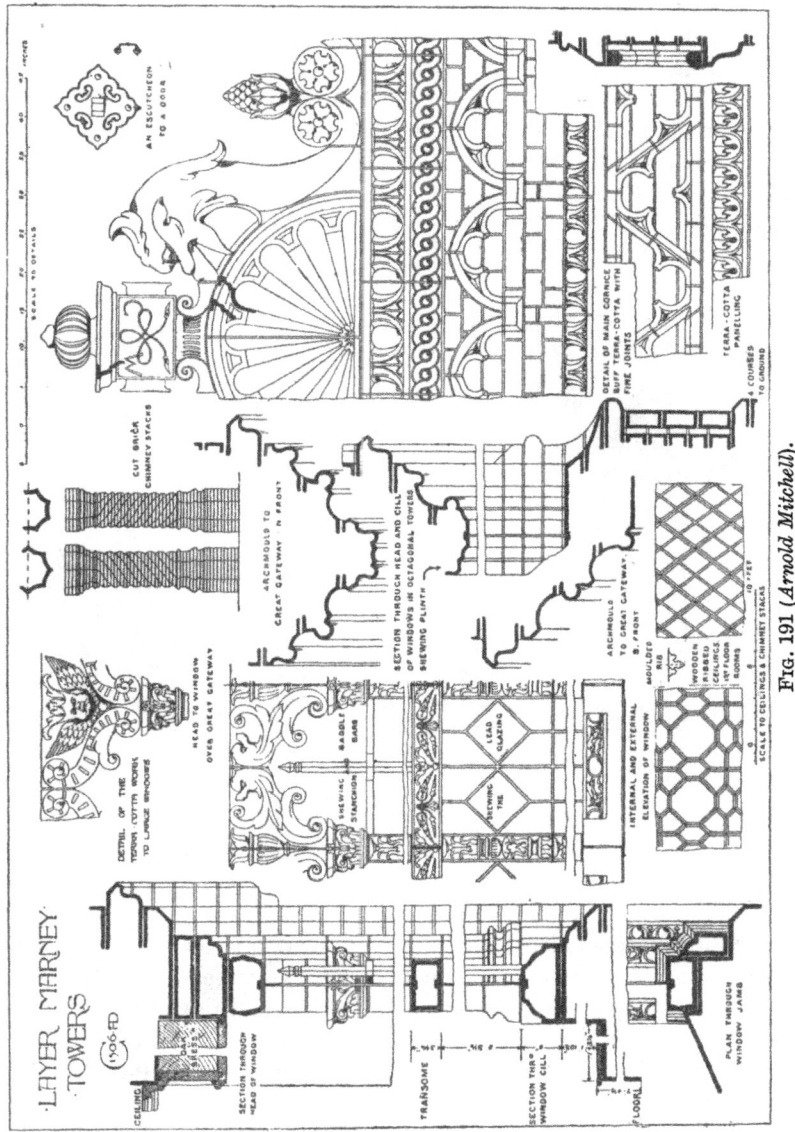

FIG. 191 (*Arnold Mitchell*).

simultaneously employed in the building and its decoration. The idea of the king was doubtless to rival Francis I.'s château de

Madrid. The nearest approach to a Classic building was possibly old Somerset House, built between 1546 and 1549, for which architects were possibly brought from Italy; but this is not certain. In the archives of Longleat, Wilts, are recorded payments to a certain John of Padua in 1544 and 1549, "pro servitio in architectura et musica." Who and what John of Padua was is unknown, and the meaning of the entries is doubtful. The theory held formerly, that he was the architect of Longleat, and also of the Duke's House, Bradford-on-Avon, in the same county, is now discredited. Even if he were, these entries would not apply, as

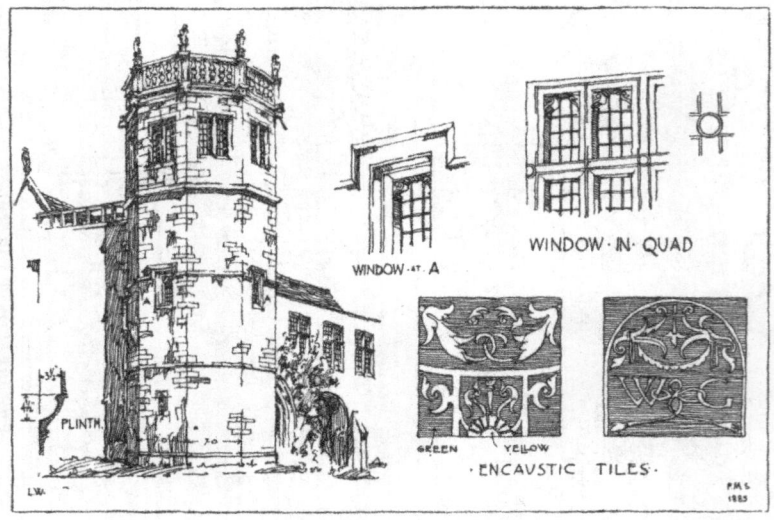

FIG. 192.—LACOCK ABBEY, WILTS.

Longleat was not rebuilt for Sir John Thynne until between 1567 and 1578, and the Duke's House is either contemporary with it or later.

The examples mentioned above form by no means a complete list of buildings in which Renaissance traits appear, but are sufficient to indicate their character and the localities in which they are to be found. The whole of the midlands and the north, with one exception, were unaffected by the movement taking place in the south and east. The exception is an oak screen in Carlisle Cathedral, which is either Flemish or French. It is in an excellent state of preservation, and is similar in character to the screens at Winchester and S. Cross.

THE RENAISSANCE IN ENGLAND

About the middle of the sixteenth century the Italian workmen who had settled here, and such French as may have come, began to leave, and their place was taken, to some extent, by Germans and Flemings. The reasons for the change are many. The excommunication of Henry VIII. by the Pope had tended to divert the trade from Roman Catholic to Protestant countries. With his death, in 1547, extravagant regal expenditure came to an end. The exchequer was empty. The nobility and people also had been severely taxed in order that the king could wage his wars with Francis of France and Charles of Germany. But German and Flemish workmen would require pay as much as Italians and French, and if no money had been forthcoming would have stopped in their own countries. The religious situation supplies a third, and the strongest, reason. Henry VIII., notwithstanding his conflicts with the pope, was a Roman Catholic. Under Edward VI. there was religious toleration. Mary was a papist. Not until Elizabeth came to the throne, in 1558, did Roman Catholic workmen here suffer any inconvenience because of their religion. But with the accession of Elizabeth things changed, and they thought it prudent to withdraw. Germany and the Low Countries were even more Protestant than England, and the new batch of workmen to arrive were probably all of that persuasion.[1]

Exode of the Italians.

The names of some German and Dutch workers in England have been preserved in documents, but little beyond their trades and the payments made to them have been recorded. The extent of their labours in this country appears to have been exaggerated. They certainly carved some fireplaces and other internal fittings, and were occasionally employed on outside work, as at Burghley, where the clock tower and the arcaded and pilastered portions of the quadrangle are probably theirs (1570-83). The two porches of the entrance front of Audley End (1603-16) and the strap-work decoration of the parapet are German in their clumsiness and heavy ornamentation, but as likely as not Englishmen, working from foreign architectural books, are responsible. The design of the tower of the "Schools" at Oxford, built by Sir Thomas Bodley about 1612, with its five storeys, each storey having its own

Germans and Dutch.

---

[1] Professor Reginald Blomfield records, in "A History of Renaissance Architecture in England," vol. i. p. 31, that Casper Vosbergh, who, together with other Germans, was employed on the work at Burghley, petitioned Lord Burghley, in 1572, "for privileges for a German Church to be founded at Stamford."

"Order" in correct sequence (Tuscan, Doric, Ionic, Corinthian, Composite), can be traced to J. T.'s translation of Bloome's book of the five columns, published four years before, or to Wendel Dietterlin's "De Quinque Columnarum," published 1593.[1] To the influence of German books may also be attributed the gateways of Caius College, Cambridge, formerly attributed to Theodore Haveus, or Heave, but probably designed by Dr. Caius himself and carried out by Englishmen.

The clumsy-proportioned columns and pilasters, the "bastard" detail and coarse carving, which are to be found in many Elizabethan and Jacobean houses, are sometimes "scored" against the German workman. He probably did not execute one-hundredth part of this work. The Englishman himself was at fault; and these unsatisfactory traits, when they exist, are due to his indifferent knowledge, skill, and taste. The old school of craftsmen that executed the fine work of the fifteenth century in this country had died out. Their successors had inherited some of their traditions, but not their skill; and in trying to adapt themselves to the new movement they fell between two stools. They might have learnt from the Italian workmen, as the French did, but the Italian feeling was too fine for them. Between English and Germans there was not only a religious bond; their tastes and artistic sympathies were also akin. This is in itself sufficient to account for the similarity of some of the English work with the work of the Teutonic countries in Europe, without the presence in this country of Germans at all. The Englishmen, however, to their credit, be it said, possessed a certain saving grace which steered them clear, in the main, of the eccentricities and coarseness of touch frequently met with abroad. They failed most when they tried to be foreign; they succeeded best when they were insular, and relied on their own traditions. For this reason the plainest buildings of the sixteenth and seventeenth centuries are generally the most acceptable.

[1] There were few English books on architecture at this time. Shute's is mentioned later. There were also two or three translations. Sir Henry Wotton's "Elements of Architecture" did not appear till 1624. The principal Italian and French publications have been referred to in previous chapters. German ones, in addition to those already mentioned, are: J. V. Frisius, or Vriese, "Perspectiva" (1559); "Architectura" (1563 and 1577); "Fountains" (1568); S. Cammermayer, "Modell Architettur" (1564); Wendel Dietterlin, "Architettura" (1594); Evelman, "Architectura Civilis Germanice" (1600), etc. Some of these no doubt were used in England, although Holinshed's Chronicles of 1577 only mentions Alberti, Vitruvius, and Serlio.

THE RENAISSANCE IN ENGLAND

One building in England, undoubtedly due entirely to a Fleming, was the Royal Exchange, London, built by Sir Thomas Gresham, which was destroyed in the Great Fire. The first stone was laid on June 7, 1566, and the building was formally opened on January 23, 1570. The architect was Henri de Pas, or Paschen, of Antwerp, who built the Hôtel des Villes Hanséatiques in that city. His foreman in London was one Heindrickx, or Henrick, who was afterwards employed at Burghley. Sir Thomas not only engaged a foreign architect and foreign workmen, but also imported from abroad the black and white marble for the paving of the open square of the Exchange. He was severely blamed by his contemporaries for his action. Harrison wrote, "But as he will answer peradventure that he bargained for the whole mould and substance of his workmanship in Flanders."[1] This extract shows that considerable ill-feeling towards foreign workmen existed in England early in Elizabeth's reign. The feeling was not confined to the craftsmen. Before her time many Dutch and Flemish merchants and traders had settled along the east coast, and in some of the southern counties, especially Kent; and after her accession their numbers multiplied. Further extracts show that their presence was equally objected to, and in 1601 Elizabeth issued an edict commanding them to leave the country. It appears therefore fairly certain that most foreign craftsmen left also, and that after that date few, if any, remained here.

<small>The Royal Exchange.</small>

Great uncertainty prevails as to who should be given the credit for the fine country houses and other buildings which rose all over England during the reigns of Elizabeth and James I. No architect, using the term in its modern sense, was employed. In some cases the owner seems to have been his own architect, with better results than follow now when that course is pursued. In others, so far as can be gathered from evidence, often incomplete and sometimes misleading, plans and sketch elevations were supplied by a "surveyor," who may or may not have been solely in the employ of the building owner. For small buildings it seems certain that the designs were made by the master-masons, head carpenters, chief plumbers, plasterers, etc. The head of each trade was responsible for the work in that trade alone; there was no such thing as a general contractor.[2] The building owner generally

<small>Designers of Elizabethan houses.</small>

---

[1] In Holinshed's Chronicles, quoted by Wyatt Papworth in "The Renaissance and Italian Styles of Architecture in Great Britain" (1883).

[2] General contractors are a modern innovation. In the north and in outlying districts of England, separate firms still tender for each separate trade.

supplied the materials; quarrying the stone, sometimes importing marble from abroad, as Sir Thomas Gresham and Lord Burghley did, cutting down the necessary trees—oak was the only wood used for carpentry and joinery, with few exceptions, until near the eighteenth century—often making the bricks, and purchasing whatever else was necessary. If Germans were employed, their work was restricted mainly to the ornamental portions, or they were engaged purely as carvers of chimney-pieces and other accessories. The carcase of each building was carried out by Englishmen, as had been done when the Italians were the employees.

John Shute.

Before the exode of the Italians, very few Englishmen designed and worked Renaissance detail. After the middle of the sixteenth century, however, many of the crude, coarse attempts, often attributed to foreigners, are by native workmen. Little is known of these men before 1570, and for many years after that date information regarding them is still meagre. The first in England to style himself architect was John Shute. In 1550 Shute was sent to Italy by the Duke of Northumberland to study architecture, and in 1563, the year of his death, he published his "Chief Groundes of Architecture." The full title page reads: "The first and chief groundes of Architecture, used in all the auncient and famous monymentes; with a further and more ample discourse uppon the same, than hitherto hath been set out by any other. Published by Ihon Shute, Paynter and Archytecte. Imprinted at London in Flete Street, near to Sainct Dunstan's churche by Thomas Marshe, 1563." This was the first attempt made in English to explain the rules and principles of Classic architecture, and that it was appreciated is proved by further editions issued in 1579 and 1584. The book is dedicated to Queen Elizabeth. The "Orders" are beautifully drawn. Each is represented by one column, with an appropriately proportioned figure alongside, and with delightful little figures engraved in the panels of the dies below the columns and larger figures. Shute describes himself as a "Paynter and Archytecte," but no known buildings are ascribed to him. The action of the duke is interesting as showing that before Elizabeth's time wealthy Englishmen realized that if their countrymen were to design in the new style, it was necessary for them to study it in the country of its birth.

John Thorpe.

Who was John Thorpe? This is a question frequently asked

which receives different answers. According to Mr. J. A. Gotch he was the architect of many of the finest of Elizabethan country houses; according to Professor Blomfield, he was mainly employed to survey houses and lands, although that writer admits that he may also have designed some buildings.[1] From Peacham's "Gentleman's Exercise," first published in 1612, it appears that there were two John Thorpes, father and son, that the former was a man of some position, and had the right to bear a coat of arms, and that he resided in the parish of S. Martin-in-the-Fields in 1592. He is described by Peacham as "my especiall friend and excellent geometrician and surveiour, whom the rather I remember, because

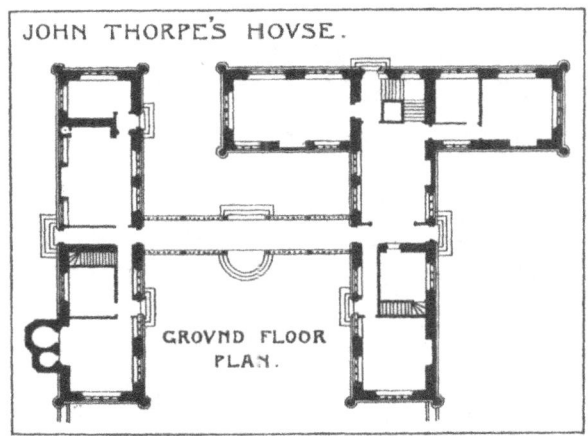

FIG. 193.

he is not only learned and ingenuous him selfe, but a furtherer and favorer of all excellency whatsoever, of whom our age findeth too few." The term "surveicur" used here must not be taken in its modern sense. Inigo Jones was surveyor to the king; Wren was called surveyor of S. Paul's, a title still employed, and in the reign of James I. designers of buildings were called surveyors, and the word "architect" was seldom employed. If the John Thorpe referred to by Peacham is the same as laid the first stone of Kirby Hall, Northants, in 1570, he must have been getting on in years in 1612, the date of Peacham's publication. Other records show that

[1] J. A. Gotch, "Architecture of the Renaissance in England"; "Early Renaissance Architecture in England"; "The Buildings of Sir Thomas Gresham," etc. R. Blomfield, "A History of Renaissance Architecture in England."

240 A HISTORY OF ARCHITECTURAL DEVELOPMENT

between 1590 and 1611 Thorpe was the surveyor of royal property, and that about the year 1600 he was in Paris, where apparently he designed one or more buildings for that city. In 1608 a translation of the " Quinque Columnarum " of Hans Bloome (Bluom or Bloem), originally published in Zurich in 1550, appeared in London under the title of "The booke of five columns." The translator is represented merely by initials, which are J. T. Whether these stand for John Thorpe is not known, but appears probable.

Thorpe's sketch-book.

Thorpe's name is best known through his sketch-book, which has been preserved, and is now in Sir John Soane's Museum,

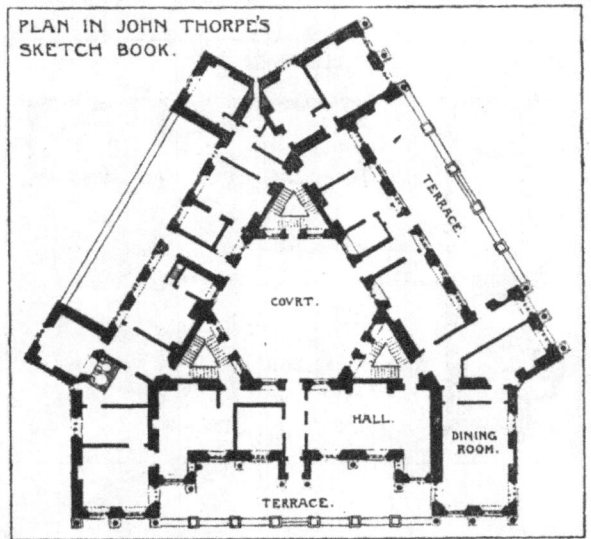

FIG. 194.

Lincoln's Inn Fields. It contains a number of plans and, in some cases, elevations of many important known houses, and of others which are unknown, together with portions of buildings, such as gables, etc., to a bigger scale, and a few large-size details. A few of these drawings are signed and dated, the dates ranging from 1570 to 1621. All the buildings represented cannot possibly have been designed by him. Some undoubtedly represent surveys he made for various noblemen and others. That he was employed on this work by no means proves that he did not also practise as an architect; in fact, it tends to prove the contrary, and it appears probable that he gained a reputation as a designer before he obtained much employment as a surveyor. That he possessed a quaint fancy is manifest in plans for houses which were not built, notably in a sketch for a house for himself, the plan of which is formed by his initials placed side by side and united by a corridor, in the centre of which is the entrance. Under the plan is written: "Thes two initials I and T, Being joyned together as you see, Is ment for a dwelling house for mee." The plan of a house with a hexagonal central court which is among his sketches, and is attributed to him, shows also considerable ingenuity. That he studied books on architecture, and exercised his imagination in design, is proved by further sketches of his which are more or less copies of drawings taken from foreign publications, but with suggested alterations.

Space does not admit of arguing the *pros* and *cons* as to the probability of Thorpe's share in the designs for such houses as Holland House, Kensington; Wollaton Hall, Nottinghamshire; Rushton Hall, Apethorpe Hall, and Lyveden New Building, all in Northamptonshire. It is quite possible that he was the architect of most; but that he did more than survey Burghley, near Stamford, Knowle, in Kent, and some others, the plans of which are in his sketch-book, is unlikely. With one building, Kirby Hall, Northamptonshire, he is closely identified. It was commenced for Sir Humphrey Stafford, whose badge, the Stafford Knot, appears frequently in the carving, but soon passed into the hands of Sir Christopher Hatton. Thorpe has written inside the plan of this house in his sketch-book—" Whereof I layd the first stone 1570." This plan differs in some respects from the plan of the house as it now exists, excluding the portions altered or added in the seventeenth century. The most important variation is that only one bay window is shown at the south-west corner instead of the pair which together now form the most striking feature of the outside (see Fig. 195). Kirby Hall proves that either Thorpe was a very bad surveyor or else a very fine architect. The latter is the more probable. Some ignorance, or wilful disregard, of correct Classic proportions may be shown in the elevations, notably in those of the quadrangle, but, before condemning Thorpe for this, the date when the house was built should be taken into account. Even the Italians who worked in England were by no means sticklers for correctness. On two of the pinnacles at the end of the courtyard are carved 1572 and 1575. These dates confirm the stated date of the laying of the

Kirby Hall.

foundation stone. Apart from some slight irregularities in proportion, there is no lack of delicacy and refinement. On the contrary, the detail throughout is full of feeling and all the more interesting because of its irregularities. The carving is in many cases excellent, and the gables, although reminiscent of Germany,

FIG. 195.

are much more refined and graceful than any in that country.[1] These good traits are probably due to Thorpe entirely, as well as the general design of the building. He was a young man when Kirby was built, and probably particularly anxious that the work

[1] The gables at the north end of the west front are probably later (see Fig. 199).

Photo: Author.
FIG. 196.—KIRBY HALL, DOORWAY IN COURTYARD.

Photo: Author.
FIG. 197.—KIRBY HALL, BAY OF COURTYARD.

[To face p. 242.

THE RENAISSANCE IN ENGLAND 243

should do him credit. If Thorpe did not act himself as master mason at Kirby, he probably supplied details, knowing full well how ignorant of Classic architecture the workmen of his time were.

In the absence of definite information regarding many particulars of Thorpe's career, one may perhaps be allowed to exercise one's imagination and fill in some of the gaps. Thorpe probably began life as a mason, had a thorough knowledge of the mysteries of his craft, and in addition was keenly interested in

Thorpe's career.

Fig. 198.

the bigger problems of design. One can picture him, about 1563, studying with avidity John Shute's recently published book, as well as foreign publications. In 1570 he lays the first stone of Kirby Hall, with no doubt that intense feeling of satisfaction which all architects experience at the commencement of their first big work. The sensation Kirby produced must have been considerable. It was one of the first, if not the first country house to be built entirely in the new manner. It probably was the means of introducing Thorpe to Sir Thomas Tresham and other large landowners of the neighbourhood. All houses in Northamptonshire built during the following fifty years are similar in feeling and detail. His knowledge of building, coupled with his success as a designer, and his high character for integrity which Peacham records, leads to his appointment as Crown Surveyor, and to his being employed to survey houses and lands for other clients in all parts of the country. On this work he was engaged until his death. But he did not allow his imagination to rust. He continued his practice as an architect, and also indulged his fancy in planning and designing buildings which he saw no immediate prospect of erecting. He remained a student until the end. In his old age he settled in S. Dunstan's parish, possibly translated Bloome's book, and collecting together his designs for buildings, copies of surveys made by him, fancy designs, and other *data*, left his sketch-book as a partial record of his life's labour. A well-spent life if the above be correct. That he was generous, as well as "learned and ingenuous," is shown by his friend Peacham's tribute: "a furtherer and favorer of all excellency whatsoever, of whom our age findeth too few."

Sir Thomas Tresham.

A great builder was Sir Thomas Tresham. Even when in prison—where he was sent more than once, owing to his religious beliefs, he being a Roman Catholic—he issued instructions as to how work should be done. The buildings associated with his name are Rushton Hall, the Triangular Lodge, Rushton, Lyveden New "Bield" and Old "Bield," and Rothwell, or Rowell, Markethouse. Thorpe may have helped him on the two first. The lodge, which stands in the woods not far from the Hall, is dated 1595 on the chimney, but was probably commenced some years earlier. The plan forms a triangle; each side has three gables; the chimney that rises in the centre is three-sided; and the windows are enclosed in trefoils. The windows of the New Bield, or Building, are similar in detail to those of Kirby and other houses in Northamptonshire, but the entablature which surrounds the building shows more thorough knowledge of Classic. Its excellence is due neither to Sir Thomas nor to Thorpe, but to one Roland Stickles, who was employed by Sir Thomas to draw it correctly, as the following letter from him, in 1606, to his employer shows: "Right worshipful, my humble duty remembered. I have made the ordnance according to your request and have made them by the symmetry or measure agreeing with the Doricke architrave, frieze and cornice. The enriching of the friezes, I refer that unto you and the workmen, and so I betake your worship unto the Almighty, who send you a merry new year in Jesus

THE RENAISSANCE IN ENGLAND

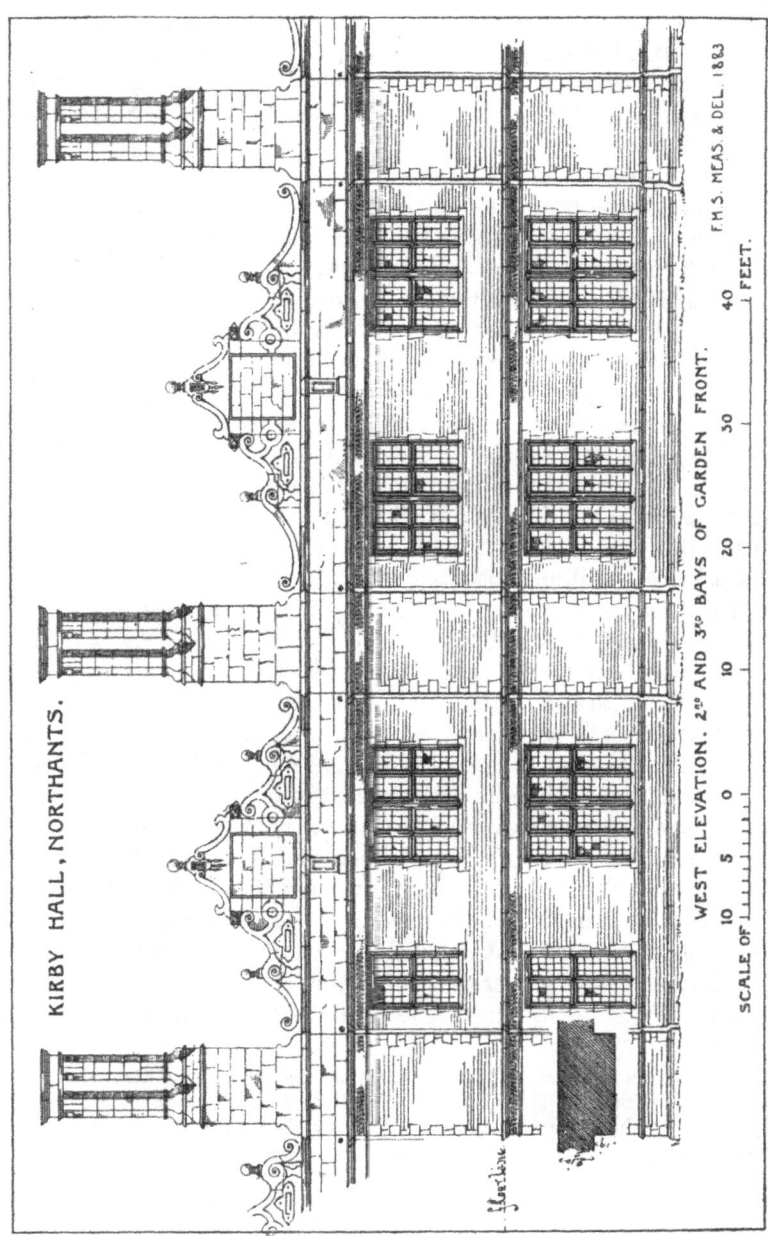

FIG. 199. (For plans, see Figs. 203 and 208.)

Christ."[1] The letter is endorsed, "Stickles moulds for building," and plainly shows that large-size details were supplied and that Sir Thomas had skilled assistance over this building at least, although its curious Greek cross plan and heraldic decoration in the frieze may have been his idea. The payments for it begin in 1596, and continue in 1605-06.

The Smithsons.

After Thorpe come the Smithsons, who between them designed many fine houses in Nottinghamshire and Derbyshire. The eldest, Robert Smithson, was his contemporary, and possibly designed Wollaton Hall, near Nottingham, although its plan and elevations show evidence of foreign study.[2] He died in 1614, and lies buried in Wollaton Church, where his record reads: "Gent, architector and survayor unto the most worthy house of Wollaton with diverse others of great account." The next is John Smithson, possibly a son of Robert, who died at Bolsover in 1634. He was succeeded by his son Huntingdon (d. 1648), whose tomb is in Bolsover Church, he being described as an architect. One of his sons was John Smithson, gent, also of Bolsover (1638-1716).[3] The principal buildings attributed to the elder John and his son Huntingdon are Bolsover Castle, including the square block, and the long gallery which stands detached, but excluding the riding school, which is later; and Hardwick Hall, Derbyshire; the present inhabited hall and the dismantled ruin within a stone's throw of it, both the work of "Building Bess" of Hardwick, Elizabeth, Countess of Shrewsbury. Barlborough Hall, near Bolsover, if not by the Smithsons, is in their manner. One trait these three buildings have in common: they are not grouped round courtyards, like so many Elizabethan and Jacobean houses, but are compact blocks. This plan, first adopted at Wollaton, was continued in the Derbyshire examples. The detail of the fireplaces, doorways, etc., at both Hardwick and Bolsover is better and simpler than in other parts of England. The feeling is almost Italian. What little figure sculpture there is is fairly good; the

---

[1] See "John Thorpe and Roland Stickles," by Mr. Harry Sirr, *R.I.B.A. Journal*, 3rd Series, Vol. XVIII. p. 377. The Robert Stickelles who, according to Wyatt Papworth, was recommended in 1597 for the office of "Surveyor of the Queen's Works," was apparently the father of Roland, and a man of some repute.

[2] Both plan and elevation are in Thorpe's book, and are not identical with the existing building.

[3] See pedigree given by Mr. Walter L. Spiers in the *R.I.B.A. Journal*, 3rd Series, Vol. XVI. p. 140.

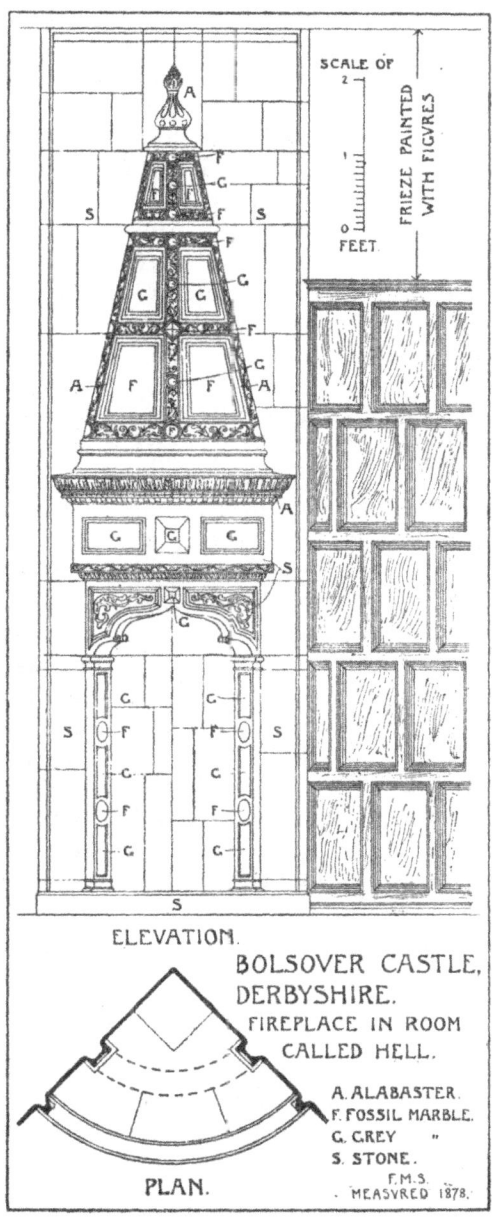

Fig. 200.

pilasters and entablatures framing the openings are well proportioned; and the carving, especially at Bolsover, is delicate and refined. Much of the last is in alabaster, which lends itself readily to delicacy. Local Derbyshire marbles, the grey and fossil, are largely used in some cases round doorways and for wall linings, as in the green bedroom of Hardwick Hall. According to Horace Walpole, John Smithson "was sent to Italy to collect designs" when Sir William Cavendish, afterwards Duke of Newcastle, contemplated additions to Bolsover Castle. These additions were probably the long gallery built by Sir William for the proper reception of Charles I. If that is so, Smithson—it is not certain whether John or his son Huntingdon went—made indifferent use of his opportunity, as the façade of the gallery, with its badly proportioned engaged and rusticated columns carried on corbels, is one of the most debased and unsatisfactory examples of the Renaissance in England. The nearly square windows, with their frolicsome frames, are effective in their boldness. The windows of Nottingham Castle are similar, and were either designed by the same architect as the Bolsover gallery or else were copied later from that building by the Duke of Newcastle.

The Smithsons' drawings. A large number of drawings by the Smithsons—about two hundred in all—have been preserved. These, unlike Thorpe's, are unbound. None are signed in full; one is initialled Jo. S.; a few have dates, which range from 1599 to 1632. Many of the plans are most carefully executed, and, besides surveys of houses and gardens, there are "details of doorways, windows, screens, chimney-pieces, and monuments, as well as drawings of panelling, of fittings, and of a few implements."[1] These drawings and Thorpe's are of the utmost value as proving that the larger Elizabethan houses were designed by architects who, in the seventeenth century, and possibly before, designed also their internal fittings. An alabaster and marble screen in front of a side chapel in Bolsover church, dated 1619, is by one of the Smithsons, and is interesting, as similar church fittings of this date are few. Many other surveyors, or architects, must have been designing throughout England in the style which the later purists ridiculed as "King Jamie's Gothic," long after Inigo Jones had commenced Whitehall. Thomas Holte, of Oxford (d. 1624), was one. Their names, however, are mostly forgotten, or preserved only in little-known documents.

[1] See article by Mr. J. A. Gotch in the *R.I.B.A. Journal*, 3rd Series, Vol. XVI. p. 41; also article by Mr. Maurice B. Adams in Vol. XIV. p. 366.

THE RENAISASNCE IN ENGLAND

Before the time of Henry VIII. the ruling idea in domestic buildings was defence. The country was far from settled, and, self-preservation being the first law, people needed protection from their fellows as much as a rocf over their heads. Buildings were surrounded by moats, the water of which washed the walls, as at Ightham Moat House, Kent, and drawbridges were a necessity, and not an ornament. As a rule there were two: the larger for horsemen, the smaller for people on foot. Small houses in the country, like the "Peel" towers of the northern border—there is

Early planning.

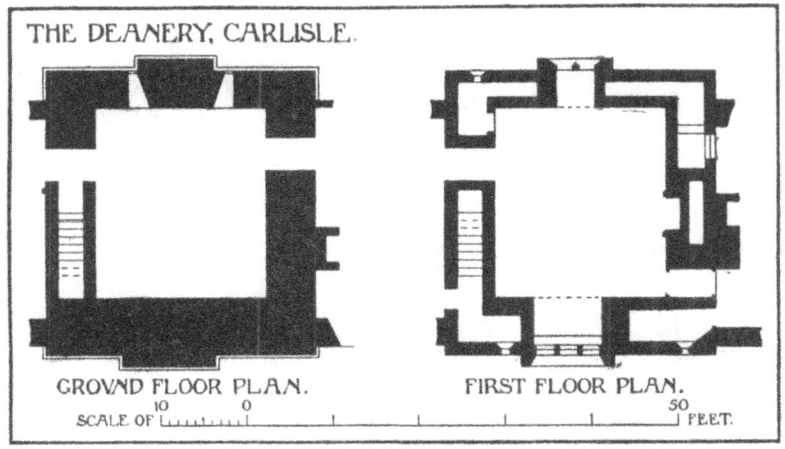

FIG. 201.

a good example at Carlisle, now part of the Deanery—Little Wenham Hall, Essex, etc., were generally compact buildings, the ground storey being for the servants or retainers, the upper storeys for the family, the only means of access from below being a narrow, winding staircase. Larger houses, like castles, were built round a courtyard, a gateway, guarded by portcullis and drawbridge, being the only entrance. The hall formed the connection between the kitchen, etc., at one end, and the principal living-rooms at the other. Otherwise no attempt at unity was made. Round the courtyard were several small doorways, each of which provided access to one or two rooms, as at Haddon Hall, Derbyshire. After the Wars of the Roses the country somewhat settled down. Drawbridge, portcullis, and machicolations were still retained, as at Hurstmonceaux Castle, Sussex, Thornbury Castle, Gloucestershire, etc., but the last especially, from force of habit more than for use.

Gunpowder had made close fighting under the walls almost a thing of the past, and machicolations, when retained, were merely an ornamental finish. The change that was taking place is further emphasized by the gradual dropping of the word "castle," and the more general adoption of "hall," "court," "place," as Oxborough Hall, Hampton Court, Brede Place, etc. The smaller manor

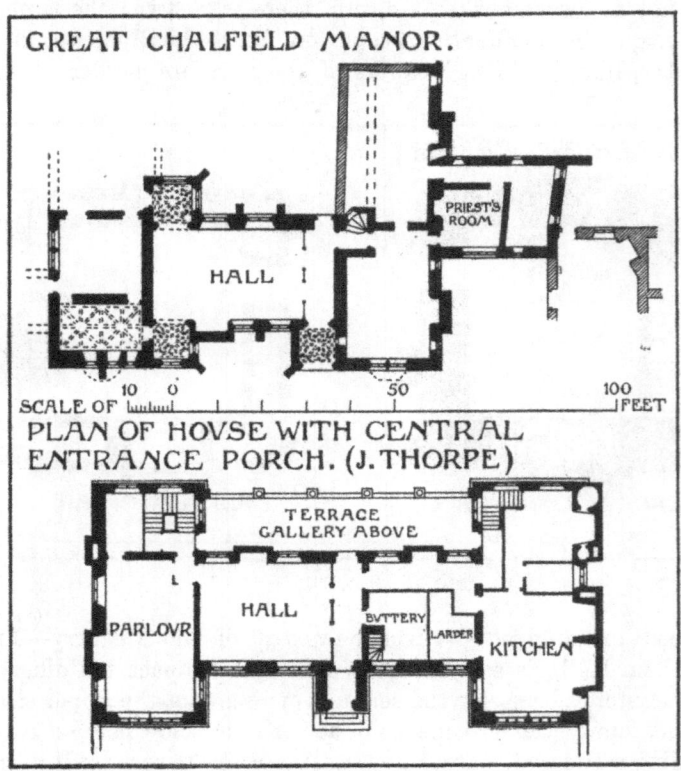

Fig. 202.

houses, such as Ockwells, Berks, Great Chalfield, Wilts, etc., were planned alike. The hall occupied the whole of the central part, and was flanked by wings, which sometimes projected in front only, in other examples at the back as well. One wing, that nearest to the entrance, was for the servants, the other for the family. The hall was neutral ground, common to both. At one end was a passage, which led from the porch in front to a door at the back, which opened into the garden or court. Beyond the passage were the buttery, pantry, kitchen, and above it was a minstrel's gallery. The passage was divided from the hall by an oak screen, in which were generally a couple of openings or doorways. The hall, as a rule, was the full height of the building, and often had an open timber roof. It was lighted by windows on both sides high up, and at the end furthest from the entrance was a raised dais, on which the dining-table for the family and guests was set. At one end of the dais was occasionally a bay window, which started lower than the other windows, only a few feet from the floor, a feature general in the college halls of Oxford and Cambridge, where the same plan was followed.

In early plans the wings are seldom exact counterparts of each other, and the entrance being to one side the elevations are unsymmetrical. Great Chalfield is more symmetrical than most, as the porch is balanced by a bay window. The first modification introduced was to arrange the rooms so that the entrance, instead of being in a corner, should be central between the wings, they being alike, and yet still open into the passage at the end of the hall, as before. This for long remained the plan of most Elizabethan houses, large and small. In the larger houses, however, the wings were extended in front (sometimes at the back as well), forming sides of an open or an enclosed courtyard, which had to be traversed before the entrance was reached. Kirby Hall is a good example. The planning is still primitive. The rooms on either side of the quadrangle can only be reached by the external doorways which open out of it. These, on one side, also give access to staircases, which lead to rooms on the upper floor; on the other side of the court the whole of the first floor was a long gallery. These many entrances were not so inconvenient then as they appear now; in fact, were probably regarded as advantageous, as the rooms round the court were arranged in suites, and reserved for guests. In the plan of Buckhurst, in Thorpe's book, several sets of rooms are each collectively labelled "A Nobleman's lodging." The courtyard of Kirby Hall is not so irregular in form as it is generally made to appear. At the south end there is some irregularity, but courtyard, forecourt, and the great avenue beyond are all on a central axis. The deceptive appearance of the plan is due to the south end of the quadrangle being considerably wider than the north. *Elizabethan planning.*

At Kirby most of the rooms are the full depth of each wing. In other words, the plan is of the type known as "single." The *Double houses.*

next modification was to place rooms back to back. Bacon, in his essay entitled "Of Building," published 1598, says, "and let all three sides (of a courtyard) be a double house, without thorough lights on the sides, that you may have rooms from the sun, both for forenoon and afternoon. Cast it also, that you may have rooms both for summer and winter; shady for summer, and warm for winter. You shall have sometimes fair houses so full of glass, that one cannot tell where to be come to be out of the sun or cold." Neither the Duke's House, Bradford-on-Avon, nor Hardwick Hall, Derbyshire, in particular, would have pleased Bacon as

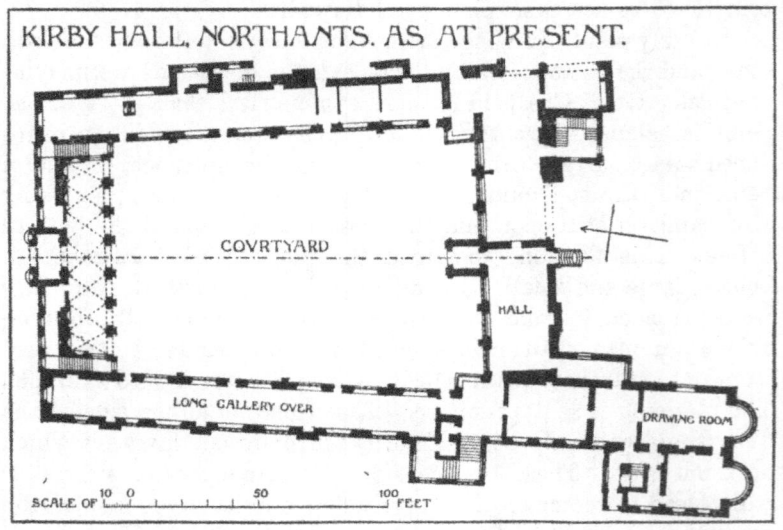

Fig. 203.

regards the last respect. No one seems to have followed exactly his advice respecting a double house on three sides, although at Buckhurst, Sussex (destroyed), Burghley, Audley End, and in a few other great houses, one or two sides have rooms back to back. Towards the end of Elizabeth's reign planning became more scientific, and pains were taken by means of corridors, galleries, etc., to knit all the parts together, to make a house homogeneous. Even in smaller houses, such as Claverton House, Somerset (destroyed), built in the first quarter of the seventeenth century, an attempt in this direction was generally made. The last change in plan worth recording was to place the hall in the centre of the main block with the porch or entrance doorway also central. The

THE RENAISSANCE IN ENGLAND 253

entrance is either in the middle of one side of the hall, as at Aston Hall, Birmingham (1618–35), or in the middle of one end, as at Hardwick Hall, Derbyshire. Some time before this modifica-

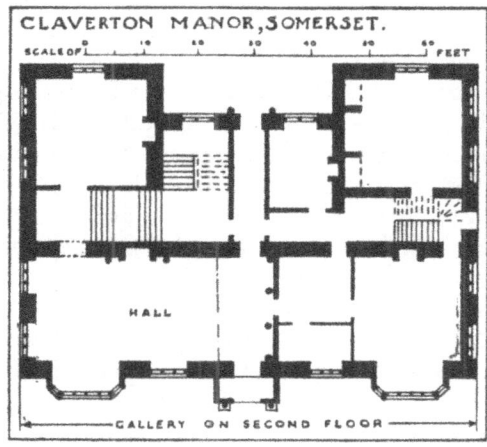

FIG. 204.

tion was introduced, a separate dining-room for the family had been provided in most large houses, and soon the hall lost its

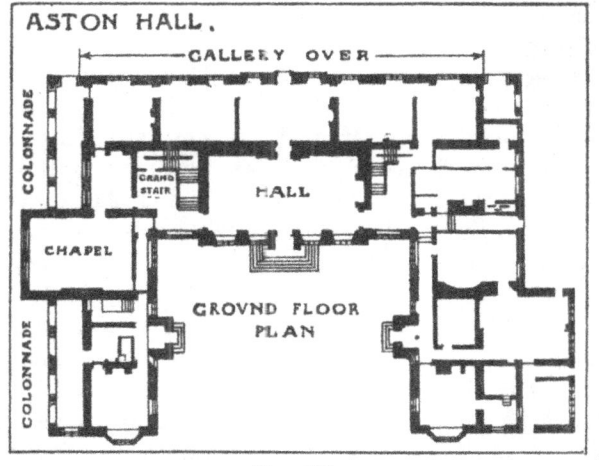

FIG. 205.

significance, ceased to be used for meals altogether, and became an entrance hall pure and simple. Opening out of it was the principal staircase hall, and surrounding it some of the chief living-rooms and

254   A HISTORY OF ARCHITECTURAL DEVELOPMENT

parlours, and the offices. Classic principles had reached so far that the chief aim in planning was symmetry. Room balanced room, bay window bay window, and projection projection. Many Elizabethan plans are real works of art, with fine vistas; the rooms being arranged for architectural effect as much as for comfort and convenience.

Long gallery.
The hall was always the principal room on the ground floor, no matter where it was placed. As a rule, it stretched across a portion of the front, but in some houses it extended from the front to the back, and was lighted from windows at both ends. This is the plan at Renishaw Hall, Derbyshire, and it appears to have been an especial favourite in the counties of Derbyshire and Yorkshire. The principal room, however, in the greater number of Elizabethan houses is the long gallery. This was always on an upper floor, often on the top floor of all, as at Montacute, Somerset, where it extends the whole length of the south front and includes the projecting bays at the end and the bay window in the centre. At Haddon Hall it is not of great extent, and is known as the ballroom. At Knole, Hardwick, Aston, Hatfield, Kirby, in houses in all parts of the country, in fact, the gallery is a great feature. As a rule it is lighted by a succession of bay windows, which greatly improve its proportions, and at the same time form recesses in which parents and their guests could sit, read, sew, or chat, and children play.

Types of plan.
The different types of plan found in Elizabethan and Jacobean houses may be summarized somewhat as follows: (1) The manor-house plan, already described, with the entrance either central or to one side. (2) The courtyard plan, as Kirby Hall, etc., with the entrance in the central block at the end of the courtyard, and the wings projecting in front to enclose a good-sized court. This was sometimes open in front, sometimes enclosed. Bacon recommends that the sides should not be equal in height to the main block. At Rushton Hall, Northamptonshire, the wings are united by a corridor in front merely one storey high. The effect is excellent. The corridor not only does not hide the higher buildings behind, but helps to give them scale. Many houses have ⊓-shaped plans, the court being in front and the porch central and projecting, and at the back a terrace. This form is stated to have been adopted in honour of Elizabeth, but this is very questionable, and it was followed as often after her death as during her reign. The H plan is a modification with a court in front and another at

THE RENAISSANCE IN ENGLAND

the back. Of houses with courts entirely enclosed on all four sides, Burghley may be taken as an example. In front is a gateway which gives access to the court and to the principal entrance at the end thereof. In this respect it follows earlier plans, such as Oxborough Hall, Norfolk. Knole House, Kent, shows another variation of the courtyard plan. The only courtyard is at the back, and is open at one end. The chief entrance is in front, and leads direct into the main portion of the building. (3) Houses planned in rectangular blocks, without courtyards. Wollaton

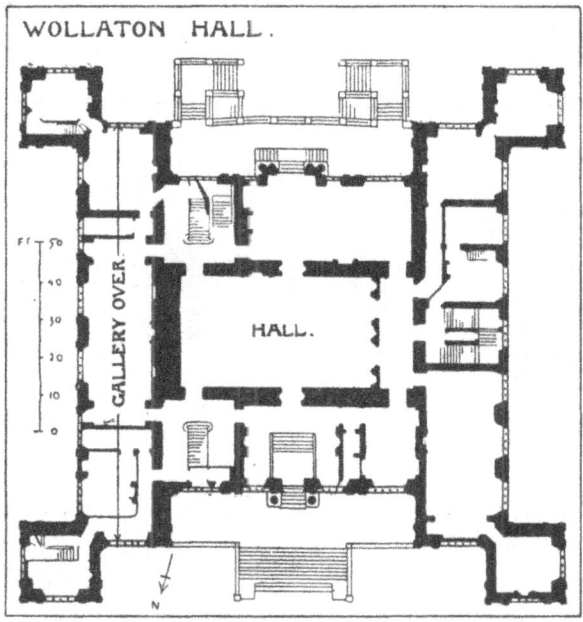

FIG. 206.—(*J. A. Gotch; B. T. Batsford.*)

Hall, Nottinghamshire, is of this type, although the rectangle is not observed exactly, as there are towers at the four corners, and projections at the front and back in addition which frame terraces. The Smithsons, as already mentioned, favoured this type, as at Bolsover Castle and Barlborough Hall, although in the latter there was originally a small open court in the centre, now covered in. At Wollaton the hall occupies this central position, and towers above the portions surrounding it. It is of great height inside, and is lighted by clerestory windows. Hardwick Hall, Derbyshire, has no enclosed courtyard. It is a large version of the manor-house type of plan. Other plans show modifications of the above-described types without possessing any marked differences; and some buildings are fantastic, like the triangular lodge at Rushton, the Greek cross Lyveden Building, Longford Castle, built round a triangular courtyard, with circular towers at the external angles, etc. The last named, however, merely follows what was a not uncommon plan in Mediæval days.

Approaches, etc.

No matter what the plan was, in front of a house was a forecourt, sometimes flanked by low buildings for stables and offices, in the manner of those at Hampton Court, but more frequently merely enclosed by a wall, as at Hardwick Hall, Kirby Hall, etc. At Hardwick the wall is crowned by a number of small obelisks,

FIG. 207.

and at each of the outside corners of the forecourt is a richly designed square pavilion. In front of the forecourt was frequently a gatehouse, or pair of lodges, as at Westwood, Worcestershire, Cotheleston Hall, Somerset, etc. At Kirby Hall the entrances are at the sides, and there is no lodge. The entrance facing the house is merely a portal. Leading up to the forecourt and house was generally a straight avenue. These avenues were often most extensive. At Kirby, notwithstanding that it led merely to the doorway mentioned, the avenue was of noble extent, and consisted of four rows of chestnut trees, with a central space of about 90 yards, and about 35 yards between the rows at each side. All the trees were planted about 9 yards apart.

Gardens.

No Elizabethan house was complete without its garden. This was generally very extensive, and was laid out formally. It included, in addition to the rose and flower gardens, orchards, grass walks, herb and kitchen-gardens, and often a bowling-green and maze, a sundial and fountain, and one or more fish ponds, partly for pleasure and partly to replenish the larder. The gardens were generally on the south side, but at Kirby Hall they stretched along the west front. At Montacute, Somerset, a formally laid-out rectangular garden is enclosed by a wall enriched with obelisks, etc., whilst at each of the outside corners stands an elaborate gazebo, or summer house. Along the south side of a house was a terrace, sometimes enclosed between wings, often extending far

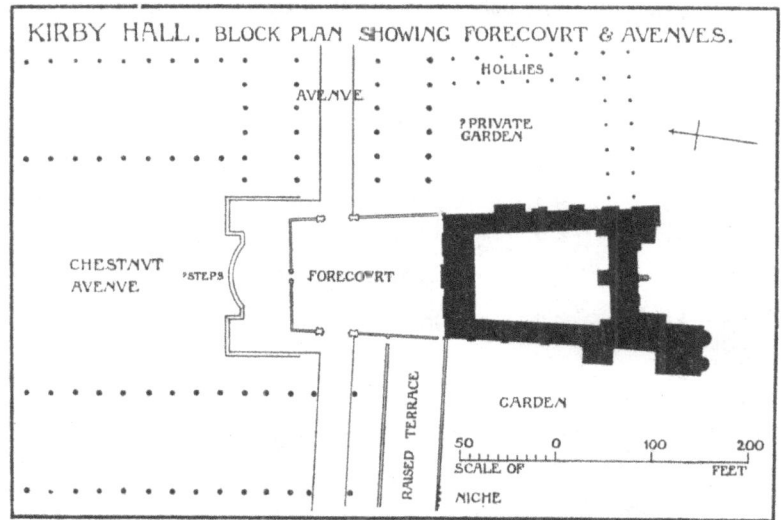

Fig. 208.

beyond. At Bramshill, Hants, the projecting wings of the building are open at each end on the ground storey and form shelters. When the fall of the ground permitted, a succession of terraces at different levels were frequently formed. At the Old Hall, Bakewell, to mention a small example, the garden is laid out in terraces. Amongst the Smithsons' drawings is a most interesting plan of a house and gardens inscribed "The Platforme of my Lo: of Exceter's house at wymbellton, 1609" (Wimbledon).

In any attempt to define the characteristics of Elizabethan and Jacobean work, one is immediately confronted by two facts. The first is that during this period the English did not succeed in forming a style possessing distinct and unmistakable traits, as the French had done along the Loire some fifty years earlier; and

Characteristics of Elizabethan.

the second is that the architects, workmen, and clients throughout England were divided into two camps. In this world half the people are generally conservative in their tastes and ideas, the other half eager for and desirous of change. In Elizabeth's reign opinion was about equally divided as to whether it were wiser to embrace the new style that came across the seas, or to retain the methods traditional in the country. In the majority of instances there was a certain amount of compromise. Both parties agreed that the mullioned and transomed window should be retained, and consequently even in buildings which are as Classic

FIG. 209.—BAKEWELL OLD HALL, DERBYSHIRE.

as the limited knowledge of the craftsmen employed rendered possible, the windows remained much as they had been in previous centuries. It is true that the heads of the lights are generally square, a few only are four-centred, and are not foliated or filled with tracery; but even in the days when the pointed arch and tracery were rampant in churches, both were dispensed with, more often than not, in secular work. On the other hand, those who wished to preserve the vernacular style saw no objection to symmetrical planning, nor to employing sometimes the semicircular arch for doorways and other important openings, and to the substitution occasionally, by no means always, of the Classic cornice for the Mediæval string. But there they drew the line. They would have none of the "Orders" outside; they declined

FIG. 210.—SOUTH WRAXALL, FIREPLACE IN DRAWING-ROOM.

FIG. 211.—ASTON HALL, LONG GALLERY.

[*To face p.* 259.

THE RENAISSANCE IN ENGLAND

to plaster their fronts with columns and pilasters. As the men who carved in the old manner had died out, they preferred that there should be no carving at all—at least, none externally. Inside a house their faith seemed to waver; and in their chimney-pieces especially, they admitted detail they would have been the first to condemn if placed outside. A case in point is the drawing-room addition at South Wraxall Manor. The large window that lights the room, and its outside surroundings, are simplicity itself. Inside there is the most barbarous chimney-piece to be found in the whole of England, an example all the more dangerous because of the dexterity and skill of the craftsmen who executed it.

FIG. 212.

Windows.

South Wraxall also illustrates well the marked increase in the size of windows which took place in Elizabeth's reign. The cry was for more light in more senses than one, for more air, more freshness. Mediæval gloom, stuffiness, and feeling of insecurity were passing away. Men felt safe. And so not only did windows increase in size and number, but the old bars and stanchions, hitherto regarded as necessary for safety, disappeared. Sometimes the lighting is overdone, as at the Duke's House, Bradford-on-Avon, Hardwick Hall, etc. Bay windows multiplied to an extraordinary extent. In former days they had been reserved for the dais ends of halls, or as oriels had projected from an important room on an upper floor. Now most rooms were lighted by them, and some rooms by nothing else. One can have too much of a good thing, and bay windows may be too numerous. They would have been a positive curse to the inmates, and eyesores from outside, if it had not been for the lead cames which broke the expanse of glass, and divided the lights of all windows into small panes, forming often elaborate patterns.

Characteristics of houses showing foreign influence.

The foreign influence perceptible in some Elizabethan and Jacobean houses may be due to Germans, Flemings, or Italians; may be direct or indirect. Work of this nature was not necessarily executed by foreigners. The traits which distinguish the houses in which this influence is strong from those in which it is barely apparent may be summarized somewhat as follows: (1) Flat roofs behind balustraded or ornamental parapets, as at Audley End, etc.; (2) gables, when there are any, fantastic in outline, as at Wollaton, Kirby, etc. (but see p. 242); (3) pilasters, columns, and entablatures in tiers all over fronts of buildings, as at Wollaton, Longleat, etc.; at Longleat (1567-78), however, the proportions are better and the detail more refined than in most contemporary and later buildings; (4) pilasters or columns flanking doorways, sometimes windows which it was desired to emphasize especially; (5) columns starting from corbels and used purely as ornaments, and half pilasters, half figures, the latter sometimes used outside, and an especial favourite for internal work, screens, fireplaces, etc.; and (6) a general heavy-fistedness in all sculpture, carvings, mouldings. Buildings possessing these characteristics may deserve the reproach of being badly proportioned, coarse in detail, and clumsy in ornament, and be regarded as bad models for the architectural student. But they form but a small proportion of our Elizabethan and Jacobean houses. The majority show few signs of foreign influence. They are neither Italian nor German, neither Flemish nor French. They are English, and in them the old traditions of English building are successfully preserved.

Vernacular building.

The simple vernacular work most typical of the period is not confined to one part of England. It is found on the moors of Yorkshire and Derbyshire, in the shires of the Midlands, off the lanes of Kent, Sussex, and Surrey, in the eastern, southern, and western counties by the sea; in fact, everywhere. Some of the buildings are in stone, others in brick, whilst several, especially smaller examples, are in traditional half-timber. The local material was invariably used. The absence of good roads and difficulties of carriage rendered that a necessity. There were, fortunately, no railways to take Sussex tiles and bricks to Cumberland, and to bring Westmorland slates and Yorkshire stone to Kent and

Fig. 213.

Fig. 214.

Surrey. The buildings, in consequence, harmonize perfectly with the landscape, a necessity that should be the first aim of every architect.

Stone buildings.

The Gloucestershire Cotswolds and the valley of the Northamptonshire Nene are particularly rich in stone examples. These are charming in their quiet dignity and perfect proportion. Even the farmhouses and smaller houses are works of art, such as the Talbot Inn, Oundle, and the house at Higham Ferrars, both in Northamptonshire. Many a hint may be obtained and many a lesson learnt from these buildings, and from larger ones, of which there is no lack. One lesson they teach is that picturesqueness lies in simplicity; another, that ornament is not necessary in architecture; a third, that windows and other absolutely necessary portions may be designed so as to obtain different effects in proportion without having recourse to pilasters to give verticality, or entablatures to produce an effect of horizontality. The long, low windows in

FIG. 215.—ABBEY HOUSE, MALMESBURY, GABLES.

many of these buildings give an appearance of breadth, without the aid of string courses, which, however, generally run above their heads, and the larger transomed windows, with their loftier mullions, an appearance of height. In most southern counties height is also emphasized by the steep-pitched, straight-sided gables, with their moulded copings and finials, sometimes obelisks, at the apex and above the corner stones. In Yorkshire and the North generally, gables are flatter in pitch, to suit the local stone slates with which most of the roofs are covered. In the larger houses in Northamptonshire—Apethorpe Hall, Lilford Hall, portions of Rushton Hall, etc.—the gables are curved in outline, but have similar finials, etc. At Montacute, in Somersetshire, the main gables are also curved, but it is doubtful if such gables are really so effective as straight-sided ones. In the eastern counties and in Kent the gables in brick are still more fantastic, owing to the presence of descendants of the Dutch and German settlers already referred to. Other gables are sometimes stepped, as at Kinnersley Castle, Herefordshire, a form, however, more common in Scotland than in England. In varying the outline of gables the English builders were departing from traditional Mediæval custom, and probably following Dutch or German models. Curly gables are practically unknown in French work, but in Germany, Holland, and Belgium straight-sided gables are the exception.

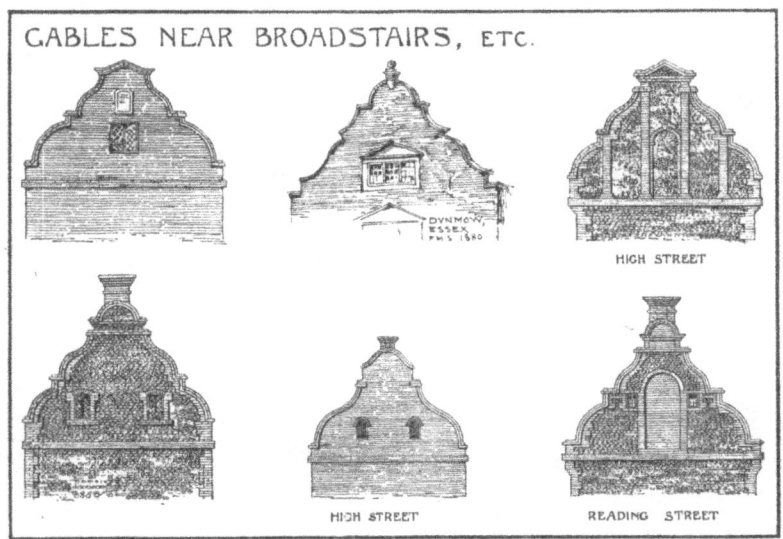

FIG. 216.

The majority of houses the walling of which is brick have sometimes brick copings to their gables, and the window mullions and jambs are occasionally of this material. Generally, however, these portions and the entrance doorways are stone. The chimneys are brick, and in houses otherwise stone built this is frequently also the case. Moyns Hall, Suffolk (c. 1590), is a typical vernacular example. The placing of its large bay windows, and its otherwise symmetrical front, show that its builders did not disdain to learn the good lessons the Renaissance taught, whilst retaining the spirit of the work of their forefathers. *Brick houses.*

Traditions lasted even longer in half-timbered houses than in those of brick or stone. Foreign books did not treat of their *Half timbered* houses, etc.

design, as, although buildings of timber construction were common abroad, the men who came to these shores were masons and

Fig. 217.

Fig. 218.

carvers, not carpenters. The last would have run little chance of employment. England had for centuries been famous for its

Fig. 219.—Moyns Hall, Suffolk.

Fig. 220.—Speke Hall, garden front.

[*To face p.* 264.

excellent carpentry; witness the fine fourteenth- and fifteenth-century open timber roofs of this country, absolutely without parallel abroad. Lancashire and Cheshire are the counties *par excellence* for half-timbered houses. Moreton Old Hall, Cheshire (c. 1550-59), is the most fascinating of all examples, with its three-storied entrance gateway at one end of a court, round the three sides of which is grouped the house. Speke Hall, near Liverpool, Park House, Oswestry, Cheshire, are well-known examples, the courtyard of the first being specially attractive. In these examples, especially Moreton and Speke, Gothic feeling is very strong. The barge-boards of the gables are cusped,[1] the timbers of the framing are bent and cut to form quatrefoils, trefoils, and curved-sided lozenges, and diagonal framing is common. In more southern counties the Gothic feeling is not so marked, partly because the timber buildings are mostly later in date, and partly because the spread of the new movement was putting men out of conceits with old ideas. In Suffolk and Kent, for instance, both counties being rich in examples, barge-boards are generally straight-edged and merely moulded, save in fifteenth-century work, and the timbers forming the framing are mainly vertical, with horizontal heads and cills, and an occasional curved brace for structural reasons.

In the word "home" is summed up the great attraction of English country houses of the sixteenth century and first half of the seventeenth. They were not built as show places or for great entertainments, and their virtues are by no means only external. They were built to be lived in. Even their smallest rooms are not without a certain stateliness, but the first and main impression the houses inside create is one of comfort. *Interiors.*

With few exceptions the rooms are panelled from floor to ceiling, or to a frieze immediately below the ceiling. This panelling, as a rule, is quiet in design, thoroughly English, and appropriate in treatment to the material. There is seldom a trace of the attempts at ornamentation and the clumsy, decorative forms that frequently disfigure the contemporary panelling of Germany, Holland, and Belgium, the only three countries on the Continent where panelled rooms are general. Occasionally, as in the ballroom at Haddon Hall, pilasters, arches, and other forms appertaining more correctly to stone, are introduced, but such examples are the exception. The panels are generally small and oblong. *Panelling.*

[1] The barge-boards are missing on the garden side of Speke.

Their repetition gives scale. Sometimes larger panels frame smaller ones in the shape of lozenges, octagons, etc., but the treatment still remains simple. In a few instances the panels are enriched with arabesque ornament, in bog-oak and holly, or some other light-coloured wood, as in the room from Sizergh Castle, Westmorland, now in the Victoria and Albert Museum. The panelling is not improved thereby. In Hardwick Hall there is an extraordinary amount of arabesque inlaying, but it is mostly in black composition, whilst in many of the panels the ornament is merely painted.[1]

Fireplaces. The simplicity so marked in the panelling hardly extends to fireplaces. No doubt the principle is sound that in every design there should be—or, at all events, may be—a rich centre; and one does not complain of the richness of Elizabethan fireplaces, but of the coarseness, exaggeration, and clumsiness of not a few. Some are all of stone or marble; in others the lower portions alone are stone—those round the big openings in which logs of wood rested on iron "dogs," whilst the overmantel is wood. Some are wood throughout, save for a protecting stone frame to the opening. At Knole, in Kent, the fireplaces are exceptionally numerous and fine, and few Elizabethan houses are without one or more examples.

Plaster work. In the craft of the plasterer the English of the sixteenth and seventeenth centuries excelled. Before the time of Elizabeth the heavy oak beams and joists of floors were moulded and exposed, or else were hidden by panelled wood ceilings. Plaster ceilings were rare. But after the middle of the sixteenth century the art advanced rapidly. The variety in design is remarkable. Some are semicircular in section, some segmental, others flat. Many of the last start from a cove above the panelling. Ribs making geometrical patterns, with pendants at their junctions, form the design generally, as at Westwood, Bolton, etc. Other ceilings are covered all over with strap-work, as in a small room at Castle Ashby. At Boughton Malherbe, Kent, the curved ceiling is decorated throughout with a flowing pattern. Sometimes ceilings are divided by oak beams and binders into panels, which are filled with decorative plasterwork, as at Hatfield, Knole, and the Laudian church of S. John the Evangelist, Leeds. The plasterer did not confine his art to ceilings. Many friezes of rooms are very

---

[1] For some examples of this inlay, see chapters on "Joinery" in "Building Construction," Vol. II.

elaborate. The most remarkable frieze is at Hardwick Hall, in the Presence Chamber. A hunting story, represented by figures,

Fig. 221.

animals, trees, etc., runs round the room in modelled plaster, which is coloured. The effect, if somewhat coarse, is very striking. The

Smithson who designed Hardwick was evidently fond of plaster decoration, and used it freely above fireplaces instead of the panelling general in other houses.

Staircases. English staircases, like other details of English interiors, have a character of their own. Stone was only used occasionally, as at Burghley, and for the principal staircase at Hardwick. As a rule, building owners relied on their own forests for material. At Burghley the staircase is enclosed by walls and covered by a raking barrel-vault, such as is frequently met with on the Continent, and suggests the presence of foreign workmen. The majority of Elizabethan staircases have open wells. All are of the type known as "newel," and fine and bold many of the newels are, nine or ten inches square, with their sides elaborately carved, as in the Charterhouse, London, etc., and surmounted by finials and often by heraldic figures. Different kinds of treatment were accorded to the sides of flights between handrail and string. At the Charterhouse the sides are arcaded, the arches springing from ugly carved and shaped pilasters; at Aston Hall they are filled with strap-work, with excellent results. A running pattern, based on the Classic acanthus-leaf foliage design, is sometimes used, but the most general treatment of all is balustrading. The balusters are generally turned, but sometimes they are shaped, and occasionally plain. They are always large in scale to be in keeping with the newels. Greater stateliness may be found in the staircases of Italy, but for variety and picturesqueness, English staircases surpass those of any other country.

Churches. Little was done in the way of church building during the reigns of Elizabeth and her immediate successors. The Reformation had quenched the fire of enthusiasm which formerly burnt so brightly. Under Archbishop Laud there was a brief rekindling, but it soon died down. He is responsible for the church of S. John the Evangelist, Leeds, built 1631–34. Outside it is Gothic, and in appearance little different from churches of the fifteenth century. Internally the arches are pointed, but the tall pews, with their carved panels and curious but interesting cresting on the top rails, the elaborate screens and other fittings, and the ornamental plaster-panels of the roof, are of the queer provincial Classic of the age. Although few new churches were built in the century following the destruction of the monasteries, old churches were by no means so neglected as their present appearance would lead one to suppose. The tombs and commemorative tablets have,

Fig. 222.—Aston Hall, staircase.

[*To face p.* 268.

with few exceptions, survived. They vary in excellence; but even the most rude have a certain quaintness—in the inscriptions if nowhere else—which render them interesting. But the other fittings—the communion table and rails, the screens, pulpits, and high-back pews—have mostly disappeared; they were swept away in the restoration mania of the last century. A few pulpits remain, and, in the west of England especially, several screens. The finest of the latter are probably in Croscombe Church, Devon. But those that still exist are but a tithe of what there was formerly. They were not Gothic—not even churchwarden's Gothic—and their destruction was regarded as a pious and praiseworthy act.

CHAPTER XII

INIGO JONES, SIR CHRISTOPHER WREN, AND LONDON CHURCHES

"LITTLE knacks are in great vogue: but building certainly ought to have the attribute of eternal, and therefore the only thing uncapable of new fashions."[1] The words are Wren's; the opinion expressed was also Inigo Jones'. The remark applies to the present time, and the advice is even more necessary to remember now than it was two hundred and fifty years ago.

Inigo Jones.

Inigo Jones occupies a unique position in English architecture; a position, moreover, which no other architect has ever occupied in any other country. Brunelleschi, when he started the Renaissance in Florence, was for a brief period somewhat similarly placed, but he was soon surrounded by a number of artists in sympathy with him. Inigo Jones for years stood alone. From 1615, when he was appointed by James I. Surveyor-General of the Works until the outbreak of the Civil War in 1642, he designed in a totally different manner from his contemporaries. But for that war and the feeling of unrest which preceded it, his influence would have been felt sooner, and his isolation not have been so great. As it is, his buildings stand like rocks, towering above a troubled sea of architectural confusion.

Early life of Inigo Jones.

Inigo Jones was born on July 15, 1573, in the parish of S. Bartholomew, Smithfield, and died on June 21, 1652. He had a long life, but only about half of it was devoted to architecture. He began apparently as a joiner's apprentice, but forsook the bench for the easel, and obtained a proficiency in drawing which stood him in good stead later. As a young man he travelled in Italy and the "politer parts of Europe." Early in the seventeenth century he was in Denmark, although on what errand and for what reason is uncertain. Thence he returned to

[1] "Parentalia," p. 261.

England, and, possibly through the influence of Queen Anne of Denmark, James's queen, was employed at Court as a designer of the scenery for masques. The first at which he assisted was "The Masque of Blacknesse," arranged by the queen herself for Twelfth Night, 1604-5. At that time Ben Jonson was the principal writer of masques, the favourite form of theatrical entertainment which succeeded the drama of Elizabeth's reign and preceded the comedies of the Restoration. When Prince Henry, the eldest son of James I., was created Prince of Wales in 1610, Inigo Jones was appointed his "Surveyor," but what work he did in that capacity is not definitely known. No existing documents connect his name with the house in Fleet Street, opposite the end of Chancery Lane, one room on the first floor of which was probably the council-room, or office, of the Duchy of Cornwall which appertained to the prince. On the ceiling are a number of H's and crowns, otherwise the design is similar to many other ornamental Jacobean ceilings elsewhere. The prince dying in 1612, Jones lost his post, and took the opportunity in the following year to revisit Italy, where he remained for about a couple of years.

His architectural career may be said to commence from 1615, when he was appointed by James I. Surveyor-General of the Works. Whether the king really understood the importance of the appointment, and how far-reaching would be the results, appears doubtful. At that time Jones had considerable reputation as an art connoisseur, so much so that he was commissioned by the Earls of Pembroke and Arundel, possibly by the king himself, to buy works of art in Italy and France, and had already shown, in his designs for masques, his inventive faculty and draughtsman's skill. But if he had actually carried out any buildings, which appears doubtful, they probably differed little from his contemporaries'. After 1615, however, no such remark can be made. In the Queen's House, Greenwich, commenced 1617, in the houses on the west side of Lincoln's Inn Fields, for the laying out of which he prepared plans in the following year, and more important still, in the Banqueting Hall, Whitehall, the first stone of which was laid on June 1, 1619, he struck a note absolutely unknown before in England. *His architectural career.*

The original Banqueting Hall was destroyed by fire on January 12, 1618-19, and Jones, as Crown Surveyor, got his chance. The new building was finished in March, 1622. It seems *Banqueting Hall.*

probable that all the king desired at first was a new hall, but the architect saw his opportunity of designing an entirely new palace which would take the place of the existing irregularly planned

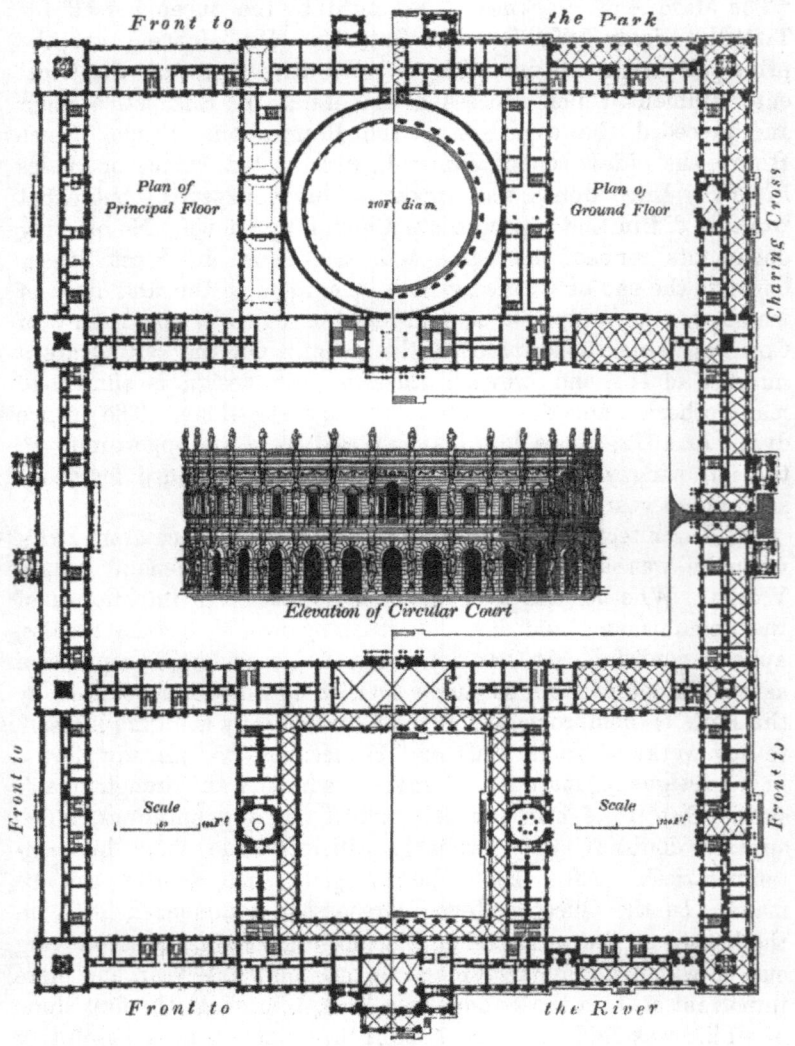

FIG. 223 (*Gwilt*).

buildings which then comprised Whitehall. He accordingly produced a plan which, if carried out, would have given the Kings of England one of the finest royal residences in the world.

Fig. 224.—Palace of Whitehall.

[To face p. 272.

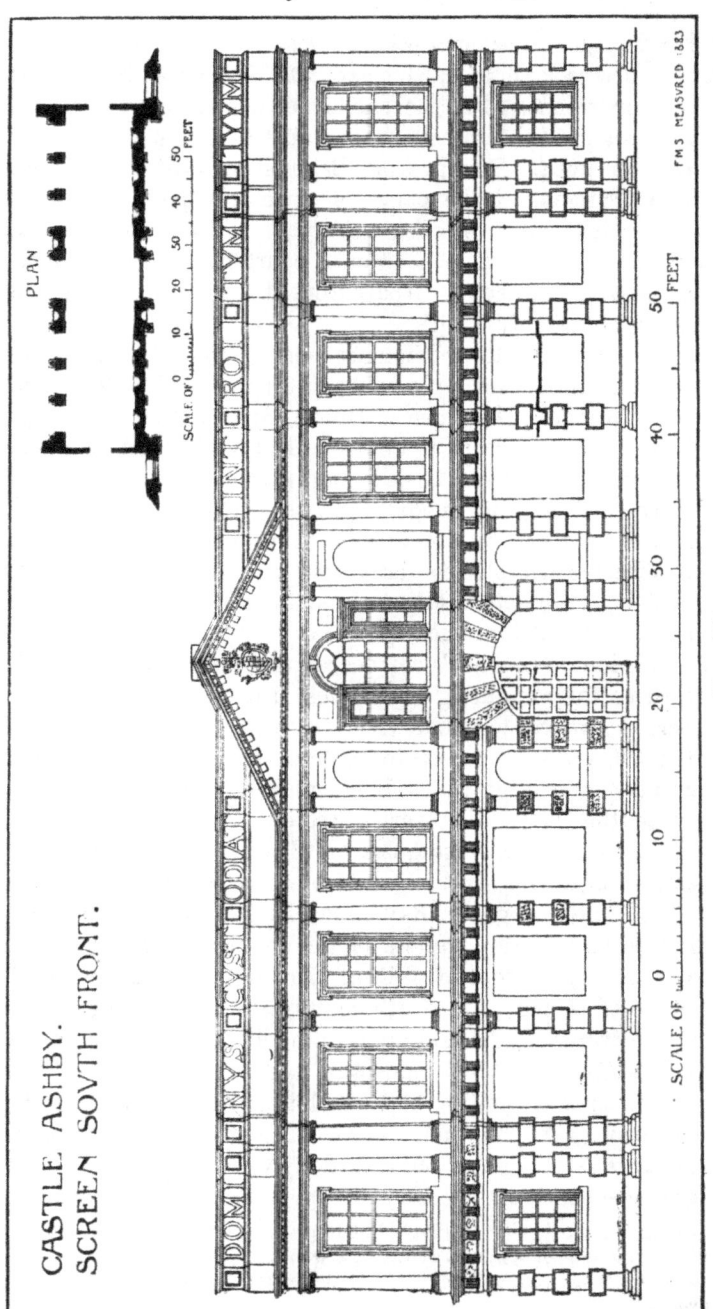

Fig. 225.

274   A HISTORY OF ARCHITECTURAL DEVELOPMENT

Extensive though the scheme was, it was not sufficiently palatial for James' successor, Charles, who, about 1639, ordered fresh plans of greater dimensions. But the exchequer was empty, the people murmuring against the excessive and unjust taxation, and nothing more was ever built. The present Banqueting Hall would have been but a fragment of the palace, and not the most important either, occupying but a small portion of one side of the great central court. On one side a circular court had been intended, about 110 feet in diameter.[1] Apart from this feature the plan is absolutely symmetrical.

1620-42. Between 1620 and the commencement of the Civil War was Jones' busiest time, when he was fully occupied with Whitehall and other buildings. The Queen's House, Greenwich, not finished until 1635, and the houses iu Lincoln's Inn Fields, have already been mentioned. In 1631 he laid out Covent Garden, with its piazza, now altered and modernized, and church of S. Paul. The last was destroyed by fire in 1795, but its portico, as rebuilt, with its massive simple columns, has a genuine Inigo Jones feeling, although the entablature and pediment may have suffered modification. He had previously, about 1620, prepared a report on the condition of S. Paul's Cathedral, and thirteen years later he commenced the rebuilding of the west front and other portions, which were destroyed, together with the rest of the church, in the Great Fire. There is no reason to deplore their loss. Fine though the front may have been in itself, it must have appeared incongruous with the more lofty, earlier Gothic work behind it. In France there are several examples of Classic west fronts tacked on to earlier buildings, but not one that is really satisfactory. About 1630 he designed Raynham Hall, Norfolk, the best authenticated and most complete of his country houses, and ten years later the south front of Wilton House, near Salisbury, with its fine suite of rooms. In Northamptonshire he had previously designed the two-storied building running across the front of the courtyard at Castle Ashby, connecting the two wings, and he is credited with the remodelling of a similarly placed front at Kirby Hall, between 1638 and 1640, and with some of the internal fittings. At Castle Ashby he also designed the panelling of a small ground-floor room to the left of his addition,[2] but it is

[1] The unfinished court of Brydon's building, at the bottom of Parliament Street, gives some idea of what its appearance would have been.

[2] Drawings of it are given in "Joinery" in the second volume of "Building Construction."

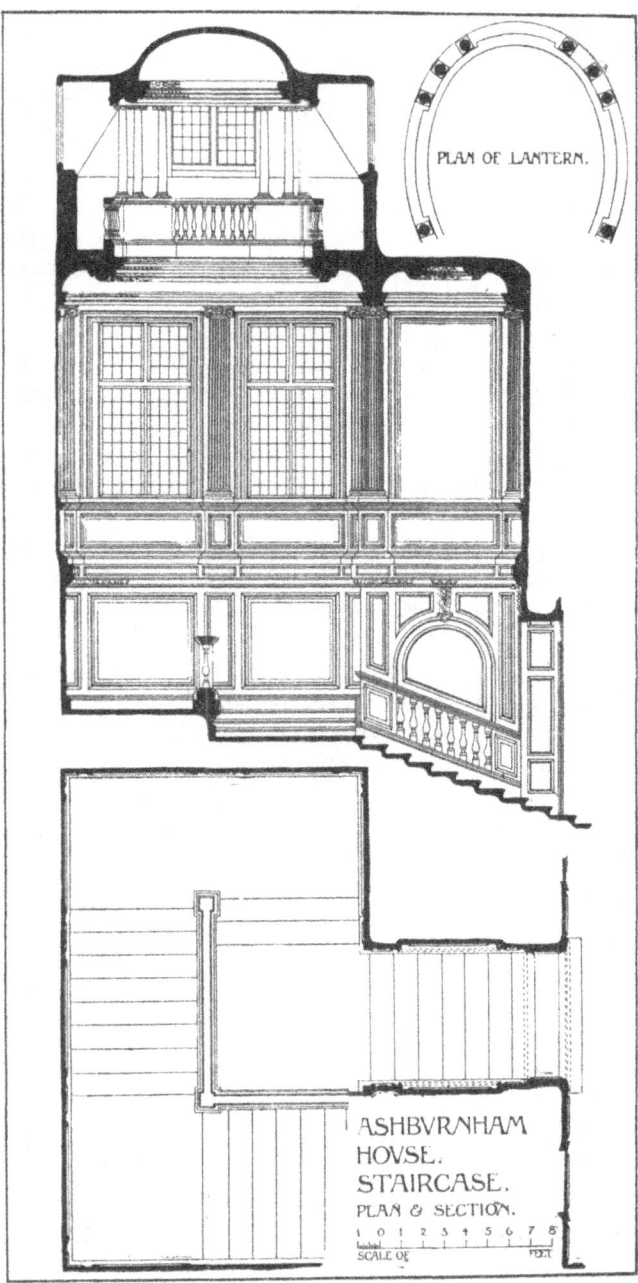

Fig. 226.

questionable if he is responsible for the fittings at Kirby. Well
designed though they are, they appear later in date and more
"Wrenian" in character, and lack the virility that generally
distinguishes his work. York Water Gate, which formerly stood
at the top of a flight of steps leading down to the river, and now
is half buried below the level of the Embankment Gardens, is
doubtless his, and dates from 1626. It was carved by Nicholas
Stone, who worked as chief mason for Jones at Whitehall and
elsewhere. Only one Gothic design can authentically be attributed
to him, namely, the Chapel of Lincoln's Inn, built between 1617
and 1623. But those who go there now to see how the architect
managed Gothic will have their labour for nothing. The building,
until about thirty years ago, was full of most interesting little
touches which although not Gothic did not conflict with the style.
These were ruthlessly "restored" away about 1880, when the
detail was "corrected," and the building made infinitely more
commonplace in consequence.

Attributed buildings.
Amongst other buildings attributed to him are portions of
Charles II.'s block, Greenwich Hospital, Coleshill House, Berks,
and Ashburnham House, Westminster, with its exceedingly dignified and beautifully proportioned staircase. These were not built
until after his death, and were carried out by his successor, Webb.
The Civil War stopped work so completely that the designs may
have been made years before they were carried out. On the other
hand, it is possible that the credit for all should be given to Webb.[1]

That Inigo Jones was a disciple of Palladio, and carried that
architect's book about with him everywhere, is an oft-told story,
but none the less a true one.[2] In his dislike of and revolt against
the detail and proportions which passed muster in his time in
England, he sometimes rather overdid correctness. He felt bound
to make a protest. If one less gifted than he could have prepared
the way he might have given freer rein to his genius. As it is,
many of his designs, and those amongst his best, are deliberately
clothed in Palladian dress. This applies particularly to his work
in London; in the country he was less severe, and, if all the
buildings there credited to him are really his, less "correct."
The Banqueting Hall resembles the Palazzo Porto Barbarano,

[1] As regards Greenwich, see article by Mr. J. A. Gotch on the Burlington-
Devonshire drawings in the *R.I.B.A. Journal*, Third Series, Vol. XVIII. pp.
317-342.

[2] His copy of Palladio's book is in the Library of Worcester College, Oxford.

INIGO JONES AND WREN

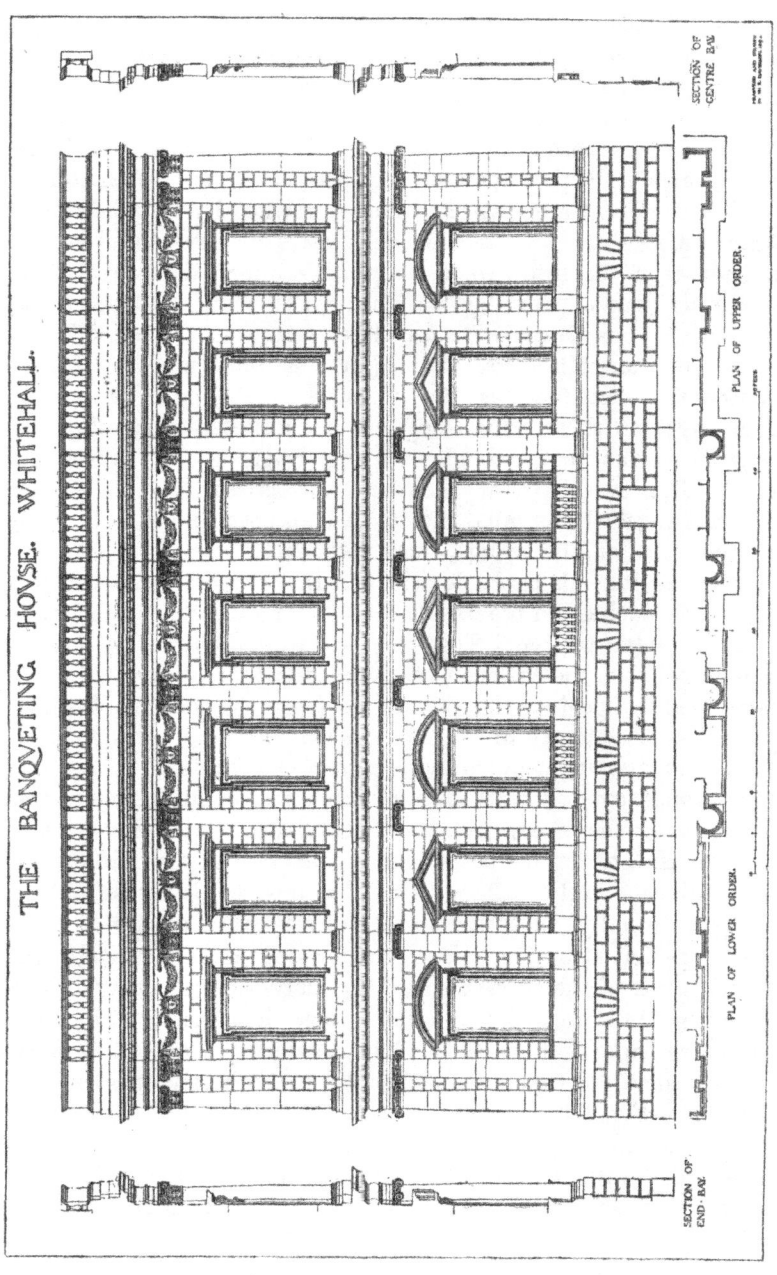

Fig. 227 (*W. R. Davidson*).

Vicenza, in the super-imposition of the Ionic and Corinthian orders, and the Casa del Diavolo and Palazzo Thiene, in the same town, in the swags uniting the capitals. In the houses in Lincoln's Inn Fields he followed his master in the rusticated basement with pilasters above running through two storeys. In the Charles II.'s block of Greenwich Hospital (possibly not his but Webb's), both storeys of the east front are rusticated stone crowned by an exceedingly heavy entablature. There are no pilasters or columns, except in the centre of the front, where engaged columns start direct from the ground and support an entablature, and at the end nearest to the river.[1] The Queen's House, Greenwich, and the York Water Gate are thoroughly Palladian. In the Lincoln's Inn Fields' houses the bands across the pilasters with Tudor rose and fleur-de-lys on them alternating, are an original touch. Equally original is the sectional plan of the front of the Banqueting Hall. The two bays at each end are pilastered; the central part has engaged columns, and its face projects slightly in front of the face of the wings, just sufficiently to allow the two columns at its ends to be detached on the outside, and yet three-quarters attached on the inside, like the remaining two columns of the central portion. This may appear a small detail to lay stress upon, but the charm of the front is largely owing to it. The same idea is repeated, on a smaller scale, in the columns flanking the entrance gateway in front of the courtyard at Castle Ashby.

The greater freedom and less correctness in detail of some of Inigo Jones' country work are probably due to his being unable to exercise the same personal supervision that he was able to give in London. The workmen did not always follow his instructions exactly. There is no appearance of this at Wilton, either externally or internally. He evidently gave the work there special attention. But portions of Raynham Hall, the central gable of the entrance front especially, are unworthy of him. At Kirby Hall parts are excellent, others less satisfactory. The chimneys are full of character; but the windows facing the courts suggest some one less versed than he in Classic proportion and detail (see Fig. 229). The rustication of the sides of the chimneys and of the walling generally, is worked in the same way as is indicated in some of the detail drawings of Whitehall. The face of the rustication is the face of the wall; the channels are sunk and are stopped at the corners. The more usual treatment is for

---

[1] For the river front see next chapter, pp. 302-4.

Photo: Author.

FIG. 228.—KIRBY HALL, FRONT ENTRANCE TO FORE COURT.

Photo: Author.

FIG. 229.—KIRBY HALL, ENTRANCE FRONT.

[*To face p.* 278.

the channels to form the face of the wall, and to run through, the rest of the wall being a series of raised panels. At Castle Ashby the proportions are good; but when thinking of Inigo Jones' work one is so accustomed to picture the Banqueting Hall, to the exclusion of everything else, that even Castle Ashby is somewhat disappointing.

Inigo Jones' principal successor was John Webb, his pupil assistant, and executor, who during his lifetime made most of his architectural drawings. Webb had an enthusiastic admiration for his master, and in his work followed faithfully the example the

John Webb.

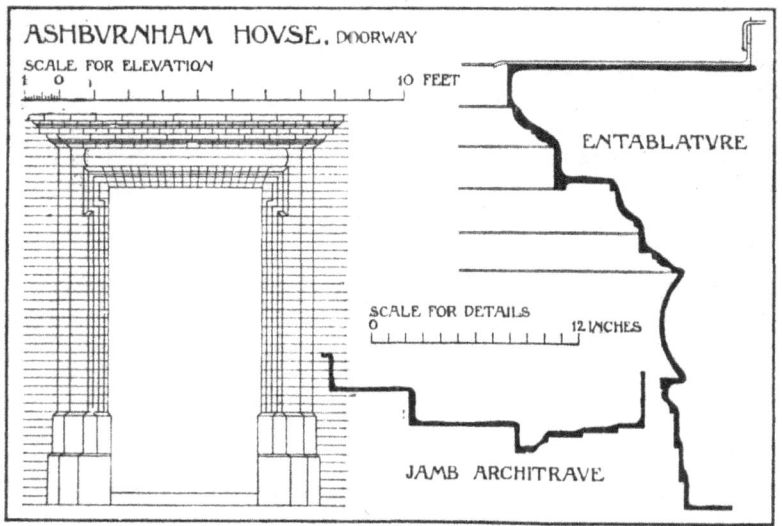

FIG. 230.

latter had set. To what extent he possessed original ability is disputed, but Mr. Gotch, in the article already referred to, gives him a higher place than he has hitherto been credited with. He commenced, or else continued, the "Charles II." block at Greenwich, and either designed himself or carried out Jones' designs at Ashburnham House, Thorpe Hall, near Peterborough, Ashdown House, Berkshire,[1] the main block of which resembles Coleshill in the same county, in the bold cornice under the eaves, in the balustrading surrounding the lead flat above the roof, and in the cupola which rises from its centre; and other buildings

[1] For further particulars of Ashdown, Coleshill, etc., see next chapter, pp. 313-15.

mostly now destroyed. In the gardens of Thorpe Hall is a delightful two-storied garden-house, evidently modelled on Michael Angelo's buildings on the Capitol, Rome. Broad pilasters run the full height from the ground to the top cornice, and alongside these are columns on the lower storey flanking the lintelled opening. The pilaster-fronted house in Great Queen Street—laid out in 1606, the houses being built about thirty years later—may be his or his master's. The front is characteristic of both men, and the same may be said of the staircase inside. For some time Webb was Deputy-Surveyor to the Crown, and had the promise of the reversion of the post of Surveyor-General at Sir John Denham's death. When that happened, however, in 1668, Wren was appointed in his stead. Webb promptly resigned his Deputyship, and soon after retired from practice and went to live in the country.

Jones' other successors.

Webb forms the connecting link between Inigo Jones and Sir Christopher Wren. Little is known about his contemporaries.

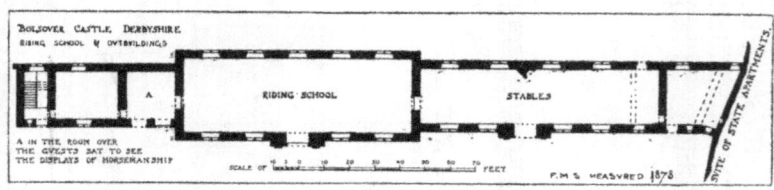

FIG. 231.

The Riding School at Bolsover Castle is attributed, by Walpole, to an architect named Marsh. It was built by Sir William Cavendish, afterwards Duke of Newcastle, the great authority of his time on horsemanship, probably before the Civil War commenced, but this is not certain.[1] It is a very fine design. The entrances to the Riding School and Stables are bold, suitable, and well-proportioned, and the numerous dormers perhaps the best of their class in the country. The rusticated columns which flank the gates alongside the building (not shown in the drawing)

[1] Bolsover Castle is not easy to date. The main block was apparently commenced by Elizabeth, Countess of Shrewsbury (Bess of Hardwick), about 1607, and finished by Sir Charles Cavendish in 1613, who probably added the forecourt and the garden alongside, with its wall forming a series of alcoves. His successor, Sir William, later Duke of Newcastle, built the detached long, or "Queen's," gallery in 1633-34 (see p. 248). The Riding School followed. The duke died in 1676.

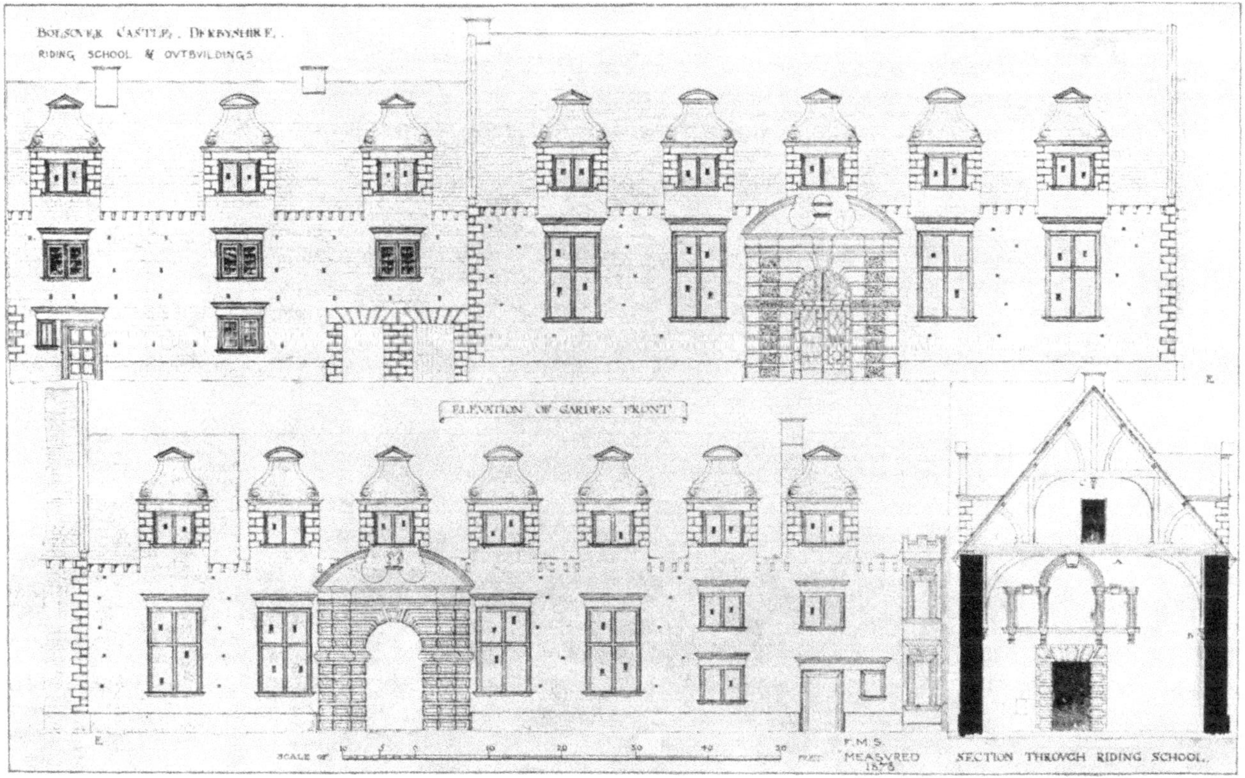

[*To face p. 280.*

Fig. 232.

INIGO JONES AND WREN

are coarse and unsatisfactory. These probably were built before the Riding School, and at the same time as the Long Gallery.

The knowledge of Classic was spreading in England before the Commonwealth began, but old traditions were far from being abandoned. The Banqueting Hall, with its pure detail and proportions, and framed-in window openings, was long finished, but the workman clung to his mullions and transoms, his string courses and gables, and preferred that the heads of his doorways should be Tudor.[1] At Oxford the conservative feeling was

Lingering old traditions.

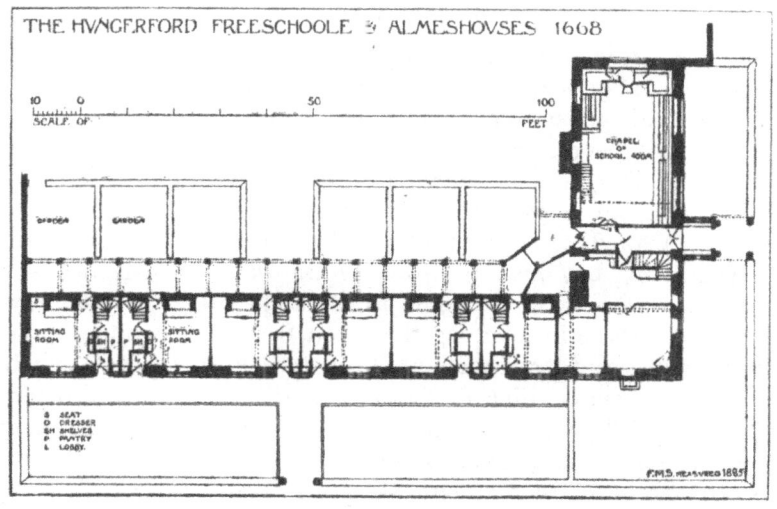

Fig. 233.

particularly strong. Between 1630 and 1640, Christ Church College staircase hall was building with a Gothic fan tracery vault. Between 1631 and 1635, Archbishop Laud made the additions to S. John's College. These have been attributed to Inigo Jones, but without foundation. That architect might have been swayed sufficiently by the surroundings to build in Gothic, but that influence could hardly have caused him to design in indifferent Classic. The confusion of ideals prevailing even after the Restoration is well illustrated in the "Hungerford Free Schoole and Almeshouses," Corsham, Wilts, dated 1668. The greater part of the outside and all the fittings of the almshouse

---

[1] They are Tudor, except that the upper portions of each head are straight, instead of being slightly curved, as in pure Tudor four-centred arches.

portion of the building are on the old lines. In the porch, however, and on the commemorative tablet on the long front, and in the fittings of the chapel that also served as schoolroom, the feeling is entirely different; and yet it appears certain that they are the same date as the rest. These portions must have been executed by another set of workmen, coming possibly from Bath, Bristol, or some other centre, who were more advanced than the local men who carried out most of the work. Still further west, in Somerset, many examples still exist, later in date than the Corsham building, which are thoroughly Gothic in spirit, and not particularly debased in detail. At Martock especially there are several; and in other villages in the county men clung to the old forms long after they had been abandoned elsewhere.

Sir C. Wren. Sir Christopher Wren was born on October 20, 1632. His father was a country clergyman, and his uncle was Mathew Wren, Bishop of Ely, who was imprisoned in the Tower for eighteen years, and only regained his freedom at the Restoration. As a boy he showed marked abilities. His Classical knowledge was considerable, but his favourite studies were mathematics and astronomy. He was a Fellow of All Souls' when only twenty-one, had a share in founding the Royal Society, and after having been Professor of Astronomy at Gresham College, London, was, in 1661, appointed Savilian Professor of Astronomy in the University of Oxford. Nothing in his career up to then had marked him as destined for the architectural profession, but in the same year he became assistant to Sir John Denham, Surveyor-General to the Crown. That was the turning-point in his career. His first work was the Chapel at Pembroke College, Cambridge, which he designed for his uncle the Bishop in 1663. It is a delightfully simple design, thoroughly Classic, and might well be fifty years later in date. In the same year he prepared plans for the Sheldonian Theatre, Oxford, which was finished in 1668. This possesses no particular architectural merit, but shows some knowledge of construction and planning. The span of the roof is 68 feet, and, in the words of Fergusson, "a larger number can see and hear than in any similar building in the United Kingdom." In 1665 Wren paid a six months' visit to France, returning early in the following year. During this visit he studied architecture diligently. "I shall bring you almost all France in paper," he writes. Most of the time he was in Paris, at that period a better school at which to study modern architecture than

Italy. Lemercier was dead, and François Mansard's best work

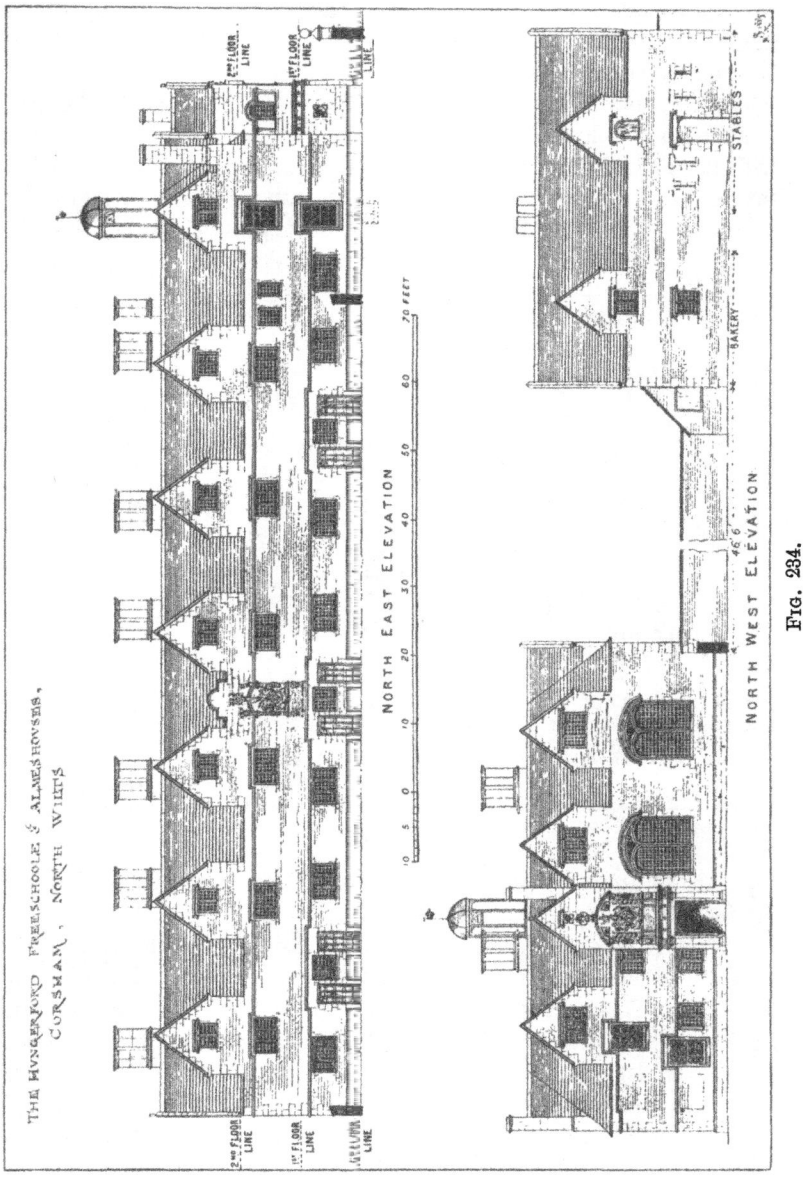

Fig. 234.

finished, but Levau, Perrault and also Bernini, were all engaged on the Louvre, and other fine buildings were being erected.

Wren's failure to reach Italy was not, therefore, so serious a loss, although actual contact with the ruins of Imperial Rome and the masterpieces of Bramante, Peruzzi, and Michael Angelo would probably have given his style that broader, bigger touch which to some extent it lacks. On his return to London he was busy with a scheme for remodelling old S. Paul's, which church had been neglected during the Commonwealth, and had fallen into a very ruinous condition. In his alterations and additions he proposed to depart from "the Gothick rudeness of the old design," and to follow "a good Roman manner." Luckily for his

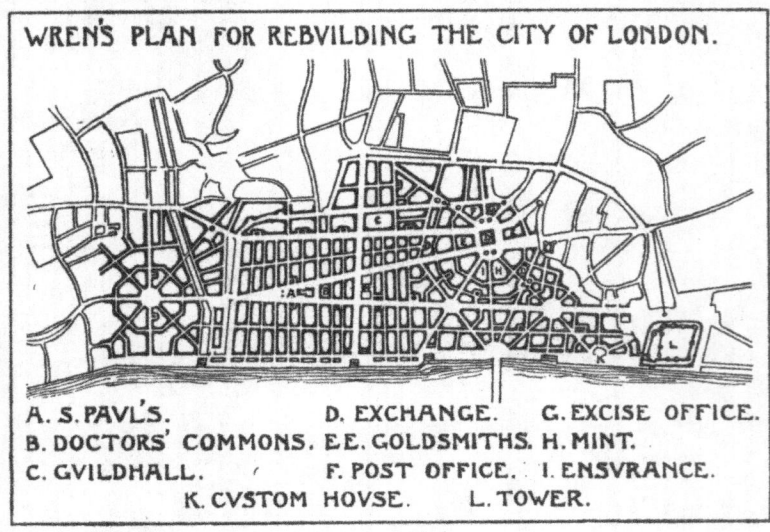

FIG. 235.

reputation, and for posterity, the Great Fire of 1666 frustrated his intentions.

Plan for rebuilding London.

The fire was Wren's opportunity; but he could not have availed himself of it so fully but for the death of Sir John Denham. Wren succeeded to his post of Surveyor-General in 1669, and hereafter the rebuilding of London was to a great extent in his hands. He did not, however, get his own way entirely. The fine scheme he prepared for laying out the city architecturally was not accepted. The cost would have been great, but the advantages greater. The golden opportunity was lost; and no such chance is ever likely to occur again. In his plan he made the Exchange the centre, and grouped round it the Post Office,

Mint, and other important buildings; making it a Forum, in fact, after the manner of the Romans. From it started four main thoroughfares and six slightly narrower streets, one of which led direct to London Bridge. S. Paul's Cathedral he isolated, making the open space in front of the west end of considerable width, narrowing as it ran westward down Ludgate Hill. Near the foot of the hill he planned a "rond point," from which radiated streets, and similar centres he placed in other parts of the city.

If Wren had never built S. Paul's Cathedral his reputation would still be great owing to the large number of churches, public and Collegiate buildings, and private houses he designed. Some of his churches are considered later in this chapter, and a few of his other buildings are referred to in the next. It would have been impossible for him to have carried out all this work, in addition to S. Paul's, if architectural design had been in the same state then that it is now; if even the conditions had been similar to those prevailing fifty years previously. Before Wren was engulfed in his numerous undertakings the seed sown by Inigo Jones and Webb had taken root, and all over England architects and workmen were in sympathy. The confusion of tongues which had prevailed for a hundred and fifty years or more was stilled, and once more men were in agreement as to what constituted architecture. The full-size details and rigid instructions which Inigo Jones had found necessary were no longer imperative. Wren could leave the carving of internal fittings to Grinling Gibbons and Cibber; and other skilled men of the time could carve the stone capitals in and outside S. Paul's without much attention from the architect. The entablatures and other mouldings could be worked according to rule, once their main dimensions were settled. That Wren, however, sometimes found it advantageous to supply full-size details is shown in a letter accompanying his design for the Library, Trinity College, Cambridge, which was commenced in 1678. He says, "I suppose you have good masons, however, I would willingly take a further pains to give all the mouldings in great; we are scrupulous in small matters, and you must pardon us, the architects are as great pedants as critics or heralds." This letter shows that in the latter part of the seventeenth century details were frequently still left to the mason. In London Wren could trust the workmen, because they had been trained under him; of the men at Cambridge he evidently had doubts.

State of architecture in c. 1670.

S. Paul's.   For some time after the fire hopes were entertained that it might be possible to retain a great deal of old S. Paul's. Fortunately these proved vain. In 1668 it was decided to destroy the dangerous portions, and the following year Wren was instructed to prepare designs for a new building. His first design was octagonal in plan, the diagonal sides being curved. In front of the west end was a domed narthex, somewhat similar to the one suggested by A. San Gallo for S. Peter's, Rome.[1] The plan is fascinating, and would have resulted in a magnificent interior, but it may be questioned if externally the effect would have been so fine as the existing building. A square, Greek Cross, or octagonal plan, is undoubtedly by far the best to show a dome to advantage; a fact already recognized by Bramante, Michael Angelo, the three San Galli, and other Italian architects, and soon to be demonstrated also by J. H. Mansard at Les Invalides, Paris. Wren realized this also. But at the time he made his design he had had little experience, and his style was still unformed. He had not, like Inigo Jones, examined on the spot the monuments of antiquity and the masterpieces of the Italian Renaissance. His few months spent in France had been invaluable, but at the same time insufficient. He had seen no really large Classic churches, and the only domes he was acquainted with were a few in Paris, notably Lemercier's dome for the church of the Sorbonne. Wren's genius enabled him to make a noble plan and fitting interior. To design an exterior, however, to such a plan is one of the most difficult problems an architect can tackle. No wonder he did not quite succeed at the first attempt. If his design had been accepted, improvements would doubtless have been introduced as the work proceeded, especially as regards the dome. But to his great regret it was rejected. It was too great a departure. The clergy with one accord cried out against it. It was so different from anything they had been accustomed to, and their especial complaint was that there was no chancel. Their idea of a cathedral was still a Latin cross, with nave, choir, transepts, and flanking aisles. The "Warrant" design followed; the one officially described, in 1675, as "very artificial (*i.e.* artistic), proper, and useful." In this design Wren gave them all they asked for, and in addition a great octagon about 110 feet in diameter. This he proposed to cover

[1] The model he prepared for this is now in the south gallery of the Cathedral, and is sufficiently large for the many beauties of the design to be apparent.

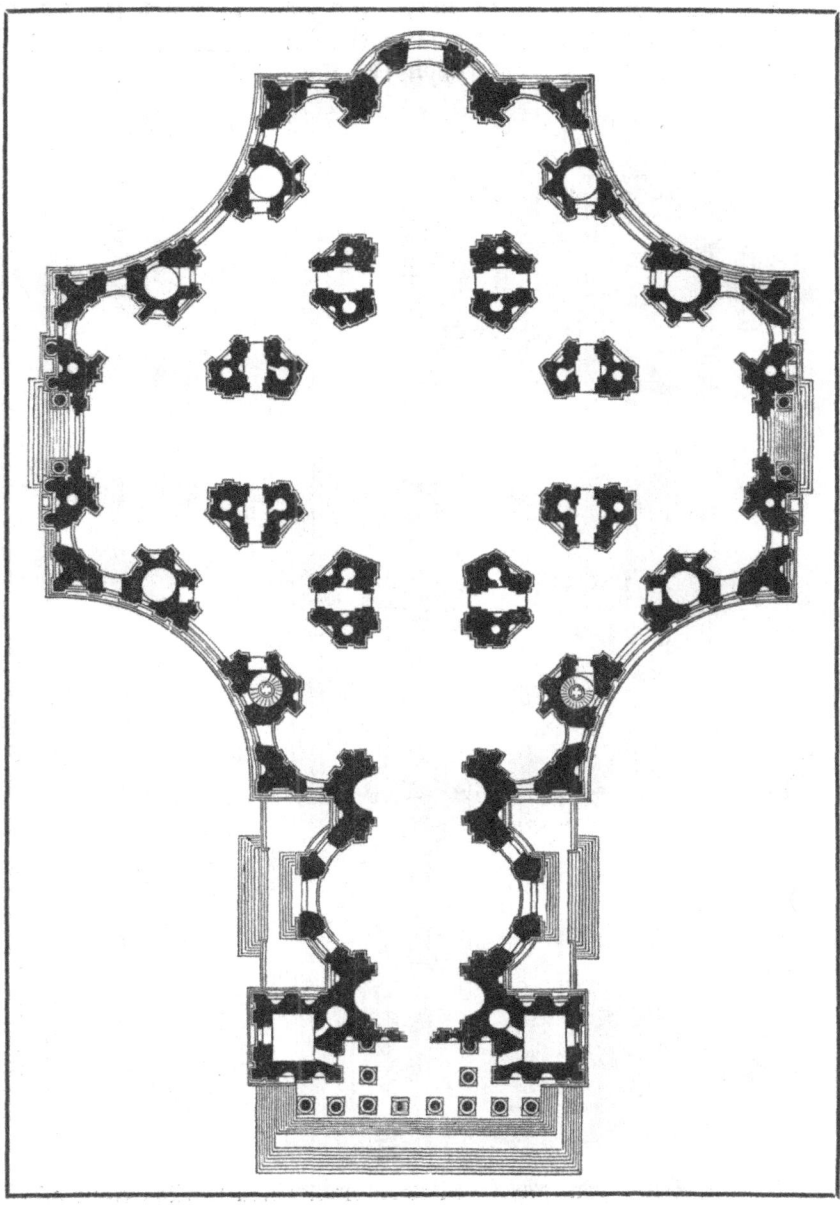

Fig. 236.—Wren's First Plan of St. Paul's.
(From W. Longman's "A History of the Three Cathedrals dedicated to St. Paul in London.")

288 A HISTORY OF ARCHITECTURAL DEVELOPMENT

by a combination of dome, tower, and spire, of which the less said the better. The Londoners of the seventeenth century had become so accustomed to a spire as the chief feature of their

Fig. 287.—Interior of Wren's Original Design for St. Paul's (*Longmans' "St. Paul's"*).

cathedral, that Wren was forced to humour them to the extent of including one in his design. But that he intended to oblige them further by putting it into execution is doubtful. The warrant

Fig. 288.

allowed him to make variations "as from time to time he should see proper," and this "liberty" he availed himself of to a considerable extent. He did not dare depart greatly from the main outline of the plan, as such departure would have been easily detected, but he introduced several modifications, the chief being reducing the number of the nave bays, by which he approached nearer to the proportions of Classic churches on the Continent, and to a corresponding extent departed from the reduplication of piers customary in Gothic churches. The exterior was altogether remodelled, and an entirely new design made for the dome and its drums.[1] The first stone of the new foundations was laid on

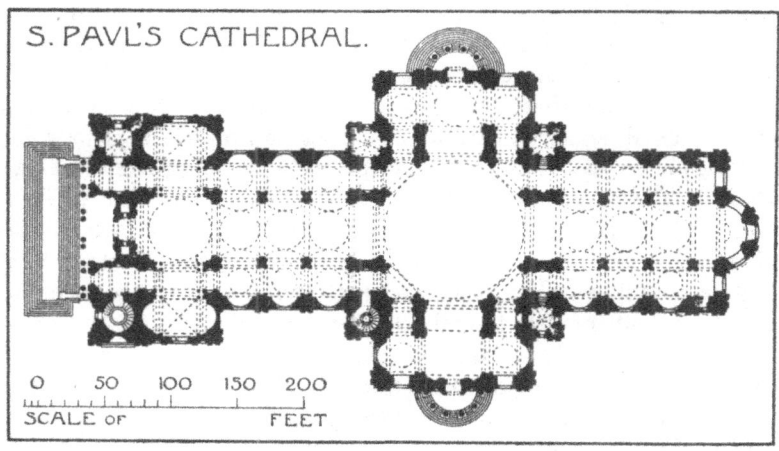

Fig. 239.

June 21, 1675, by Wren himself, and the top stone of the lantern thirty-five years later by his son and by Edward Strong, chief mason, son of Thomas Strong, who assisted Wren to lay the first stone.

The skilful construction of the dome and the great beauty of the peristylar drum have already been referred to (see pp. 162-4). A tower or spire may be a more appropriate landmark in the country and equally effective in a small town; but for a great city nothing can compare in dignity with a dome. The ribs of the dome of S. Paul's spread themselves out as though to embrace the whole city, and extend a welcome to its inhabitants. The

The dome.

[1] Several designs were made, some of which have been preserved. The present magnificent result was by no means obtained at a first or even second essay.

VOL. III. U

domes of S. Peter's, Rome, and Florence Cathedral are greater, and the dome itself of the former possibly finer, but taking drum and dome together, neither of the above can compare in beauty of outline with Wren's crowning triumph. It not only looks well from afar, towering above the city, but such fascinating peeps of it are also obtainable from the narrow streets surrounding the cathedral.[1] S. Paul's means more to London than S. Peter's to Rome; more even than its cathedral means to Florence. S. Peter's is on the outskirts; S. Paul's not only is central, but is placed on the highest ground in the city, and dominates the whole.[2]

<small>Side walls of S. Paul's.</small> In the "Warrant" design the aisle walls were only of one storey, and little higher than the top of the side vaults. In execution Wren raised these to the same height as the nave walls, following, in this respect, the example set at S. Peter's. There can be no doubt that he was right in doing so. Few now will endorse Gwilt's statement that the upper portion of the aisle walls is "an abuse that admits of no apology. It is an architectural fraud." The upper walls buttress the supports of the dome. They also take the place of and perform the same functions as the lofty pinnacles that rise above the haunches of flying buttresses in Gothic churches. That they are continuous and not a series of isolated members does not make them fraudulent, neither does it diminish their utility. On the contrary, their utility is increased by their solidity. Behind them are the flying buttresses. To have allowed these to show from outside would have destroyed entirely that feeling of repose, essential to success in Classic design, which was acknowledged by Alberti at Mantua, by Michael Angelo at Rome, and by other great masters of the Renaissance. The construction of the domes of S. Paul's has also been termed a fraud. If to conceal an inner dome and a cone by an outer dome of timber and lead deserves this reproach, why should it not be applied equally to the thousands of mediæval churches in which vaults of stone are covered by high-pitched roofs? If either deserves it, which is doubtful, the latter deserve it more, as in a Gothic church vault and roof are entirely separate and distinct.

---

[1] I remember vividly the view I once had through a top window of a house in Paternoster Square. The dome and a spandril of blue sky filled the frame, and the effect was stupendous.

[2] The inscription on the tablet, dated 1688, in Panyer Alley, off Paternoster Row, reads:

"When y^e have sought the Citty round
Yet still this is the highs^t ground."

Fig. 240.—Interior of S. Paul's, London.

[*To face p.* 291.

In S. Paul's the cone carries the timbers of the outer dome, which without it could only have been constructed with difficulty.

In the interior the customary Classic ordinance of pilastered piers supporting arches, with an entablature above, is followed. Only the cornice of the entablature, however, is continuous. The frieze and architrave are omitted over the arches between the pilasters. Above the cornice is a lofty attic from which springs the vault, cut into by the tall clerestory windows. The bays of

Interior.

FIG. 241.

the nave and choir are oblong, and are divided from one another by transverse arches. A barrel vault, as at S. Andrea, Mantua, and in portions of St. Peter's, Rome, was out of the question, owing to the need for high side-lighting. In churches abroad, such as S. Giorgio Maggiore, Venice, S. Roch, Paris, etc., in which the bays are oblong, and similar lighting was required, the vault is of the Welsh groin type (see p. 131). This cannot be said to be a beautiful form. Wren improved on it vastly at S. Paul's by making the central part of each bay a saucer dome, surrounded by a broad and highly enriched band which separates it from the irregularly shaped pendentives below. At the crossing, under the dome, Wren was confronted by a difficulty owing to the shape of his piers which made the openings on the cardinal sides of the octagon considerably wider than the openings on the diagonal sides. It was essential, however, that the upper arches of the latter should in appearance be identical, at least superficially, with the barrel vaults opening into nave, choir, and transepts. To have made them so in reality was impossible. His drum and dome would have been unsupported. He overcame the difficulty by partially filling in the arches on the diagonal sides with spandrils which are recessed a few inches behind the moulded archivolts, and are quite plain. Ornament would only have emphasized them, and Wren was probably wise in leaving them as they are. At the same time the effect is not satisfactory, and the spandrils are but a makeshift. It looks as though Wren, when he settled the plan of his piers, did not consider the arches above. A Gothic architect would not have fallen into that error. The lack of apparent strength at the springing of the arches, and the slenderness of the pilasters immediately below, create a feeling of weakness at the very place where the opposite is most desired. Apart from this defect the design at the crossing and the ingenuity displayed in the treatment of the spaces surrounding it are great, and both from the floor and the galleries, especially from the latter, the perspective effects are very striking.

City churches. In 1667 an Act of Parliament was passed for the rebuilding of thirty-nine of the City churches. Most of these fell to Wren's lot. The task that confronted him was no easy one. Money was far from plentiful. The sites in most cases were cramped and irregular; seating accommodation had to be provided for large congregations; and the narrow, inartistic requirements of the Protestant ritual and its lack of elasticity were a serious hindrance to architectural effect. No separation was desired between clergy and congregation; no long chancel to give an air of space and of mystery. This was fortunate in one sense, as in most cases no room was available. A Communion table sufficed, standing in many cases in the body of the church, and separated from it only by a rail. Even when room was plentiful, as at S. James, Piccadilly, a shallow recess, only a few feet deep, was all that was thought necessary for a chancel. The churches were purely congregational, and every inch of their area had to be utilized. Few, if any, are twice their width in length, the majority are about two to three, whilst many are approximately square.

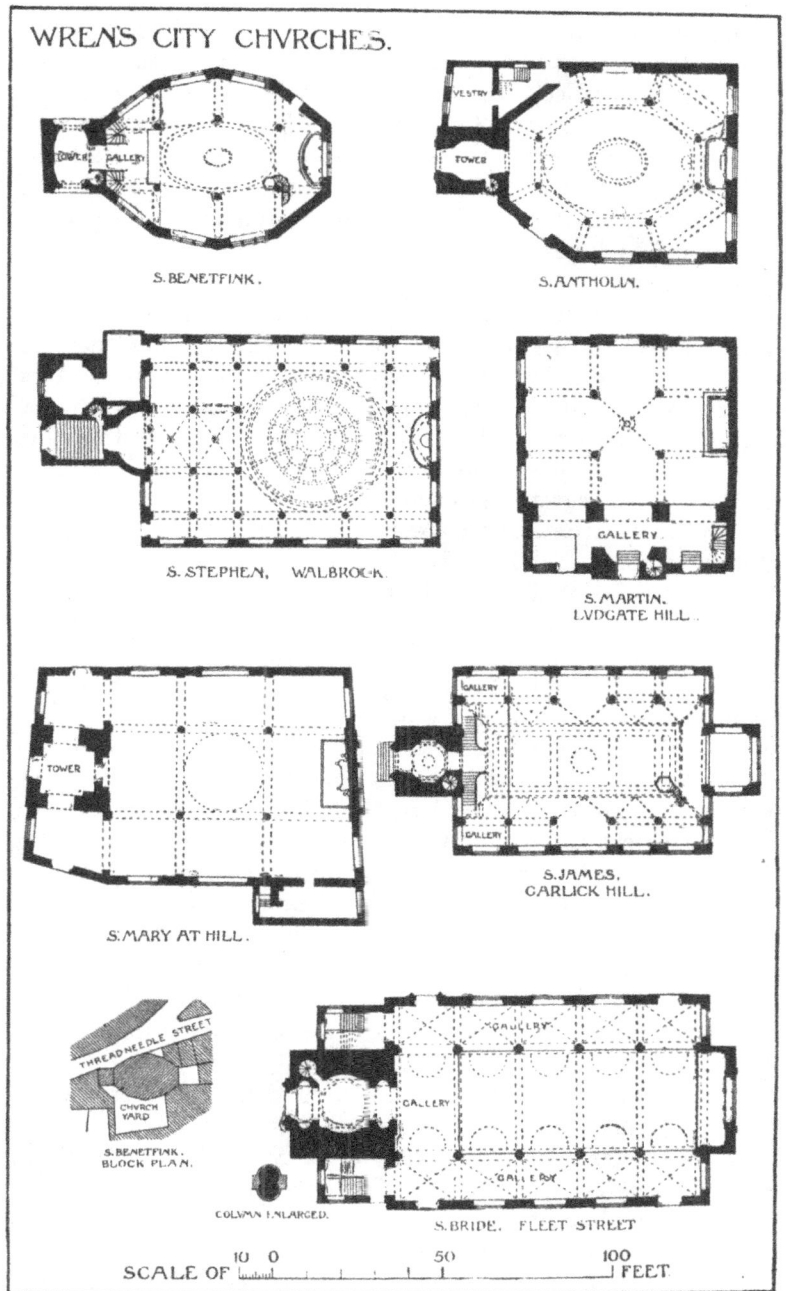

FIG. 242 (*I. Clayton*).

Oblong churches.

Of the fifty or more churches Wren designed for London, about three-quarters are oblong in plan, and are either barrel-vaulted or flat-ceiled, both vaults and ceilings being generally panelled. At S. James, Garlick Hill, a good effect is obtained by a deep upper cove at the sides, cut into by the windows, whilst the centre of the ceiling is flat. About twenty-five of the vaulted or flat ceiled churches have aisles, and about a dozen are aisleless. The majority present no particular points of interest, either in plan or internal treatment. The necessity of providing for a large congregation obliged Wren to have galleries in many cases. There is no particular objection to galleries when they are well managed, and do not cut into the sides of columns. As a rule he avoided this mistake, and carried the galleries on piers, the columns supporting the vault or ceiling starting from the gallery floor or from the top of the gallery front. At S. Bride's, Fleet Street, however, the columns, which are in pairs, are cut into, and in a particularly aggressive manner. This defect spoils what otherwise would have been the finest interior of any of his vaulted churches. The beauty of these inside—and many are undoubtedly beautiful—lies mainly in their breadth of treatment, absence of fussiness, old-world feeling of reposeful quiet, and the charm of their fittings. The high panelled dado on the walls; the similar dadoes surrounding the columns to raise their bases above the pews; the reredos behind the altar, often of noble dimensions and elaborate design; the fronts of many of the galleries; the organ-cases, beautifully carved in many instances; even the pews themselves; are all well worthy of study. The pulpits are placed well forward and raised high, so that all could hear the preacher. Many are approached by winding staircases, with turned or carved balusters, whilst above is that practical and often beautiful feature, common also in Jacobean pulpits, the sounding-board. Very effective also are the painted and gilded wrought-iron uprights in many churches to receive the mace, sword, etc., when the Lord Mayor attends service in state.

Domed churches.

Wren's genius displays itself best in those churches, mostly either of Greek cross plan or approximately square, which are domed. The smaller ones, such as S. Mary, Tower Hill, are planned like the numerous smaller Byzantine churches of the ninth and tenth centuries, and many small Renaissance churches in Italy, with a dome over the central square, barrel vaults over the four arms, and a flat ceiling at each corner. The largest and most beautiful of the larger domed churches is S. Stephen, Walbrook. Here the dome is the full width, exclusive of the narrow outer aisles along the north and south sides, and the plan is reminiscent of the larger churches of the East, such as Daphni, near Athens. The resemblance is probably accidental, and ends with the plan. The treatment is very different. The dome is carried on eight arches, which start from an entablature supported on columns. Wren showed emphatically in this church what can be done within a simple rectangle without any breaks or projections. He obtained his results in a large measure through the outer aisles, as without these half the columns would have been unnecessary, and the existing perspective effects unobtainable. The church was begun in 1672, and was therefore among the first of those to be rebuilt.[1] At that time he was working on his design for S. Paul's, and was evidently enamoured of the dome. S. Benet Fink (destroyed), S. Mary, Tower Hill, S. Swithin, Cannon Street, and S. Antholin (destroyed), are all domed churches commenced between 1670 and 1680. It is a thousand pities that two churches with such interesting plans as S. Antholin and S. Benet Fink could not have been preserved. In 1680 he also commenced All Saints, Northampton, a square church with a central dome, in plan similar to S. Mary, Tower Hill. Its interior ranks second only to S. Stephen, Walbrook. The fine portico of Ionic columns at the west end was the forerunner of many similar porticoes, but of the Corinthian order, by later architects.

The exteriors of Wren's City churches are generally severely plain, but none the less effective on that account. The walls are principally of red brick, the crowning cornices, with or without a balustrade on top, and the architraves surrounding the large, semi-circular headed windows being of Portland stone. The only ornamentation is frequently the carving on the keystones of the windows, which looks all the better owing to the simplicity of its surrounding. Such spare money as was available was reserved for the towers and spires, frequently for the latter alone, as many of the towers themselves are quite plain. Most of the churches were so hemmed in by houses that they could be little seen, whereas the spires rising above the houses marked the different parishes, and therefore received architectural treatment of a more elaborate character.

Exteriors.

[1] Mr. G. H. Birch in "London Churches of the Seventeenth and Eighteenth Centuries" says 1676–78.

296 A HISTORY OF ARCHITECTURAL DEVELOPMENT

Towers, spires, etc.

Wren is stated to have designed, for London alone, thirty spires or steeples, eleven of stone, the rest of timber covered with lead; and in addition more than a dozen towers without an upper feature. Some of the stone spires better deserve the title of

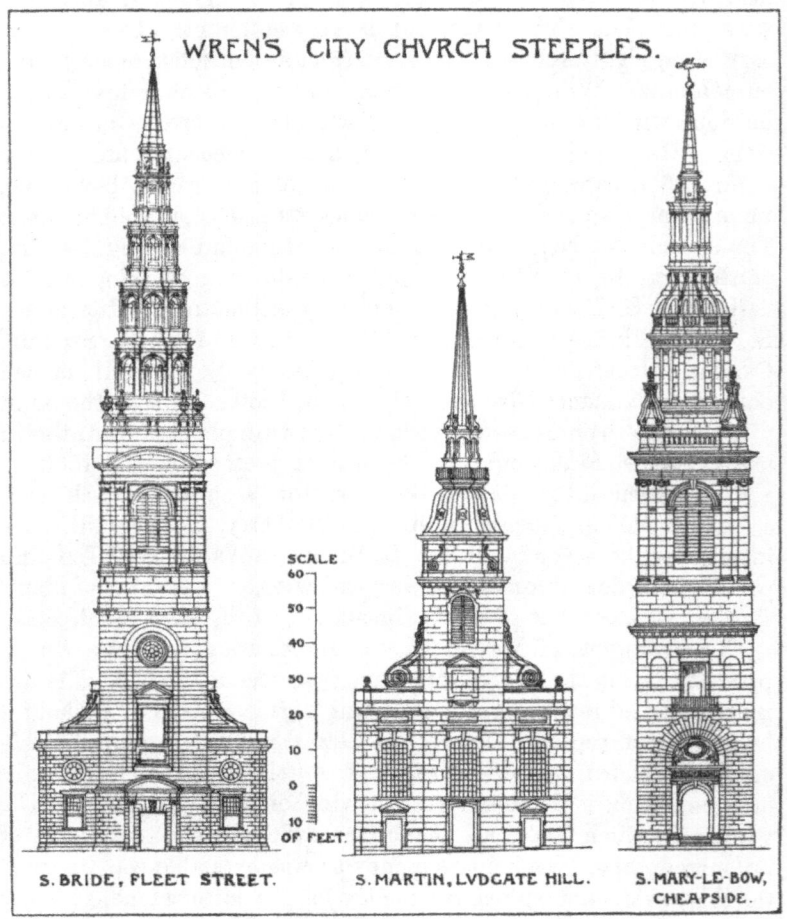

Fig. 243 (*I. Clayton*).

lantern; those, for instance, of S. Stephen, Walbrook, S. Magnus, London Bridge, and S. James, Garlick Hill. In the first-named the lantern, beautiful though it is in itself, is quite independent of the very plain tower below, and appears like an after-thought. The same remark applies to some other examples. At Christ

Church, Newgate, the relation of tower to lantern is excellent, although the actual top of the latter is unsatisfactory. The finest stone towers and spires are undoubtedly those of S. Mary-le-Bow, Cheapside, and S. Bride, Fleet Street. There is perfect harmony between upper and lower portions in both, and the proportions are excellent. S. Bride's spire has been criticized as being too "telescopic," but on the whole it is, perhaps, the more effective of the two. The towers are very similar, but S. Bride's cannot boast a doorway so fine as that which forms the entrance to the Cheapside church. The variety in design of the lead spires is extraordinary. From the simple straight-sided spire of S. Margaret Pattens to the most perfect example of all, that of S. Martin, Ludgate Hill, all shapes and outlines are to be found. The spire of S. Martin's rises perfectly from its tower. Not only is it a very beautiful object in itself, but it combines so well from all points with the great dome of S. Paul's that rises beyond and above it; now standing out alongside it, now cutting through and emphasizing its great mass. In either case the combination makes one of the finest architectural pictures in the world.[1] In designing the spires for the churches in the vicinity of S. Paul's Wren undoubtedly considered their effect in relation to his cathedral. S. Martin's produces the most striking results, but almost as good can be seen from other positions with the spires of other churches.

S. Dunstan in the East, with its stone spire carried on four flying arches, as at S. Nicholas, Newcastle, is one of Wren's few attempts at a Gothic spire. His tower for S. Michael, Cornhill, is also Gothic; but that was built in place of the one damaged at the Great Fire. This is stated to have been his last work, and to have been finished only in 1721, two years before his death. In S. Mary Aldermary, Wren essayed a Gothic interior, and succeeded passably well. The fan vault is quite good, and the series of saucer domes where pendants generally come is sound constructurally, and possibly an improvement æsthetically. *Wren's Gothic.*

In 1723 Wren died, at the great age of 90. He was badly treated towards the end. Half of the "noble" £200 a year he received for the work at S. Paul's was docked in 1697, and in 1718 he was deprived by George I. of the office of Surveyor- *Death of Wren.*

---

[1] A finer picture still is obtained by riding down Ludgate Hill, looking back all the time and seeing the dome gradually rise higher and higher above the west front.

General, which he had held since 1669. His great achievement was to consolidate English Architecture. Inigo Jones had prepared the way, but his example might have been ignored if some one less virile had been his successor. But Wren set his face against "little knacks." In any comparison with his great French contemporary, J. H. Mansard, he has the advantage. The dome of the church of Les Invalides is very stately, but it has not the nobility of the S. Paul's dome. Versailles in mere extent far excels Hampton Court or Greenwich, but either of the latter is better in scale, and finer in composition. Wren's originality may not have been great, but he succeeded because he observed the exhortation of the Preacher: "Whatsoever thy hand findeth to do, do it with all thy might."

N. Hawksmoor. There is greater originality in the work of his successors, John Vanbrugh and Nicholas Hawksmoor. The buildings of the former are domestic, and are referred to in the next chapter. Hawksmoor also built houses, but his principal achievements are ecclesiastical. Born in 1661, he was a pupil of Wren, who evidently held him in high esteem, as the various offices he filled under his master prove. He was Deputy-Surveyor of Chelsea, Supervisor of the Royal Palace for Charles II. at Winchester, Clerk of Works at Kensington Palace and at Greenwich, and assisted at S. Paul's until its completion. After Wren's death he continued the work at Greenwich, and also acted as assistant to Vanbrugh at Blenheim and elsewhere. In 1708 a commission was appointed for building fifty new churches. Wren was one of the Commissioners, and took good care that his old pupil got his share. Hawksmoor designed S. Mary Woolnoth, Lombard Street, S. George, Bloomsbury, and Christ Church, Spitalfields. The west towers of Westminster Abbey were also built by him, some writers say from Wren's design, but as the actual towers were not commenced until twelve years after that architect's death, the probability is that the sole credit is due to Hawksmoor. And very creditable they are. The design has great vigour. The cornices that form such marked horizontal lines may not be Gothic, but they impart a strong feeling of breadth and solidity. It is sincerely to be hoped that no attempt will ever be made to tamper with what has become history. The Spitalfields church has one of the finest interiors in London, vastly improved by the removal of the side galleries, although their removal has made the double tier of windows in the aisle walls look somewhat absurd. The tower of the west end has real originality and considerable beauty. Hawksmoor failed sometimes because he attempted. Such failures are more praiseworthy than a timid man's successes. The portico of this church is a case in point. At S. George's (1720-30) he introduced a more "correct" portico at the west end, but his originality bubbles over in the tower behind at one side, crowned by a stepped spire. The exterior of S. Mary Woolnoth shows what a strong man Hawksmoor was. The lower portion of the front is grand in its rugged simplicity, the windows are powerfully designed, and both inside and out the church is full of interest.

Other churches of the eighteenth century are briefly mentioned now so that the whole of the next chapter can be devoted to domestic work. James Gibbs' S. Mary-le-Strand is famous for the architectural richness of its façades, its semicircular portico at the west end, and its graceful tower and steeple. Gibbs was luckier than Wren in being able to build where his church could be well seen, and in having sufficient money at his command to use stone throughout for the exterior. S. Martin-in-the-Fields (1721-26) is the best known of his other churches. It stands splendidly with a fine portico in front, raised on a stylobate of many steps which confers great dignity on the front. Few London churches have received so much abuse as S. John, Westminster, designed by Thomas Archer. To appreciate its good points one must live near it. To the casual observer its exterior is somewhat forbidding. But it improves on acquaintance. S. George, Hanover Square, the work of John James, of Greenwich (1713-24), was apparently the first church to have a portico of Corinthian columns, although S. George, Bloomsbury, and S. Martin-in-the-Fields have each a similar feature, and were building at the same time. Churches had been built with porticos before, but not of the Corinthian order. Inigo Jones' portico of S. Paul, Covent Garden, was Doric; Wren's portico of All Saints', Northampton, is Ionic. S. Leonard, Shoreditch (1736-40), by George Dance, sen., is one of the latest Classic churches with architectural expression. In another fifty years Horace Walpole was singing the praises of Gothic, and practising it—with variations. The architects of the first quarter of the eighteenth century—Hawksmoor, Vanbrugh, Gibbs, James, Archer, Kent—were all men of distinction. Each had his own characteristics: Hawksmoor and Vanbrugh, originality and rugged strength; Gibbs and Kent,

J. Gibbs and others.

refinement; Archer and James, a certain clumsiness. But in the main they were animated by the same spirit, and their work collectively is harmonious. It coincides with what is termed the Augustan Age of English literature, when Addison, Pope, Swift, Steele were contemporaries. The architecture also may be called Augustan, in the sense that it was based on the buildings of Imperial Rome, but it hardly deserves the broader, bigger meaning which belongs to the term when applied to literature.

CHAPTER XIII

FROM SIR CHRISTOPHER WREN TO SIR WILLIAM CHAMBERS; A CENTURY OF ENGLISH ARCHITECTS AND THEIR BUILDINGS, c. 1670–1770.

SOME of Inigo Jones' and Webb's houses were mentioned in the last chapter, and enough was said to show that both in plan and appearance they differed considerably from earlier Jacobean and Elizabethan. Webb, an ardent Royalist, continued the traditions of his great master; but his opportunities were not numerous, as until the Restoration few new private houses were commenced. What Wren's domestic work would have been like if he had not had Jones and Webb as forerunners is difficult to imagine. As already mentioned, his architectural training had been almost *nil* when he found himself with an immense practice, embracing work of all descriptions. How he must have blessed the few months he spent in France! The influence of that sojourn is marked in some of his earlier buildings, and never entirely left him. His grasp was never so masculine as Jones'; his knowledge of architecture never so profound. But he had a keen insight into what was possible and right. He made few mistakes, because he never ventured much. His first design for S. Paul's was his most original effort. His secular work is always sound, always dignified, but shows no striking signs of originality. *Introduction.*

The most important of his domestic buildings are Greenwich Hospital and Hampton Court Palace, both referred to again later, but neither is completely his. At Greenwich he followed Inigo Jones and Webb; at Hampton Court he unfortunately had to add to an existing building, and consequently could not display fully his powers of planning. Moreover, the large court that he intended in front of Wolsey's great hall was never carried out. The Library of Trinity College, Cambridge, that he built about 1678, has not the severity of Jones' work; in fact, in some portions, notably in the filling in of the semicircular heads of the ground-floor arcade, the feeling is almost Jacobean. Sansovino's Library at Venice, *Wren's buildings.*

which he had probably heard about although not seen, may have suggested to him the main lines of the design, but the Cambridge Library lacks the essential features which give such distinction to the Venetian. The design of old Temple Bar (*c.* 1671) is weak, although, on historical grounds especially, all must regret its removal. Far stronger is the entrance to the Temple (*c.* 1684), which Inigo Jones himself might have been proud to acknowledge. When this front was completed Wren had been twenty years in practice, and had therefore been learning his lesson in the best school a man can have. The long façade of Christ's Hospital, London, now destroyed, was another fine work, and one of the most successful of his in which brick predominated. The pilasters on the front, built of small bricks with "putty" joints, were well raised above the ground on plain lofty plinths. Other large buildings of his are Chelsea Hospital (*c.* 1682), Winchester Palace (*c.* 1683), Kensington Palace (*c.* 1690), including the Banqueting-room, or Orangery, in the gardens, and Morden College, Blackheath (*c.* 1694). All are distinguished by great reticence and good proportion and detail. The same qualities exist in the numerous private houses attributed to him, some of which are mentioned later.

Greenwich Hospital.

Shortly after Wren was appointed Crown Surveyor, Charles II. decided to make extensive additions to the palace commenced by Jones or Webb at Greenwich.[1] The plan Wren prepared is masterly. He balanced the existing block facing the river, marked A on plan, by another, marked D, and behind placed two other blocks, B and C, with a colonnade in front of each. The width of the quadrangle between the river blocks is about 280 feet, whereas the space between the colonnades is narrowed to 115 feet, which agrees with the frontage dimension of the Queen's House. This stands on the central axis of the whole scheme 160 yards away, and forms the end of the vista.[2] The narrowing of the space between the blocks at the back was not only a happy inspiration, improving considerably the perspective, but it also gave Wren an excuse for emphasizing the north corners of these by the two existing domes, which stand so well in the picture. These are excellent in design, but the general result is spoilt by

[1] For authorship, see footnote, p. 276.

[2] If the house had not existed, the effect might have been still finer, as the ground rises very suddenly behind it; and if the vista could have been carried to the top of the hill, a wonderful result might have been obtained.

Fig. 244.—Greenwich Hospital, view from the river.

the meanness of the work below and at the sides, excluding, of course, the colonnades, which are well-proportioned and dignified. All these portions apparently are Wren's. The work attributed to him includes the river front of block D, which is a repetition

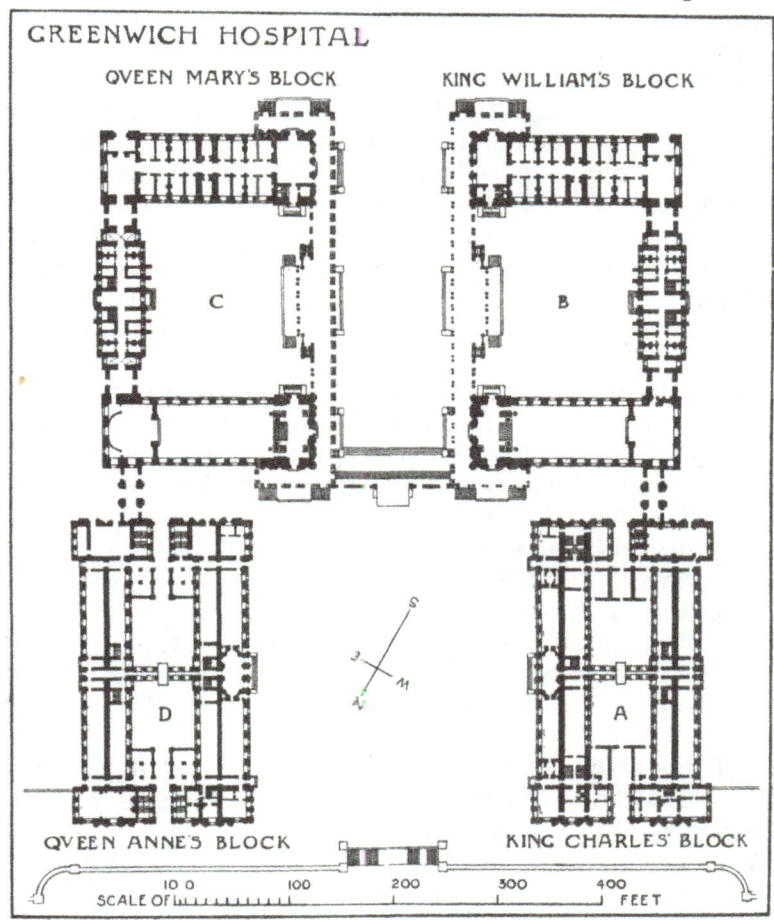

Fig. 245.

of A, the north and south fronts of blocks B and C, and the colonnades connecting these fronts. The east elevation and river front of block A were probably completed before he appeared on the scene, with the exception of the tall attic which he added.[1]

[1] The date on the panel of the entablature under the left-hand pediment (Car: II Rex. a: reg: XVI), and the sculpture in the pediment above, were

The river front of block A may be regarded as the combined work of Jones, Webb, and Wren. It is a double front, inasmuch as behind it are two wings separated from each other by a courtyard. Tho plan is therefore expressed on the elevation, which has two centres, each consisting of four engaged columns arranged in pairs. These start from within a foot of the ground, and support pediments. The walls flanking the centres are pilastered, and in this respect the design recalls Whitehall, although otherwise it is very different. The appearance of the building as it stands is not altogether happy. A pediment dying against an attic is never satisfactory. Moreover, the height of the attic overpowers the lower portion, and appears to be thrusting it into the ground. Even without the attic the building would not have had the appearance of rising from it. Both Jones and Webb were generally so anxious that their buildings should produce this effect, and took such pains to obtain it, that it seems probable that either the front was designed to rise direct out of the river, or else that a terrace was intended in front at a lower level than the present ground.[1]

Later men at Greenwich. After Wren was retired, the work at Greenwich was continued by Vanbrugh, Hawksmoor, Campbell, and Ripley, the west side of block A not being built until 1814 by Stuart. If Campbell really designed the south fronts of blocks A and D, they do him great credit. They are amongst the most successful portions of the palace. The courtyard front of block B, and portions of the front of the same block facing west, are by Vanbrugh. They are exceedingly interesting, but not altogether convincing. Like everything of his they are noble in scale and stamped with individuality.

Hampton Court. The additions Wren made to Hampton Court for William and Mary (*c.* 1689) are more homely. Greenwich is mainly stone; Hampton Court red brick with Portland stone dressings. Nowhere are these materials combined more harmoniously. In many buildings in which they are used together the effect is spotty, because the stone is scattered, and no attempt made to mass it. Wren did not make this mistake. The centre of each of the garden fronts is stone throughout; the architraves of the ground and first-floor windows are connected by panels of stone;

probably carved when the attic was added. The panel and tympanum under the right-hand pediment are still in block state.

[1] If there was more plinth below the columns, the height of the attic would, of course, not appear so excessive.

Photo: Author.
FIG. 246.—HAMPTON COURT, SOUTH FRONT.

Photo: Author.
FIG. 247.—HAMPTON COURT, FOUNTAIN COURT. [*To face p.* 304.

in the pilasters at the corners courses of brick and stone alternate; and the crowning cornice and balustrade and the deep strong course below are stone, tying the whole together. Over the centre of the garden east front is a pediment which stops against the top storey, and comes under the main entablature. This is the chief fault in the design. If a pediment cannot be used at a crowning feature, it is best not to use one at all. There is no pediment over the centre of the south front, and its absence is not missed. Inigo Jones never misapplied the pediment, and the later architects, whatever other faults they possessed, steered clear of this. Over the large windows which light the suite of reception rooms on the first floor are several circular windows. One cannot help feeling that these are a mistake, and would have been better omitted. The majority are dummies. Owing to the great height of the reception rooms, Wren had an opportunity of obtaining the expanse of plain walling which is so effective in the palaces of Italy, and so seldom possible outside that country. But he sacrificed it. Where there are no circles there are brick swags, carved excellently, no doubt, but quite meaningless and altogether unnecessary. In the cloistered Fountain Court there are similar circles, some of which are actually windows. These have elaborately carved stone frames, and their effect, in consequence, is better than the plainer circles on the fronts. The most delightful portion of Wren's work at Hampton Court is the colonnade of columns in pairs which forms the Royal entrance. It is similar to the Greenwich colonnades, except that the Order is Ionic instead of Doric. Equally charming, but in a different way, is the garden wall, with its happy blending of stone and brick in the pilasters and its stone coping. The gardens themselves, and the long vistas through the trees, are not the least of the attractions The wonderful wrought-iron gates, probably executed by Huntingdon Shaw, were designed by Jean Tijou, a Frenchman, who also designed the fine screens in S. Paul's Cathedral.

Wren belonged essentially to the seventeenth century, the second half. S. Paul's was still unfinished when the century ended, and he later designed a few buildings, of which Marlborough House, Pall Mall, is one, but the major part of his work was done. One of his last designs was for the Westminster Dormitory, which was carried out after his death with considerable modifications. He outlived his contemporaries. When he died in 1723, a younger school was rising. Hawksmoor,

Eighteenth-century architecture.

Vanbrugh, Gibbs, Kent, Campbell, Wood, and others continued his methods, but in some respects departed from them. To what extent is shown in subsequent pages.

Sir John Vanbrugh (c. 1666–1726).

How Vanbrugh obtained his architectural knowledge is not recorded; even when and where he was born are uncertain, 1666 being the year generally stated. When still in his teens he was sent to France, and on his return was appointed an ensign in the army. Whether he ever saw active service, why he went to France, are unknown. He may have gone to study architecture, and divided his time between that art and the theatre. He undoubtedly obtained there his insight into dramatic composition which he afterwards turned to such excellent account. His position as a playwright was established before he began Castle Howard in 1702. Hawksmoor was his assistant at Blenheim, and that architect's practical experience must have been a great help. The sympathy between the two men was evidently great, and there is some similarity in their work. The centre of the entrance front of Seaton Delaval, for instance, recalls somewhat the lower part of the west façade of Hawksmoor's S. Mary Woolnoth. Both men were full of ideas, strong, original, and, Vanbrugh especially, masters of composition.

Reynolds' appreciation of Vanbrugh.

The plans of Blenheim and Castle Howard, which are described in detail later (see Figs. 258 and 260), and Vanbrugh's treatment of the elevations, account for Sir Joshua Reynolds' appreciative remarks in his lectures about that architect's work: "In the buildings of Vanbrugh, who was a poet as well as an architect, there is a greater display of imagination than we shall find perhaps in any other, . . . he had originality of invention; he understood light and shadow, and had great skill in composition. To support his principal object, he produced his second and third groups, or masses. . . . No architect took greater care that his work should not appear crude and hard, that is, that it did not abruptly start out of the ground without expectation or preparation." This is high praise, and it is deserved. His buildings do rise from the ground, largely because of the semi-basement below the principal floor, and although they may be ponderous, they are saved from being unpleasantly so by this very quality. They possess dignity, and they have the "attribute of eternal." The wings, or "second groups," are always subordinate in height and architectural expression to the centre. Blenheim excels especially in this respect. Its detail may not be

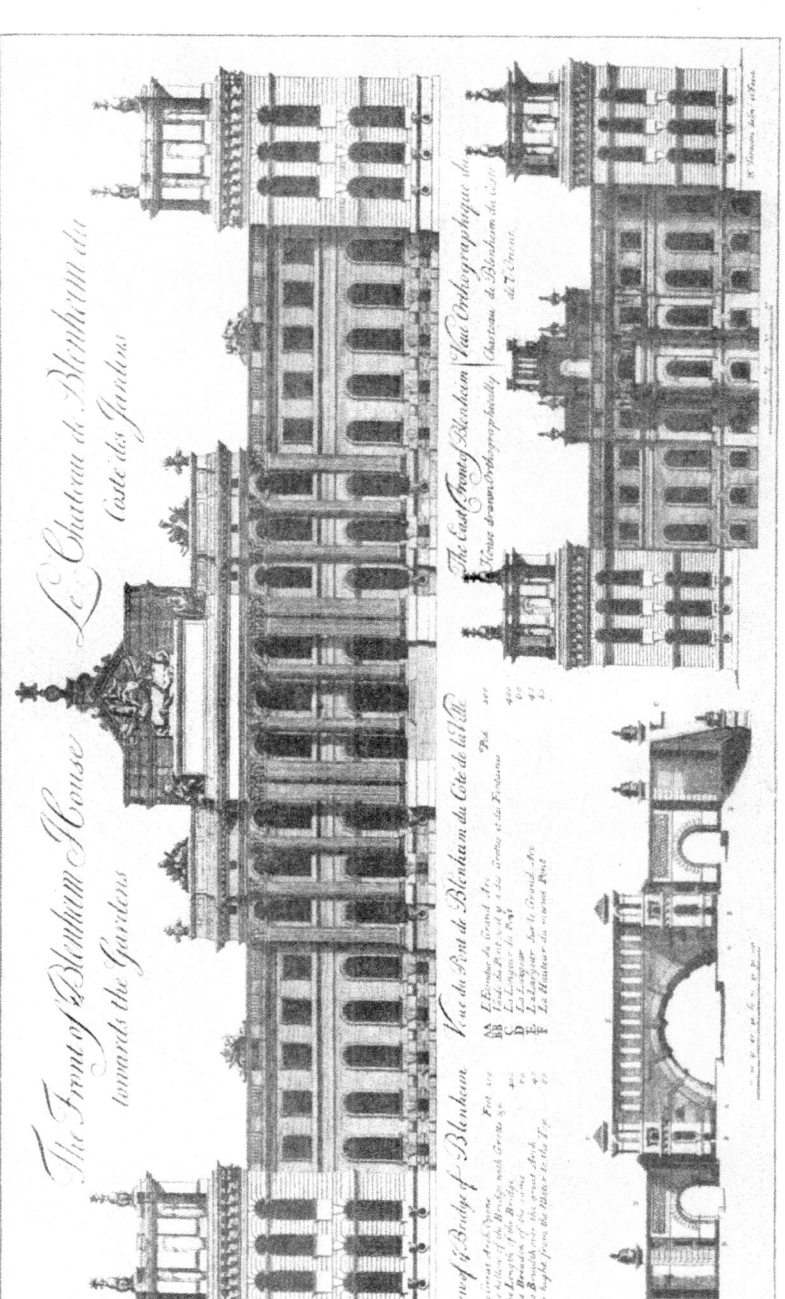

FIG. 248 (*R. I. B. A. Journal*, vol. vii, 1890).

first-rate, but its composition is masterly. Castle Howard, built some years before, is far less impressive. The idea is the same, but the result is not quite achieved. The building succeeds in appearing heavy without looking big. Vanbrugh generally treated his garden fronts with less severity than his entrance fronts. His lighter touches he reserved for the former. This is most apparent at Seaton Delaval, where the entrance almost has the ruggedness of old Newgate, whilst at the back the Ionic portico is a masterpiece of delicacy. Although he carried out a large amount of work, he had his share of annoyances in connection with it. The Duchess of Marlborough—" may a Scottish ensign get her," he writes—dismissed him from Blenheim, refused to pay him money due for work done, and even issued special instructions that he and his wife, who had come to Blenheim with a party of friends, were not to be allowed to see the house and grounds.[1] Pope and Swift satirized him, and Walpole could not abide him, but Reynolds' opinion on art matters is worth more than the opinions of all three together. The public's attitude towards his work was summed up by a writer of the day in the couplet:

> "Lie heavy on him, earth! for he
> Laid many heavy loads on thee."

Hawksmoor's career was outlined in the last chapter. At Oxford he built the Clarendon Press buildings, a sturdy, although somewhat forbidding, pile, with a fine Doric portico, and portions of All Souls and Queen's Colleges. The work attributed to him at Greenwich, the west side of block C, facing the courtyard, and the east side of block D, is exceedingly dull. On the whole his churches are much better than his other buildings. *Nicholas Hawksmoor (1661–1736).*

Gibbs was born at Aberdeen in 1682, studied for some time in Rome, and came to London about 1710. S. Bartholomew's Hospital is the best example of his secular work in the metropolis, simple, dignified, and fine in scale, but his *chef d'œuvre* is the Radcliffe Library, Oxford, built between 1737–47. It is a rotunda. Above a simply treated basement, with its eight arched and pedimented doorways, rises the main drum enriched by sixteen pairs of Corinthian columns. These support the unbroken entablature and balustrade. Gibbs' study of the Colosseum had taught him not to break entablatures, and how dignified is their *James Gibbs (1682–1754).*

---

[1] Leigh Hunt's "The Dramatic Works of Wycherley, Congreve, Vanbrugh, and Farquhar."

308 A HISTORY OF ARCHITECTURAL DEVELOPMENT

sweep on a curve. The reading-room is lighted principally from the windows in the upper drum which carries the dome, the windows in the main drum lighting the side recesses and galleries above. Gibbs published a monograph in 1714, "Bibliotheca Radcliviana," of this building. He was also the author of " A Book of Architecture," "Rules for drawing the several parts of Architecture," the latter one of the safest guides a student can have for the " Orders," and other books.

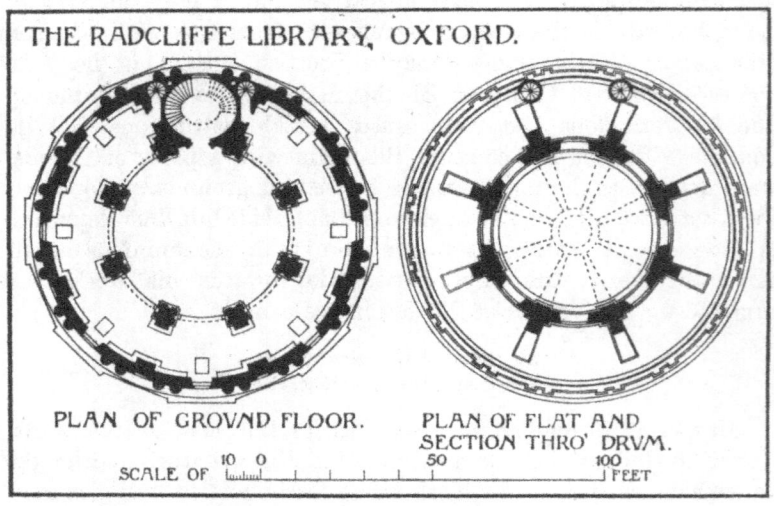

Fig. 249.

Colin Campbell and William Kent (1684–1748).

Colin Campbell (*d.* 1734) is best known by his "Vitruvius Britannicus," which did for English eighteenth-century Architecture what Blondel's book did for French. The title shows the trend of thought in England at the time. Campbell paid Palladio the compliment of copying his Villa Capra (see Fig. 76) at Mereworth, Kent, with all its porticoes, but he could do more original work. His Houghton Hall, Norfolk, and Wanstead House, Essex, have many good points (see Fig. 256), and the excellence of the additions attributed to him at Greenwich has already been mentioned. Both Campbell and William Kent worked for the Earl of Burlington, and it is difficult to say to which of the trio should be given the credit for much of the work for which the last undoubtedly paid. Burlington House, Piccadilly, before it was spoilt by the addition of the top storey, was a dignified, refined

FIG. 250.—PALLADIAN BRIDGE AT WILTON HOUSE.

FIG. 251.—PRIOR PARK, BATH.   [*To face p.* 309.

façade. The earl's villa at Chiswick was based on the Villa Capra, but the folly of treating all four sides alike was not repeated. There are no staircases or entrances at the sides, and only a less important staircase at the back. The energy of all concerned was concentrated on the superbly planned staircases and finely designed portico in front.[1] Buildings undoubtedly Kent's are the Treasury, Whitehall, and the Horse Guards, the Parliament Street front of which was finished by J. Vardy. Kent was a painter before he was induced by Lord Burlington to study architecture, but there is none of the littleness, often associated with painters' architecture, about either of the buildings mentioned. Both are well proportioned, simply detailed, and the compositions of both fronts of the Horse Guards are exceedingly effective. Kent understood light and shade, and was not afraid of projecting boldly both his central block and his side wings. He deserves the thanks of all architects for his edition of "Designs of Inigo Jones," although most of the actual drawing was done by Flitcroft.

A little-known architect of the middle of the eighteenth century is Robert Morris. His Bridge at Wilton is a delightful composition. The arch and lintel have probably never been so happily blended. The design was repeated with but trifling differences of detail in the grounds of Prior Park, Bath. The house at Prior Park is the work of John Wood, who, with his son, also John, laid out portions of Bath in such splendid fashion. The front and sides of Prior Park are dull. Its splendour lies in the terrace that stretches on either side of it, and in the portico and outside staircase at the back, with flights of steps leading down the hill. Occupying a magnificent position overlooking the city and surrounding country, it forms one of the most striking architectural pictures to be found in England. In Bath itself, the father built the north side of Queen's Square, the Circus and the north and south parades; the son followed with the Crescent and Gay Street. The buildings in these are somewhat disappointing. What is so fine is the survey. Bath, at least that portion laid out by the Woods, is planned as a city should be, on architectural lines and symmetrically, with wide streets opening out into wider spaces.[2] The first stone of the elder Wood's Exchange at Liverpool,

Robert Morris and John Wood (d. 1754).

---

[1] Lord Verney described the villa as "too small to inhabit and too large to hang one's watch in."

[2] In no city in England is the eighteenth-century "atmosphere" so strong as in Bath. Sir Lucius O'Trigger on the North Parade waiting for Lucy who is on

now the Town Hall, was laid in 1748, the building being opened in 1754. It suffered severely from fire in 1795, and has been added to so considerably since that only the shell remains, and even that has been altered.

Architects of second half of eighteenth century.

George Dance, sen. (1695–1768), was the City architect, and in that capacity designed the Mansion House. His son George (1741–1825) is best known as the architect of Newgate. Its rugged exterior was a relief after the florid modern work that surrounded it. It possessed the great virtue of appearing what it was. Modern buildings often do not express on the outside the purpose for which they are built, but Dance did not fail in this respect. He kept a grim hold of his subject. The façades were unbroken, but for the doorways and a few slits. The latter were not windows. Behind each was a hollow in the thickness of the wall, with a circular stone post in the centre. The reason for these posts is not clear. They may have been intended to soften the depth of the shadow, and may have done so when new, but before Newgate was pulled down they were black with age and quite undiscernible from outside.[1] Towards the end of the eighteenth century Dance laid out Finsbury Square, and shortly afterwards Alfred Place, alongside Tottenham Court Road, and the two crescents terminating it—a nice little piece of town planning. The houses are now being rebuilt. The effect of the west side of Finsbury Square as a whole is exceedingly good. Some of the houses are individually worth studying, and the neighbouring streets also contain respectable examples of one hundred and twenty years ago.

James Paine (1716–89), Sir Robert Taylor (1714–88).

James Paine was one of the most prolific of country house designers of his time. Gosforth House, Yorkshire, Thorndon Hall, Essex, and many others are his. In 1761 he planned Kedleston Hall, Derbyshire, one of the finest planned houses of its type (see Fig. 262), which was finished by the Adams. His contemporary, Sir Robert Taylor (1714–88), also did a great deal of work. Ely House, Dover Street, shows that he was a master of proportion, and that his detail was good. Its front was held up to derision by Pugin in his "Contrasts," who shows drawings comparing it

the South is a real person in Bath; and Gay Street recalls *The Beggar's Opera*, which, according to the wits of the time, "Made Rich" (the manager who produced it) "gay, and Gay rich."

[1] They were shown to me by the late Mr. Mountford when the walls were being pulled down. He said the reason for them baffled him.

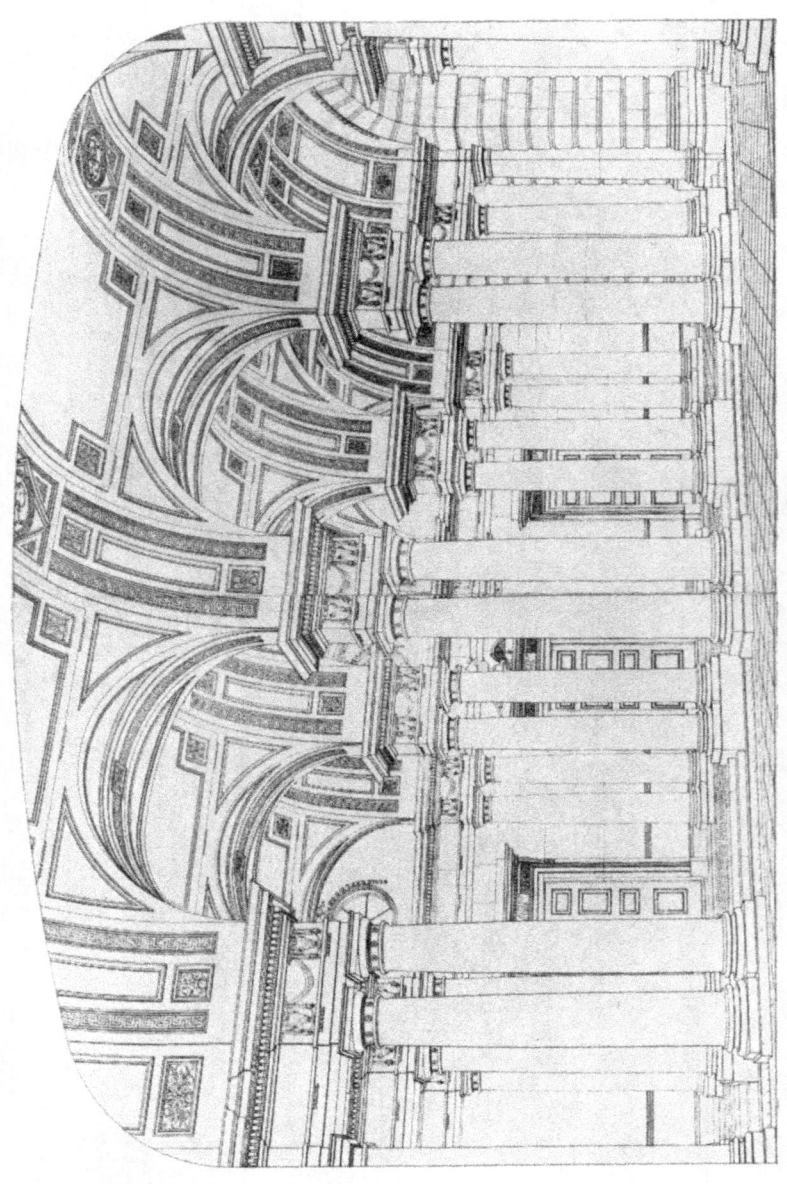

Fig. 252.—Somerset House, Entrance Vestibule.
(*Frederic Miller, from "Building News," 1881.*)

[*To face p.* 311.

with Ely Place, Holborn,[1] but the whirligig of time has once more brought Ely House into favour, and Pugin's "true" style is neglected.

The principal works of Carr of York are the Crescent at Buxton, a sturdy, dignified front, and Harewood House, Yorkshire. The latter is a very fine composition. It consists of a central block, pilastered and crowned by an entablature and balustrade, and two side blocks on a line with it. The side blocks are the same height as the centre and are also pilastered, but the entablature of each is lower, and above is an attic. The portions of the building which connect the centre and sides are only two storeys high, and are also slightly recessed. *Carr of York.*

The century finished with Sir William Chambers and Robert Adam. These two men, absolute contemporaries, followed different ideals. Chambers did his utmost to keep the old flag flying, to preserve to the end of the century the traditions which Wren had upheld at the beginning. To a great extent he succeeded. His river front of Somerset House ranks as one of the greatest architectural achievements of the eighteenth century. It is fine now with the Embankment in front; it must have been finer still when the river washed its walls. The setting back of the upper storeys so as to form a terrace in front above the basement is a happy idea; and the open peristyles under the cornice of the main building one of the most effective methods ever devised for separating, and at the same time uniting, different blocks. The tooling of the rustications of the terrace front is worth careful study. It is beautifully executed and of great variety. The actual façade facing the Strand is but ordinary, but the open vaulted vestibule that gives access to the courtyard is a masterpiece of delicate, refined detail. Chambers knew when to be bold, as the terrace front facing the river and the archways at the sides of the courtyard show. But he did not, like, possibly, Hawksmoor and Vanbrugh, believe in bigness merely for bigness' sake. *Sir William Chambers (1726-86).*

The brothers Adam posed as reformers; but they did not carry their reformation very far. It took the form of diminution. Their besetting sin was littleness. Robert, by far the ablest of the family, when left to himself, was bolder and more masculine. The man who measured Diocletian's palace at Spalato knew what big work was. Edinburgh University, especially the front to *Robert Adam (1728–92).*

[1] "Contrasts, or a Parallel between the noble edifices of the Middle Ages and corresponding buildings of the present day," 1836.

the street, is a strong design. It is unfair to judge him by the fittings and interiors generally of the many buildings in London attributed to the "firm." All "etchings by Rembrandt" were not "bitten" by that master, and all "Adam Ceilings" are not by the brothers. They set the fashion in the last quarter of the century, and had dozens of imitators. The amount of work, however, they carried out was very great. They and their army of workmen designed anything and everything, from a door-scraper to a palace. Their internal decorations and fittings, when really theirs, are often very beautiful, although the work always errs on the side of smallness. Their furniture has not quite the charm of Louis Seize, neither does it equal the work of slightly earlier English cabinet-makers. The French work is quite as small in detail as the Adams', but it conveys a sense of purity, whereas the feeling raised by the other is one of "finikiness." The "Adelphi," the streets of which they named after themselves, still exercises a certain fascination—especially individual rooms therein—and must have looked well from the river when vessels could reach the quay below, and the great arched tunnel storehouses for merchandise ran under the terrace above.[1] The screen across the front of the Admiralty, Whitehall, which partially conceals Ripley's dull building behind, although it possesses the usual fault, is one of the most charming of Robert's works. The east side of Fitzroy Square is still dignified, notwithstanding that the stucco decoration that the brothers used on every possible occasion, externally as well as internally, is peeling off the frieze. Many houses designed by them still exist in London, and for the most part are well planned, if allowances are made for sanitary details better understood now than then, and, when retaining their original decoration and fittings, very delightful dwellings. Robert Adam showed he could plan in the great circular hall he added to Sion House, in the house he built for Lord Derby in Grosvenor Square, Luton Park House, Bedford, etc. At Kedleston the decorations are his, but the plan is Paine's.

Country houses after 1640.

In order to trace the development of country house plan and design in the eighteenth century it is necessary to go back to before the Commonwealth. Previous to then the courtyard plan had been general, and this was not altogether abandoned for some

[1] See drawing in "Works in Architecture of Robert and James Adam," published 1778.

time. Houses of ⊓ and H plans continued to be built until near the end of the seventeenth century. But what may be termed the "block" plan finally drove out of the field the earlier forms. The change originated with Inigo Jones, was continued by Webb, and to him therefore belongs some of the credit. The difficulty of apportioning the amount depends largely on who designed

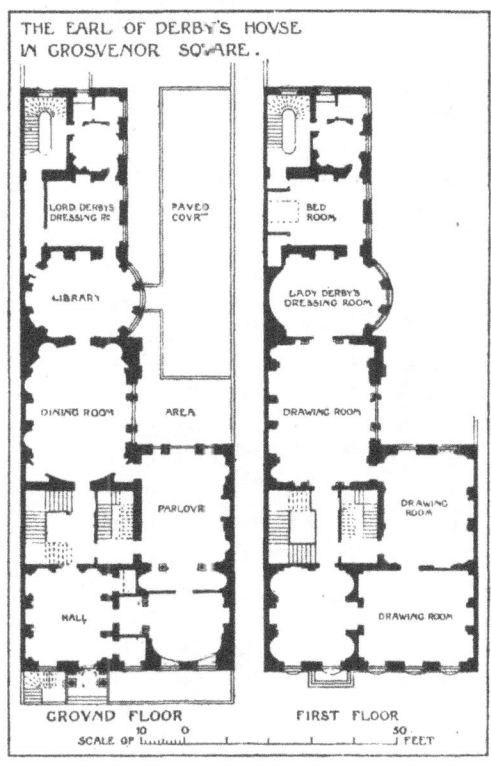

FIG. 253.

Coleshill and Ashdown Houses, in Berkshire. They were carried out by Webb, but the designs for both may have been made by Jones. The design of Coleshill is apparently his without doubt, but there is little proof that he had anything to do with the other, which was not commenced until long after his death. In plan and general design these two houses are the forerunners of the type which prevailed all through the eighteenth century. Wren accepted it, and departed little from it.

Planning. In plan the smaller houses of this type consist merely of a rectangular block, which contains the living-rooms, servants' quarters, bedrooms, etc. In larger houses two forms were followed. In one, there is still only one block, rectangular in form and oblong, but the central portion is made more important and higher than the side portions. In the other there are three, sometimes more, separate and distinct blocks. The central block contains the principal rooms, and in front of it, to the right and left, are two independent blocks, which contain on one side the kitchen and offices, on the other the stables. The only connection between the main and side blocks is by corridors. The side blocks are always lower and subordinate in all respects.

Single block plan. The Queen's House, Greenwich (1617-35), marks the commencement of the new era in planning. It is a simple rectangle, within which, however, are two small courts for light, lingering evidence of the departing plan. All its rooms are disposed symmetrically. Raynham Hall, Norfolk (c. 1636), has also a rectangular plan, but there are small breaks at the back, and in front two wings project about 10 feet. At Coleshill House, Berks (c. 1650), there are no projections, and the plan is a simple oblong. This is divided into three by two cross walls. The central division, which is slightly wider than those on either side, contains on the ground floor the entrance hall, in which is a great double staircase, and the salon. The position of the staircase marks a new departure in planning. The hall, which began by being the dining-living room, then became an entrance hall pure and simple, now only justified its dimensions by containing the stairs. This was the first serious attack on its importance. It gradually decreased in size until, not without a struggle on its part to maintain its dignity, it became in the last century the narrow mean passage familiar to all. At Coleshill the principal floor is raised well above the ground,

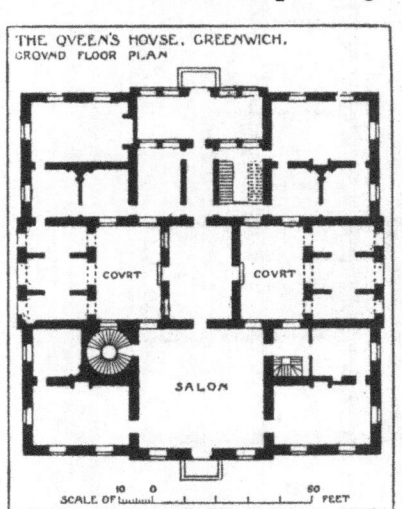

FIG. 254.

with a semi-basement below which contains the kitchen and offices. The adoption of this lower ground floor or semi-basement, which is general in the plans of both Inigo Jones and Webb, had two important results. The first was the necessary introduction of outside staircases leading from the ground to the principal floor, which afterwards played so important a part in large eighteenth-century country houses; and the second the gradual shrinkage of inside staircases. In Elizabeth's reign the staircase was a great feature, because the principal rooms, apart from the hall, were

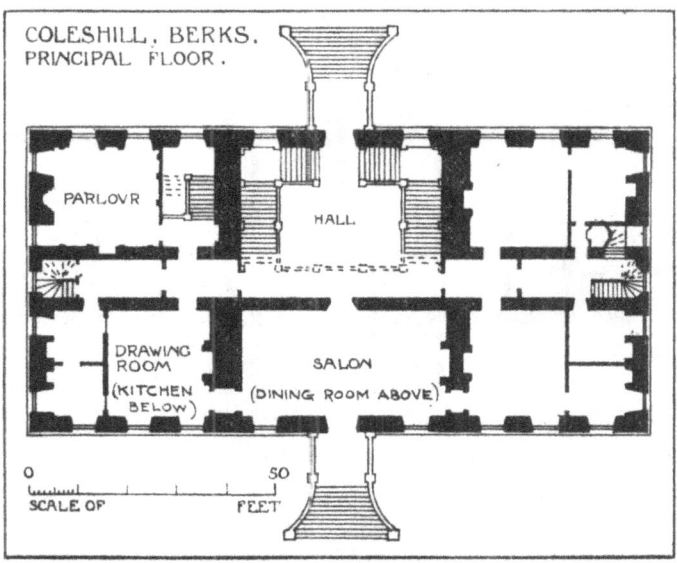

Fig. 255.

generally on an upper floor, and good access to them was a necessity. But when the principal sitting-rooms are grouped round a hall, and the upper floor contains only bedrooms, with an occasional reception-room as at Raynham, the need for fine staircases is not so great. For some time, however, they continued to be large and stately, and all through the eighteenth century they retained their importance in the smaller houses. But not in the large country mansions. One of the most curious characteristics of these is the comparative meanness of the stairs from ground to first floor.

In the majority of large houses in single blocks the kitchen and offices are on the lower floor, and the whole of the principal

316   A HISTORY OF ARCHITECTURAL DEVELOPMENT

Single block large houses.

floor is devoted to reception-rooms, with occasionally some bedrooms. The larger examples differ only from the smaller in the greater number and size of the rooms. Wanstead House, Essex (now destroyed), built by Campbell in 1720, was long regarded as the best example of its class, both in plan and elevation. It extended about 260 feet in length, and was about 75 feet wide. The central portion, which merely projected a few inches in front of the remainder, was about 110 feet long and three storeys high, whilst the sides were only two. This centre, moreover, derived

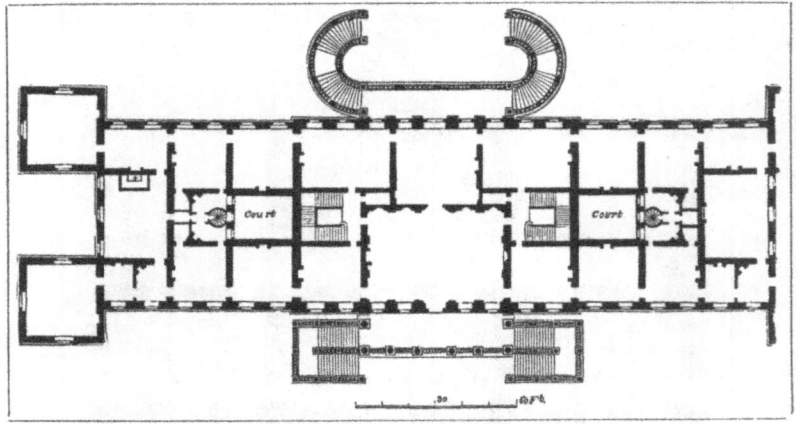

FIG. 256.—WANSTEAD HOUSE, ESSEX (*Gwilt*).

additional emphasis from its portico, which, as is shown later, was regarded as an essential adjunct to every large house.

The three-block plan.

The three-block plan started in the middle of the seventeenth century. It may have been evolved out of the earlier courtyard plan, but more probably was imported from Italy, or from France, where François Mansard's château of Balleroy (see p. 203) had been commenced in 1626. The two earliest examples in England are probably Stoke Park, Northants, and Ashdown House, Berks. The latter, by Webb (*c.* 1665), consists of a lofty central rectangular block, with two low wings, and two smaller detached blocks of outbuildings standing forward some little distance, and framing the house proper, as at Balleroy. At Stoke a new feature, *i.e.* new in England, is introduced in the shape of colonnaded corridors, quadrants in plan, which connect the main portion with the front wings. Wyatt Papworth says that Sir Francis Crane, who built the house, " brought the design from Italy," and he dates it about 1630–34. Inigo Jones was employed on the work, and it is possible that the plan as well as portions of the elevations are his. He was as capable of producing an Italian plan as any Italian.

The curved corridors in front which are the distinctive characteristics of Stoke, became a great favourite with later eighteenth-century architects, especially Vanbrugh. Both Blenheim and Castle Howard are planned on these lines. At Castle Howard the main block, which in front is narrow, is joined *Block plan with corridors: Blenheim.*

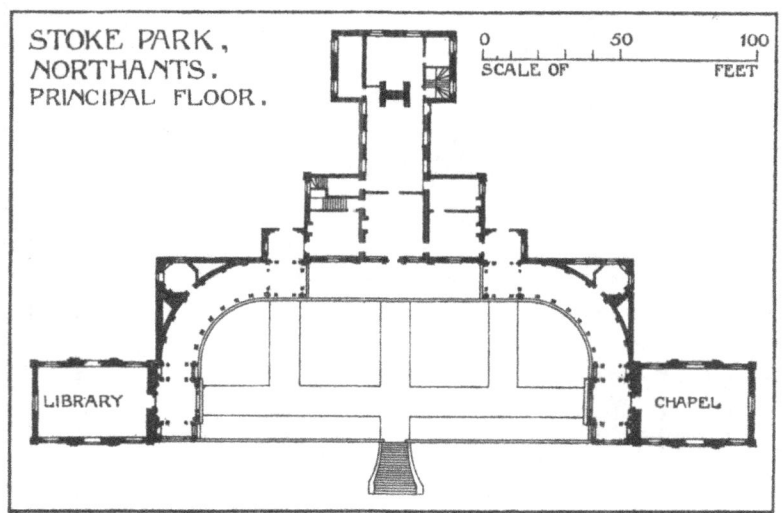

FIG. 257.

to the wings by corridors and arcades. At Blenheim the three portions are more separate. In front of the central block is the great courtyard, with the stable court on one side and the kitchen court on the other, both surrounded by buildings. The plans of the main blocks of these two mansions agree in most respects; in the great central entrance hall flanked by two staircases; in the salon behind the hall opening to the garden; in the vista through the house from front to back; and in the fine suite of rooms, with through communication, on either side of the central saloon, making a total length of over 300 feet. The doubling of the staircase is characteristic of the age. An imposing staircase was not a necessity, because all the sitting-rooms being on the ground floor, decent access to bedrooms was all that was absolutely necessary. Either

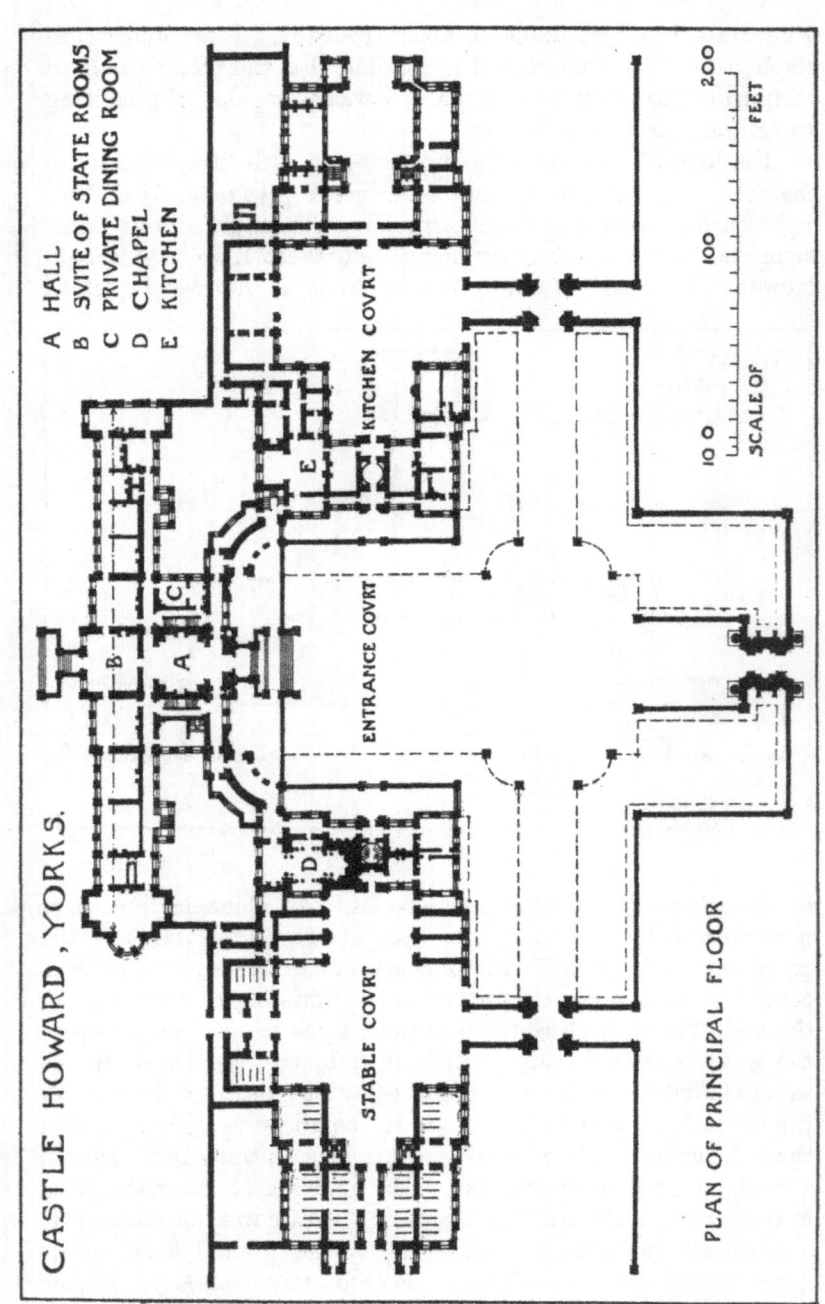

Fig. 258.

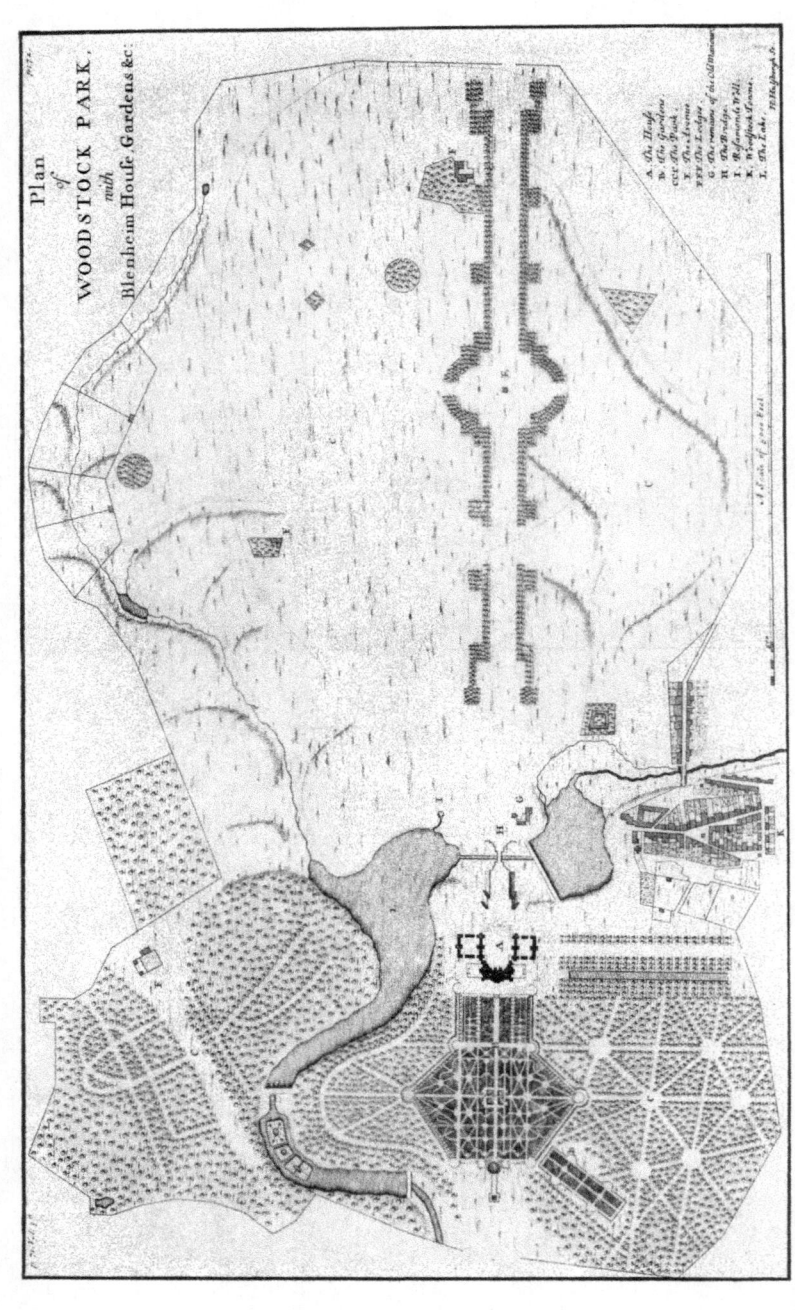

[*To face p.* 319.

Fig. 259.

of the staircases provided would have sufficed; but then the plan would not have been absolutely symmetrical. One sympathizes thoroughly with these eighteenth-century architects in their desire for symmetry, but they carried it to extremes. They ignored the fact that only a small portion of the outside of a large building can be seen at any one time; that inside one cannot see through thick walls, and that what exists beyond is of little moment, save when vistas are possible. To depart from strict symmetry may make a plan look less pretty on paper, but efficiency will

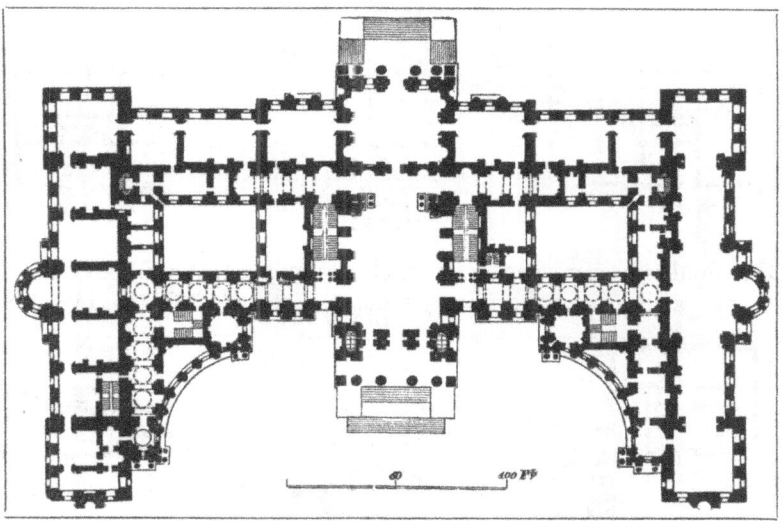

FIG. 260.—BLENHEIM, MAIN BLOCK (*Gwilt*).

probably be increased thereby. The same applies to elevations. Provided the main lines are symmetrical, it is refreshing to be able to note a variation here, a slight difference there. Every one admits that designs for ornament are better if two sides are not identical; and, provided that sufficient balance is preserved, the same applies to architectural compositions. To decide the balance necessary and the departure permissible is an art.

Houghton Hall, Norfolk, designed by Campbell in 1723, is a good example of central and side blocks, connected by curved corridors. At Holkham, also in Norfolk (*c.* 1735), Kent placed his wings overlapping the front of the main block so that two short straight corridors sufficed as connections. In addition to the wings in front he placed two corresponding ones at the back,

<small>Other three-block plans.</small>

320 A HISTORY OF ARCHITECTURAL DEVELOPMENT

and thus framed his central block on both sides. On paper the plan looks superb. Whether it is so satisfactory in reality may

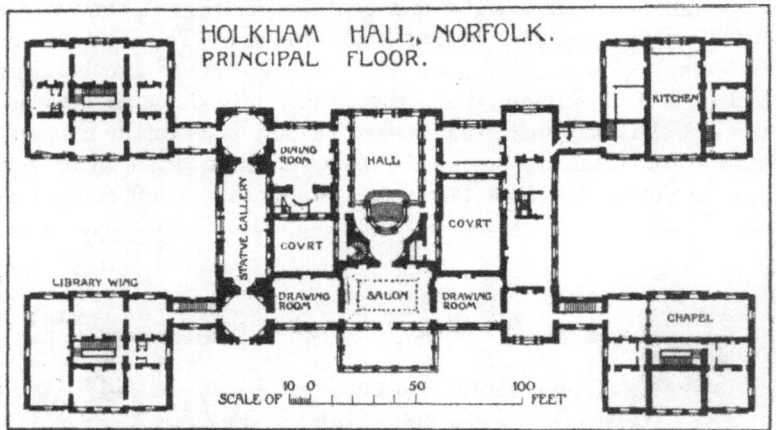

Fig. 261.

be doubted. In front the kitchen wing balances the visitors' wing; at the back the library wing, the chapel. The dining-room

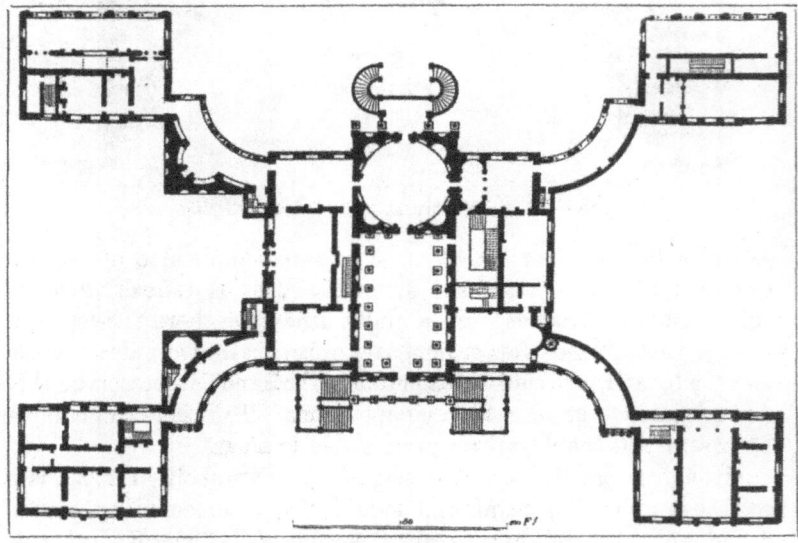

Fig. 262.—Kedleston Hall (*Gwilt*).

is shown far from the kitchen, but a very little rearrangement of rooms might cure that defect. A separate kitchen block has

A CENTURY OF ENGLISH ARCHITECTS

great advantages, and its disadvantages are often exaggerated, and can easily be got over by a properly fitted serving-room. Kedleston, which was begun by Paine and finished by Robert Adam, also has four flanking blocks and a central block. These are connected by curved corridors no longer colonnaded and open in front, as at Stoke, but enclosed by walls liberally windowed towards the forecourt in front and towards the garden at the back. Paine designed more country mansions than any other contemporary architect. The majority are single, self-contained oblong blocks, but many are of the three-block plan. Gosforth, Northumberland, Thorndon Hall, Essex, and Wardour House, Wilts, show three varieties. Of this type also is Standlinch,

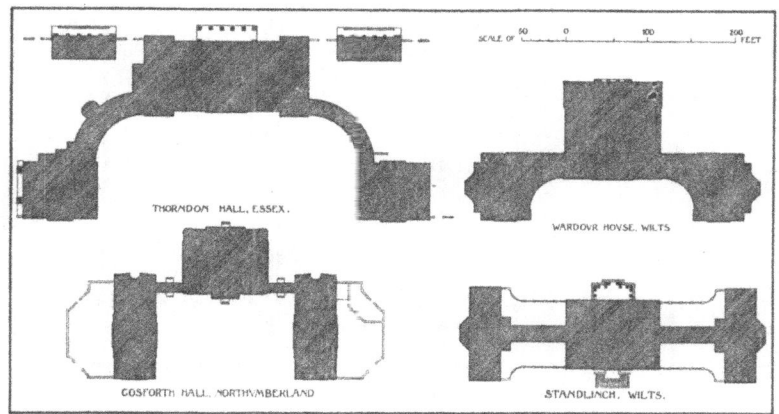

FIG. 263.

Wilts, by John Wood, junior, but instead of the subordinate blocks being in front, they are on a line with the central block, and the corridors connecting them straight. The three-block plan was sometimes adopted for smaller houses, and with considerable success. A house at Beaconsfield, Bucks, by Thomas Millner, illustrated in "Vitruvius Britannicus" (Vol. II. Plate 47), is a good example. But the most original is Vanbrugh's Seaton Delaval, in Northumberland (*c.* 1720). As an example of stately planning on a comparatively small scale it is incomparable. The house is a square, with the addition of an octagonal turret at each corner, and a newel staircase forming a projection in the centre of each side. In front is the entrance-hall, with a room on either side, and at the back is the salon, about 70 feet

322 A HISTORY OF ARCHITECTURAL DEVELOPMENT

long, the full width of the house. Between the salon and the small rooms in front are corridors leading to the staircases. On each side of the entrance forecourt is an arcaded cloister which masks and at the same time affords access to the kitchen block on one side and the stables on the other. Other similar buildings, both large and small, might be mentioned, but the above are sufficient to show how fond eighteenth-century architects were of

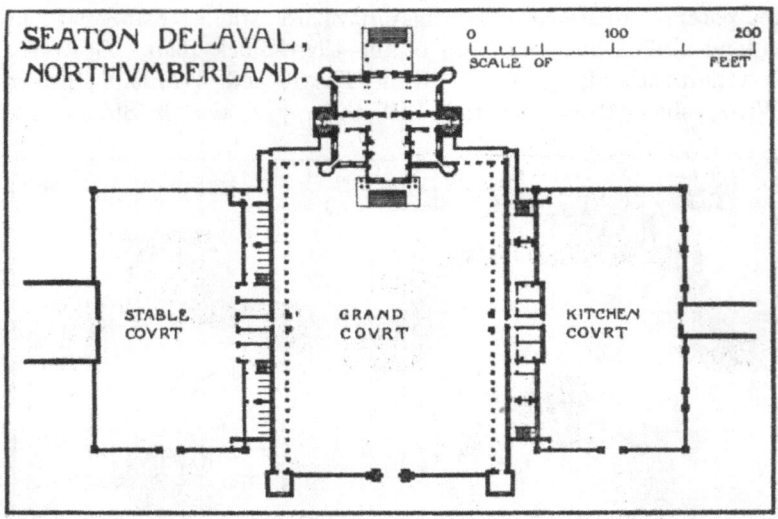

Fig. 264.

this type, and the extent to which they had departed from the courtyard plan of the Elizabethan men.

Faults.   These plans have been condemned by some who maintain that utility and convenience are sacrificed to effect. The accusation is true up to a certain point, but the sacrifice has been exaggerated. These were mostly state houses, designed for state occasions. In that respect their plans are unrivalled. The man who prefers "to live in one room" would no doubt find the suites of apartments tedious. But these houses were not built for such. The times were still ceremonious; stateliness was still counted a virtue, and utilitarianism was not yet rampant. One must judge the houses by the age in which they were built. That may have been artificial, but it was also dignified, and a little more dignity in both houses and the age would not be amiss now.

Great though the changes are in planning introduced by Inigo Jones, the differences in the treatment of exteriors due to him are still more marked. The models he set, however, were not followed immediately. Old traditions were too strong. Before his time all houses were gabled, except a few large ones which had lead flats. The simple, straight-sided gable, which is merely the end wall of a roof with the pitch of which it agrees, continued to be employed in small houses all through the seventeenth century and well into the eighteenth. In fact, in country districts it was never entirely abandoned. For it, in the seventeenth century, was sometimes substituted a curved-sided gable crowned by a pediment, the origin of which is Flemish. Inigo Jones designed such gables for the wings of Raynham Hall, and for portions of the front of Kirby Hall, and Webb followed suit at Thorpe Hall, Northants. There are many gables of this type in England on houses built mostly between 1640 and 1680, such as Swateley Hall, near Uxbridge, Kew Palace, the riding school, Bolsover Castle, etc. (see Fig. 232). In Lincoln's Inn Fields and Great Queen Street, Jones and Webb started the Palladian treatment of carrying large and well-proportioned pilasters through two storeys, but this was not followed generally until the eighteenth century. Their successors preferred that each storey should have its own order, in this respect following their Elizabethan forefathers.[1] They got their proportions better, however. The pilasters are generally entasised, and above them is a regulation entablature. In the front of Christ's Hospital there were Ionic pilasters, but in his purely domestic buildings Wren either omitted pilasters altogether or else used the French type, introduced by Lemercier and F. Mansard, which have neither capitals nor bases. Such are the brick and stone pilasters at the angles of Hampton Court, the smooth stone pilasters of a house in West Street, Chichester, and the still more characteristically French channelled pilasters of Marlborough House, Pall Mall. The house at Greenwich, shown in Fig. 265, is fairly representative of the vernacular work of the middle of the seventeenth century. It is of brick entirely, and the windows have the wood mullions and transoms usually found in work of that period.

Exteriors.

---

[1] An exception is in the quadrangle of Kirby Hall (see Fig. 197). Thorpe may have got the idea from Du Cerceau, whose "Les plus excellents Bastiments" he certainly knew, or the considerable projection of these pilasters suggests that the mediæval buttress was in his mind, which he clothed in a Classic dress.

Buildings such as the last mentioned, however, showed little architectural advance. They were but an aftermath. The advance was made at Coleshill House and Ashdown House. Whether Wren ever saw either is uncertain, but their characteristics are also those of the greater number of houses built by him and also by his successors. Both houses are "boxes" covered by a pitched roof, Coleshill House being a long box and Ashdown a tall one. They belong to the "astylar" type; there are no pilasters on the walls. At the angles are quoins. At the eaves is a great cornice,

Fig. 265.

from which the roof starts direct without the intervention of any parapet, blocking course, or balustrade. The roof is hipped on all sides, and there are no gables. At the ridge is a wood balustrade, which surrounds a lead flat, from the centre of which rises a lantern. The fronts of both houses rely for effect on their proportions and the spacing of their windows. They are quite plain, save for the entrance doorway on the principal floor, which is well raised above the ground by the semi-basement below, and approached by a flight of outside steps. At Ashdown House the central window on the upper floor over the doorway is richer in design than the others. The picturesqueness of the earlier age, obtained by broken plan and broken outline in elevation, was passing away, and was being succeeded by symmetry and dignity. Coleshill and Ashdown are not unpicturesque; but their picturesqueness is more subdued, and is the result of their simplicity and sobriety.

The differences between houses built before *c.* 1650, and those of the succeeding hundred years or more, are largely due to the changes in window design. Windows of the earlier period are invariably stone mullioned; the majority of the later period have sashes. The sash window is essentially English. One may almost say it is never met with in France, where long casement windows are general; and it is uncommon in other countries. Abroad it occurs most frequently in Holland and in some parts of Germany. When it was first used in this country is uncertain, but at the beginning it was not the convenient contrivance that it is now. "Double-hung" sashes were unknown, and the casings very rough. The bottom sash was rarely hung. Sometimes it was fixed altogether; in other cases it could be opened, but had to be wedged up to prevent its falling. It is doubtful if Inigo Jones ever used sash windows. The ones in the Banqueting Hall are probably much more modern. It was difficult in his time to obtain glass large enough even for those comparatively small panes. The windows of the additions he made at Kirby Hall, Northants, still retain their old glazing, and show one method he adopted. In the lower half of each window are two iron casements; the upper half does not open. Both portions are filled with many small panes, separated

Windows.

Fig. 266.

by lead cames. The more general method, however, was a solid wood frame, divided into four lights by a wood mullion and transom, with iron casements where required, and lead lights throughout. Window openings had to be treated as "voids"

326 A HISTORY OF ARCHITECTURAL DEVELOPMENT

that was essential; and the effect could be obtained by sash windows, solid wood frames, or by iron casements, as at Kirby.

Façades of large country houses. There is nothing playful in the façades of large eighteenth-century country houses. The chief characteristic is dignity. Drawings fail to do them justice. Even photographs convey but a faint idea of the effect they produce, as their fine scale, one of their principal assets, is difficult to realize. Their rooms are always lofty, 18 to 20 feet being not uncommon dimensions, which are sometimes exceeded. They are essentially sober in design. To the credit of the eighteenth-century architect be it said that, whatever his faults might be, he was never rococo. Some fronts are pilastered, like Chatsworth, originally built by Talman, a contemporary of Wren; Easton Neston, an exceedingly fine design by Hawksmoor; Harewood House, by Carr of York, described on a previous page; portions of Blenheim, and some others. The pilasters seldom start from the ground level, but from the top of a rusticated basement which forms the front of the semi-sunk ground floor, and run through the principal and upper floors to a main entablature. This is generally surmounted by a balustrade. The treatment is essentially Michaelangeloesque and Palladian. The majority of these houses, however, have no pilasters, save those behind the columns of a portico. Even the corners are plain. They owe their effect to their mass, grouping, spacing of windows, and proportions generally. They stand well, owing to their semi-basements, and with few exceptions possess the virtue which Reynolds ascribed to Vanbrugh's buildings of not "abruptly starting out of the ground without expectation or preparation."

Porticoes and outside staircases. The short flight of steps outside the front door at Coleshill developed in the eighteenth century into the magnificent staircases which are so fine a feature of many of these houses. Amongst the most elaborate are those of Lord Burlington's villa at Chiswick, and Prior Park, Bath (see Fig. 251). Above them rises the portico which was considered indispensable. Both porticoes and staircases have been ridiculed as useless, unnecessary, and extravagant. The same might be said of any embellishment. If a sculptor had been called in to carve the centre of these buildings, most of those who decry the porticoes would have been the first to express approval. The principle is the same whatever form of ornamentation is adopted. The accentuation of the principal portion of any design has at all times, and in all styles, been recognized as legitimate and right; and that ornament should be massed and not scattered about is an acknowledged rule. To produce an effect of richness by architectural forms, by the use of columns and entablatures, by the play of light and shade, is surely more praiseworthy in an architect, than for him to rely for his effect mainly on the efforts of a worker in another art. These men regarded architecture as the mistress of the arts, and to the best of their ability maintained her supremacy. They felt no antagonism towards the other arts, but they held that the beauty of a building should lie mainly in its proportions, balance, detail, and composition generally; in other words, in its architecture; and not in its embellishment by either sculpture or painting. In the hands of dull men this sometimes led to dull work. First-rate sculpture might have attracted attention and prevented the dullness from being apparent. But if the sculpture or other ornamentation had been mediocre, what otherwise was merely dull would have become disagreeable.

The porticoes, as a rule, are crowned by pediments. An exception is on the garden side of Seaton Delaval, where there is balustrade instead. The rule was not followed in this case because the central portion of the building behind rises higher, and the pediment is therefore on that. It was in no spirit of pedantry that Vanbrugh and his contemporaries and successors refused to follow the example set by Wren at Hampton Court and Greenwich, and plaster a pediment against an attic. They felt, and rightly, that a pediment should be the crowning feature of a building, and that although the precedent of the Romans might be claimed for its misuse, that was no reason why they should follow suit. They did not hesitate about pediments over doorways and windows, because, as pointed out in a previous chapter, these are complete and, so to speak, independent features; whereas the pediment over the central portion of any house is the pediment of the house itself, and out of place if it does not occupy the highest position. *Pediments.*

The smaller houses, both in town and country, have the same characteristics as the larger, and possess the same virtues. Some are in stone; as at Bath and its vicinity, at Stamford, and in Cumberland, Yorkshire, wherever, in fact, that material was plentiful. But the majority are in brick. Hardly a town in England, from Shrewsbury, which is particularly rich in examples, to Dover; from the coast of Norfolk to the Land's End, has not several. They are quiet and unobtrusive. They do not catch the eye and arrest attention, but like their French contemporaries *Smaller houses.*

they well deserve attention. The fronts are either of red brick throughout, or red bricks are used only for quoins, window heads, cornices, strings, etc., and the walling is of "stocks," which in colour range from "white," as in Suffolk, through shades of yellow almost to red, according to locality. Not their least charm is their workmanship. The heads of windows and the "aprons" under them are frequently of rubbed brick with "putty" joints, their slightly different colour and texture making a pleasant contrast with the walling. Rubbed bricks were sometimes used for pilasters, as in Wren's front of Christ's Hospital, and often for doorways, as in the fine examples in King's Bench Walk, the Temple. The bricks of the window heads are frequently cut into shapes above each opening, as in the house in the Pallant, Chichester, in Essex Street, Strand, etc. The crowning cornice is often of wood, especially when it comes immediately under the eaves. Otherwise it is of brick or stone, whichever material the walling is, and above it is generally a parapet. In some buildings the cornice is not at the top, but is surmounted by an attic. This is more usual when the wall is pilastered than when plain. The one rich spot is the entrance doorway. The variety in design of these in London alone is remarkable. The principal windows always have sashes, but it is no uncommon occurrence to find the earlier solid mullioned frame and lead lights used in servants' wings, outbuildings, etc. Windows, casings, and frames are generally nearly flush with the outside face of a wall, being recessed about an inch. In 1709 an Act of Parliament was passed that no door or window frames were to be set nearer to the outside face than four inches. For the succeeding thirty years or so the Act appears to have been more honoured in the breach than in the observance.

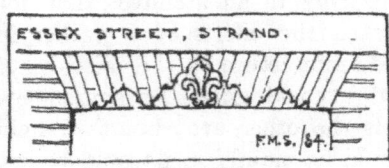

Fig. 267.

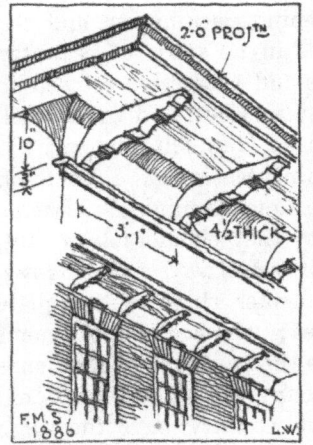

Fig. 268.—Cornice of House, Poole, Dorset.

Recessed window frames generally denote that a house belongs to the second half of the century. The intention was to prevent the spread of fire. But a walking-stick is as much a protection against rain as the Act was against fire, and the restriction no longer holds good in London and some other centres. In no detail of a building is the tendency towards littleness, which set in about the middle of the eighteenth century, more marked than in the bars of sash windows. In Queen Anne's reign they were an inch and a half, in large buildings sometimes two inches or more, wide, and they gradually got thinner and thinner, until towards the end of the century they are often not more than three-quarters of an inch in width. The majority of smaller houses, like the larger, have no pilasters, but in not a few, especially in towns, a single pilaster is placed near, not on, each outside angle, so that the cornice above it can return on the face of the wall without any awkwardness resulting. Most of the pilasters are straight-sided, and excellent examples of the bricklayers' skill.

The interiors are as pleasant and reposeful as the exteriors. Until about 1750 all the principal rooms were panelled in wood from floor to the cornice against the ceiling, low panels below and high ones above, the two rows divided by a chair rail. After that time the upper panels were frequently omitted, and only the lower retained as a dado; or else the walls were panelled with the "stucco" of the Adams and other firms. The variety in design of the staircases is considerable, but a family likeness runs through all. In larger houses they are often placed in the entrance hall, which is frequently paved with large stone octagons and small marble or slate squares. In smaller houses they are more frequently at the back. *Interiors.*

Neither outside nor inside is there anything startling about these smaller houses. But they are delightful to live in; their proportions and detail are so soothing. They represent the winter and not the spring of a great architectural movement. They may not be important works of art, but they command respect; and remind one pleasantly of the days when sons addressed their fathers as "Honoured Sir," when ladies curtsied, and gentlemen knew how to bow.

CHAPTER XIV

THE NINETEENTH CENTURY IN ENGLAND:
A POSTSCRIPT

THE eighteenth century was but half finished when two movements were set on foot which were destined to break up the traditions which had become vernacular in this country. The first is known as the Greek revival, the second as the Gothic. These two revivals would not have enjoyed such success, if architectural style had possessed a tithe of the vitality that distinguished it a hundred years previously, and if the time had not been one of general unrest. The factors that caused the great French Revolution of the end of the century affected other than economic conditions. Men witnessed long-cherished ideals trampled underfoot, and laws, they had believed immutable, overturned with the greatest of ease. If architectural style had been strong it might have stood firm amidst the general upheaval. But it had begun to weaken before the revivals commenced. It was played out; and even if there had been no revivals and no revolution, it could not long have survived. Fresh blood was imperative; and the only pity is that men could not agree whence it should come. The result of the disagreement was that throughout the whole of the nineteenth century architecture was in a disorganized, chaotic condition. As Professor Donaldson said, "We are all in a state of transition; we are wandering in a labyrinth of experiments." Only in the last decade was there anything approaching an understanding as to the lines on which progress was possible and right.

Greek revival.

The Greek revival may be said to start with the visit to Greece in 1751 of James Stuart and N. Revett. Greece had been a sealed book for some centuries, and it was only with considerable difficulty and at some risk that these two artists were able to take their measurements and make their sketches. They remained in the country five years, returning to England in 1755. In 1762 was published the first volume of their "Antiquities of Athens," which to this day remains a standard work. It contains drawings of the finest buildings of the most glorious period of Greek art. The list of subscribers to the volume shows how widespread was the interest it created, and includes the names of the wealthy art patrons of the day; the names of painters and sculptors, headed by Sir Joshua Reynolds; David Garrick, the actor; and, what is of more interest, the names of builders, carpenters, and others engaged in the building trade. Additional impetus was given to the movement by the purchase from Lord Elgin in 1816 of much of the sculpture from the frieze and pediment of the Parthenon, and other marbles, and their shipment to England. Greece and her colonies rapidly supplanted Italy and the old Roman colonies as the chief training ground for architects. Cockerell spent many years studying at first hand ancient Greek art; and many other men did likewise. In the mean time the powerful Dilettanti Society lent their aid, and provided funds for visits, explorations, and publications of the results obtained. Under their auspices the fourth volume of Stuart and Revett's work appeared in 1816, and amongst other publications, for which they were partly responsible, are "The Antiquities of Ionia," Wilkins' "Magna Græcia," Penrose's valuable treatise on the Parthenon, and Cockerell's "Ægina and Bassæ." The last was not published until 1860, by which time the movement was on the wane.

At the beginning of the revival archæological correctness was insisted upon, and attempts were made to make buildings devoted to most opposite uses all appear externally like Greek temples. Most of the examples are "correct," but cold and lifeless. In Liverpool there are several, the majority being designed by John Foster, City Surveyor until 1839, who was fellow traveller with Cockerell in Greece. In London, S. Pancras church, *c.* 1820, with its caryatid porch and "Erechtheum" entrance portico, is notable as an instance of clever copying of the "letter" of Greek art. The work of Cockerell and Harvey Lonsdale Elmes comes under another category. Cockerell's admiration for and knowledge of antique Greek work were unsurpassed, but he never allowed it to become his master. The Taylor Institute at Oxford, the Bank of England, Liverpool, the Sun Fire Office, Threadneedle Street, and the London, Liverpool and Globe Insurance Building, Liverpool, have pure and beautiful detail, but that is not their sole charm. They possess real originality as well. Elmes was more Græco-Roman in his taste; in that respect following Sir John Soane, who, in the

Buildings of the Greek revival.

Bank of England, London, chose the circular temple at Tivoli as his model. S. George's Hall, Liverpool, commenced in 1838, is the culminating triumph of the revival. Elmes won it in competition when only twenty-three, and he died at the age of thirty-three, when it was little more than half finished. Its completion was entrusted to Cockerell, who designed the internal fittings, and also made the original sketch for the sculpture in the pediment over the south portico. This was afterwards redrawn, with some slight alterations, by Alfred Stevens, the sculptor, and the figures were carved by Nicholls. For fine scale and stateliness the building has no equal in this country, and probably none abroad. It is Roman in its bigness, symmetrical plan, and fine peristyles. Only in the interior did Elmes follow pure Greek models. The north portico inside is a delightful design, with Greek Doric columns of grey Tallacher stone. Other important buildings of the revival, in addition to those already mentioned, are University College, London, by Wilkins, with its stately Corinthian portico and fine outside staircase, the British Museum, by Sir Robert Smirke, and the Royal Exchange, by Sir William Tite, the last possessing little character.

Partial break with tradition. If the Greek revival had stood alone there would have been no absolute break with tradition. In the early days of the movement, insistence on correctness in detail created a barrier between architects and workmen, and upset the relations which had previously prevailed; but otherwise existing traditions were but little disturbed. The principles of architectural design remained unchanged. Greek Doric or Ionic porticoes, with suitable mouldings, supplanted Roman Corinthian, but that was only an alteration in detail. In the later buildings of the revival there was genuine development. Cockerell and Elmes lifted the movement out of the archæological rut in which it started. If their efforts had been unopposed, if they had received the undivided support of their brethren, the confusion of the latter half of the last century would have been avoided, and the threads of tradition have remained intact. In France, where the revival was contemporary with ours, they were not broken. In that country merely a fresh stream was turned into the current and mingled with it; clearing the waters and making them sparkle. In England the result might have been equally good, but for the counter factor, the Gothic revival. In France that was weak; in England it obtained the absolute mastery and overwhelmed the other.

THE NINETEENTH CENTURY IN ENGLAND 333

A year or two before the publication of Stuart and Revett's "Antiquities of Athens," Horace Walpole commenced his villa at Strawberry Hill, near Richmond, with its tower and drawbridge, its cloisters and other affectations of mediævalism. The detail of Gothic was there, but the spirit was sadly lacking. The next sensation was caused by the building, between 1810 and 1820, by William Beckford of Fonthill Abbey "in the Gothic style." In 1805 John Britton commenced the issue of his "Architectural Antiquities of Great Britain," followed by his "Cathedral Antiquities of England." Both helped to draw attention to the old monuments in this country which, it must be admitted, had either been shamefully neglected or else disgracefully "restored." Next came Rickman, with his "Attempt to discriminate the styles of architecture in England from the Conquest to the Reformation," and Augustus Pugin with "Specimens of Gothic Architecture." The revival was now established. The flame of enthusiasm was fanned by the novels of Sir Walter Scott and others; in fact, the "Romantic" movement in literature largely urged forward the Gothic movement in art. The extent to which Mediævalism had caught the popular fancy in the middle of the century, was made evident by the famous tourney at Eglinton Castle in 1855, when lists were erected, a Queen of Beauty enthroned, and knight and squire once more broke a lance in Merrie England.

<small>Gothic revival.</small>

So far the two movements had run concurrently, not exactly amicably, but without strong outward manifestations of hostility on either side. In 1836, however, Augustus Welby Pugin, son of the above named, threw down the gauntlet with his "Contrasts," in which he compared the "noble edifices of the Middle Ages and corresponding buildings of the present day." "The true principles of Pointed or Christian Architecture," also by him, followed a few years later. The "War of the Styles," as it was termed, was soon in full swing. It is somewhat difficult to realize now with what bitterness the war was waged. Much ink was spilt, and many invectives hurled on both sides. Professor Cockerell was captain of the Classic camp, and Augustus Welby Pugin was the leader of the Goths. Two men more different in temperament it would be difficult to imagine. Cockerell, President of the Institute, Professor of Architecture at the Academy, and Royal Academician, was a man of intense refinement, exquisite taste, and considerable knowledge. A courtly gentleman, he was no match in a war of words for his fiery, outspoken opponent. Pugin owed much of

<small>"War of the Styles."</small>

his versatility and impetuosity to his forbears, who were French. He did not mince his words. He said the Classic men were "besotted in their mongrel compositions;" that "a man who paganizes in the Universities deserves no quarter," that Cockerell's work there, the Taylor Institute, was an "unsightly pile," and could commend itself only to those who approved the "gin palace" style of design; that Tite's Royal Exchange was "another stale dish of ill-adapted classicisms;" and that Sir Francis Chantry's figure of James Watt in Westminster Abbey was "so offensive in its present position that if Sir Francis did really so design it, he deserves to be crushed under its great pedestal, to prevent him again committing so great an outrage on good taste." The war of the styles undoubtedly had the effect of making men keen, and in a sense was stimulating. But in other respects it was disastrous. When men are divided, hopelessly at variance, and about equal in strength, a see-saw game is in progress; first one side is uppermost, then the other, and the result is that advance is impossible.

Houses of Parliament.

The most distinguished example of the Gothic revival is the Houses of Parliament, Westminster, commenced in 1837, a year before its famous rival in the other style, S. George's Hall, Liverpool. These two contemporary buildings are monuments of the confusion in architectural ideals which prevailed in the first half of the last century. The conditions of the competition for the Houses of Parliament stated—"The style is to be Gothic or Elizabethan." Sir Charles Barry, who was successful, was little in sympathy with the Greek movement, and yet certainly did not belong to the Gothic camp. His previous work had been in free Classic. The Travellers' and Reform Clubs in Pall Mall are more or less copies of Italian Renaissance palaces. But for the conditions of the competition Barry would probably have submitted a design more on the lines of Inigo Jones' Whitehall. As it is, the plan is Classic; it is the detail only that is Gothic; or as Pugin, who gave Barry valuable assistance over the latter, put it, the building has "Tudor details on a Classic body." It is very warmly clad. No other building, ancient or modern, has façades so covered with ornament and detail.

Restoration mania.

The middle of the century is chiefly remarkable for the Great Exhibition of '51, which brought the manufacturer to the front and drove the artist to the wall; and for the commencement of the "restoration" mania, which, supported by the Cambridge

Camden Society and the great body of the clergy, swept the land in the sixties and seventies. Sir George Gilbert Scott was the central figure. The ancient cathedrals were scraped, re-chiselled, recarved, refitted, in some cases almost rebuilt. A clean sweep was made of everything that was not Gothic, and even Gothic itself was not always sacred. Windows which had been inserted in place of earlier ones, in order to obtain more light, or else to frame the splendour of painted glass, were removed to make way for modern versions of what might have been. Oak benches, screens and panelling of crude but interesting design by Elizabethan and Jacobean men, which showed the churches had not been so neglected after the Reformation as the restorers tried to make out, were condemned as unsuitable, and disappeared. Before the restorers began, the history of England was written in and about these old buildings. They were full of memories of the multitudes which had worshipped within their walls, and of the craftsmen who had laboured to make them beautiful. Every stone could tell a story. The marks of the chisels of the original workers were to be seen on carvings and mouldings. The carvings no doubt were mutilated in places, the mouldings broken. But they were genuine. The great mistake the restorers made was not to realize that what one cannot exactly make out, one cannot with certainty restore; and that when the design is clear, restoration is unnecessary. It is true that in many churches alterations and additions had been made which, in the agreement of all, were tasteless, and not to be endured. Some dated from the beginning of the century, when James Wyatt, of "execrable memory," as Pugin called him, was the chief offender. But such additions might have been removed without subjecting the buildings to such wholesale restoration and refitting. When churches were so far dilapidated as to necessitate almost rebuilding, they might surely have been allowed to remain as historical monuments, a little judicious attention preventing their total collapse. Fountains, Tintern, Glastonbury, are not less valuable to architectural students, are not less interesting to all who care for Gothic art, because they are ruins. On the contrary, they are more valuable, more interesting, more beautiful, than ninety-nine out of a hundred restored churches.

Sir Gilbert Scott first made his mark by winning in 1840 the international competition for the church of S. Nicholas, Hamburg, and for the next five and thirty years he occupied a commanding

Zenith of Gothic.

position in the architectural world. In the time of Pugin, fifteenth-century English Gothic was regarded as the only style worthy of imitation. Scott's churches are mostly based on thirteenth- and fourteenth-century work, and the inspiration was not always from English sources. French and Italian influences, however, are more marked in the churches of the brilliant group of men comprising Butterfield, Burges, Street, Bodley, Pearson, etc., who were partly his contemporaries, partly his successors. Space does not permit of any attempt to treat of their achievements; but they, together with George Gilbert Scott, jun., son of Sir Gilbert, John Bentley, John D. Sedding, and more than one architect still living, designed churches as beautiful as any built in the Middle Ages, and full of originality. The movement was at its zenith about 1880. It had taken nearly a century to build up; the archæology that marred the earlier work had disappeared, and the movement had become progressive; and yet it collapsed with startling suddenness. Why? The probable reason is the unsuitability of the style for anything but churches. Street's Law Courts, despite the care bestowed upon them, and the excellence of portions, notably the principal entrance and great hall, showed conclusively the futility of attempting Gothic for a public building. And there are thousands of public and private secular buildings now to one church. To have retained Gothic for churches, and developed Classic for other buildings, would have been to perpetuate the confusion which had harassed architecture throughout the century. Gothic had to go; not because it was less beautiful, but because it was less adaptable. One may regret the result, but it was inevitable. The requirements of the day must be the first consideration in building. It was by observing them closely in the past that architecture gained its high position, and it is only by similar observance in the present and future that the art can once more rise triumphant.

"Queen Anne." Whilst architects were fighting as to which was the proper style to use for public buildings and churches, private houses were left to the builder. Cromwell Road and many squares in South Kensington show the slough into which domestic architecture had been allowed to sink. The reaction started about 1860. Stucco and Welsh slate, which had hitherto reigned supreme, were banned, and red brick and red tiles took their place. A few years previously these materials had been used for churches by Butterfield,

Bodley, Street, and Brooks—Scott's churches are of stone—and as early as 1842 Hardwick had built the Library at Lincoln's Inn in brick with stone dressings. In the sixties Bodley built parsonages at Pendlebury and Scarborough and a group of five houses at Malvern in red brick with tiled roofs. At the same time Nesfield built the Lodge by the Broad Walk in Regent's Park. About 1870 Mr. Norman Shaw startled the architectural world with Lowther Lodge, Kensington, and the offices for Messrs. Shaw, Savill & Co., Leadenhall Street, London, Barings' Bank following a few years later; and Mr. Philip Webb built Lord Carlisle's house, Kensington, and some offices in Lincoln's Inn Fields. The new style was promptly christened "Queen Anne." It was at once fiercely attacked, and as warmly defended. The scattered remnants of the two camps, Gothic and Classic, united in condemnation. But their opposition was of no avail. All over the country houses of red brick and tile sprang up with picturesque outlines, irregular plans, small leaded panes for windows—a reaction against plate glass—white paint, dormers, barge boards, finials, and other excrescences. Most of the buildings were totally unlike the quiet, stately old houses of the beginning of the eighteenth century, and many were full of affectations, but the idea underlying the movement was sound. It led to the revival of the love for the "house beautiful" which was almost dead in England.

Close on the heels of the Queen Anne movement followed a foreign invasion. Greater facilities for travel had brought the Continent within reach of all. Architects crossed the Channel, sketch book in hand, and in Normandy and Brittany, along the Loire and the Rhine, jotted down picturesque "bits," to be worked in afterwards in their designs. The few weeks abroad and the hurried sketching, although better than idleness at home, were a poor substitute for the "grand tour" and the serious study which eighteenth-century architects engaged in. They worked on big lines; studying buildings as a whole, and grasping the big essentials of architecture. The sketch-book men worked on small lines; picking up trifles; without time to do more than skirmish round a building. And so planning on a grand scale, with the surroundings of a building considered equally with the building itself, became almost a lost art in England. *Sketchbook architecture.*

The art of stately planning is now reviving, and a more chastened version of Classic has supplanted Queen Anne and sketch-book vagaries. Once again attention is being paid to the *Plea for unity.*

precepts of Palladio and other great Italians of the sixteenth century, and to the work of Inigo Jones and Wren. The tendency became marked in the last decade of the last century, and since then has daily been growing in volume. At first there were fears that this might prove but another phase that would "fret its hour upon the stage," and then collapse, as other movements had collapsed. For a short time that seemed possible. A cry arose from a few that tradition was nought; that salvation lay in ignoring it. The advent of "art nouveau" was a blessing in disguise; inasmuch as it showed how false the cry was. Its immediate result was to stiffen and consolidate the movement in the exactly opposite direction, and to unite men who before had been at variance. The buildings of the present century throughout England show in the main a harmony of aim and expression which has been unknown in this country for a hundred years. There is now no war of the styles. Once again there is agreement as to the main principles on which design should be based. And yet there is no stifling of originality. The work of to-day is far more individualistic and original than when one specified cut-and-dried style or another had to be strictly followed. In the latter half of the last century changes were so rapid that few men were able to remain long enough on one tack to make real headway. As soon as they were beginning to feel that they were moving, the wind changed, and they had to begin again on another tack if they did not wish to drop out of the race. It is sincerely to be hoped that we have done with changes. Not that architecture should stand still. It must advance and develop; but it can only do this properly when there is agreement. Architecture prospered most in the past under a bond of union and under the influence of tradition. Similar conditions are essential still, if the real advance of to-day is to be strengthened and maintained.

INDEX

ABACUS, upper (pseudo-dosseret), 22
Abbeville—doors of S. Vulfran, 198
Abbiate Grasso, church at, 54–56
Adam brothers, 310–312
Adams, Maurice B., cited, 248 note
Alberti, Leon Battista, family and career of, 25–26; superintendents of his work, 26, 45; Palazzo Rucellai by, 38–39; panelled pilasters by, 63; S. M. de' Miracoli (Rome) by, 123; Greek cross plan churches by, 124; S. Andrea (Mantua) by, 129–132 and note; S. Francesco (Rimini) by, 130, 138–139; "De Re Ædificatoria," 25–26, 105; otherwise mentioned, 50, 54, 70
Alessi, Galeazzo, 109, 114–115
Alfriston, wood and plaster house at, 226
Amadeo, Gio. Antonio, 60
Amati, 124
Amboise—
 Castle, 169–170, 172
Ammanati, Bartolommeo, 32, 109, 110
Anderson quoted, 97
Anet, Château d', 190–191
Angers—
 Corbel cornices at, 183
 Hôtel de Pincé, 183
Angerville-Bailleul Château, 179–180
Anne, Queen of Denmark, 271
Anne de Bretagne, 186
Antwerp—
 Hôtel des Villes Hanséatiques, 237
 Jesuit church façade at, 189
Apethorpe Hall, Northants, 241, 262
Apses, 121, 125
Arcading—
 Borghese, 112
 Genoa University, 115
Archer, Thomas, 299, 300

Arches (see also Vaults)—
 Four-centred, 281 note
 Lintel in combination with, 94
 Pairs of columns, starting from, 99
 Three-centred, 181
 Window—intrados and extrados not concentric, 31, 40–41
Architect-clerks of works, 44–45
Architects of the Renaissance—
 Italian, 13, 14
 French, 185
Arezzo—
 S. Maria delle Grazie, 27
 Strozzi Palace, designs of, 27
Arles—Amphitheatre, vaulting of, 141 note²
Arnolfo, 15, 31
Ashburnham House—staircase of, 275–276; doorway of, 279
Ashdown House, Berks, 279, 313, 316; style of, 324–325
Aston Hall, Birmingham—plan of, 253; gallery of, 254, 259; staircase of, 268
Astylar palaces, character of, 30
Athens—
 Arch of Hadrian, 63 note², 65
 Erechtheum, 23
 Parthenon—destruction of, 47 note; sculpture from, 331
Attics—
 Different treatment of, 31
 Drum, 160
 Greenwich Hospital, at, 304
 Rome, not common in, 79
 Vault springing from, instances of, 130
Audley End, 235, 252; foreign influence shown by, 260
Averlino, Antonio, see Filarete

INDEX

Avignon—
  Jesuit church façade at, 139
  S. Didier, 169
Azay-le-rideau Château—
  Canopies at, 180
  Description of, 177, 178
  Façade of, 181
  Oratory of, 184
  Towers of, 179

BACON quoted, 252, 254
Badges, 182
Banner holders, 37
Barge-boards, 265
Bari, window arches, 41
Barisanus of Trani, 4 *note*²
Barlborough Hall, 246, 255
Barozzi, Giacomo, *see* Vignola
Barry, Sir Charles, 334
Basilican architecture in Italy—influence of, 4; examples of, 20
Basilican Churches, spacing in, 22 *note*
Bakewell Old Hall, 257-258
Balleroy Château, 203, 316
Bath, Wood's work at, 309
Batter, 162
Beaconsfield, Bucks, house at, 321
Beaudouin, J., 185
Beaugency—Hôtel de Ville, 172 *and note*; cornice, 180
Beauvais Cathedral, 199
Beckford, Wm., 333
Benevento, bronze doors at, 4 *note*²
Bentley, John, 336
Bergamasco, Guglielmo, 64, 96.
Bergamo—
  Cathedral buttresses, 137
  " Masters' " work at, 60
  S. Maria Maggiore—Colleoni Chapel, 60
Bernini, Giovanni Lorenzo, colonnade by, 107; Piazza of S. Peter's, 146; design for the Louvre, 207 *and note*²; otherwise mentioned, 69, 109, 112, 123
Berthelot, Gilles, 177
Bianchi, P., 124
Bianco, Bartolomeo, 115
Billard, 192
Birch, G. H., cited, 295 *note*
Blackheath—Morden College, 302

Blashfield, Messrs., quoted, 80-81, 122
Blenheim—
  Corridors of, 317
  Exterior of, 306
  Pilasters at, 326
  Plans of, 319
Blois—
  Château—
    Francis I.'s wing, cornice of, 180
    Gaston d'Orléans wing, 204-205
    Louis XII.'s wing, 170, 171-172, 176; arcading of, 181
    Outside staircase, 176
  Château de Bury, 175, 179
  Hôtel d'Alluye, 171, 172; arches of, 181
Blomfield, Prof. R., cited, 190, 239; quoted, 235 *note*
Blondel, J. F., publications of, 221 *note*; cited, 193 *note*², 207 *and note*¹
Bloom (Bluom, Bloem), Hans, " De Quinque Columnarum " by, 240
Boccaccio, 2, 3
Bodley, G. F., 336-337
Bodley, Sir T., 235
Boffrand, Germain, 217, 220
Bohier, Thomas, 176
Bologna—
  Astylar buildings common in, 69
  Building materials of, 60
  Palazzo Bevilacqua, 60-61
  Palazzo Davia (Bargellini), 115-116
  Palazzo Elefantussi, 111
  Romanesque architecture in, 4 *note*¹
  S. Petronio, 5
Bolsover—
  Castle, internal decoration of, 246-247; riding-school, 280 *and note*, 323; long gallery, 281
  Church, 246, 248
Bolton Hall, ceilings in, 266
Books on architecture—
  Renaissance—
    English, 236 *note*, 238
    French, 191, 192, 212, 213
    German, 236 *and note*
    Italian, 25-26, 49, 85 *note*, 92, 104-105
  Eighteenth century, 308
Borgognone, 60 *and note*

Borromini, Francesco, 69, 109, 112, 126
Botticelli, 7
Boughton Malherbe, Kent, ceiling at, 266
Bourges—Jacques Cœur's house, 186
Boussart, Simon, 185 *and note* [1]
Braccio, length of, 16 *note* [2]
Brackets—
 Louis XV., 218
 Scroll, 139
Bradford-on-Avon—Duke's House, 252, 259
Bramante, —, training of, 54; two periods of, 54; cloisters of S. Maria della Pace, 61; in Rome, 71, 75; Il Tempietto, 74; design for S. Peter's, Rome, 141-143, 145, 151; pilastered façades by, 79; estimate of, 53, 75-76: otherwise mentioned, 50, 69, 96, 122, 123, 125
Bramshill, Hants, 257
Brécy Château, 203-204
Brescia—
 "Masters'" work at, 59-60
 Municipio, 59
 Palazzo Martinengo, 116-117
 Prigioni, 59-60
 S. Maria de' Miracoli, 59, 135-133; dome and roof, 61
Brick—
 Dome of, 120
 English stone-built houses' chimneys of, 263
 Northern Italy, prevalence in, 52
 Palladio's use of, 101, 111
 Portland stone in conjunction with, 304-305
 Roman Renaissance, 78
 Rubbed, 328
Briçonnet, Cardinal, 171
Brittany—
 Half-timbered fronts in, 227
 Renaissance work in, 186-187
Britton, John, 333
Broadstairs, gables near, 263
Brogi, Sig. Giacomo, cited, 34 *note*
Bronze-founding in Italy, 4 *note* [2]
Bronze rings, banner-holders, and lanterns, 37, 38
Brooks, J., 337
Brunelleschi, Filippo, training and education of, 6-9, 14; guilds of, 11 *note* [2], 14; patron of, 12; bronze panel by, 14 *and note* [2]; at Rome, 14; construction of the cathedral dome at Florence, 16-19, 155-160; S. Spirito, 20, 22-23; S. Lorenzo, 21-23; design for Palazzo Riccardi, 31, 32; for the Pitti, 32; Church of the Angels, 122; Pazzi Chapel, 124; fondness of, for continuous entablature, 23-24; capitals by, 65; death of, 9; estimate of, 24, 25; nature of work of, 5; mentioned, 4, 270

Buckhurst, Sussex, 251, 252
Bullant, 192
Buoni family, 64
Buontalenti, Bernardo, 34 *note*, 109, 112
Burges, W., 336
Burghley, 235 *note*, 237, 241, 252; clock tower and quadrangle of, 235; plan of, 255; staircase at, 268
Burlington, Earl of, 308
Bury, Château of, 175, 179
Butterfield, W., 336-337
Buttresses—
 Internal, 290
 Renaissance forms of, 137
Buxton—the Crescent, 311
Byzantine churches compared with Classic, 127
Byzantine tradition and influence in Italy, 4, 61

CAEN—
 Hôtel de Valois (d'Ecoville), 186
 S. Pierre, 186, 198
Caius, Dr., 236
Calvaries, 187
Calvo, M. F., 105
Cambridge—
 Caius College—gateways, 236
 Camden Society, 334-335
 King's College—screen, 232
 Pembroke College Chapel, 282
 Trinity College Library, 285, 301-302
Campbell, Colin, 304, 308, 316, 319
Canopies over niches, 180
Caparrà, il (Niccolo Grosso), 38
Capitals—
 Corinthian, 22

Capitals—*continued.*
 Renaissance, 65-66
 Swags between, 102
Caprarola, Palazzo, 93
Caradossa, 56
Carlisle—
 Cathedral, oak screen in, 234
 Deanery, 249
Carnarvon Castle, 226
Carr of York, 311, 326
Carving, *see under* Decoration
Castle Ashby, 266, 273, 274, 276, 278-279
Castle Hedingham Keep, 226
Castle Howard, Yorks., 307, 317-319; plan of, 318
Catherine de' Medici, 11, 176, 182, 184, 191, 193
Cattaneo cited, 3 *note*
Cavendish, Sir Charles, 280 *note*
Cavendish, Sir Wm. (Duke of Newcastle), 248, 280 *and note*
Ceilings, timbered and plastered, 266
Cellini, Benvenuto, 7, 229
Challuau, Château, 173
Chambers, Sir Wm., 311
Chambiges, Pierre, 189
Chambord, Château de—
 Cornice of, 180
 Keep of, 179
 Pediments of, 194
 Plan of, 178
 Slate panelling of, 183
 Staircase of, 174-176
 Window-heads of, 181
Chantilly, Château de, 192
Chantry, Sir Francis, 334
Charles VIII., King of France, 169-171
Charleval Château, 192
Chatsworth, 326
Chaumont, Château de, 178-179, 184 *note* 1
Chenonceaux, Château de—site and dates of, 176-177; tiling in, 184; towers of, 179
Chichester—
 Pallant, house in the, 328
 West Street, pilasters of house in, 323
Chimneys, brick, 263
Chiswick—Lord Burlington's villa at, 309 *and note*,[1], 326

Choisy cited, 16 *note* [3]
Christ Church, Hants, 231
Cibber, 285
Cigoli, Luigi, 112
Citta di' Sforvinda, 49
Classic churches—
 Byzantine compared with, 127
 Gothic compared with, 130, 131, 133, 136
Claverton House, Somerset, 252-253
Cockerell, Professor, 331-333
Colbert, 207
Coleshill House, Berks., 276; exterior features, 279; plan, 313-315; staircase, 326; style, 324-325
Colombe, Michel, 172
Columns—
 Attached pilasters in combination with, 91-92
 Banded, 191, 195
 Engaged, compared with pilasters, 134
 Fluted spiral, 95
 Intercolumniation, 124
 Pairs of, arches starting from, 99
 Piers in combination with, 101 *note*
 Recessed, 90
 Rusticated, 95, 111
 Twisted, 110
Como Cathedral, 64 *note*, 180; archivolt design in, 58; windows of, 59
Constantinople—
 Church of Holy Apostles, 222
 S. Sergius and Bacchus, 19 *note* [1]
 S. Sophia, pendentives in, 151
 S. Theodore, 121
Contractors, general, 237 *note* [2]
Conway Castle, 226
Cornice—
 Attic above, 30-31
 Corbel, 183; arched corbel, 172
 English eighteenth century, 328
 French châteaux, of, 180
 Lighting difficulties due to, 38
Coqueau, Jacques, 185
Corridors, curved, 317-321
Corsham, Wilts—
 Hall, 264
 Hungerford free schoole and almeshouses, 281-283
Cortona—La Madonna del Calcinaio, 126, 154

INDEX

Cothelston Hall, Somerset, 256
Courtyards of Genoese palaces, 115
Cowdray Park, Sussex, 231
Crane, Sir Francis, 316
Cremona—
    Baptistry dome, 160
    Palazzo Publico, 51
Cronaca (Simone Pollaiuolo), 27, 32, 36, 43
Croscombe church, Devon, 269
Cuiffagni, Bernardo, 132 *note*
Curtoni, Domenico, 114

D'ALLUYE, BARON, 174
d'Angelo, Baccio, 36, 41
da Cortona, Pietro, 123
da Laurana, Luciano, 54
da Majano, Benedetta, 27, 28, 32
da Majano, Giovanni, 229–230
da Majano, Giuliano, 27
da Settignano, Desiderio, 25
da Vinci, Leonardo, 8, 50, 171 *and note*
Dance, George (sen.), 299, 310
Dance, George (jun.), 310
Daviler quoted, 213
de Brosse, Salamon, 185, 196
de Chavannes, Puvis, 222 *note*[2]
de Cotte, Robert, 213, 217
de Coucy, Robert, 13
de Lespine, Jean, 183
De l'Orme, Philibert, career of, 191; work on the Tuileries, 193; mentioned, 177, 185, 188, 189
de Luzarches, Robert, 13
de' Medici, Catherine, *see* Catherine
de' Medici, Cosimo, 6, 11, 31, 48
de' Medici, Giovanni (Leo X.), 11, 70, 171
de' Medici, Giulio (Clement VII.), 11
de' Medici, Lorenzo, 11, 12
de' Medici, Piero, 49
De Montferrand, 164 *note*
de Montigny, Grandjean, cited, 45 *and note*[2], 46 *note*
de Pas (Paschen), Henri, 237
Decoration—
    Architectural *v.* sculptured, 326–327
    Billet design, 53
    Candelabra system of, 187
    Carving—
        Keystones, of, 217, 218

Decoration—*continued*.
    Carving—*continued*.
        Newels, of, 268
        North Italian, 65
        Panelling, of, 184
    Colour, 115, 184
    Coloured marbles, by, 135
    Cornice, *see that heading*
    Figures, 110, 115
    Figures turning into pilasters, 110
    Florentine and North Italian use of compared, 64–65
    Fresco painting, 37
    Frieze, *see that heading*
    Majolica plaques, 188
    Marble, in, 54, 60, 135
    Medallions in frieze, 23
    Panelling—
        Arabesque inlaying on, 226
        Carved and painted, 184
        Sculptured, 132 *note*
    Panthéon, of the, 222 *and note*[2]
    Plasterwork, 266–268
    Sgraffito, 36–37 *and note*
    Shadow as, 36
    Shields, 37
    Slate, 183
    Stucco, 79, 312
del Duca, Giacomo, 120
della Francesca, Piero, 54
della Porta, Giacomo, 69, 109, 139; work of, on the Farnese, 82; work on S. Peter's (Rome), 146
della Robbia, Girolamo, 188
della Robbia, Luca, 7, 169 *and notes*
della Rovere, Giuliano (Pope Julius II.), 70
Denham, Sir John, 280, 282, 284
di Matteucio, Cola, 125
Diane de Poitiers, 176, 182, 191
Dijon—
    Hôtel de Vogüé, 195–196
    S. Michel, 199
Dilettanti Society, 331
Distemper, 78
Domes—
    Centering of, 158
    Cities, in, suitability of, 289
    Concave compartments of, 19 *and note*[1]
    Double, 154 ff.
    Drums of, 152

INDEX

Domes—*continued.*
  Examples of—
    Florence Cathedral, 155–160
    London—S. Paul's, 162–164
    Paris—Les Invalides, 122, 164–165;
      Panthéon, 164, 166–167
  Galleries in, 158
  Italy, mediæval prevalence in, 4
  Large and small, in combination, 128, 136
  Materials of, 152; brick, 120
  Renaissance prevalence of, 119
  Shapes of, 152 ff.
  Windows in, 152
Domesday Book, 229 *note* [1]
Donaldson, Prof., quoted, 330
Donatello, doorways by, 7–8 *and note* [1]; with Brunelleschi, 14, 25; shields by, 25, 37; feeling for the beautiful in work of, 25 *note*
Doors, bronze, 4 *note* [2]
Doorways, Tudor, 281 *note*
Dosio, Giovanni Antonio, 112
Dosserets, 22
Drawbridges, 249
du Cerceau, Baptiste Androuet, 196 *note*
du Cerceau, Jacques Androuet, 192, 323 *note*
du Cerceau, Jean, 196
Durago, Rocco, 115

EASTON NESTON, 326
Ecouen, Château d', 192
Edinburgh University, 311–312
Edward VI., King of England, 235
Eglinton Castle, tourney at, 333
Elgin Marbles, 331
Elizabeth, Countess of Shrewsbury, 246, 280 *note*
Elizabeth, Duchess of Urbino, 50
Elizabeth, Queen of England, 235, 237
Elmes, Harvey Lonsdale, 331, 332
England (*for particular churches, houses, towns, etc., see their names*)—
  Architect, early use of term, 238–239
  Country houses after 1640, 312 ff.; single block plan, 314–316; three block plan, 316–322
  Country houses of eighteenth century —exteriors, 323 ff.; windows, 325; façades, 326
  Early planning in, 249

England—*continued.*
  Elizabethan and Jacobean houses—
    Approaches of, 256
    Carving in, 236
    Ceilings of, 271
    Characteristics of, 257 ff.
    Designers of, 237
    Fireplaces of, 266–268
    Foreign influences in, traits showing, 260
    Gardens of, 256–257
    Half-timbered, 263–265
    Halls of, 253–254
    Interiors of, 265
    Long galleries of, 254
    Materials of, 260–261
    Panelling in, 256
    Planning of, 251 ff.; types of plan 254–256
    Staircases of, 268
    Stone, 262
  Flemish work in, 230
  Gothic revival in, 302 ff.
  Greek revival in, 330–332
  Italian architects and craftsmen in, 228–230 *and note*; exode of, 235
  Queen Anne style, 336–337
  Renaissance in—
    Beginning of, 228
    Compromise of vernacular style with, 258
  Restoration mania in, 335
  Surveyors in, connotation of term, 239
Entablature (*see also* Cornice and Frieze)—
  Absence of, from Byzantine churches, 127
  Columns, over, 22–23
  Continuous, 23–24, 63; broken and unbroken compared, 100–101
  Examples of—
    Hôtel de Beauvais (Paris), 212
    Libreria Vecchia (Venice), 99
    Palladio's—Casa del Diavolo, 102
  Merging of divisions of, 23
  Position of, in astylar buildings, 30–31
  Slight projection, example of, 103
  Topmost, projection of, 39–40 *and note* [1]
  Vault springing direct from, 130
Eugenius IV., Pope, 24

FAÇADES, western, of churches, 137 ff.
Fancelli, Luca, 26 *and note*, 45, 50
Fenestration, *see* Windows
Fergusson quoted, 28 *note*[3], 115 *and note*[2], 145, 282
Ferrara, council at (1438), 6
Fiesole—Badia arches, 23
Figeac, old houses in, 227
Filarete (Antonio Averlino), 70; career of, 48; relations with Lombard Masons' Guild, 51; writings of, on architecture, 105; "Trattato," 49
Flitcroft, —, 309
Florence—
  Apprenticeship in, 7
  Archbishop's Palace, 112
  Arti (guilds) of, 11
  Baptistry—
    Bronze doors of, 5, 14 *and notes*
    Dome of, 159-160
  Bargello, bronze panels in, 14 *note*[2]
  Brunelleschi's works in, 24
  Cathedral—
    Building of, 15
    Dome of, 5, 119-120, 122, 153; construction of, 16-19, 155-160
    Nave arches of, 22
    Plan of, 15
    Singing gallery designed for, 25 *note*
  Churches—
    Angeli, 121, 122
    S. Annunziata, 45, 123
    S. Croce—character of, 4; spacing in, 22; pulpit in, 27
    S. Lorenzo—
      Dome of, 19 *note*[1], 119
      Interior of, 22
      Laurentian Library, 89-90
      Plan of, 21
      Sagrestia Nuova, 89
      Sagrestia Vecchia, 8 *and note*[1], 20
    Santa Maria Novella, 16, 139
    S. Spirito—dome of, 19 *note*[1], 119; plan and section of, 20
  Foundling Hospital, 24, 25
  Greek refugees in, 6
  Loggia dei Lanzi, 7, 22
  Neo-platonic academy at, 9
  Palaces—
    Later, 111-112
    Plans of, 42-44

Florence—*continued*.
  Palaces, astylar—
    Façades of, 37
    Rustications of, 34-36
    Stability in, sense of, 38
  Palaces, pilastered, examples of, 38 ff.
  Palazzo Antellesi, 37
  Palazzo Antinori, 36, 37
  Palazzo Bartolini, 36, 41
  Palazzo Gondi, walling of, 35, 36; staircase of, 44
  Palazzo Guadagni, 36; sgraffito work on, 37; stone seating of, 38; window arches of, 40-41
  Palazzo Larderel, 112
  Palazzo Montalvi, 37, 40
  Palazzo Nonfinito, 112
  Palazzo Pandolfini, 41-44, 83
  Palazzo Pitti—
    Courtyard façade of, 110
    Designer of, 31
    Drawing of, cited, 34 *note*
    Luxembourg a copy of, 196
    Original form of, 32-33
    Plan of, 33
    Size and proportions of, 40
    Windows of, 33-34; arches, 40
  Palazzo Quaratesi (de Rast)—
    Designer of, 31
    Illustration of, 32
    Rustication of, 34
    Shields on, 25, 37
    Windows of, 40
  Palazzo Ricasoli-Zanchini, 40
  Palazzo Riccardi—
    Additions to, 32 *note*
    Brunelleschi's design for, 31-32
    Designer of, 27
    Plan of, 43
    Proportions of, 32
    Section of upper storey of, 39
    Shield on, 37
    Stone seating of, 38
    Walling of, 34, 36
    Windows of, 112; arches, 40
  Palazzo Rucellai—
    Design of, 38
    Rustication of, 35, 40
    Size and proportions of, 40
    Window arches of, 41
    mentioned, 27, 37

Florence—*continued*.
  Palazzo Strozzi—
    Designers of, 32
    Lighting of upper storey of, 38
    Plan of, 42, 44
    Rustication of, 35, 36
    Section of upper storey of, 39
    Shield on, 37
    Size and proportions of, 40
    Stone seating of, 38
    Window arches of, 40
  Palazzo Strozzino — rustication of, 34; courtyard of, 44
  Palazzo Uffizi courtyard, 112
  Palazzo Uguccioni, 112
  Palazzo Vecchio—design of, 31; windows of, 40
  Paving and building of, 31
  Pazzi Chapel
    Arches and entablature in, 23
    Domes of, 19
    Façade of, 19, 24-25
    Loggia of, 94
    Plan of, 124; plan and section, 18
    Windows in, 152
  Shields as decoration in, 37
Florentine Republic—
  Fortifications of, 24, 28
  Position of, in the fifteenth century, 10, 47
  Stone quarries of, 34, 52, 65
Folembray, Château, 173
Folfi, Mariotto di Zanobi, 112
Fontainebleau, 173, 185, 188-189
Fontana, Carlo, 109
Fontana, Domenico, 109, 146
Fonthill Abbey, 333
Foster, John, 331
France—
  (*for particular châteaux, churches, towns, etc., see their names*)—
  Architects of, 185
  Carvers of, 172-173
  Châteaux—
    Badges on, 182
    Examples of, 174-178
    Façades of, 180-181
    Internal treatment of, 184
    Material of, 182-185
    Plans of, 178-180
  Gothic revival in, 169-170
  Institut de, 209

France—*continued*.
  Modern architecture in, 224-225
  Renaissance in—
    Louis XIV. period, architects of, 206
    Louis XV. period, 217 ff.
    Originality of work of, 224
    René's introduction of, 169
    Second period, 189 ff.
    Start of (end of fifteenth century), 171
  Windows in, 325
Francis I., King of France, 192; in Italy, 171; badge of, 182; châteaux of, 173, 188
Frieze—
  Caradosso's, at Milan, 56
  High-relief groups (Maisons), 206
  Medallions in, 23
  Plaster, 267
  Windows in, 38, 99, 102

GABLES—
  Brick copings to, 263
  Elizabethan, varieties in, 262-263; Kirby Hall, 242
  Fantastic, 260
  Flemish, 323
  Semicircular, 61, 64
Gabriel, Jacques Ange, 216, 221
Gaddi, Taddeo, 16 note [1]
Gaillon, château at, 186
Galilei, Alessandro, 140
Galleries of London churches, 294
Gallienus, 53
Genoa—
  Annunziata, 135
  Painted walls in, 37
  Palazzo del Municipio, 115
  Palazzo Durazzo, 115
  S. Maria in Carignano, 114
  Site and palaces of, 115
  University, 115, 116
  Villa Cambioso, 114
Germany—
  Old houses in, 227
  Panelling in, 265
  Windows in, 325
George I., King of England, 297
Ghiberti, Lorenzo, 4 note [2], 7; bronze panel by, 14 *and* note [2]; Brunelleschi's colleague, 17

INDEX

Ghirlandajo, 7, 88
Giacondo, Fra, 143
Gibbons, Grinling, 285
Gibbs, James, 299, 307-308
Giorgio, Francesco di, 45
Giotto, 16 note [1]
Girolamo di Fiesole, 172
Glastonbury—
  Abbot's kitchen, 226
  George Inn, 226
  Tithe-barn, 226
  Tribunal House, 226-227
Gloucester—New Inn, 226
Gnoli, Sig. Domenico, *cited*, 71 note
Gosforth Hall, Northumberland, 321
Gosforth House, Yorks, 310
Goujon, Jean, 190-191
Gotch, J. A., cited, 239 *and note*, 248 *note*, 276 note [1], 279
Gothic architecture—
  England, in—Wren's, 297; nineteenth century revival, 333
  Italy, in, 1, 4-6
Gothic churches compared with Classic, 130, 131, 133, 136
Great Chalfield Manor (Wilts), 227, 250-251
Greenwich—
  Exterior of house at, 323-324
  Hospital—Charles II.'s block, 276, 278; Wren's work on, 302-304; later work, 304; Versailles compared with, 298
  Queen's House, 271, 278, 314
Gresham, Sir Thos. 237
Grosso, Niccolo (Caparrà), 38
Guimiliau, Calvary at, 187
Guingamp — Nôtre Dame de Bon Secours, 187
Gwilt quoted, 290

Haddon Hall, 227, 249; ballroom, 254, 265
Halls, 314
Hamburg—S. Nicholas, 335
Hampton Court Palace—
  Great hall, carving in, 230 *note*
  Pilasters of, 323
  Wolsey's portion of, 230
  Wren's work on, 304-305; limitations imposed on, 301
Hardwick, —, 337

Hardwick Hall, Derbyshire—
  Arabesque inlaying in, 266
  Forecourt of, 256
  Gallery of, 254
  Marble decoration in, 248
  Plan of, 255-256
  Plasterwork in, 267-268
  Staircase at, 268
  mentioned, 246
Harewood House, Yorks, 311, 326
Harfleur Château façade, 195
Harrison quoted, 237
Hatfield, 254
Hatton, Sir Christopher, 241
Haveus (Heave), Theodore, 236
Hawksmoor, Nicholas, originality of, 298-299; relations with Vanbrugh, 306; work at Oxford, 307
Heindrickx (Henrick), 237
Hengrave Hall, Suffolk, 231-232
Henri II., King of France, 175-176, 182, 189
Henri IV., King of France, 189
Henry VIII., King of England, 228, 232-233, 235
Henry, Prince of Wales, 271
Hever Castle, 226
Higham Ferrars, Northants, house at, 261
Holbein, Hans, 230
Holinshed's Chronicles quoted, 237 *and note* [1]
Holkham Hall, Norfolk, 319-320
Holland, windows in, 325
Holte, Thomas, 248
Houghton Hall, Norfolk, 308, 319
Hubsch cited, 222 *note* [1]
Hurstmonceaux Castle, Sussex, 227, 249

Ightham Moat House, Kent, 249
Île de France, châteaux in, 188
Institut de France, 209
Il Rosso, 189
Isabella d' Este, 50
Italy (*for particular districts, towns, churches, etc., see their names*)—
  Bottega training in, 6-9
  Byzantine and Basilican traditions in, 4
  Carvers of, 172
  Circular plan churches in, 123-124

Italy—*continued.*
  Exteriors of churches in, 136-137
  Gothic architecture in, 1, 4-6; decline of, 50-51
  Grecian cult in, 6
  Greek cross plan churches in, 124-127 *and note*
  Jesuit churches in, 118, 128, 139
  Leading powers in, before Renaissance, 10
  Materials in, differing with locality, 52
  North, Roman remains in, 52
  Octagonal churches in, 122-123, 128
  Position of, in fifteenth century, 2
  Renaissance in—
    Individual, importance of, 13, 76, 109
    Influences affecting, 5
    Literary, 2-4
    Nature of, 1, 4
    Painting, independent position of, 9 *and note* [1]
    Reaction after, 106-107
    Spread of, 49-50
    Start of—in Milan, 48; in Florence, 52
    Suitability of buildings of, 29
  Seventeenth and eighteenth century buildings in, 106 ff.
  Square plan churches in, 120-122

JAMES I., King of England, 270-271
James, John, 299, 300
John of Padua, 234
Jombert, Charles Antoine, 221 *note*
Jones, Inigo, early life of, 270-271; unique position of, 270; Banqueting Hall, Whitehall, 271-272, 274, 276-278; work during 1620-1642, 274-275; Lincoln's Inn Chapel, 275; Coleshill, 313; Stoke Park, 317; exteriors by, 323; windows by, 325; original touches by, 278; retirement of, 280; otherwise mentioned, 68, 93, 239, 248, 305
Joyner, Michael, 230 *note*
Julius II., Pope (Giuliano della Rovere), 70, 141

KEDLESTON HALL, Derbyshire, 310-312; plan of, 320-321

Kent, William, 299-300; works by, 308-309, 319
Keystones, projecting carved, 99 *note*
Kew Palace, 323
Kinnersley Castle, Herefordshire, 263
Kirby Hall, Northants—
  Avenue of, 256
  Chimneys of, 278
  Description of, 241-242
  Entrance of, 256, 278
  Exterior of, 242-243, 245
  Foreign influences shown by, 260
  Gables of, 243, 260, 323
  Gallery of, 254
  Gardens of, 257
  Plan of, 251-252; block plan, 257
  Quadrangle of, 241, 323 *note*
  Rustication of, 278
  Windows of, 278, 325
  otherwise mentioned, 239, 274, 276
Knowle House, Kent—
  Courtyard of, 255
  Fireplaces in, 266
  Gallery of, 254
  Surveyor of, 241

LA MADONNA DI SANTO BIAGIO FUORI MONTEPULCIANO, 124-125, 154
La Muette Château, 173
La Rochelle—Hôtel de Ville, 195
Lacock Abbey, 230, 232, 234
Lance, Adolf, *cited*, 185 note [2]
Lannion—houses in La Place, 184
Lanterns—
  Bronze, 38
  Lighting by, 152
Lassurance, Cailleteau, 213, 217
Lassurance, Jean, 217
Laud, Archbishop, 268, 281
Laurana, Francesco, 169
Lavenham Guildhall, 226
Layer Marney Towers, Essex, 232-233
le Breton, Gilles, 188-189
Le Mans Cathedral, tomb in, 169
Le Nôtre, 216
Le Pautre, Antoine, 206, 210
Le Pautre, Jean, 212
Leduc, 206
Leeds—S. John the Evangelist, 268
Lemercier, Jacques, career and works of, 200-201; Val-de-Grâce, 206; pilaster treatment by, 323; pay of, 185

INDEX

Lemuet, 206
Leo X., Pope, 11, 70, 171
Lescot, Pierre, 185, 189-191
Letarouilly *cited*, 79
Levau (Leveau), Louis, 206, 214; work on the Louvre, 207-208; Vaux-le-Vicomte Château, 209
Lighting of churches (*see also* Windows)—
  Classic architecture, in, 136
  Lanterns, by, 152
  Les Invalides and Le Panthéon domes, 164, 167
Lighting of upper storeys, 38 (*see also* Windows)
Lilford Hall, Northants, 262
Lincoln—"Jew's" house, 226
Lintels—
  Arches in combination with, 94
  Pairs of columns joined by, 100
Little Wenham Hall, Essex, 226, 249
Liverpool—
  Bank of England, 331
  Exchange (Town Hall), 309-310
  London, Liverpool and Globe Insurance Building, 331
  St. George's Hall, 332
Loches—
  Hôtel de Ville, architect of, 185
  La Chancellerie, 177
Lodovico, Duke of Milan, 54
Loggie, 34
Loire district, châteaux, etc., of, 175 ff.
Lombardi (Solari), Martino, 64
Lombardi, Santo, 64
Lombardi family, 52, 96
Lombardo, Moro, 62, 64
Lombardo, Pietro, 61, 62, 64, 102
Lombardy, Romanesque buildings in, 40 *note* 1
London—
  Adelphi, 312
  Admiralty, Whitehall, 312
  Alfred Place, 310
  Bank of England, 332
  Baring's Bank, 337
  British Museum, 332
  Brydon's building, Parliament Street, 274 *note* 1
  Burlington House, Piccadilly, 308-309
  Charterhouse, 268

London—*continued*.
  Chelsea Hospital, 302
  Chiswick, Burlington's villa at, 309 and *note* 1, 326
  Christ's Hospital—pilasters of, 302, 323; rubbed bricks in, 328
  Churches—
    Chapel Royal, St. James's, 230
    Christ Church, Newgate, 296-297
    Christ Church, Spitalfields, 298-299
    City churches, rebuilding of (1667), 292 ff; interiors, 294; exteriors, 295; towers and spires, 296-297
    Lincoln's Inn Chapel, 276
    S. Antholin, 293, 295
    S. Benet Fink, 293, 295
    S. Bride, Fleet Street, 293-294; spire, 296-297
    S. Dunstan in the East, 297
    S. George, Bloomsbury, 298-299
    S. George, Hanover Square, 299
    S. James, Garlic Hill, 293-294, 296
    S. James, Piccadilly, 294
    S. John, Westminster, 299
    S. Leonard, Shoreditch, 299
    S. Magnus, London Bridge, 296
    S. Margaret Pattens, 297
    S. Martin-in-the-Fields, 299
    S. Martin, Ludgate Hill, 293, 296; spire, 297 *and note*
    S. Mary Aldermary, 297
    S. Mary at Hill, 293, 294, 295
    S. Mary-le-Bow, Cheapside, 296-297
    S. Mary-le-Strand, 299
    S. Mary Woolnoth, Lombard Street, 298-299
    S. Michael, Cornhill, 297
    S. Pancras, 331
    S. Paul, Covent Garden, 274, 299
    S. Paul's Cathedral, *see that heading*
    S. Swithin, Cannon Street, 295
    S. Stephen, Walbrook, 293, 295, 296
    Westminster Abbey, 229
  Colour effects in, 63 *note* 1
  Covent Garden, 274
  Cromwell Road houses, 336
  Ely House, Dover Street, 310
  Ely Place, Holborn, 311
  Essex Street, Strand, window in, 328

London—*continued.*
  Finsbury Square, 310
  Fire of, 284
  Fitzroy Square, 312
  Great Queen Street, house in, 280
  Grosvenor Square—Lord Derby's house, 312, 313
  Horse Guards, 309
  Kensington—
    Broad Walk, lodge in, 337
    Holland House, 241
    Lord Carlisle's house, 337
    Lowther Lodge, 337
    Palace, 302
  Law Courts, 336
  Lincoln's Inn—
    Chapel, 276
    Gateway, panels of, 230
  Lincoln's Inn Fields—
    Pilaster design in, 323
    Soane's Museum, 240
    West side houses, 271, 278
  Mansion House, 310
  Marlborough House, Pall Mall, 305, 323
  Newgate, 310 *and note*[1]
  Royal Exchange (old), 237
  Royal Exchange (present), 322, 334
  S. Bartholomew's Hospital, 307
  Somerset House, 311
  Somerset House (old), 234
  Sun Fire Office, Threadneedle Street, 331
  Temple—
    King's Bench Walk, 328
    Wren's entrance to, 302
  Temple Bar (1671), 302
  Treasury, Whitehall, 309
  University College, 164 *note*, 332
  Westminster—
    Abbey, *see* Westminster Abbey
    Dormitory, 305
    Houses of Parliament, 334
  Whitehall—
    Banqueting Hall, 271-272, 274, 276-278
    Gateway to, 230
    Wren's scheme for rebuilding of, 284-285
  York Water Gate, 276, 278
Longford Castle, 256
Longhena, Baldassare, 109, 127-128

Longhi, Martino, 112
Longleat, Wilts., 234, 260
Louis XI., King of France, 168-169
Louis XII., King of France, 170, 171
Louis XIII., King of France, 192, 206
Louvre, Paris—
  Banded columns and pilasters of, 191
  Courtyard of, enlarged, 206
  Earliest portions of, 192-193
  East façade of, 207-208
  Lemercier's work on, 200
  Lescot architect of, 189-191
  Plan showing dates of, 193
  Tuileries connected with, 208-209
Lugano, capitals in, 65
Luton Park House, Bedford, 312
Lyveden New Building, Northants, 244

MADERNO, CARLO, 69, 109, 112, 146
Madrid, Château de, 173, 188, 233-234; towers, 179
Maisons-sur-Seine Château, 205-206 *and note*[1]
Malatesta, Sigismondo, Duke of Rimini, 138
Mansard (Mansart), François, 200; works by, 203 ff.; pilaster treatment by, 323
Mansard, Jules Hardouin, 213 ff.; Wren compared with, 298
Mantegna, Andrea, 54
Mantua—
  Ducal Palace, 110
  Palazzo del Tè, 109
  Palazzo Giustizia, 109-110
  S. Andrea—
    Description, plan, and section of, 129-132 *and note*
    Façade of, 138
    Fancelli's work on, 26 *note*, 45
    Lighting of, 136
    Panelled pilasters at, 63
    West front of, 30
  S. Sebastiano, 124, 138
Marble—
  Central Italy, prevalence in, 52
  Decorative use of, 54, 60, 135
  Venetian use of, 65
Marie de' Medici, 196
Mariette, 221 *and note*
Marlborough, Duchess of, 307

INDEX

Marney, Lord (1523), 232
Marot, Jean, 201, 206; "Le Grand Marot" cited, 205 note, 212
Marseilles Cathedral, 169 and note[2]
Marsh, —, 280
Martock, Gothic work at, 282
Mary Tudor, Queen of England, 235
Massimo, Angelo, 77, 85, 86
Massimo, Pietro, 77, 85
Masters of Building Guilds, work by, 59–60, 64
Maxstoke Castle, 226
Mazarin, 207
Mazzoni, Giulio, 79
Medici family, 11; mausoleum of, 89 (see also de' Medici)
Mereworth, Kent, 308
Mezzanine, 77, 79
Michael Angelo, birthplace of, 69; career of, 88–89; Farnese completed by, 82; Laurentian Library, 89–90; buildings on the Capitol, 91–94; Palladio influenced by, 99; designs for S. Peter's, 144–145; façade, 140; dome, 160; estimate of architectural work of, 89–90; otherwise mentioned, 7, 8, 112, 122, 138
Michelozzi, Michelozzo, patron of, 12; works of, 27; design for Palazzo Riccardi, 32; at Venice, 48; at Milan, 50
Middleton cited, 16 note[2]
Milan—
  Cathedral—
    da Vinci's work for, 50 note[1]
    Filarete's work on, 49
    Renaissance ideas in, 50–51
  Ospedale Maggiore, 48–49
  Palazzo Marino, 114–115; entablatures, 23
  Renaissance beginning at, 48–50
  S. Ambrogio, 51
  S. Carlo Borromeo, 124
  S. Eustorgio—Capella Portinari, 50
  S. Lorenzo, 4; alterations in, 75 note; plan of, compared with that of S. Peter's, 143 and note
  S. Maria delle Grazie—
    Candelabra pilasters of, 54
    da Vinci's work at, 50
    Plan of east end, 57
    Section of east end, 58

Milan—continued.
  S. Maria della Grazie—continued.
    mentioned, 122
  S. Maria presso S. Satiro, 54–56
  S. Satiro, 121 note; dome, 19 note[1]
  Via degli Omenoni, decorations in, 110
Milan, Duchy of—
  Apprenticeship in, 51
  Building materials of, 52
  Masons' guild of, 51
  Territory of, 47
Moats, 249
Models by Florentine architects, 44
Modes, W., cited, 48 note
Montecavallo, Antonio, 71 note
Montacute, Somerset—
  Gables of, 262
  Gallery of, 254
  Garden of, 257
Montepulciano—La Madonna di Santo Biagio, 124–125, 154
Moore, C. H., quoted, 19 note[2]
Moreton Old Hall, Cheshire, 265
Morlaix, 115 note[1]
Morris, Robert, 309
Mountford, Mr., cited, 310 note[1]
Moyns Hall, Suffolk, 263, 264

NANCY, 221
Nantes Cathedral, tomb in, 172
Naples—
  Alfonso's Archway, 27
  Porta Capuana, 27
  S. Annunziata, 133
Napoleon I., 208
Narthex in Renaissance churches, 138; S. Peter's, 140
Naves, 128
Newcastle—S. Nicholas, 297
Nesfield, —, 337
Newton House, near Yeovil, 264
Nicholas V., Pope, 27, 70, 141
Nicholls, —, 332
Nîmes—
  Baths of Diana, 63 note,[2] 141 note[2]
  Maison Carrée, 53, 223–224
  Pont du Gard near, 141 note[2]
Nonesuch Palace, near Cheam, 232–233
Northampton—All Saints, 295, 299
Nottingham Castle, 248
Noyon Cathedral, 212

OCKWELLS, Berks., 227, 250-251
Olivieri, P., 128
Orcagna, 5, 7
Orleans—
  Agnes Sorel's house at, 181 *and note*
  Hôtel de Ville (original), 171, 172; cornice, 180
Ornament, *see* Decoration
Orvieto Cathedral, 5
Ossuaries, 187-188
Ottoman empire, rise of, 47
Oundle, Northants—Talbot Inn, 261
Oxborough Hall, Norfolk, 255
Oxford—
  All Souls' College, 307
  Christ Church College, 281
  Clarendon Press buildings, 307
  Queen's College, 307
  Radcliffe Library, 307-308
  S. John's College, Laud's additions to, 281
  Schools, tower of, 235-236
  Sheldonian Theatre, 282
  Taylor Institute, 331

PADUA, Squarcione's school for painters at, 9
Paine, James, 310, 312
Palermo Cathedral, 152
Palladio, Andrea, career of, 99; Basilica at Vicenza, 99-101 *and note;* Palazzo Thiene, 102, 103, 111; Il Redentore (Venice), 129, 133, 139; S. Giorgio Maggiore, 128, 138-139; comparison of, with Sansovino, 99-100; Inigo Jones' study of, 276 *and note*[2]; quoted, 175; mentioned, 61, 69, 96
Palustre, Léon, cited, 170-173, 188, 189, 192
Papworth, Wyatt, quoted, 237 *note*[1], 316-317; cited, 246 *note*[1]
Paris—
  Churches—
    La Madeleine, 223-224 *and note*
    S. Etienne du Mont, 198
    S. Eustache, 198
    S. Paul and S. Louis, 139
    S. Roch, 130, 201
    S. Sulpice, 224
    Sorbonne, 200-201
    Val de Grâce—buttresses of, 137, 206; brackets of, 139; dome of, 155

Paris—*continued.*
  Ecole des Beaux Arts, 186, 191
  Entrance gateways in, 218
  Hôtel Amelot (1, Rue S. Dominique), 219-220
  Hôtel Carnavalet, 189, 217
  Hôtel de Beauvais, 210-212
  Hôtel de Sully, 196
  Hôtel des Invalides, dome of, 122, 164-165, 213
  Hôtel Lambert, 209-210
  Hôtels, eighteenth century, 220 *and note*
  Louvre, *see that heading*
  Luxembourg, Palais du, 196-197
  Map of (1800), 220 *note*
  Palais Bourbon, 213
  Palais Royal (Cardinal), 200
  Panthéon (S. Geneviève)—dome of, 154, 164, 166-167; plan and section of, 222-223
  Place de la Concorde, 221
  Place des Victoires, 213
  Place Vendome, 213-214
  Tuileries—
    Columns and pilasters of, 191; early portions of, 193-194; Louvre connected with, 208-209
Park House, Oswestry, 265
Parma—Madonna della Steccata, 121
Paul III., Pope, 80
Pavia—
  Certosa, 64 *note;* façade, 60, 127; cloisters, 180
  "Masters'" work at, 59
  S. Michele, 51
Pavillon, 180
Peacham, quoted, 239
Pearson, —, 336
Pediments, 304, 305, 326
Peel towers, 249
Pendentives, 151
Penshurst Place, 226
Perrault, Charles, 208
Perrault, Claude, 206-208
Perspective—
  Chancel painted in, 54
  Gardens painted in, 77
  Panels, 64
  Renaissance painting, in, 8, 9 *note*[2]
  S. Maria della Salute, of, 128
Peruzzi, Baldassare, career of, 84;

frieze windows adopted by, 38 : work on Villa Farnesina, 84 ; Palazzo Pietro Massimi, 85-88; plans for S. Peter's (Rome), 141-143; estimate of, 85; mentioned, 69, 79, 96, 111, 112

Petrarch, 2, 3, 6

Piacenza—
Cathedral dome, 154-155
Palazzo Communale, 51
Palazzo Farnese, 78-80

Pienza—
Palazzo Piccolomini, 39 *and note*, 110
Rossellino's work at, 27

Piers—
Classic and Gothic churches compared as to, 133
Columns in combination with, 131 *note*
Few *v.* many, 134

Pilastered fronts, examples of, 38 ff.

Pilasters—
Angles, at, 56 *and note*[2] ; near outside angles, 329
Banded, 191, 195
Columns in combination with, 91-92
Engaged columns compared with, 134
French type of, 214, 323
Pairs, grouping in, 71-72
Panelling of, 56, 63 *and note*[2], 181 ; in slate, 183
Pilasters on, 91
Recessed behind window frames, 177
Rustication of, 110-111
Two storeys, carried through, 158, 323

Pilon, Germain, 191
Pintelli, Baccio, 123
Piranesi *cited*, 159 *note*

Pisa—
Byzantine influence in, 4
Cathedral dome, 4
S. Maria della Spina, 5 *note*

Pisano, Andrea, 5, 14 *note*[1]
Pisano, Giovanni, 5 *note*
Pisano, Niccola, 3, 5
Pistoja—Madonna dell' Umilta, 122
Pius II., Pope, 27, 45, 70
Pius V., Pope, 146
Plasterwork, 266-268

VOL. III.

Plougastel-Daoulas, Calvary at, 187
Pollaiuolo, Simone, *see* Cronaca
Poole, Dorset, cornice of house at, 328
Porticoes, 140, 295, 299, 307, 326-327
Prato—S. Maria delle Carceri, 19 *note*[1], 124-125
Primaticcio, 188, 189
Prior Park, Bath, 309, 326
Pugin, Augustus Welby, 333; cited, 310-311 *and note*

QUOINS, 203

RAINALDI, Carlo, 109, 126, 128, 139
Rainaldi, Girolamo, 69, 109, 126
Raphael—Palazzo Pandolfini designed by, 42; cartoon by, 110 *note*[1]; influence of, 95; plan of S. Peter's (Rome), 143; mentioned, 69, 96, 105
Raschdorff, J. C., cited, 111 *and note*, 112
Ravello, bronze doors at, 4 *note*[2]
Ravenna—S. Vitale, 4, 19, 119, 128
Raynham Hall, Norfolk, 274, 278, 314, 315 ; gables, 323
Records Office Museum, 229 *note*[1]
René I., King, 169
Renishaw Hall, Derbyshire, 254
Revett, N., 330-331
Reynolds, Sir Joshua, *quoted*, 306
Riccio (Rizo), Antonio, 63, 96
Richelieu, Card., 192, 206 ; town of, 201-203
Rickman, T., 333

Rimini—
Alberti's work at, 26
Roman arch at, 52
S. Francesco—entablature of, 100 ; side chapels of, 132 ; exterior of, 137-138

Ripley, —, 304
Rochester keep, 226
Rodari, Tommaso, 59
Roman architecture, entablature unbroken in, 24
Romanesque architecture in Italy, traditions and influence of, 4 *note*[1], 19
Romanesque buildings in Lombardy, 40 *note*[1]
Romanesque churches, 51 ; window arches of, 41

2 A

Romano, Giulio, 69, 109–110
Rome—
  Aqueduct of Claudius, 83 *note*
  Arch of Titus, 42, 99 *note*
  Art centre at (sixteenth century), 68–69
  Astylar buildings common in, 69
  Basilica of Constantine, 22, 137
  Baths of Caracalla, 137
  Baths of Diocletian, 22, 137
  Baths of Gallienus, 159 *and note*
  Capitol, Michael Angelo's buildings on the, 91–94
  Casa di Bramante, 73
  Churches—
    Gesù, 139 ; section of dome, 153
    S. Agnese, 126–7 *and note*
    S. Andrea della Valle, 128–9, 137, 139
    S. Costanza, 22
    S. Giovanni de' Fiorentini, 96
    S. Giovanni in Laterano, 140
    S. Ignazio, 128–30
    S. Lorenzo fuori le Mura, 3 *note*.
    S. Maria de' Miracoli—plan of, 123 ; drum and dome of, 123–4, 152 ; portico of, 140
    S. Maria del Popolo, 188
    S. Maria della Pace—cloisters of, 61, 74 ; plan of, 75, 123
    S. Maria di Loreto, 120
    S. Maria di Monte Santo, 123, 124 ; portico, 140
    S. Maria in Campitelli, 139–140
    S. Maria in Trastevere, 22
    S. Maria Maggiore, 21
    S. Paolo fuori le Mura, 22 *note*
    S. Peter's. *See that heading*
    S. Pietro in Montorio—Il Tempietto, 94
  Colosseum—
    Entablature of, 24, 39–40
    Influence of, on northern façades, 97–98
  Early Renaissance work in, 70–76
  Foreign architects in, 69
  Open spaces in, 2
  Palaces :
    Façades of, 79
    Late examples of, 112–113
    Material of, 78
    Plan of, 77
    Sites of, irregular, 77

Rome—*continued*.
  Palazzi Pietro and Angelo Massimi, 77–78, 85–88 ; loggia, 94
  Palazzo Barberini, 107, 112–113
  Palazzo Borghese :
    Arcade of, 112
    Courtyard of, 74, 77 ; entablatures, 23
    Site of, 77
    Stateliness of, 107
    Windows of, 79
  Palazzo Cancelleria, 54, 71–73 ; brickwork, 78
  Palazzo dei Conservatori, 91–93
  Palazzo del Museo Capitolino, 91–92
  Palazzo del Senatore, 91–92
  Palazzo di Venezia, 70–71
  Palazzo Farnese, 80–83
  Palazzo Giraud (Torlonia), 54, 73
  Palazzo Linotte, 79
  Palazzo Maccarani, 77–78
  Palazzo Niccolini, 96
  Palazzo Poli, 113–114
  Palazzo Sacchetti, 79–80
  Palazzo Spada alla Regola, 79
  Pantheon, 42 *note*,^{2} ; columns, 124
  Piazza del Campidoglio, 91–94
  Piazza del Popolo, 107
  Scala di Spagna, 107
  Temple of Castor and Pollux, 52–53
  Theatre of Marcellus, 24, 98
  Vatican, court of, 74–76
  Villa di Papa Giulio, 92–94
  Villa Farnesina, or Chigi, 38, 84–85
Roofs—
  French sixteenth century, 180
  Hipped, 202, 203
  Keel-shaped, 191
  Slates, of, in Loire district, 183
Rossellino, Bernardo, 26 *and note*, 27, 45, 70 ; Rucellai and Piccolomini, 39 *and note*
Rothwell (Rowell) Market-house, 244
Rouen—
  Ancient Bureau des Finances, 186
  Cathedral, tomb in, 186
  Hôtel du Bôurgtheroulde, 182, 186
  Palais de Justice, 186
  S. Vincent, 197
Rovezzano, 229–230
Rushton Hall, Northants, 241, 244 ; plan, 254 ; triangular lodge, 256

INDEX

Rustication—
　Basements treated by, 31
　Development of, 110–111
　Late Renaissance, 110
Rydge, Richard, 230 *note*

S. Germain-en-Laye Château, 173, 188
S. Germigny les Prés, 121 *note*
S. Paul's Cathedral, London (destroyed by fire), 274
S. Paul's Cathedral, London—
　Attic of, 130
　Cross section of, 291
　Crossing, defect at, 292
　Dome of—
　　Construction of, 162–164, 290–291
　　Estimate of, 290–291
　　Form of, 154
　　Section through transept and, 153
　　Various designs for, 289 *and note*
　　Views of, 290 *and note* [1], 297 *and note*
　Drum of, 162–163
　Flying buttresses of, 137
　Interior of, 291–292
　Model of, by Wren, 286 *note*
　North elevation of, 289
　Piers in, 133
　Plan of, 289
　Screens in, 305
　Side walls of, 290
　Site of, 290
　"Warrant" design for, 286–290
　West front of, 140
　Windows of, 131, 162–163
　Wren's first plan of, 287
S. Peter's, Rome—
　Attic of, 79, 160
　Bronze doors of, 48
　Colonnade of, 107, 146–147
　Cupolas of, 146
　Date of commencement of, 118
　Dimensions of, 150–151
　Dome of—
　　Construction of, 160–161
　　Form of, 153
　　Section of, 161
　　Time occupied in building, 146, 161 *note*
　Drum of, 145–146, 160
　Early plans for, 141–143

S. Peter's, Rome—*continued*.
　Entablature of, 100–101
　Entrance front of, 146–149
　External ordinance of, 145 *and note* [1]
　Interior of, 149
　Internal ordinance of, settled before Michael Angelo, 144–145
　Later additions to, 146
　Lighting of, 136
　Michael Angelo's work on, 144–145
　Models of, 144–160
　Nave piers in, 133
　Nave plans for, 143
　Orientation of, 141 *note* [1]
　Pendentives in, 151
　Piazza of, 146
　Piers in, 150–151; nave, 133
　Plan of, 147
　Pronaos plan for, 143–144
　Sculpture in, 149
　Towers designed for, 149
　West front of, 140
　otherwise mentioned, 28, 122, 130
S. Petersburg—S. Isaacs, 164 *note*
S. Thégonnec, Calvary and ossuary at, 187
Saint-Simon, *quoted*, 213
Salisbury cathedral, 140
Sambin, Hugues, 199
Sampierdarena—Villa Scassi, 114
San Gallo, Antonio da, models by, 44; Farnese palace, 23, 81–84; S. Maria di Loreto, 120; La Madonna di Santo Biagio, 124–125; estimate of, 27–28; otherwise mentioned, 69, 70, 96
San Gallo, Antonio da (younger), Palazzo Sacchetti by, 79–80; designs for S. Peter's, 143, 151
San Gallo, Bastiano da, 42
San Gallo, Giovanni Francesco da, 42
San Gallo, Giuliano da, models by, 44; Gondi staircase, 44; plan for S. Peter's, 143; La Madonna delle Carceri, 124–125; estimate of, 28; otherwise mentioned, 36, 70, 96.
Sandstone, rustications of, 34
Sanmicheli, Michele, career and works of, 95–96; windows by, 103; rustication by, 110–111; influence of, 114; mentioned, 31, 69
Sansovino, Andrea, 96

Sansovino (Tatti), Jacopo, career of, 96; work in Rome, 96; in Venice, 96–101 *note*; Giants' Staircase spoiled by, 63; windows by, 38, 103; rustication by, 111; influence of, 114; comparison of Palladio with, 99–100; mentioned, 52, 61, 69
Saumur—Nôtre Dame des Ardilliers, 212–213
Scamozzi, Vincenzo, 105, 109, 114
Scarpagnino, 96
Scott, Sir George Gilbert, 335–336
Scott, Leader, quoted, 17 *and note*[1]; 60 *note*; cited, 45 *note*[1], 50 *note*[1]
Sculptors in collaboration with architects, 25
Seaton Delaval, Northumberland, 306, 307, 327; plan of, 321, 322
Sedding, John D., 336
Semi-basements, 315
Serlio, —, 105, 185, 189
Servandony, 224
Sforza, Francesco, Duke of Milan, 48–49
Sgraffito work, 36–37 *and note*
Shaw, Huntingdon, 305
Shaw, Norman, 337
Sherington, Sir Wm., 232
Shute, John, 238
Siena—
  Cathedral, 5 *and note*
  Palaces in, character of, 45
  Palazzo Piccolomini, 27, 37; window arches of, 41; character of, 45
  S. Giuseppe, 126
  SS. Pietro e Paolo, 126
  Villa Santa Colomba, 111 *and note*.
Simone, 132 *note*
Sirr, Harry, cited, 246 *note*[1]
Sizergh Castle, Westmorland, 266
Sketch-book architecture, 337
Slate, 183
Smirke, Sir Robert, 332
Smithsons, 246, 248
Soane, Sir John, 240, 331–332
Sohier, Hector, 186
Soissons—Pavillon des Arquebusiers, 212
Solari, Cristoforo, 59
Solari, Guiniforte, 60
Solari, Martino (Lombardi), 64
Solari family, 64 *and note*

Soufflot, J. G., 222
South Wraxall Manor, Wilts, 227; exterior and fire-place, 259
Speke Hall, near Liverpool, 264
Spiers, Walter L., cited, 246 *note*[3]
Spires, 296–297
Squarcione, Francesco, 9
Stafford, Sir Humphrey, 241
Staircases—
  Chambord Château, at, 175
  Double, 317, 319
  English—Elizabethan, 268; seventeenth and eighteenth century, 275, 314–315
  External, 91, 176, 326; Gondi Palace, 44
  Newel, 175–176; carved, 268
  Spiral, 113
Standlinch, Wilts, 321
Stanilas, 221
Steeples, 296–297
Stephens, Alfred, 332
Stickles, Roland, 244–246 *and note*[1]
Stoke Park, Northants, 316–317
Stone—
  Bolognese working of, 60
  Caen and Loire district, of, 182–183, 186
  Florentine use of, 34, 52, 65
  Portland, brick in connection with, 304–305
  Staircases of, 268
Stone, Nicholas, 276
Street, G. E., 336–337
Strong, Edward, 289
Strong, Thomas, 289
Stuart, James, 330–331
Stucco—
  Exterior decoration, as, 312
  Florentine palaces, in, 36–37
  Interior panelling of, 329
  Palladio's work in, 101
Sutton Court, Surrey, 232
Swags, 102, 223, 278; brick, 305
Swatley Hall, near Uxbridge, 323
Symmetry, 319
Symonds, J. A., quoted, 2, 3, 5, 7 *note*, 10; cited, 9 *note*[1], 132 *note*

TALMAN, 326
Taylor, Sir Robert, 310
Terra-cotta work in England, 230, 232

INDEX

Thorndon Hall, Essex, 310, 321
Thorpe, John, career of, 243-244; house of, 239, 241; plan in sketch book of, 240; Kirby Hall, 242-243, 323 note
Thorpe Hall, near Peterborough, 279, 280; gables, 323
Tijon, Jean, 305
Tiles—
  Domes, on, 152
  French châteaux, in, 183-185
  Lacock Abbey, at, 232
Tite, Sir Wm., 332, 334
Tivoli—Hadrian's villa, 19 note [1], 71
Todi—
  S. Crocifisso, 126
  S. Maria della Consolazione, 125 and note
Torch-holders, 37
Torrigiano, Pietro, 228-229 and notes
Toulouse, Renaissance buildings in, 187-188; Hôtel d'Asseza, 188, 193
Tours—
  Cathedral—tomb in, 171, 172; cupolas and cloister staircase of, 193
  Fontaine de Beaune, 173
Towers of churches, 297
Trani, bronze doors at, 4 note [2]
Tregastel, ossuary at, 188
Tresham, Sir Thos., 243, 244
Trinqueau (Pierre Nepveu), 185
Turin—La Superga, 154
Turks, rise of (fifteenth century), 47

VALENÇAY, château de, 179
Vanbrugh, Sir John, 299, 306
Vardy, J., 309
Variation in plans and elevations, 319
Vasari, Giorgio, date of, 109; Uffizi courtyard by, 112; work at Pistoja, 123; cited, 16 note [1], 41, 44, 229 note [2]; quoted, 8, 14, 71, 141 note [2], 145
Vaults (see also Arches)—
  Barrel, pierced by oblong openings, 88
  Entablature springing directly from, 130
  Groin lines, emphasizing of, 43 note
  Slices, built in, 141 note [2]
  Welsh-groin, 131 and note
Velasquez, 38

Venetian Republic (for particular towns see their names)—
  Building materials of, 52
  Byzantine influence and traditions in, 4, 52, 61
  Masons' guild in, 51-52
  Territory comprised by, 49
  Unique style of, 61
  Zenith and decline of, 47
Venice—
  Churches—
    Il Redentore, 129, 133; façade, 139; section of dome, 153
    S. Giorgio Maggiore—
      Façade of, 102, 138-139
      Lighting of, 136
      Monastery of, 48
      Piers in, 133-134
      Plan and section of, 129
    S. Maria della Salute—plan of, 127; description of, 128; interior of, 134; dome of, 154
    S. Mark's, Sansovino's work on, 96
    S. Salvatore, 135
    S. Zaccharia, 61-62
  Ducal Palace, 63-64
  Libreria Vecchia, 98-101 and note; frieze windows, 38
  Marble the material of, 65
  Palaces, balconies and windows of, 62
  Palazzo Cornaro, 96, 98, 114; rusticated columns, 111
  Palazzo Corner Spinelli, 63
  Palazzo Grimani, 97
  Palazzo Pesaro, 114
  Palazzo Rezzonico, 114
  Palazzo Vendramin Calergi, 62-63, 99 note, 102
  Procurazie Nuove, 114
  Sansovino's work in, 96-99
  Scuola di S. Marco, 64
  Scuola di S. Rocco, 64
  Seventeenth and eighteenth century work in, 117
  "Tentative" renaissance work in, 64
  Zecca (Mint), 111
Verney, Lord, quoted, 309 note [1]
Verona—
  Gran Guardia Antica, 112, 114
  Loggia (Fra Giacondo's), 60
  Painted walls in, 37

Verona—*continued*.
 Palazzo Bevilacqua, 95, 111
 Palazzo Canossa, 95-96
 Palazzo dei Diamanti, 60
 Palazzo Pompei, 95
 Porta de' Borsari, 53, 71
 Porta del Palio, 95, 110-111
 Porta Nuova, 95
 Porta S. Zeno, 95
 S. Bernardino—Capella Pellegrini, 95
 S. Zeno, 51
Versailles, 213-216; Trianons, 216
Vestibules, 122
Viart, Charles, 172
Vicenza—
 Basilica Palladiana, 98-101 *and note*
 Casa del Diavolo, 102, 278
 Municipio (Loggia del Capitanio), 102
 Palazzo Porto Barbarano, 101, 103, 276
 Palazzo Thiene, 102, 103, 111, 278
 Palazzo Valmarano, 102, 103
 Palladio's work in, 99 ff.
 Rotonda (Villa del Capri), 103-104, 308
Vignola (Giacomo Barozzi), birthplace of, 69; works of, 92-93, 139; Palazzo Farnese (Piacenza), 79-80; work on S. Peter's (Rome), 146; square-planned churches by, 121; publication of, 92, 105
Vignon, Pierre, 223
Villers-Cotterets Château, 173, 188, 191
Viollet-le-Duc, 224
Viterbo—SS. Francesco e Paolo, 121
Vitré, Renaissance decoration at, 186-187
Vitruvius, 105
Vittoni, Ventura, 122-123
Volterra—Palazzo Ricciarelli, 34
von Geymüller, Baron H., cited, 51 *note*, 56 *note* [1], 58 *and notes*, 73, 125, 143, 151
Vosbergh, Caspar, 235 *note*

WALLS—
 Decoration of, *see* Decoration
 Rusticated, 34-36
 Stuccoed, 37
Walpole, Horace, villa of, at Strawberry Hill, 299, 333; quoted, 248

Wanstead House, Essex, 308, 316
Wardour House, Wilts, 321
Webb, John, Coleshill by, 313; Ashdown, 313, 316; Thorpe Hall, 323; estimate of, 279-280; mentioned, 276, 301
Webb, Philip, 337
Wells—
 Bishop's Palace, 226
 Cathedral, 140, 148-149
 Vicar's Close, 226
Westminster Abbey, 229
Westwood, Worcestershire, 256; ceilings, 266
Whistler quoted, 10, 38
Wilkins, 332
Wilton House, near Salisbury, 274, 278; bridge, 309
Wimbledon—garden of Lord Exeter's house, 257
Winchester—
 Cathedral, 231
 Palace, 302
 S. Cross (near), 231
Windows—
 Alternation of large and small, 79, 97
 Arches of, 31, 40-41
 Bay, multiplication of, in England, 259
 Churches, of—different countries compared, 131 *note* [2]
 Classic and Gothic contrasted, 59, 136
 Dais of halls, of, 251
 Dormer, 180, 194
 Drums, in, 152
 Elizabethan houses, of, 258-260
 Farnese and Pandolfini palaces, of, 83
 Florentine early Renaissance, character of, 40
 Framed in, 41, 53; Filarete's designs of, 49
 French châteaux, of, 181
 French middle Renaissance, 194
 Frieze, in, 38, 102
 Grilles of, 217
 Keystones of, carved, 217
 Louis XV., 217
 Mediæval, 53
 Recessed panels, in, 91

INDEX

Windows—*continued*.
  Recesses of, pilastered, 33-34
  Recessing of, 328-329
  Sash, in England, 325
  Spacing of, 62
  Straight-headed (Palladio's), 103
  Voids, as, 41
Wollaton Hall, Notts, 246 *and note* ², 260; plan of, 255
Wolsey, Card., 230 *and note*
Wood, John, 309
Wood, John (jun.), 321
Wren, Sir Christopher, family of, 282; early works of, 282; S. Paul's, 162, 164; scheme for rebuilding of London, 284-285; rebuilding of City churches, 292 ff.; interiors, 294; exteriors, 295; towers and spires, 296-297; Greenwich hospital, 302-304; Hampton Court, 304-305; death of, 297; estimate of, 301, 302; comparison with Mansard, 298; quoted, 207 *note* ², 270; mentioned, 239, 313
Wren, Mathew, Bishop of Ely, 282
Wyatt, James, 335

YOUNG, JOHN, tomb of, 229 *and note* ¹

THE END

www.ingramcontent.com/pod-product-compliance
Lightning Source LLC
Chambersburg PA
CBHW032027150426
43194CB00006B/186